NEW GOVERNMENTS
IN EUROPE

NEW GOVERNMENTS IN EUROPE

The Trend Toward Dictatorship

By

VERA MICHELES DEAN
JOHN C. DEWILDE
BAILEY W. DIFFIE
CHARLES A. THOMSON
MILDRED S. WERTHEIMER

WITH AN INTRODUCTION BY
RAYMOND LESLIE BUELL

REVISED AND ENLARGED

*A Publication of
the Foreign Policy Association
Incorporated*

THOMAS NELSON AND SONS

NEW YORK   1937

PREFACE

UNTIL recently, it has been customary for students of government to devote the greater part of their attention to the study of parliamentary institutions. It was assumed that with the spread of popular education the principles and methods of democracy would eventually prevail among all enlightened peoples.

The events of the post-war period have seriously shaken these assumptions. Today three leading countries in Europe are under the rule of authoritarian dictatorships, which have come into existence because of the failure of previous systems of government to settle pressing domestic and international problems. The world today is witnessing what Spengler calls the return of the Cæsars.

Although authoritarian rule has dominated the world during the greater part of its history, present-day dictatorships differ widely from the arbitrary régimes which prevailed in many countries before the World War. In the first place, the three leading dictatorships of the present day rest on a system of ideas which gives a sense of direction to the state and restrains dictators from indulging in purely whimsical rule. In the second place, dictatorship in Russia, Italy, and Germany relies upon public opinion to a much greater degree than is supposed. Although political officials in each of these countries

ruthlessly suppress opposition to the existing system, they recognize that their position depends on
their success in enlisting the active support, if not
the enthusiasm, of a large element in the public.
Soviet leaders are constantly resorting to propaganda
devices to make the principles of Communism popular among the people. In Italy Mussolini frequently
makes dramatic appeals from the balcony of Palazzo Venezia and organizes vast parades and other
spectacles. In Germany Hitler did not seize power
by means of a military *coup d'état,* but by the
pressure of a vast propaganda system which he had
patiently organized and directed for years. From
the constitutional point of view, present-day dictatorships may be largely irresponsible, but all of
them realize the importance of winning the support
of public opinion. It is not too much to say that the
majority of the people in Russia, Italy, and Germany support their present leaders in the belief,
which may or may not be well founded, that these
men are moved by more disinterested devotion to
the national good than is demonstrated by political
leaders in supposedly democratic countries.

When Russia adopted Communism in November
1917, and when Italy turned to Fascism after the
famous march on Rome in 1922, defenders of democracy remained undisturbed. They explained that
party government had never taken root either in
Italy or in Russia, and that these countries had
merely turned from one form of dictatorship to another. Their optimism was severely shaken, however, when the German Republic was overthrown
by Hitler in 1933. The Weimar Constitution, drawn
up in 1919, has been hailed by publicists as the most
democratic in the world—a model which all other

states should adopt. Yet in 1933 the Weimar system
succumbed to a Nazi dictatorship.

Among the Great Powers the three remaining exponents of democracy are France, England and the
United States. While these countries have experienced democratic rule during a much longer period
than Germany, it is by no means certain that they
will not adopt some form of dictatorship. In all three
countries growing discontent has been expressed with
the pettiness of parliaments, the irresoluteness of administrations fearful of overthrow at the next elections, and the dominance of local and group interests
at the expense of the general good. If democracy
cannot develop a type of leader and political organization which will consider the interests of the forgotten man—if democracy cannot cope with the
problems created by the defects of capitalism—then
peoples in despair will turn to more authoritarian
rule.

In France growing discontent with the Republic
—provoked by constant changes in ministries, a
financial policy that increased the cost of living in
a period of dwindling employment and trade—came
to a head after the Stavisky affair of January 1934.
Alexandre Stavisky, a notorious swindler and gam-
bler, managed to gain control of the municipal pawnshop in Bayonne, with the complicity of government
officials. Through issuing bonds upon the supposed
security of pawnshop pledges, he defrauded insurance companies and private individuals to the
amount of two hundred million francs. Not only
were the Mayor of Bayonne, a deputy, and several
journalists implicated in this swindle, but a member
of the Cabinet, who had written letters calling the
attention of insurance companies to the possibility

of investing in these bonds, was compelled to resign. The Stavisky scandal, which in many respects
is similar to a dozen scandals recently revealed in
the United States, was the match that touched off
the growing indignation of many Frenchmen with
the parliamentary régime. For two days in February
mobs in Paris actually fought the police, the troops,
and the mobile guards. Quiet was restored only after
the formation of a non-partisan cabinet headed by
Gaston Doumergue, the seventy-one-year-old ex-
president. The Paris riots did not represent the work
of a patiently organized and well-disciplined movement against the Republic. They were merely the
spontaneous outbursts of various sections of opinion
against the six hundred "dictators" who occupy the
Palais Bourbon. It is also significant that, although
the Chautemps and Daladier cabinets which preceded the Doumergue ministry managed to secure
votes of confidence from parliament, they both resigned office because of the fury of the mob. If public opinion cannot properly vent itself through constitutional methods, it will make itself heard through
extra-legal channels.

The Doumergue government, composed largely of
old men, constitutes a truce between the Right and
the Left. Unless this government carries out radical
reforms and adopts a constructive foreign policy,
Fascist sentiment in France, already pronounced
among several organizations of young men, may continue to grow.

In Great Britain many voices also declare that
the traditional forms of parliamentary government
cannot cope with the problems created by tech-
nology. In August 1931 the party system was virtually abandoned when Prime Minister MacDonald

forced the resignation of the Labor Cabinet and established a National government composed of four Conservatives, three former Laborites, and two Liberals. This action only served to increase underlying dissatisfaction with the existing methods. The Fascist League organized by Sir Oswald Mosley won the support of the Rothermere papers in the winter of 1933–34. Certain leading personalities, such as Sir Stafford Cripps, also attempted to commit the Labor party in favor of government by means of emergency powers—a movement which was defeated when the party executive on January 25, 1934 adopted a strong resolution adhering to the principles of parliamentary government.

Discontent with existing forms of governmental procedure also arose in the United States at the end of the Hoover Administration. Here a widespread revulsion set in against the policy of using government machinery to increase the profits of private business, while doing little to combat unemployment. Universal disgust was also felt at the revelation of corruption in municipal government. Fortunately a presidential election in November 1932 gave the American public a constitutional outlet for their discontent. The result was an overwhelming victory for the opposition candidate, Franklin D. Roosevelt.

Although ostensibly a party Democrat, President Roosevelt developed an administration which constitutes a radical departure from any previous form of government the American people has experienced. He did not abolish the Constitution, nor did he assume any illegal powers; he did, however, induce Congress to vest in him far-reaching control over the economic life of the country. This control was

delegated not to the ordinary Cabinet departments
but to a series of new agencies, chief of which were
the National Recovery Administration, the Reconstruction Finance Corporation, and the Agricultural
Adjustment Administration. Under this system the
powers of Congress, of the Cabinet, and of the
States were vastly reduced.

That the American government had not become
a dictatorship similar to those existing in Soviet
Russia, Fascist Italy, or Hitlerized Germany was
indicated by the fact that Congress remained the
ultimate source of authority; that fair elections were
held; that universal suffrage continued in effect;
that it was still possible to appeal to the courts
against the acts of public officials; and that freedom
of the press, speech and radio were not curtailed.
The Roosevelt Administration, moreover, did not
ferret out opposition by a system of espionage and
secret police. Nor did it attempt to suppress the
Labor Unions.

The underlying purpose of this new system of administration was to bring about economic recovery
and at the same time reform our economic and social system. While the methods employed by President Roosevelt involve many unique departures,
they respect the underlying principles of democracy.
If the Roosevelt system succeeds in meeting the
economic and social crisis, democracy will be vindicated in the United States. Should the Roosevelt
Administration fail, it is not improbable that
Fascism and Communism will continue their march
across the world.

In view of recent developments, the Foreign
Policy Association believes that the publication of
this book describing the principles and methods of

the new governments of Europe is of timely importance. Since its establishment in 1925, the Research Department of the Foreign Policy Association has closely followed political developments in
every part of the world. The results of its studies,
which have been based not only on a careful examination of documents, both official and unofficial, but
also on widespread travel and first-hand contacts,
have been presented in fortnightly publications, now
called *Foreign Policy Reports*. The present volume
is based largely on a collection of the reports devoted to the new governments of Europe, but revised so as to bring them up to date.

The introductory chapter on the theories of Democracy, Fascism and Communism, and the sections
on Fascist Italy and Communist Russia have been
written by Dr. Vera Micheles Dean, the section on
Germany by Dr. Mildred S. Wertheimer, both members of the Foreign Policy Association staff. The
section on Spain, which portrays the effort of a
country to realize Socialism by parliamentary means,
has been written by Bailey W. Diffie, instructor at
the College of the City of New York. The final
chapters on the new Baltic republics, where Fascist
sentiment seems to be growing, are the work of
Malbone W. Graham, professor of political science
at the University in California at Los Angeles.

RAYMOND LESLIE BUELL
President, Foreign Policy Association

PREFACE TO REVISED EDITION

Since this book first appeared in 1934, the new dictatorships in Europe have continued to attract world-wide attention. In defiance of the League of Nations, Fascist Italy has succeeded in conquering Ethiopia; and, in violation of the Treaty of Versailles, Nazi Germany is building up an enormous military establishment and has reoccupied the Rhineland. In contrast to Italy and Germany, Soviet Russia has vast undeveloped resources and is relatively underpopulated. Consequently, it continues to be an ardent defender of the *status quo*. During the last few years, it has become disillusioned with the League of Nations, and even with its allies. More and more, it depends for its security on its own powerful army, which has increased from 562,-000, when Hitler came to power in 1933, to 1,300,000 at the present time. In order to assure the loyalty of its population in wartime, Soviet Russia has modified its agricultural policy, and in December 1936 adopted a new constitution which is described in following chapters.

Despite the "war against bolshevism," the internal régimes of Soviet Russia and the Fascist dictatorships seem to be converging toward a common pattern. In the Soviet Union, while the State continues to own the means of production, new differences in class and wealth have begun to appear. The gulf separating the new governing hierarchy from the workers seems almost as wide as under private capitalism. Under the speed-up or Stakhanov system, wide variations in the income of workers have arisen. Moreover, today the principle of private property is admitted to an increased degree. The new constitution of 1936 admits the principle of inheritance. Certainly Soviet Russia has failed to create the Communist society envisaged by Marx and Lenin.

In Nazi Germany and Fascist Italy a trend toward state capitalism has taken place during the past three years, which is producing a politico-economic régime similar to that in Soviet Russia. In November 1936 Mussolini imposed a capital levy of 20 per cent on real property—a drastic step toward nationalization, imposed by the financial burden of the Ethiopian war. In Germany two-thirds of the business of the country consists of government orders financed largely by borrowed money. When the limit of debt capacity is reached, the Nazi régime will also be confronted with the question of expropriation. The German four-year plan aiming at self-sufficiency in raw materials has accentuated state intervention. In both Germany and Italy, labor and capital are regimented, while class distinctions are steadily being reduced.

In the development of huge military establishments, the three dictatorships of Europe are also following parallel policies. Critics of these régimes insist that the dictatorships could not exist except on a basis of militarism. It is true that each dictatorship has employed militaristic symbols as one means of maintaining internal discipline and rallying the nation to a gigantic collective effort. But primarily

these huge military establishments reflect a conflict
of traditional national interests. Soviet Russia arms
not because it enjoys the sight of huge armies, but
because it fears an attack by Germany and Japan.
Italy arms for the purpose of establishing an empire
and extracting from the rest of the world a recognition of its position as a great power. Nazi Germany follows a similar course to overcome the inequalities established in the Versailles Treaty and
wrest concessions from an unwilling France and
Britain. If the diplomatic situation justifies it, these
German armaments may also be used for territorial
expansion in Central Europe and the Soviet Union.

Military considerations have prompted each dictatorship to aim at self-sufficiency, and today all
three are operating virtually on the basis of a war
economy. In the case of Germany and Italy at least,
self-sufficiency is extremely difficult because raw
materials are lacking. So far, synthetic substitutes
are proving inferior in quality and excessive in price.
As a result of militarism and *Autarkie*, the standard
of living of both the German and Italian dictatorships seems to be falling. Finally, the dictatorships
are characterized by a totalitarian attitude toward
life, under which the individual counts for nothing
except an instrument of the state. Freedom of
thought and expression, parliamentary institutions
and all forms of effective governmental responsibility have disappeared. In Soviet Russia no departure
from the party "line" is tolerated. In politics as well
as in art, rigid conformity is the rule. After a visit
to Soviet Russia, the famous French novelist André
Gide, who recently became a Communist, wrote:
"I doubt whether in any other country today, even
in Hitler's Germany, the spirit is less free, more

curbed, more terrorized, more enchained [*vassalisé*]."[1] What impressed M. Gide was the "extraordinary uniformity" and the complete "depersonalization" of the masses.

In Fascist Italy and Nazi Germany this same disregard of personality, the same fanatical devotion to totalitarian power exists. The Fascist régime in Italy, while it still resorts to arrests, seems to have consolidated itself so strongly that the wholesale repressive measures found in the Soviet Union and Germany are no longer necessary. In the latter country the offense of economic sabotage, i.e., the attempted expatriation of capital, is now punished with death. Mass trials of Social Democrats are held, concentration camps remain full, and Communists such as Edgar André are executed for offenses committed before the Nazis came to power.

Despite the aggressive tendencies of the Fascist dictatorships, the three leading democracies of Britain, France and the United States seem to have gained strength during the last war. In each of these countries the "Fascist" groups threatening to overthrow the democratic process have lost ground. Profiting from the example of the German republic, both Britain and France have enacted legislation prohibiting the maintenance of private armies and the wearing of uniforms by political groups. Following the enactment of such legislation in England and the East End riots, Oswald Mosley's movement, which never was important, began to dwindle. The inherent strength of British democracy was indicated not only by Mr. J. H. Thomas's removal last June from the British Cabinet on account of budget leaks,

[1] André Gide, *Retour de l'U.S.S.R.* (Paris, Gallimard, 1936), p. 67.

but by the dignity and promptness with which Britain in December solved a grave constitutional crisis caused by the desire of Edward VIII to marry a twice-divorced American. In France even more striking developments have taken place, as result of which French democracy seems to be steadily strengthening itself. The groups sympathetic to fascism received a striking rebuff in the elections of June 1936 which brought to power a Popular Front government headed by Léon Blum. Confronted by grave social unrest marked by a remarkable series of stay-in strikes, the Blum government quickly secured concessions from the French employers and obtained the evacuation of factories. In the summer of 1936 the French Parliament enacted a far-reaching series of social reforms and in September the government devalued the franc. Altogether the Blum cabinet wrought a peaceful social transformation in France while maintaining the principles of French civilization. Toward the end of the year, the shrill accusations of the reactionaries had begun to decline and business recovery seemed to be taking place. Finally, in America, democratic ideals seem to have been vindicated by the enormous majority received by President Roosevelt in the November elections. It may be significant that the voices of Father Coughlin, Doctor Townsend and Huey Long, all of whom might have served as the vanguard of an American Fascist movement, are no longer heard. The United States, too, is making necessary social changes by means of the democratic process. It is perhaps of significance, moreover, that economic recovery is taking place in all the democratic countries while conditions seem to be deteriorating in Germany and Italy. Only in Spain has democracy suf-

fered a setback. Whatever the outcome of the civil
war—some form of dictatorship seems inevitable.

As a result of the growing conflict between democracies and dictatorships, there is a danger that war
may occur. The problem is to devise an international
settlement which will make it possible for democracies and dictatorships to live peacefully side by
side. Such a settlement involves economic concessions on the part of the democracies if, in return, the
dictatorships will agree to give up their ambitions
for further territorial expansion. Many liberals, however, insist that by virtue of a different attitude
toward life, no compromise between totalitarian and
democratic powers is possible. While admitting the
differences in philosophy between these types of
régime, two facts should be remembered. First, the
totalitarian régimes have adopted extremist policies
and, indeed, in some cases have come into existence
partly because of the defects of an international
political and economic system for which the great
democracies have been largely responsible. Second,
the democracies have continued to adhere to liberalism by virtue of a long tradition and a standard of
living superior to that in the countries which have
become dictatorships. The difference between the
dictatorships and the democracies, is one of degree.
Nations, like individuals, are possessed of dual personalities warring against each other. The baser aspects of these personalities emerge triumphant when
the traditional controls break down. These controls
are undermined when political and social institutions fail to provide the masses with a minimum
degree of security and self-respect. Liberty is a
fundamental quality of human existence, but men
en masse abandon it when insecurity reaches an un-

bearable point. There is therefore no impassable gulf between the dictatorships and the democracies. Given a rising standard of living and recognition of the legitimate nationalist aspirations of the dictatorships, one may expect a moderation in their policies. Moreover, if democracies today are not aggressive, it is due not to superior virtues but to the fact that they have all the territory they want and are comparatively well-fed. Glorification of war and a distorted nationalism in the dictatorships is to a large extent the reflection of economic needs which have not been satisfied.

It should not be forgotten that while France and Britain achieved national unity as early as the 13th century, the process of national unification in the case of Germany and Italy was delayed until the latter part of the 19th century and is only now being completed. To take the case of Germany, this delay in achieving unity is due to a number of geographical and historical causes. At the time when France and Britain were establishing their national existence, Germany was involved in a series of wars rising out of the pretensions of the Holy Roman Empire, which reduced the country to a prolonged state of disintegrated feudalism. Again unlike Britain and France, Germany was not protected by natural frontiers. In the case of France, the Pyrenees and the Rhine set a limit to the necessities of self-defense. But no such natural barriers existed in the case of Germany. As a result, it spent centuries in fighting wars for the control of the indefinite plains extending into East Prussia and Central Europe. In the absence of a natural boundary "the conqueror only believed in security when he had destroyed the enemy state."[2] The German wars therefore became wars of extermination. At the end of the Thirty Years' War, which was terminated with the Peace of Westphalia in 1648, Germany had been completely desolated.

The efforts to achieve national unity in Germany during the 19th century need not be recounted here. But the World War, the peace settlement and the defects of the post-war economic and political system led the German people to turn to Hitler, in many cases with a sense of joy and relief. Dictatorship is a technique—brutal and dangerous perhaps— of forming a nation.[3] The three great dictatorships of Europe today are in the grip of a profound revolutionary process which inevitably produces individual injustices and the violation of democratic principles. Such has been the history of every revolution in the past. As these revolutions consolidate themselves, present excesses may be moderated and more liberal principles gradually accepted.[4] The return to moderation will largely depend on whether the world is to be plunged into a new war or whether an international settlement can be peacefully effected.

If the world makes it clear that it will resist further acts of aggression on the part of the Fascist dictatorships, it is reasonable to believe that, confronted with the alternative of a world settlement or a declining standard of living, the dictatorships

[2] Cf. Henri Pirenne, *Histoire de l'Europe des Invasions au XVI Siecle* (Brussels, 1936), p. 208.

[3] Cf. Erich Voegelin, *Der Autoritäre Staat* (Wien, Springer, 1936).

[4] In an interesting book, Benedetto Croce declares that every conservative reaction of the 19th century has been followed by a return to liberalism. Cf. his *History of Europe during the 19th Century* (New York, Harcourt, Brace, 1933).

will choose the former. An international solution will strengthen the remaining forces of moderation in the dictatorships and it is only by means of such a settlement that the excesses of the dictatorships may be removed. Whether a world war will arise either between Nazi Germany and Soviet Russia or the Fascist dictatorships and the outside world will depend largely on the willingness and ability of the democratic powers to make economic concessions removing the legitimate grievances of relatively over-populated countries and at the same time resisting any further treaty violation. While the following pages are not devoted to the international aspects of this problem, they do give the reader a detailed and clear picture of the type of state which has come into existence during the last few years—a picture which is essential to an understanding both of the problem of modern government and of international relations.

The present edition of this book, which first appeared in 1934, has been thoroughly revised. Several new authors appear, thus Mr. John C. deWilde has brought down to date and expanded the German chapters, while Mr. Charles A. Thomson has written an account of the causes and progress of the Spanish revolt. Owing to limitations of space, the section on the Baltic has been omitted. Those who wish to keep abreast of the rapidly changing developments in the new governments of Europe will find material of value in the current publications of the Foreign Policy Association.

RAYMOND LESLIE BUELL

January 1937

CONTENTS

CONTENTS

CONTENTS

THE
ATTACK ON DEMOCRACY

WE are living in a period when the most coura-
geous face moments of profound discouragement,
when the hopes for social and international appease-
ment salvaged from the wreckage of the World War
seem sadly illusory. It is natural that in such a period we should seize on every creed which contains
a promise, no matter how vague, of new relations
between men and states. The more chaotic the world
around him, the more distraught his mind and soul,
the more urgent is man's desire to believe in something outside himself, to surrender to the tide of
a mass movement, little as he knows where this
movement may lead him. It is only too easy, in
an age of recurring crises, to be stampeded into acceptance of authority, no matter what its source, and
to demand that the Western heritage of political and
economic traditions be jettisoned in favor of a new
system, be it Fascism or Communism. Yet the very
prevalence of mass hysteria makes it supremely important to assay, with as much detachment as one
can summon, both that which it is proposed to surrender and that which it is hoped to achieve.

Loss of faith in traditional institutions and traditional patterns of life—intellectual skepticism and
emotional instability—have marked not only political and economic speculation, but art and litera-

ture since the World War. To the generation nurtured on Victorian faith in human progress and the ultimate goodness of mankind the war was a catastrophe, shattering a world of unrealized ideals. The war severed a historical nerve connection which no amount of political surgery has succeeded in restoring. Confronted by the unprecedented strain of a world conflict, countries which had appeared dedicated to democracy resorted to the methods of dictatorship, and drastically curtailed, or altogether suspended, individual liberty for the sake of the common cause. The liberal state, once committed to the policy of *laissez faire*, assumed control of economic activities to a degree unprecedented in modern history. The unlimited powers which individuals had been willing to grant the state for the duration of the emergency could not be laid aside overnight. War had exalted the state and diminished the individual. Peace, with its manifold problems and its heritage of economic disorganization culminating in world-wide depression, only emphasized the helplessness of the individual and his need for an authoritarian state. In this sense, 1914 marked the end of an era which had made a cult of democracy, individual liberty and economic *laissez faire*.

From the Renaissance and the Reformation the Western world has inherited a conception of the dignity and worth of the individual which even now it finds it difficult to discard. The French Revolution, defying the tyranny of monarchs and the glaring inequalities of a society built on privilege of birth, asserted the right of all individuals within the state to political liberty and equality. The driving force of this revolution came from the middle class, which desired to exercise political powers commensurate with its economic achievements. This class regarded the state as a necessary evil, whose functions should be strictly limited by a written constitution, and never allowed to interfere with individual liberty. It demanded that the business of government be transacted not by a few irresponsible ministers closeted with the king or the king's mistress, but in the full light of day, through elected assemblies representing the will of the people. To assure its control of political power, it demanded the extension of suffrage, liberty of association and the press, free access to the courts and educational facilities. To assure its control of economic power, it demanded that the state adopt a policy of *laissez faire,* abstain from interfering with trade and industry, and give full scope to individual initiative in the acquisition of property. The political theories of the French Revolution closely paralleled the economic practices sponsored by the Industrial Revolution. Historically the birth of democracy coincided with that of capitalism. The nineteenth century may thus be described as a period of capitalist democracy.

That century opened on a world which seemed to hold unlimited possibilities of progress. There were still frontiers to conquer, hinterlands to explore, markets and raw materials to develop. Man felt that his vigor had not yet been tested, and was ready to challenge nature in laboratory, field and factory. The increase in production made possible by the machine seemed to hold out a promise of indefinite improvement in the standard of living. Armed with the twin weapons of industry and science, man thought he could fearlessly confront the future, rising from one peak of progress to the next. The full-

blooded optimism of that period was both ruthless
and sentimental.

This optimism, this faith in material progress, had
a far-reaching influence on political and economic
institutions. The middle class, entrenched in parliament, could afford to be relatively generous. It
resisted the introduction of universal suffrage and
improvement in the living conditions of the rising
industrial proletariat, but seldom resorted to violence. Meanwhile the workers were confident that,
with strong trade-union organization, with able and
honest leadership, they too would soon reach the
level of economic prosperity achieved by the middle
class. Not that this period was free of strikes and
lockouts, of conflicts between capital and labor.
These clashes, however, were not yet fought out as
ultimate issues, to be solved only by resort to
violence and thoroughgoing revolution. Common
agreement still existed regarding the basic conceptions of the political and economic system, and the
conflicting groups were not only able, but willing,
to air their differences in parliament and the press.

These two factors—common agreement regarding
basic concepts and willingness to discuss existing
problems—facilitated the successful operation of
democracy in the nineteenth century. Democracy
prospers in societies with a fairly simple political
and economic organization, in which the issues at
stake are not complex, are easily understood by the
average man, and lend themselves to clear-cut and
dramatic discussion in representative assemblies.
Democracy presupposes readiness on the part of the
majority, in parliament or outside, to give the minority a hearing, and willingness on the part of the
minority to accept, even if it attacks, the policies

of the majority as long as the latter holds power. Democracy has functioned most successfully in countries like Great Britain and France, where a homogeneous population, no matter how divided by individual and party differences, is closely bound by similar traditions, and usually refuses to sacrifice the welfare of the nation as a whole to party or local interests. It has also functioned most successfully in periods when economic conditions have been sufficiently sound and elastic to prevent sharp class differentiation and conflicts between various classes over control of property. Where the disposition to rational discussion of fundamental problems is lacking, where differences between political or economic groups appear irreconcilable, where these groups prefer to fight out the ultimate issues involved rather than effect a compromise, where a continuing state of crisis, of emergency, exists— democracy no longer functions with success, and must sooner or later yield to some other form of government.

It is to the presence of these factors that the current reaction against democracy may be traced. The increasing complexity of modern life has created a multiplicity of technical problems which cannot be properly understood by the electorate or efficiently solved by discussion in popular assemblies. The intricacies of currency stabilization, the manifold difficulties raised by adjustment of wages and prices, are beyond the scope of both the voters and their representatives, who prefer to leave them in the hands of a strong executive. The prolonged economic crisis has only increased the individual's desire to throw the burden of his personal problems on the shoulders of the state. Finding himself unable to

cope with the economic anxieties which assail him
on all sides, the individual is ready to surrender a
large portion of his liberty in return for economic
security, which he believes it the task of the state
to assure. The state is alternately implored and
bullied by various groups of the population—industrialists, farmers, taxpayers, war veterans, unemployed—to assume ever growing powers and to
enter spheres of activity from which it had previously been barred in the name of individual liberty
and private initiative.

At the same time the economic crisis tends to
sharpen political conflicts, and reduces the willingness of various classes to settle these conflicts by
peaceful means. Emergencies demand rapid and decisive action, for which democratic institutions are
essentially unsuited. Parliamentary debates, ab-
sorbing and important in normal times, become dangerous obstacles to effective action in moments of
crisis. The population begins to demand that authority be concentrated in the hands of a few leaders.
These leaders, in turn, insist that they can act
decisively only if not hampered by the necessity of
constantly consulting the electorate or its representatives.

Democracy is attacked not only on the ground
that its political institutions are ill devised to cope
with modern problems, but because it is identified
with capitalism, which has failed to assure the perpetuation of material prosperity. It is contended
that political equality, as guaranteed by written
constitutions, has become illusory—that it is drastically curtailed, if not altogether nullified, by
glaring economic inequalities which capitalism has
failed to correct. Nor do critics of democracy believe

that the economic inequalities which have developed under capitalism can be corrected by democratic methods.

The attack on capitalist democracy has been particularly violent in countries like Germany and Italy, which lack democratic traditions. In both countries the reaction against democracy, while differing in some of its manifestations, has taken the form of Fascism. This tendency toward Fascism springs, in the first place, from disillusionment with the outcome of the World War and the events of the post-war period. Italy, it is true, was among the victors, and satisfied its principal territorial ambitions in Europe. It failed, however, to obtain colonies in Africa, which it regards essential as an outlet for its rapidly growing population. If Italy was embittered by what it described as a Pyrrhic victory, Germany was overwhelmed with a sense of humiliation and despair. A nation which had been inordinately proud of its military prowess and technical achievements had been forced to yield to the superior numbers of the Allies and accept a Draconian peace. Millions of Germans believed that defeat had been brought about by the treachery of liberals, socialists and pacifists, who had given the army a "stab in the back," and had blindly subscribed to President Wilson's Fourteen Points, few of which had found place in the peace treaties. Nor did the events of the post-war period serve to assuage Germany's moral wounds. Severe inflation ruined a large section of the middle class and fanned the discontent of industrial workers. The failure of the League of Nations to correct the inequities of the Versailles treaty and the reluctance of the Allies to meet Germany's demands with regard to reparation and arms equality, perpetuated the Germans' sense of injury and humiliation. The Weimar republic had little opportunity to strike roots in German soil.

Both in Germany and Italy democratic institutions were charged with incompetence, indecisiveness, inability to meet the problems of the post-war period. The necessity for a strong government, for centralized and unlimited authority, was stressed on every hand. At the same time the trend toward Socialism and Communism, encouraged by the success of the Bolshevik revolution in Russia in 1917, alarmed the industrialists and the middle class, who feared destruction of private property and resulting economic chaos. The appearance of Fascism in Germany and Italy constituted, on the one hand, a revolution against democracy and liberalism and, on the other, a reaction against Communism and all forms of left extremism.

That discontent with existing institutions should have taken the form of Fascism, rather than Communism, was due primarily to the presence in both Germany and Italy of a strong middle class, which had been lacking in Russia, and whose political importance has been underestimated by Marxist philosophy. The Marxist assumption that, with the progress of industrialization, society inevitably divides into two irreconcilable groups—a small handful of capitalists, and masses of industrial proletariat—is not supported by the experience of Western states. Nor does the middle class, as argued by Marxists, tend to join Communist ranks when it becomes impoverished and proletarianized. The middle class is a broad term, which covers several social and economic groups—professional men, technical experts, small merchants and shopkeepers,

clerks and skilled workers. The average member of
the middle class may have risen from humble be-
ginnings, from the ranks of peasants or industrial
workers. In the course of his career, however, he
cultivates a standard of living patterned on that of
the wealthy, acquires some property, perhaps a
house of his own, and develops ambitions for the
future of his children. The middle class usually lacks
the class consciousness of industrial workers, as well
as their organization. It can seldom act coherently
or harmoniously on political and economic issues.
It is knit together, however, by a sense of professional dignity, by attachment to personal property
and domestic privacy. To this class Communism,
with its demand for state control of property, with
its emphasis on the dictatorship of the proletariat,
which presupposes destruction of the middle class,
is distinctly repugnant as a solution of its problems.
Even when the white collar worker is reduced to the
lowest level of subsistence, when he is forced to
tramp the streets in search of employment, when he
has lost the white collar, symbol of his class, he is
not yet ready to throw in his fate with Communism.
Little Man, what now? asks the German writer
Hans Fallada in his poignant novel depicting the
plight of a humble member of the middle class, and
his answer is that the little man, even on the verge
of starvation, will turn Nazi rather than Communist.
This attitude of the middle class has been cleverly
utilized by Nazi propaganda in Germany to assure
the triumph of Fascism against both liberalism and
Communism.

The middle class seeks in Fascism not only protection against revolution from the left, not only
economic security, but a new faith in life, a new

assurance and inspiration which would contrast, on the one hand, with the agnosticism of the liberal state and, on the other, with the materialism of the Communist philosophy. After years of disillusionment with political and economic institutions, the traditional conceptions of home, love and religion, of frantic search for new values, mankind inevitably experiences a period of reaction, and passionately, even hysterically, seeks new gods to worship. Fascism attempts to fill this need by its emphasis on the conception of the state as a mystic entity, representing the continuance of a nation's spirit through the ages; by its demand that the individual surrender his will to supreme and unquestioned authority; by its support of religion, its demand for purification of morals, its championship of the home and family, and the glamour it confers on the military virtues of men and the housekeeping skill of women.

The mystic aspects of Fascism make an especially powerful appeal to the young generation, adrift in a crumbling world without star or compass. It is consequently not surprising to find a predominance of youth in Fascist ranks. The generation born just before or during the war knows little of democratic institutions or the spirit of liberalism. Its conscious years have been spent in an atmosphere of hopelessness and instability. This situation has been particularly acute in Germany, which has suffered severely from intellectual unemployment. Students leaving the universities had no outlook except further study, since all professions were overcrowded and vacancies were at a premium. Lack of opportunity for work fostered a dangerous spirit of resentment against existing governments, which had failed to assure the possibility of employment, and created a whole group of *déracinés*, restless and ready for any adventure. Enforced idleness stirred the desire for direct action, for channels which could use up the excess energy of youth. Fascism offers such a channel. It accepts youth with all the defects of its virtues—its intransigeance and violence, its arrogance and enthusiasm, its disregard of tradition and precedent, and its readiness to undergo supreme sacrifices for a cause which has fired its imagination. Fascism stresses the advantages of physical vigor, athletic prowess, youthful leadership, and gives the young generation an opportunity to exercise its lungs and muscles, if not its intellect, on the parade ground and in training camps. Fascism takes complete charge of the education of the young, insulates them against all contacts with the outside world, and inoculates them with its doctrines. A generation trained under such conditions would furnish excellent cannon-fodder should the Fascist state embark on a policy of territorial expansion. In fact, it is difficult to see how youth could long be restrained from demanding to be transferred from the parade-ground to the battlefield. The dangers of this situation are particularly acute because this young generation knows nothing of the horrors of modern warfare, has been taught to scorn the searing portrayals of Remarque and Barbusse, and considers the dangers of war far preferable to the stagnant atmosphere of peace without employment.

Another cause which has contributed to the rise of Fascism is the despair of the average individual, his desire to find warmth and security in contact with masses of his fellow beings. Individualism has flourished in periods relatively free of economic pressure, where opportunity still waited around the corner, and the individual was able to shape his own destiny. When the possibilities for individual development disappear, when economic difficulties apply a brake to individual initiative, the average man is less ready to challenge the world, and more willing to submit to authority as long as that authority undertakes to clothe and feed him. This tendency of the individual to become merged in a group, a collectivity, which offers him a modicum of protection against economic insecurity is not without danger. The individual who is normally kind, generous and tolerant may, when absorbed in a group, be easily swayed by mob emotion, and may condone, or even participate in, acts of violence which his better judgment would ordinarily condemn. No matter what his integrity and force of character, he may yield to mass pressure to preserve his job, his life, the security of his family, and in so doing may commit acts which his conscience repudiates. A mass movement seeks and finds its lowest level. The actions of a crowd may achieve supreme heroism. More often they result in shocking injustice or brutality.

The masses, however, do not act long without guidance—they crave leadership. Their selection is based on no process of rationalization. Most frequently it is determined by emotional factors. Not that the masses necessarily follow a worthless or inept figure—neither Hitler nor Mussolini could be described in these terms—but they demand from their leaders personal magnetism, glowing oratory, rather than demonstrated ability. This emotionalism of the masses, their desire to identify themselves with a man whom they can regard as a superior being, a symbol of their confused desires, has been capitalized by Mussolini and Hitler with striking success.

The political system of Fascism faithfully mirrors the various trends which go to make up the Fascist state of mind. Fascist philosophy conceives the state as a "totalitarian" entity, which absorbs the individual as well as all groups—the church, the school, the trade union—and in which alone the individual can fulfill his destiny. This concept is expressed in Mussolini's famous phrase: "Everything within the state; nothing outside the state." Within the framework of the Fascist state all human activities and interests must be coördinated under government control. Individual liberty is entirely subordinated to the interests of the state, which are paramount. If it threatens to conflict with the aims of the state, it must be curtailed or destroyed.

The Nazi program in Germany declares that "common welfare comes before individual welfare." By its exaltation of the authoritarian state, Fascist philosophy challenges both liberal agnosticism and Marxist materialism. To the individual weary of skepticism and emphasis on material ends, Fascism offers a philosophy which prescribes discipline and acquiescence in authority, and at the same time glorifies the romantic elements of national tradition. Thus Fascist Italy exalts the glamourous memories of imperial Rome, while Nazi Germany glorifies the simple virtues of the German race.

Fascism rejects the conception of popular sovereignty and the traditional institutions of democracy. Parliaments are regarded not only as obsolete and useless, but as a grave obstacle to efficient administration. According to the Fascists democracy, which may have had a *raison d'être* in the nineteenth century, is today an anachronism. Sovereignty resides not in the people, but in society organized as a state. The great mass of citizens, argues Fascism, is too ignorant or too concerned with narrow private and local interests to undertake the complicated task of government. This task must devolve on a chosen few, a governing élite, selected not by popular suffrage, which is a blundering method, but from the ranks of the Fascist party, on the basis of merit.

This governing class, in turn, must be led and animated by a man who can give expression to its ideals—*Il Duce* in Italy, *Der Führer* in Germany. This leader, once he has seized power, becomes the object of a sentiment closely akin to divinization. Mussolini has frequently expressed the conviction that he is a man of destiny, fated to guide Italy to a brilliant future. Hitler, when he addresses the throngs of his adherents, becomes mystically exalted, and speaks in terms of almost sensuous delight of his spiritual communion with the masses.

The supremacy of the state—which in practice means the dominance of the Fascist party—requires ruthless suppression of all opposition by word or deed. The introduction of Fascism in Italy and Germany has been accompanied by the exile, imprisonment or murder of political opponents, even when these offered no resistance to the new régime; suspension of civil liberties; suppression of all organs of public opinion and substitution of a colorless official press; and strict regulation of economic activities.

Fascism recognizes the importance of private initiative in industry, trade and agriculture. This is one of the important factors of its appeal to the middle class and the conservative peasantry, who fear that Communism would suppress private property. At the same time Fascism contends that private initiative should serve the interests of the state, and never interfere with them. Fascism recognizes the existence of the class struggle, of conflicts between workers and employers, but demands that such conflicts be adjusted by peaceful means, and should never be allowed to disturb public order. For the network of scattered and conflicting economic interests characteristic of the capitalist system, Fascism would eventually substitute a co-ordinated "corporative" state in which workers, employers and consumers would harmoniously co-operate under the ægis of the government, and where a council representing professional and economic interests would replace outworn parliaments selected on political lines.

In a period of political and economic disruption, Fascism exercises a strong fascination over the minds of men in all countries. Not only has it triumphed in Italy and Germany, but it has won adherents in traditionally democratic states like Great Britain and France. Fear of Fascism, moreover, has served as an excuse for the introduction of authoritarian government in Czechoslovakia and Austria, which believe that the menace of Germany, co-ordinated under Nazi rule, cannot be successfully met by democratic régimes. The German Social

Democrats, considered the strongest and best organized Socialist party in Europe, yielded to Fascism without a struggle because they stubbornly refused to resort to violence, and insisted on dealing with the Nazi movement by constitutional methods. Yet Fascism has not swept Europe unchecked. When in February 1934 Gaston Doumergue organized a cabinet of strong men following a series of anti-parliamentary riots, the French Socialist Confederation of Labor staged a general strike, warning the government that it would not tolerate adoption of Fascist measures. In Austria the Social Democrats, who had ruled Vienna since 1918, put up a desperate fight in February 1934 against the attempt of Chancellor Dollfuss to establish a Fascist system modeled on that of Italy. The ruins of Vienna's municipal apartment houses serve as a silent monument to the heroic decision of workers led by a handful of intellectuals to die rather than accept suppression of liberty and democracy as they conceived them.

Should Fascism finally triumph over liberalism and Socialism in Europe, will the workers submit to Fascist rule, as they have in Germany and Italy, or will they turn to Communism as a last resort? The middle class prefers Fascism, under which, for the time being, it retains control of private property. Have the European workers, in Marx's phrase, "nothing to lose but their chains," or will they, too, shun the thought of a Communist system modeled on that of the Soviet Union? Thus far Communism appears to have made little headway outside of Russia, where it has achieved a lasting victory. The workers have been less successful than the middle class in producing strong and daring leaders; no Communist Hitler or Mussolini has yet appeared on the European scene. Nor does the technique of government championed by Fascism and Communism offer much choice to workers nurtured in Social Democratic traditions. Both Fascism and Communism denounce parliamentary methods and economic *laissez faire*. Both advocate dictatorship and suppression of individual liberties. Neither hesitates to employ violence against its opponents. Both envisage an ultimate stage at which all citizens, usefully employed for collective ends—whether in field or factory, whether with hand or brain—will peacefully coöperate under the benevolent supervision of the state. But if, in the Fascist state, political power and control of economic resources are vested in representatives of the middle class, in the Communist state they are wielded by representatives of the workers. Is there as sharp a cleavage between workers and other social groups in leading European states as there was in Russia in 1917? Are the workers ready to destroy the middle class? Or will they prefer to accept its rule, as long as it maintains order and a modicum of material well-being? It is possible that Communism may spread in backward agrarian countries whose economic system resembles that of Russia on the eve of the Bolshevik revolution, like Bulgaria and Yugoslavia, but it seems doubtful today that it will triumph in industrialized countries as long as the middle class continues to be replenished from the ranks of the workers.

Even should Communism sweep Europe in the wake of Fascism, it is by no means certain that it would everywhere assume the same form as in the Soviet Union. Fascism and Communism may be articles of export, as claimed by both their protagonists and their opponents. No political or economic system, however, can be made to fit all countries like a standardized garment. Racial characteristics, national traditions, divergences in economic development could not fail to influence the form which Fascism or Communism might assume in different countries. Fascist Italy and Nazi Germany, starting from similar points of philosophical departure, are already following divergent roads, and might even be found arrayed against each other in a European conflict. It is consequently idle to hope that, should all Europe turn Fascist, international conflicts would be eliminated and peace immediately restored. Fascism has proved a disruptive force in international relations. Abroad as at home Fascism repudiates democratic concepts and parliamentary methods. It ridicules the deliberative procedure of the League of Nations; it demands settlement of international conflicts at small conferences of great powers, free from responsibility to public opinion; it glorifies war. By exalting the national state, Fascism perpetuates and embitters existing international differences. Communism, unlike Fascism, preaches international peace—but peace only between workers of all nations, who are simultaneously urged to suppress other social classes. The Communists argue that wars are provoked by the unbridled greeds and hatreds of capitalists and imperialists; that, once all states have adopted Communism, they will unite in an international proletarian community, and war will become obsolete. It remains to be seen, however, whether the interests of workers throughout the world, in countries so different in economic development as Great Britain and Yugoslavia, are any less conflicting than those of the middle class. If democracy, as contended by those who deride it, has failed to assure international peace and economic cooperation, Fascism and Communism have yet to demonstrate their ability to achieve these ends.

While dictatorship of the Right or Left temporarily has a powerful appeal for the masses, everywhere distracted by the economic crisis, it is fraught, in the long run, with the gravest dangers. By suppressing individual responsibility and initiative, it may simplify the daily life of the average man, but it stultifies him, and robs him of all power to formulate opinions on political and economic questions. Dictatorship creates a society where unquestioning obedience, secured and maintained by force, is substituted for intelligent and often fruitful dissension, where thought on all subjects is strictly regimented, and opposition is driven underground. By abolishing parliamentary procedure and muzzling public opinion, dictatorship leaves no alternative except civil war. The very violence of the methods which a dictatorship must necessarily employ to maintain itself in power is bound to provoke, sooner or later, an equally violent reaction which, with the passing of years, may bring about another swing toward democracy.

For with all its faults, democracy offers the individual a way of life superior to that prescribed by dictatorship. Where democracy functions most successfully, as in the Scandinavian countries, society finds it possible to achieve a balance of economic interests without repression of any social group, and permits each individual to develop to his full spiritual stature in an atmosphere of peace which fosters the finest flowering of civilization. Democracy is a far more difficult method of government than dictatorship. It makes much greater demands on the intelligence and unselfishness of the individual, and confronts him with more arduous tasks. Yet democracy does not force the individual to accept a rigid political or economic system. Its very lack of cohesion, often ridiculed by Fascists, renders it more elastic than dictatorship, more adaptable to changing conditions, and permits a wider range of peaceful political and economic experimentation. The breakdown of democracy in countries like Germany and Italy need not be interpreted as the death verdict of democracy elsewhere. If, as President Roosevelt has stated, "the machinery of democracy has failed to function" in recent years, this is due not only to defects in democratic institutions, but to "inertia on the part of leaders and on the part of the people themselves," who have permitted "the operations of government" to fall into the hands of special groups and, in a sense, have allowed democracy to go by default. The present crisis challenges the people of traditionally democratic countries like France, Great Britain and the United States to organize the state in such a way that it can cope effectively with the social problems created by the machine age without sacrificing the political and economic liberty of the individual. The success of democracy in meeting this challenge depends, in the last resort, on the willingness of each citizen to look beyond the immediate preoccupations of his daily life and develop a long-range view of the needs of society as a whole.[1]

[1] For further discussion of this subject, *cf.* G. D. H. Cole, *A Guide Through World Chaos* (New York, Knopf, 1932); Harold J. Laski, *Democracy in Crisis* (Chapel Hill, University of North Carolina Press, 1933); José Ortega y Gasset, *The Revolt of the Masses* (New York, Norton, 1932); John L. Strachey, *The Coming Struggle for Power* (New York, Covici-Friede, 1933).

FASCIST RULE IN ITALY

Nowhere in Europe, perhaps, were the doubts and disillusions engendered by the World War so sharply crystallized as in Italy. Nominally a victor, Italy regarded its share of the Versailles settlement far from commensurate with its sacrifices in wealth and manpower. War-weariness and discontent facilitated the rise of the Fascist party, which undertook to terminate the parliamentary system and to reorganize Italy's economic life along corporative lines. Fascism, essentially opposed to capitalist democracy, encountered little opposition in a country which had had little experience with parliamentary institutions, and had remained relatively unaffected by modern capitalism.

The unification of Italy, begun with the revolutions of 1821 and 1848, has been effected under conditions of considerable difficulty. The Italian *Risorgimento,* which had rallied all liberal and patriotic elements under the leadership of Mazzini and Cavour, and had given intellectual impetus to the process of unification, was essentially the movement of an *élite.* The Italian people as a whole, divided for centuries into semi-feudal principalities, oppressed by foreign rulers and absorbed in matters of local concern, had no sense of national unity, no knowledge of freedom and no experience with par-

liamentary institutions. "We have made Italy," said
the statesman D'Azeglio in 1861, "now we must
make Italians."

The country, poor in natural resources, was further weakened by a conflict of economic interests
between the North, which had begun to develop its
industries, and the agrarian South, whose progress
was hampered, first by absentee landlordism, and
later by the indifference of the central government.
Italy, like Germany, discovered that it had emerged
on the international scene too late to profit by
colonial expansion, which seemed to offer the only
outlet for a rapidly growing population. Conscious
of a brilliant past, Italy found it difficult to accept
a position which it regarded as that of a proletarian
among nations.

The form of government adopted by the Kingdom of Italy in 1861 was the product not so much
of Italy's political experience as of the cult for
liberalism and democracy which then reigned in
Western Europe. The *Statuto* granted by Charles
Albert to Piedmont in 1848 became the constitution
of the new kingdom. It provided for a monarch,
and a Parliament consisting of a Chamber of Deputies elected on a narrow franchise and a Senate, the
members of which were appointed by the King for
life from among twenty-one specified categories.
Legislative power was to be exercised jointly by the
King and the two chambers.

Parliamentary government, imposed from above
at a time when a large minority of the population
were illiterate, never became thoroughly acclimated
in Italy's political life. The deputies, as in other
countries, represented local rather than national
interests, and were frequently out of touch with the

broad masses of the population. The political leaders who succeeded Cavour—Minghetti, Depretis,
Crispi, Giolitti—enjoyed a personal, more than a
party following, and the formation of each new
cabinet involved a considerable amount of intrigue
and compromise. Elections, especially during Giolitti's several terms as Prime Minister, were accompanied by fraud and violence. The absence of political tradition and the diversity of the country's
interests prevented the emergence of a single group
which could be regarded as the ruling class.

ITALY'S POLITICAL LIFE, 1861–1914

During the fifty-three years which elapsed between the establishment of the kingdom and the
outbreak of the World War, Italy was continuously
governed by liberals, first of the Right and, after
1876, of the Left. The liberals achieved a considerable measure of success in creating national unity
and in solving Italy's most pressing economic problems. The Socialist party, organized in the early
nineties, began to participate in parliamentary work
at the beginning of the present century, and obtained a series of important social reforms, including
the electoral law of 1912, which increased the number of voters from over three million to more than
eight and a half million. Socialism, which drew its
chief support from the small bourgeoisie (*piccola
borghesia*) and the intellectuals, was weakened in
1912 by a cleavage between its moderate and radical
elements. The former seceded under the reformist
Bissolati, while the latter remained within the party,
and attempted to find a remedy for the growing
social unrest in the ranks of the proletariat. Meanwhile the Nationalist party, formed in 1910, advo-

cated a policy of expansion and imperialism.[1] The
country's renewed interest in colonial questions
found practical expression in the Italo-Turkish war
of 1911–1912, as a result of which Italy obtained
Tripoli and Cyrenaica.[2]

ITALY AND THE WORLD WAR

At the outbreak of the World War, the Italian
government decided that it was not bound by the
Triple Alliance to join the Central Powers in a war
which it regarded as one of offense, and made a
declaration of neutrality. Public opinion, however,
was divided. The Nationalists demanded, while the
Socialists opposed, Italy's entrance into the war.
The Prime Minister, Salandra, stated that the country's policy would be dictated by "sacred egoism."
After some hesitation Benito Mussolini, an extreme
Socialist and the editor of the party organ, *Avanti*,
suddenly pronounced himself in favor of intervention on the side of the Allies.[3] Expelled from the
party, he founded his own newspaper, *Il Popolo
d'Italia,* in Milan, where he was followed by the
more revolutionary Socialist elements. Mussolini
welcomed the war as a prelude to revolution. In
1915 he organized his followers in *Fasci d'Azione
Rivoluzionaria,* and instructed them to be ready
for everything—"for the trenches as well as for the

---

[1] The leaders of the Nationalist party—Enrico Corradini,
Luigi Federzoni, Roberto Forges-Davanzati—became prominent
in Fascist circles.

[2] For the history of Italy, 1859–1915, *cf.* Benedetto Croce,
A History of Italy, 1871–1915 (Oxford, Clarendon Press, 1929);
F. Quintavalle, *Storia dell' Unità Italiana* (Milan, Hoepli, 1926);
Luigi Villari, *Italy* (London, Benn, 1929); G. Volpe, *L'Italia in
Cammino* (Milan, Treves, 1927).

[3] For Mussolini's earlier years, *cf. Benito Mussolini,* My
Autobiography (New York, Scribner's, 1928); Margherita Sarfatti,
Dux (Milan, Mondadori, 1926).

barricades." [4] When Italy finally entered the war in May 1915, he greeted the event as a definite triumph of popular sentiment over a cautious government. [5]

During the war, in which he participated as a private, Mussolini denounced the defeatism of the Socialists and advocated the use of force for its suppression. He favored centralization of power in the hands of the government, as well as restrictions on the freedom of speech and of the press. The defeat which the Italian army suffered at Caporetto in October 1917 aroused both the government and the country, and a fresh drive against the enemy resulted in 1918 in the victory of Vittorio Veneto. Mussolini exulted at the breakdown of the Central Powers: Italy, he said, would now enjoy a new springtime, a new *risorgimento*, and would at last obtain its appointed place in the sun.

The hopes of Mussolini and his followers were dealt a severe blow by the wave of war-weariness which swept over the country in 1919, and by the results of the Paris Peace Conference which, in their opinion, left Italy with a "mutilated victory." The army, returning from the front to reap the reward of its sacrifices, found that the more profitable posts had meanwhile been occupied by those who had stayed safely at home. The cost of living had risen considerably, with no corresponding adjustment of salaries. The lower bourgeoisie, the civil employees and the intellectuals, many of whom were faced by unemployment, were in a worse economic plight than the peasants and industrial workers. The country was seething with disillusion and discontent.

[4] Mussolini, *Diuturna* (Milan, Imperia, 1924), p. 15.
[5] *Ibid.*, p. 52.

GROWTH OF SOCIALISM AFTER THE WAR

The Socialists, who had bitterly opposed Italy's participation in the war, now openly assailed the government for its failure to keep the country out of the conflict, and attacked officers and soldiers who ventured to appear publicly in uniform. Impressed with the success of the Soviet government, the Socialists advocated revolution by violent means as the only solution of Italy's problems. In the elections of 1919, held on the basis of proportional representation, the Socialists won an outstanding victory, returning 157 candidates to the Chamber of Deputies, and capturing the government in over two thousand municipalities. This success, however, marked the high tide of Italian Socialism. Strikes and disorders inspired by Socialists reached a climax in September 1920, when workers occupied the metallurgical factories of Lombardy and Piedmont. Neither the government nor the industrialists offered any resistance, and the workers, finding that they could not operate the factories without capital or technical experts, evacuated them after a few days. The revolutionary leaders suffered a loss of prestige. The Socialist party was further weakened in 1921 by the secession of its Left wing elements, which formed the Maximalist Communist party.[6]

ORGANIZATION OF FASCIST GROUPS

Meanwhile, two new political groups were attracting those opposed to the Socialist program. The *non-expedit,* by which the Church in 1857 had advised Catholics to abstain from political activities,

---

[6] Ivanoe Bonomi, *Dal Socialismo al Fascismo* (Rome, Formiggini, 1924).

was permitted to lapse in 1919 when a priest, Don Luigi Sturzo, organized the Popular party, with a democratic program "inspired by Christian ethics." [7] On March 23, 1919, Mussolini formed the first *Fascio di Combattimento,* modeled on the earlier *Fasci d'Azione Rivoluzionaria.*[8] These *fasci* were to devote their efforts to the restoration of public order and the suppression of Socialism. Fascism recruited its early adherents from the Nationalist party and from the ranks of the bourgeoisie, especially among World War veterans. Its program at that time was "a little of everything," combining democratic, republican, nationalist, monarchist and anarchist ideas,[9] tinged with a romantic idealization of Italy's destiny. The Fascists were entirely ineffective in the elections of 1919, when Mussolini himself was defeated at the polls.

In the autumn of 1920, however, Mussolini and other local leaders formed armed bands of Fascists (*squadre*), which carried on a vigorous campaign against Socialists and Communists. The propertied classes—landowners and industrialists—irritated and alarmed by constant disturbances of public order, gradually turned to Fascism. In the elections of 1921, thirty-five Fascist candidates, including Mussolini, were elected to the Chamber of Deputies, chiefly on the Nationalist ticket. Once in Parliament, Mussolini broke with the Nationalists, declared himself to be anti-monarchical and republican,

[7] Luigi Sturzo, *Italy and Fascismo* (London, Faber and Gwyer, 1926).

[8] Dino Grandi, *Il Fascismo* (Rome, Licinio Capelli, 1922), p. 52. The name *fascio* is taken from the word *fasces*—the Roman symbol of the lictor's power, which consisted of rods bound about an ax; it was borne in public processions before consuls and magistrates, and signified the union of all powers in one.

[9] *Ibid.,* p. 61.

and in August 1921 concluded a "pact of pacifica-
tion" with the Socialists. Neither of the two groups,
however, succeeded in persuading the rank and file
of its followers to abstain from acts of violence.
The Fascists outside Parliament finally prevailed
upon Mussolini to abandon his program of cooperation with other parliamentary groups.

Thereafter, the National Fascist party, formed on
November 6, 1921, engaged in a bitter struggle with
both Socialists and Popularists. On both sides hos-
tilities were marked by extreme violence. The government was not sufficiently strong to restore order
and, with the backing of industrialists, gave the
Fascists a free hand, hoping to find in them an ally
against Socialism. "Such conduct on the part of the
government," says the Fascist historian Villari,
"would have been wholly reprehensible in an orderly society, but Italy in 1919–1922 was nothing
of the kind." [10]

THE "MARCH ON ROME"

A number of observers believe that by 1921 Socialism was in retreat, and that the threat of a Bolshevik revolution had practically disappeared.[11] The
economic crisis had passed. The parliamentary crisis,
however, showed no signs of improvement. Successive Prime Ministers, summoned from the ranks of
Liberals, Socialists and Popularists, failed to rally
the Parliament and the country to a national program directed at the solution of the country's pressing economic problems. In the summer of 1922 the

[10] Luigi Villari, *The Fascist Experiment* (London, Faber and
Gwyer, 1928), p. 39.
[11] Bonomi, *Dal Socialismo al Fascismo,* cited, p. 147; Villari,
The Fascist Experiment, cited, p. 38; Gaetano Salvemini, *The
Fascist Dictatorship in Italy* (New York, Holt, 1927).

Fascists were offered subordinate positions in the cabinet. Mussolini refused, saying that he would not "reach power through the service entrance," or sacrifice his ideals "for a miserable dish of ministerial lentils." [12] At the party congress held in Naples on October 24, 1922, Mussolini made a *volte face,* and declared his allegiance to the King. This declaration won him the sympathies of many sections of the population, notably the army, which had previously been repelled by his republican principles. The Fascists, efficiently organized as a militia, and armed with the connivance of the government, were ready and eager for action. In October they occupied the large cities, taking possession of city halls, railway stations and postoffices. On October 27 the Fascist militia assembled at Civitavecchia, north of Rome, under the leadership of a "quadrumvirate"— General De Bono, De Vecchi, Michele Bianchi and Italo Balbo—and began the famous "March on Rome." The following day the militia entered the capital, where it met with no resistance.[13] On October 29 the King summoned Mussolini, who had remained in Milan, to form a cabinet, which he did on October 30. The Fascist revolution had taken place.

Opinion differs widely regarding the necessity of a revolution in 1922. Opponents of Fascism claim that the country had entered on a period of convalescence in 1921, and that the number of strikes

[12] Mussolini, *Discorsi della Rivoluzione* (Milan, Imperia, 1923), p. 77.
[13] On October 28 the cabinet, headed by Prime Minister Facta, decided to proclaim martial law and to oppose the March on Rome. On the advice of army leaders the King refused to sign the decree proclaiming martial law. *Cf.* Count Carlo Sforza, *Makers of Modern Europe* (Bobbs Merrill Company, 1930), Chapter XXXI, "Facta, or the Immediate Origins of Fascism."

had decreased in spite of a reduction in salaries.[14]
They believe, moreover, that the post-war parliamentary crisis was not indicative of the decadence
of democracy in Italy, and that it could have been
overcome by peaceful means if both Fascism and
Socialism had transferred their struggle to the constitutional sphere.[15] Mussolini, however, asserts that
the legal transformation of the state by means of
elections under a new electoral law, which he had
suggested before the March on Rome, had been
blocked by the government on the ground that it
would disturb public order; the problem had become, therefore, "one of force." [16] Parliamentary government, in his opinion, had been reduced to impotence after the war. He declared that the Fascist
revolution was directed not against the constitutional organization of the state, but against the
political group which for four years had failed to
give a government to the country.

The policies and acts of the Fascist government
have also given rise to diverse interpretations. The
Fascist revolution, effected by a former Socialist who
had held anti-bourgeois, anti-clerical and anti-
royalist views, has been denounced as the triumph
of a "White Guard" of industrial and agrarian
capitalists,[17] later supported by the Catholic Church.
The Fascist government has been attacked at one

[14] Bonomi, *Dal Socialismo al Fascismo,* cited, p. 89 *et seq.*
Bonomi estimates that 79,296 agricultural workers went on strike
in 1921, as compared with 1,045,732 in 1920, and 644,564 industrial
workers, as compared with 1,267,667 in 1920.

[15] *Ibid.; cf.* also Guglielmo Ferrero, *Four Years of Fascism*
(London, King & Son, 1924).

[16] *Cf.* Mussolini's speech at the Fascist party congress in
Naples, October 24, 1922. Mussolini, *Discorsi della Rivoluzione,*
cited, p. 78.

[17] Francesco Nitti, *Bolchévisme, Fascisme et Démocratie*
(Paris, "Progrès Civique," 1926).

and the same time for reaction in politics and radicalism in the economic field. The Fascists, meanwhile, claim that they have created the only political and economic structure which can assure Italy's orderly development, as well as its progress in world affairs. No general conclusions regarding the character of the Fascist state can be reached until the theory of Fascism has been examined, and its practical application analyzed.

CHAPTER I

THE THEORY OF FASCISM

FASCISM traces its intellectual origins to Machiavelli's *The Prince,* through Georges Sorel, Hegel, Nietzsche and Vico. From Machiavelli it has learned that the preservation of the state justifies recourse to force, and that politics are distinct from ethics. In the syndicalism of Sorel it finds intuition and passion exalted above reason, and direct action advocated even when it involves violence. To Hegel it owes the conception of the state as a mystical entity, superior to individuals, who find realization only in acceptance of the law. Vico's theory that political institutions are not immutable, but undergo transformation in accordance with time and place, has proved of practical value in Fascist politics. The thinker who has been acclaimed as the prophet of Fascism, however, is the Italian economist Vilfredo Pareto,[1] whose lectures at the Univer-

---

[1] Vilfredo Pareto (1848–1923), *Traité de Sociologie Générale* (Paris, Payot, 1921, 2 vols.); *Trasformazione della Democrazià* (Milan, "Corbaccio," 1921). *Cf.* G. H. Bousquet, *Vilfredo Pareto: Sa Vie et son Œuvre* (Paris, Payot, 1928). "Fascism may to a

sity of Lausanne Mussolini attended during his so-
journ in Switzerland in 1902. Pareto believes that
no social cycle can last indefinitely, and that the
cycle of "demagogic plutocracy," which he identifies with the nineteenth century, may disappear
when new elements arise, armed with knowledge,
force and will-power. No form of government, in his
opinion, is superior to any other in an abstract sense;
the test of a "good" government is whether or not it
is adapted to the society in which it is established.
The governing class—the *élite*—must rely on both
force and consent if it is to remain in power. Pareto
lived to see the advent of Fascism, some aspects of
which, notably its restrictions on the freedom of the
press, he subjected to searching criticism.

LACK OF PROGRAM

Fascism takes pride in the fact that it has no
program. To those who accused him of vagueness,
Mussolini replied in 1922 that Italy lacked, not
programs, but men and will-power.[2] Fascist writers
declare that Fascism is, above all, action and sentiment.[3] "Fascism as an idea is indefinable. It is a
fact which is taking place."[4] In its emphasis on
facts rather than theory, Fascism represents a revolt
against positivism, which permeated Italian education before the war, and against all social philoso-

large extent be regarded as an experimental proof of the doctrine
[of Pareto]." Sergio Panunzio, *Che Cos'è il Fascismo* (Milan,
Alpes, 1924), p. 77. For Pareto's influence on Mussolini, *cf.*
Sarfatti, *Dux*, cited, p. 69. The futurist poet, Marinetti, is also
regarded as a precursor of Fascism.

[2] Mussolini, *Discorsi della Rivoluzione,* cited, p. 27.

[3] Alfredo Rocco, *The Political Doctrine of Fascism,* Address
delivered at Perugia, August 30, 1925, published in Carnegie En-
dowment for International Peace, *International Conciliation,*
October 1926, No. 223, p. 394.

[4] Panunzio, *Che Cos'è il Fascismo,* cited, p. 75.

phy based solely on speculation. Fascist leaders, the
greater part of whose life has been spent in conflict, either at the front or in the field of politics,
place more reliance on action than on intellect.
"Every time we have taken up a volume," says
Turati, former Secretary-General of the party, "there
has resounded in our ears the cry of alarm, the sound
of the trumpet, and we have had to fling away our
book and take hold of the rifle." [5]

Fascism, however, chooses to be symbolized by the
book as well as the rifle (*libro e moschetto*). It is not
merely action; it has a theory. This theory is essentially in conflict with the historical materialism
of Marx, which conceives history as a predetermined
class struggle inevitably resulting in the collapse of
capitalism. Political and economic factors, according
to Fascism, are neither predetermined nor eternal,
but mobile and subject to change in different historical environments. Nor are the state or the individual concerned solely with material ends. Society
is profoundly influenced by such spiritual factors as culture, religion, custom and tradition, and
strives to preserve them for future generations.

FASCIST SLOGANS: AUTHORITY, ORDER, DISCIPLINE

Unlike Marxism, Fascism holds out no promise of
a millennium.[6] It offers, however, the prospect of an
ordered and disciplined existence within the framework of the state. The Fascist state is conceived not
as an aggregate of groups and individuals, but as
a spiritual entity which survives and transcends

[5] Augusto Turati, *A Revolution and its Leader* (London,
Alexander Ousley, 1930), p. 40.
[6] "We shall promise nothing special. We shall not assume the
appearance of missionaries who are the bearers of revealed truth."
Mussolini, *Discorsi della Rivoluzione*, cited, p. 61.

successive generations. "For Fascism, society has historical and immanent ends of preservation, expansion, improvement, quite distinct from those of the individuals which at a given moment compose it; so distinct in fact that they may even be in opposition." [7] Individuals are merely the means by which society achieves its ends. When it is objected that such worship of the state is nothing less than a new form of idolatry, Fascist writers reply that it constitutes a "religion of the spirit," which saves the mind from "the abject blindness of materialism." [8]

The individual, according to Fascism, is subordinated to society, but not eliminated. He remains an element of society "however transient and insignificant he may be." [9] The individual, however, cannot lead an existence distinct from that of the state. He owes a duty to the state, and in the exercise of this duty may be called on to sacrifice everything, including life. The preëminence of duty is regarded as the highest ethical value of Fascism. The Fascist state is not merely an administrative organization, concerned with political or economic issues; it is "totalitarian," embraces all interests and activities, whether of groups or individuals, and permeates the spiritual content of life. Nothing can exist outside or above the state. "One cannot be Fascist in politics . . . and non-Fascist in school, non-Fascist in the family circle, non-Fascist in the workshop." [10]

Where Fascism departs most radically from the

---

[7] Rocco, *The Political Doctrine of Fascism,* cited, p. 402.
[8] Giovanni Gentile, *Che Cos'è il Fascismo* (Florence, Valecchi, 1925), p. 36.
[9] Rocco, *The Political Doctrine of Fascism,* cited, p. 402.
[10] Gentile, *Che Cos'è il Fascismo,* cited, p. 38.

accepted doctrines of liberalism, socialism and democracy is in its conception of the liberty of individuals and groups. Individual rights are recognized by Fascism only in so far as they are implied
in the rights of the state.[11] The conditions that make
for the free development of the individual are to be
safeguarded. Fascism, however, does not accept a
bill of rights "which tends to make the individual
superior to the state" and empowers him "to act
in opposition to society."[12] Freedom, whether political or economic, is a concession on the part of
the state, and can be granted only on condition that
it be exercised in the interest of society as a whole
and within the limits set by social exigencies. Fascism recognizes that individual ambition is "the
most effective means of obtaining the best social
results with the least effort," and regards a degree
of economic liberty compatible with the social good.
This liberty, however, must be severely curbed
whenever it threatens to result in economic conflict
and disturbance of public order. Measures of class
self-defense, such as strikes and lockouts, are therefore prohibited by Fascism. Economic justice is to
be achieved, not in consequence of class struggle, but
by means of Fascist syndicates subject to the authority of the state.[13] It is particularly important,
according to Fascism, that peace should be preserved
in a country like Italy, which is poor in natural
resources.

"Public order must not be disturbed for any motive,
at any cost. Italy must have economic peace in order
to develop its resources. . . . It is necessary for syndical-

---

[11] Rocco, *The Political Doctrine of Fascism,* cited, p. 403.
[12] *Ibid.,* p. 403.
[13] *Ibid.,* p. 406–407.

ism and capitalism to realize the new historical reality:
that they must avoid bringing matters to the breaking-
point, must avoid war between classes, because when
such a war is fought within the nation, it is destructive.
. . . The government is at the orders of neither group.
The government stands above all groups in that it represents not only the political consciousness of the nation
today, but also all that the nation will constitute in the
future." [14]

THE INDIVIDUAL AND THE FASCIST STATE

The subordination of classes and individuals to the
state creates no ethical problem for Fascism, which
believes that "the legitimate will of the citizen is
that which coincides with the will of the state." [15]
If this be true, opposition is not only unreasonable,
but reprehensible. Should opposition nevertheless
appear, it must be regarded as a social disease, to be
eradicated as promptly as possible from the body
politic. The method advocated in such cases is that
of violence. "Discipline must be accepted," says
Mussolini. "When it is not accepted, it must be
imposed." [16] Fascist theory distinguishes between
private violence, which is arbitrary and anarchic,
and violence directed to social ends. The latter is
"willed by God and by all men who believe in God
and in the order and laws which God certainly desires for the world. . . ." [17] Such violence is holy
and highly moral.[18]

[14] Mussolini, *La Nuova Politica dell' Italia* (Milan, Imperia,
1924), Vol. II, p. 136–139.
[15] Gentile, *Che Cos'è il Fascismo*, cited, p. 34.
[16] Mussolini, *Discorsi della Rivoluzione*, cited, p. 17.
[17] Gentile, *Che Cos'è il Fascismo*, cited, p. 31.
[18] *Ibid.*, p. 31. *Cf.* also Mussolini, *Discorsi della Rivoluzione*,
cited, p. 19: "Violence is not immoral. Violence is sometimes
moral. . . . When our violence is a solution of a cancerous situation, it is highly moral, sacrosanct and necessary."

The form of government advocated by Fascism differs fundamentally from that sponsored by liberal and democratic thinkers. Fascism rejects the conception of popular sovereignty.[19] Democracy, which may have had meaning in the nineteenth century, has no place in the modern state, with its multiplicity and variety of functions. Sovereignty resides, not in the people, but in society juridically organized as a state. The great mass of citizens is incapable of undertaking the difficult task of government. This task, in Fascist theory, devolves on "the chosen few," an *élite* selected for their peculiar gifts. In practice, this governing class (*classe dirigente*) is recruited from among men noted for their loyalty to the Fascist party. "Fascism and the Fascist governing class are born together." [20] Presumably, until Italy has been thoroughly "fascistized," the range of choice for positions of responsibility will remain comparatively limited.

The governing class, in turn, must be led by a man who can crystalize its ideals. Fascism has found such a leader in Mussolini. His energy, personal magnetism and political success have won admiration even outside the immediate circle of his supporters, with the result that, for many Italians, he has come to personify the spirit of a new Renaissance. Mussolini believes that he has been chosen by fate to create a new and greater Italy.[21]

[19] Mussolini, *Discorsi della Rivoluzione,* cited, p. 21: "You know that I do not adore that new divinity, the masses. It is a creation of democracy and socialism. Only because they are many they must be right. Nothing of the kind. The opposite is true, that numbers are contrary to reason."

[20] Roberto Cantalupo, *La Classe Dirigente* (Milan, Biblioteca di Coltura Politica, 1926).

[21] *Cf.* Mussolini, *Discorsi del 1925* (Milan, Alpes, 1926). "Every great movement must have a representative man who suffers all the passion of that movement and carries its flame

The injection of a new spirit into national life is regarded by Fascism as one of its major accomplishments. "Our battle," says Mussolini, "was directed primarily against a state of mind, a mentality of renunciation, a spirit always more ready to avoid than to accept responsibility." [22] Fascism claims to have replaced the pessimism and discouragement of the post-war years by confidence in Italy's future, and to have substituted direct action for political apathy and confusion. The Fascist conception of the state as a mystical source of authority, and its recognition of religion as a necessary element in modern society, challenge the "agnosticism" of the liberal, anti-clerical state, committed to a policy of *laissez faire*.

FASCISM AND ITALIAN YOUTH

Fascism has found its most ardent adherents among World War veterans, especially those who had entered the war while still in their youth. These soldiers, many of whom had not yet come in contact with democratic institutions, spent their most impressionable years at the front, and there learned the value of direct action, discipline and submission to authority. They became, moreover, imbued with the desire to reap the fruits of victory. Fascism offered an avenue of escape from post-war weariness and disillusionment, as well as an instrument for the realization of nationalist aspirations. They turned to Fascism as to a "springtime of the nation," and from them Fascism acquired both the defects and

within him." *Cf.* Pietro Gorgolini, *La Rivoluzione Fascista* (Turin, Silvestrelli and Cappellato, 1923), who extols Mussolini as the "Man" called on by destiny to rescue Italy from the old political régime.

[22] Mussolini, *La Nuova Politica dell' Italia*, cited, Vol. II, p. 52.

qualities of youth—self-confidence, violence, defiance of opposition, as well as spontaneity, buoyancy and a sense of adventure.[23] The predominance of youth in Fascist ranks explains a number of phenomena, such as hero-worship of Mussolini, glorification of virility, emphasis on sport and physical education, and the juvenile punishments meted out to opponents, notably administrations of castor oil. The Fascist anthem, *Giovinezza,* originally a song of the *Arditi,*[24] extols youth in the same breath with Fascism.

> *Giovinezza, Giovinezza,*
> *Primavera di belleza.*
> *Nel fascismo è la salvezza*
> *Della nostra libertà.*[25]

The youthful energy released by Fascism has been directed not only to the development of Italy's resources, but to expansion of the national boundaries as well. The rapidly growing population cannot be adequately supported within the country's present boundaries, while emigration is regarded as an unsatisfactory solution, since it deprives Italy of both manpower and financial resources. Fascist Italy, therefore, seeks new worlds to conquer, and finds precedent and inspiration in the history of imperial Rome. The glorious past is constantly invoked, and many Fascist customs and institutions are modeled on those of the Roman Empire. The urge to expand, which sprang originally from economic neces-

[23] *Cf.* Robert Michel's *Socialismus und Fascismus in Italien* (Munich, Meyer and Jessen, 1925), p. 313; Herbert W. Schneider, *Making the Fascist State* (New York, Oxford University Press, 1928), pp. 350–351.

[24] Italian shock troops during the World War.

[25] "Youth, youth, springtime of beauty, Fascism is the safeguard of our liberty."

sity, has been consecrated by exaltation of the nation's spiritual heritage. This tendency has found
literary expression in the work of the poet Gabriele
d'Annunzio, who led the Fiume expedition in 1920.

CHAPTER II

THE FASCIST PARTY

THE National Fascist party was officially organized at a congress held in Rome on November 6,
1921. The program adopted at the congress stated
that the party was "a voluntary militia placed at
the service of the nation," which based its activities
on three fundamental principles—"order, discipline,
hierarchy." It is estimated that at that time the
party numbered 151,644 members, and included merchants, manufacturers, professional men, government employees, teachers, students, landowners and
agricultural workers.[1] Many of the members had
joined Fascism for personal ends, and were little
concerned with its ideals. Mussolini frequently has
deplored the original composition of the party. The
Fascist revolution, he said in 1924, had been effected by a party hastily formed at a time when
rigid selection presented practical difficulties. To
his opponents, who accuse Fascism of violence and
illegal acts, Mussolini answers that the revolution
had thrown together "the good and the bad, the
ascetics and the men eager for lucre, idealists and
profiteers." [2] "The one weak point about the new

[1] Cf. Odom Por, Fascism (London, Labour Publishing Company, 1923), p. 122.
[2] Mussolini, La Nuova Politica, cited, Vol. III, p. 180–181.

régime," says the Fascist writer Villari, "was that
not all the persons surrounding Mussolini were up
to his standard, either intellectually or morally. . . .
In the case of Fascism, moreover, as it was a movement essentially of young men, there was also a lack
of experience and other faults of youth." [3]

Opponents of Fascism charge members of the
party with a series of outrages following the March
on Rome, such as floggings, forcible administrations
of castor oil, illegal seizure of newspapers, wreckage
of private houses and offices, and a number of murders. They claim that these outrages went unpun-
ished, for the most part, due both to the connivance
of the police and to the fact that the cases were
tried by Fascist judges and juries. Moreover,
it is asserted that a number of Fascist offenses were
wiped out by the amnesty granted on December 22,
1922, which covered all crimes committed for a "national end," and by subsequent amnesties. [4] The
Fascist government denies that members of the
party have engaged in illegal activities, except in
some isolated instances, and claims that every effort
has been made to remove such offenders from the
ranks of the party.

FUNCTIONS OF THE PARTY

The functions of the party were defined by its
supreme organ, the Grand Council, [5] in a statute
adopted in 1926 and amended in 1929. [6] It reaffirms

---

[3] Villari, *The Fascist Experiment*, cited, p. 63.
[4] *Cf.* Salvemini, *The Fascist Dictatorship in Italy*, cited;
Giacomo Matteotti, *The Fascisti Exposed* (London, Independent
Labour Party, 1924).
[5] The Grand Council was established in 1923.
[6] The amended statute was published in the official organ of
the party, *Foglio d'Ordine; cf. Corriere della Sera*, December 22,
1929.

the principle that the party is a civil militia at the service of the state, whose object is "to achieve the greatness of the Italian people." Fascism, it declares, is not merely a political program; it is, above all, a faith, professed and translated into action by its militant followers, the new Italians. The party is an essential factor in the organization of the state, and is indispensable to the existence of the régime.

The nucleus of the party is the *fascio di combattimento*, the local party organization, which must rally all Italians distinguished for the Fascist virtues of "loyalty, honesty, courage and intellect." The *fasci* are organized in provincial federations, which are subject to the authority of the National Directorate and the Grand Council; the latter determines the program of action which is to be followed by the party in all fields of national life. The members of the party are subject to a hierarchy (*gerarchià*) of local, provincial and national secretaries, acting under the supreme command of the leader—*Il Duce*—the title given to Mussolini. The Secretary-General of the party is appointed for three years by the King on proposal of the head of the government; he acts as secretary of the Grand Council and may be invited to participate in the work of the Council of Ministers. Roberto Farinacci, appointed Secretary-General of the party in December 1925, at the height of anti-Fascist agitation, pursued a policy of violence and intransigeance against those suspected of opposition to the government. He was replaced in 1926 by Augusto Turati, who inaugurated a milder policy. Following Turati's resignation in 1930, Giovanni Giuriati, president of the Chamber of Deputies, was appointed to that office; he was succeeded in 1932 by Achille

Starace, who occupies that office at the present time.

In 1926 the Grand Council decided to admit no one to the party except those who "graduate" from the Advance Guard (*Avanguardisti*), the Fascist organization of young boys. On March 4, 1931 it voted to admit no fresh elements to the party until 1932.[7] In the autumn of 1932 the party inaugurated a "back to the people" policy, and announced that it would receive applications for membership. On July 23, 1933, however, Mussolini ordered that no members should be enrolled in the party after August first except those graduating from Fascist youth organizations, thus barring further enrolment from the ranks of adults. The Fascist badge (*tessera*) is given to new Fascists only after careful scrutiny of their antecedents and qualifications. The party statute, as amended in 1929, provides that persons admitted to the party must take the following oath: "I swear to follow without discussion the orders of *Il Duce*, and to serve the cause of the Fascist revolution with all my strength and, if necessary, with my blood." A disciplinary court under the presidency of the Secretary-General of the party examines all cases in which members fail to exhibit the prescribed Fascist virtues. Offenders may be warned, admonished, suspended and, in the gravest cases, expelled from the party.

COMPOSITION OF THE PARTY

In October 1935 the total membership of the party was estimated at 7,328,420, enrolled in *fasci* (the local party organizations) and the *Opera Nazionale Balilla* (the Fascist organization of children and

[7] *Corriere della Sera,* October 27, 1933.

youths),[8] while the remainder were registered with
various Fascist syndicates and associations. The
government expects that as Fascism penetrates into
national life the basis of selection to the ranks of
the party will be correspondingly broadened, and
that the party will eventually be fused with the nation. "The Fascist party," says a Fascist publicist,
"must not become a closed professional class. Fascists should not represent themselves as the only national element in a population of forty-two million." [9] The party, in turn, is expected to serve as
a training school for the ruling class (*classe dirigente*). This class, according to Mussolini, must not
withdraw to an ivory tower, remote from the masses.
It must, on the contrary, establish direct contact
with the needs and aspirations of the people, and
thus become a truly "popular régime." [10]

CHAPTER III

THE POLITICAL STRUCTURE OF THE FASCIST STATE

THE extent to which Fascism has transformed the
state in accordance with its doctrines may be ascertained only after a study of the political and eco-

[8] The *Opera Nazionale Balilla*, established by a law of April
1926, comprises four organizations: *Balilla* (boys aged 8 to 14);
Avanguardisti (Advance Guard—boys aged 14 to 18); and *Gio-
vani Italiane* (girls aged 14 to 18). The *Opera Nazionale Balilla*
is placed under the control of the Ministry of National Education.
Cf. Balbino Giuliano, "L'Opera Nazionale Balilla," *Lo Stato
Mussoliniano* (Rome, Rassegna Nazionale, 1930), p. 256.

[9] Virginio Gayda, "I Cicli del Fascismo," *Il Giornale d'Italia,*
October 10, 1930.

[10] Mussolini, *Discorsi del 1926,* cited, p. 339.

nomic changes introduced since 1922. Fascist
leaders claim that the March on Rome, while
it involved no social upheaval and resulted in
little bloodshed, was a revolution in the broadest
sense of the term. This revolution has left its marks
on the political and economic structure of the state.
The power of the monarch has been curtailed; government has been entrusted to a single party and
primarily to its leader, Mussolini; and the Fascist
Grand Council has become a constitutional organ,
while the Chamber of Deputies has been reorganized and shorn of many of its previous functions.
The maintenance of public order has been confided
to a voluntary militia recruited from Fascist ranks,
all opposition has been suppressed, and a special
tribunal has been established for crimes against the
safety of the state. The government has prohibited
action by either workers or employers in defense of
class interests, and has created a system of Fascist
syndicates which alone represent the interests of the
two groups, subject to control by the state. Finally,
changes have been effected in education which are
intended to produce a new spirit in Italian youth,
and pave the way for complete "fascistization" of
national life.

When the Fascist party came to power, it expressed the intention to preserve the existing political structure, and to govern within the framework of the *Statuto*.[1] Later, however, Mussolini
came to the conclusion that Italy could not be
"fascistized" without alteration of the constitution.
"We must violate the *Statuto*," he declared in 1925.[2]

[1] *Cf.* address of Mussolini in the Senate, November 27, 1922,
Gorgolini, *La Rivoluzione Fascista*, cited, p. 111.
[2] Mussolini, *Discorsi del 1925*, cited, p. 97.

He defended his position by claiming that the
Statuto no longer corresponded to the needs of the
country and had, in fact, been revoked by the march
of events.[3] Fascism, he said, intended to do no more
than prune the constitution of the overgrowths
which had gradually obscured its original meaning.
He denied that any constitution could be regarded
as immutable. "Are we dealing with archeology or
with politics . . . ? Constitutions are but instruments resulting from given historical conditions,
which undergo birth, development and decline."[4]
The avowed aim of the government, at that time,
was to conserve, not revolutionize, the constitution.

THE EXECUTIVE POWER

Mussolini's first act was to assert the preëminence
of the executive over the legislative power. In the
past, he claimed, the executive had been merely a
puppet of Parliament. This condition could be
tolerated no longer. The ultimate source of executive power presented a constitutional problem. In
the early days of Fascism, Mussolini had declared
himself opposed to the monarchy. In 1922, however, he made a concession to popular sentiment,
especially in the ranks of the army. He said: "We
shall leave monarchy outside our game, because
we think that Italy would look with suspicion on a
transformation of the government which would
eliminate monarchy."[5] He believed that the King
would not find it to his interest to obstruct the
Fascist revolution. Should the monarchy attempt
to resist, "we would have to abolish it, as it would

---

[3] Mussolini, *Discorsi del 1928* (Milan, Alpes, 1929), p. **101**.
[4] *Ibid.*
[5] Mussolini, *Discorsi della Rivoluzione,* cited, p. **32**.

be a question of life or death." [6] Still later, he expressed the conviction that "the unitary régime of Italy rests solidly on the House of Savoy," and that the monarchy, by reason of its origins and historical development, could not oppose the new national forces.[7]

Mussolini's expectations were realized. The House of Savoy appears to have accepted Fascism without reservations. Both Victor Emanuel III and Prince Humbert, the heir to the throne, have participated in Fascist functions and, outwardly at least, have sanctioned the acts of the Fascist government. The King's acceptance of Fascism has been denounced by anti-Fascists as treason to the constitution. When a young anti-Fascist, De Rosa, attempted to assassinate Prince Humbert in Brussels in 1929, he defended his act on the ground that the prince had proved unworthy of Italy's faith in the monarchy.[8]

The "Head of the Government"

Constitutionally the executive power is still vested in the King.[9] Actually, however, a significant transformation has been effected by the law of December 24, 1925, concerning "the attributes and prerogatives of the head of the government" (*Il Capo del Governo*).[10] This law is intended to legalize the

[6] *Ibid.*, p. 33.

[7] Speech at Fascist Congress in Naples, October 24, 1922, *ibid.*, p. 80.

[8] *Cf. Le Procés De Rosa* (Paris, Valois, 1930), particularly the testimony of MM. Nitti and Trachiani, pp. 64 and 78. De Rosa was tried in Brussels in 1930 by the Court of Assizes, and condemned to five years' imprisonment. His counsel made a sweeping attack on the Fascist government, and was supported by a number of anti-Fascists called as witnesses.

[9] Article 5 of the *Statuto* provides that the King alone possesses executive power.

[10] *Gazzetta Ufficiale del Regno d'Italia*, No. 301, December 29, 1925. p. 5067.

position and functions of the Prime Minister, who had hitherto been recognized by parliamentary practice but had remained unknown to the constitution. It states that the executive power is to be exercised by the King with the aid of his government. The government is composed of the Prime Minister and other ministers. The Prime Minister is the "head of the government"; he is nominated and recalled by the King alone. He directs and coördinates the work of the government, and is responsible to the King for its general political direction. No question can be included in the agenda of either chamber without the consent of the Prime Minister. He has power to ask that any bill rejected by either chamber be reintroduced when at least three months have elapsed since the first vote. In such a case vote by secret ballot takes place without further discussion. If the government, meanwhile, has proposed amendments to the bill, discussion is limited to these amendments. The Prime Minister may likewise demand that a bill rejected by either chamber be transmitted to the other, there to be examined and voted upon; this provision is intended to reduce to a minimum the delay formerly occasioned by parliamentary procedure. Finally, the law provides various terms of imprisonment for any act directed against the life, liberty or integrity of the Prime Minister. The law of November 25, 1926 on the defense of the state goes further, and prescribes the death penalty for such acts.[11]

When presenting the law concerning the head of the government to the Chamber of Deputies, Alfredo Rocco, Minister of Justice, stressed the fact that the Prime Minister was a true *capo del governo*, not

[11] *Gazzetta Ufficiale*, No. 281, December 6, 1926, p. 5314.

merely *primus inter pares:* on him, and not on the
Council of Ministers, devolves the task of coordinating and directing the work of his colleagues.
"Our Prime Minister," said Rocco, "is the recognized
head of the great political, economic and moral
forces of the country and those represented in Parliament, the evaluation of whose importance is subject to the decision of the sovereign." [12] The government, he explained in the Senate, "can no longer
express conflicting political thoughts; it must be the
expression of a single political thought, of a single
conception of the state; else there would be paralysis,
such as existed during the years which preceded
Fascism." [13] It is significant that the law contains
no reference to parliamentary responsibility on the
part of the Prime Minister.

In practice, Mussolini has undertaken the work
of several ministries in addition to the office of head
of the government. At the present time Il Duce holds
four out of thirteen cabinet posts—internal affairs,
war, navy and air. The post of Minister of Foreign
Affairs is occupied by his son-in-law, Colonel
Galeazzo Ciano.[14]

Promulgation of "Decree-Laws" by the Executive

The scope of the Prime Minister's power has been
further broadened by the law of January 31, 1926,
concerning the power of the executive to promulgate
decrees having the force of law.[15] The *Statuto* provides that the legislative power shall be exercised

[12] Alfredo Rocco, *La Trasformazione dello Stato* (Rome, "La
Voce," 1927), pp. 199-202.
[13] *Ibid.,* p. 204.
[14] *New York Times,* June 10, 1936.
[15] *Gazzetta Ufficiale,* No. 25, February 1, 1926, p. 426.

collectively by the King and the two chambers.[16] The Italian government had frequently invoked this article to adopt legislative measures by means of decree-laws (*decreti-leggi*). This practice became more deeply rooted during the World War and the early years of Fascism. In 1924, when public opinion had been aroused by the Matteotti affair,[17] Mussolini declared that he would no longer resort to such decrees. The law of 1926, however, provides that decrees may be promulgated regarding the execution of the laws, the exercise of the executive power, and the organization of state administration. Decrees having the force of law may also be issued in extraordinary cases where urgent action is required. Such decrees must be published immediately in the the official gazette, and submitted to Parliament without delay; they cease to be in force after two years if they have not meanwhile been adopted by Parliament. The Fascist government defends the law of 1926 on the ground that it regulates and limits a power which otherwise would be subject to abuse. Opponents of Fascism, however, declare that the government has frequently promulgated legislation by decree without giving it publicity, that it has failed to consult Parliament within the prescribed period of time, and that the law of 1926 legalizes a dangerous encroachment of the executive power on the legislature.[18]

Three other legislative measures have served to broaden the scope of the executive power and to consolidate the position of the Fascist government. A law of December 24, 1925, authorized the govern-

[16] Article 2.
[17] *Cf.* p. 73.
[18] *Cf.* Francesco Ferrari, *Le Régime Fasciste Italien* (Paris, Editions Spès, 1928), pp. 114–115.

ment to dismiss civil and military employees who
had failed to give a guarantee of their fidelity to
duty or had placed themselves in a position incompatible with the general policy of the government.[19]
This law, which was first announced as a transitional
measure, was prolonged, and extended to local administrative employees, teachers in elementary
schools and other grades of public service; its provisions were permanently embodied in a decree of
January 3, 1927, regarding the legal status of civil
employees. By a law of December 24, 1925, the government was empowered to amend the penal code,
to modify the civil code and to reorganize the system
of judicial administration.[20] In accordance with this
law, the government undertook the re-codification of
civil and penal laws, adopted a new penal code in
1931, and in 1926 established the Special Tribunal
for the Defense of the State.[21] Finally, a law of
December 31, 1925, authorized the government to
modify the laws concerning public safety, and to
promulgate a single law on the subject.[22] The provisions of this law were given effect by a decree
of November 6, 1926, which regulates all questions
relating to public safety.[23]

THE GRAND COUNCIL

The consolidation of the Fascist government
raised two important issues—the extent to which
the Fascist party had become a permanent factor in
national life, and the method of assuring its continuance in power. Mussolini's favorite slogan is

[19] *Gazzetta Ufficiale,* No. 2, January 4, 1926, p. 11.
[20] *Ibid.,* No. 301, December 29, 1925, p. 5066.
[21] For discussion of the work of this tribunal, *cf.* p. 94.
[22] *Gazzetta Ufficiale,* No. 4, January 7, 1926, p. 34.
[23] For analysis of the provisions of this decree, *cf.* p. 91.

durare (to last). He recognizes, however, that this aim can be achieved only by means of the "fascistization" of Italy. An attempt to settle both issues simultaneously is made in the law of December 9, 1928, which establishes the Fascist Grand Council as the supreme coördinating organ of the state, and vests it with the power to regulate succession to the government.[24]

Composition of the Council

The Grand Council is charged with the task of coördinating all the activities of the Fascist régime. The head of the government is "by right" president of the Grand Council; he alone can convoke it and determine its procedure. The secretary of the Fascist party serves as secretary of the Grand Council. The membership of the council falls into three categories. The first category is composed of the *quadrumviri* who participated in the March on Rome and who are appointed to the council for an unlimited period of time. The second category includes the presidents of the Senate and Chamber of Deputies; the Ministers of Foreign Affairs, the Interior, Justice, Finance, National Education, Agriculture and Forests, and Corporations; the commander-general of the militia; the secretary and the two vice-secretaries of the Fascist party; the president of the Royal Italian Academy; the president of the Special Tribunal for the Defense of the State; the presidents of the National Fascist Confederations and of the National Confederations of Fascist Syndicates of Industry and Agriculture. Members of this category

[24] *Gazzetta Ufficiale*, No. 287, December 11, 1928, p. 5978; amended by law of December 14, 1929, *ibid.*, No. 292, December 17, 1929.

form part of the Grand Council as long as they hold
their respective offices; they are nominated by royal
decree on proposal of the head of the government,
and may be recalled at any time. Finally, the head
of the government may nominate for three years,
with the right of reappointment, any persons who
have "deserved well of the nation and the cause
of the Fascist revolution."

Members of the Grand Council receive no remuneration. No member may be arrested or subjected to police procedure without the authoriza-
tion of the council. No disciplinary measures may be
taken against any member of the council who is at
the same time a member of the Fascist party without the approval of the council. The meetings of the
council are secret, and are usually held at night.
The *communiqués* of the council's proceedings are
generally brief, and more concerned with the action
adopted than with the discussion which may have
preceded it.[25]

*Relations of the Council with the State and the
    Party*

The Grand Council is vested with both consultative and advisory functions. It acts as a consultative
body in "all cases specified by law." These include
the statutes, ordinances and policies of the Fascist
party; the nomination and recall of Fascist officials
and other members of the party organization; and
the selection of candidates for the Chamber of
Deputies. The advice of the Grand Council must
be sought on all questions of a constitutional

[25] For a record of the early years of the council, *cf.* Partito
Nazionale Fascista, *Il Gran Consiglio nei Primi Cinque Anni dell'
Era Fascista* (Rome, Libreria del Littorio, 1927), p. 69.

character. These include all bills concerning the following subjects: succession to the throne; the attributes and prerogatives of the Crown; the composition and functions of the Grand Council, the Senate and the Chamber of Deputies; the attributes and prerogatives of the head of the government; the right of the executive to issue decrees having the force of law; the organization of syndicates and corporations; relations with the Holy See; and international agreements involving territorial changes. In addition, the Grand Council acts in an advisory capacity on all political, economic and social questions which the head of the government may submit to it.

The Grand Council, however, is not merely a consultative and advisory body; it is, in a sense, the ultimate source of both executive and legislative power, subject only to the control of the head of the government, and responsible to him alone. On proposal of the head of the government, the Grand Council draws up a list of names which are to be submitted to the Crown in the event of vacancy, and from which the King is to select Mussolini's successor. The Grand Council also prepares the official list of four hundred candidates to the Chamber of Deputies, which is presented to the voters for a plebiscite, and directs the application of the corporative system.

By the law of December 9, 1928 the Grand Council, which was and remains the governing body of the Fascist party, was transformed into a constitutional organ of the state, charged with effecting a synthesis of the country's political, economic and social forces. In a speech to the Senate on November 8, 1928, Mussolini declared that this legalization

of the Grand Council would have far-reaching implications. "The National Fascist party has in this
manner been incorporated in the state and has become one of its fundamental institutions. . . . Thus
is completed the evolution by which the National
Fascist party, from a simple private association like
the parties of the old régime, has been transformed
into a great institution of public law, the fundamental instrument of the régime. . . . Fascism
henceforth identifies itself with the nation and with
the state. To say Grand Council of Fascism is
equivalent to saying Grand Council of the nation
and the state." [26] The law was approved by the
Chamber of Deputies without discussion. In the
Senate, however, it met with considerable opposition.
"This bill," said Mussolini, addressing the Senate
on November 15, 1928, "has given rise to compre-
hensible and respectable hesitations, but also to ob-
lique manœuvres and to insulting vociferations." [27]
The Senate finally passed the bill by a vote of 181
to 19, with two absentions.[28]

Criticism of the Council

The chief criticism directed against the Grand
Council by opponents of Fascism is that it con-
stitutionalizes and perpetuates the rule of a single
political party, while materially curtailing the functions of both King and Parliament. Anti-Fascists
claim that no reforms of a constitutional character

[26] *Corriere della Sera*, November 9, 1928.
[27] *Ibid.*, November 16, 1928.
[28] The following senators voted against the law: Abbiate,
Albertini, Bergamasco, Bergamini, Bollati, Casati, Cornaggia,
Croce, Della Torre, Diena, Paterno, Federico Ricci, Ruffini, Stop-
pato, Valenzami, Vigliani, Volterra, Wollemborg and Zupelli.
Senators De Cupis and Nava, who were present, abstained from
voting.

can henceforth be initiated by the Chamber of Deputies, and that the Grand Council thus blocks political and economic evolution by peaceful means. Fascist spokesmen assert that the Grand Council does not limit the power of the King, but merely facilitates his selection of a successor to the post of head of the government. In their opinion, the Grand Council does not supplant Parliament, since its functions are largely consultative; its existence simply reaffirms the principle established by the *Statuto,* that the government must enjoy the confidence of the monarch rather than of Parliament. Finally, they believe that the Grand Council fulfills the indispensable function of assuring both unity and continuity in administration.[29]

THE CHAMBER OF DEPUTIES

The Fascist party, as has already been pointed out, rejects the doctrine of popular sovereignty and regards parliamentary institutions as both harmful and obsolete. Nevertheless, Mussolini did not undertake to reform Parliament immediately on his advent to power. In his first speech to the Chamber of Deputies on November 16, 1922, he stated that his appearance there was an act of deference. "I could," he said, "make of this dim gray hall a bivouac of Fascist soldiers. I could close Parliament and constitute an exclusively Fascist government. I could, but do not wish, at least at first, to do this." He warned the Chamber, however, that "it must feel its peculiar position, which makes its dissolution possible within two days or two months." [30] Speaking in

[29] *Cf.* Giovanni Corso, *Lo Stato Fascista* (Rome, Libreria del Littorio, 1929), p. 457.
[30] Mussolini, *Discorsi della Rivoluzione,* cited, p. 104.

the Senate on November 27, 1922, he said: "Who prevents me from closing Parliament? Who prevents me from proclaiming a dictatorship of two, three or five persons . . . ? No one!" He added that he had subordinated egoism to the supreme interests of the country, and had decided to confine the Fascist movement to the limits of the constitution.[31]

The Fascist party, which soon absorbed the Nationalist party, did not at the outset appear intransigeant toward other political groups. The first Fascist cabinet contained two Liberals, two Popularists and two Social-Democrats.[32] Fascist co-operation with these parties, however, was more nominal than real. In 1923 the government broke with the Popular party, and in 1924 with the Social-Democrats. These breaks were the outward sign of a widening rift between the government and the Chamber, which Mussolini described as the last refuge of forces hostile to Fascism.[33] The Chamber was finally dissolved, and new elections were called for April 6, 1924.

The Elections of 1924

These elections were held under the terms of an electoral law by which the country was divided into fifteen large constituencies, in each of which the various parties were to present their respective candidates. The party whose lists secured relatively the largest number of votes was to obtain two-thirds of the 535 seats in the Chamber of Deputies,

[31] Gorgolini, *La Rivoluzione Fascista,* cited, p. 111.
[32] The Liberals were Gentile and De Capitani; the Popularists were Tangorra and Cavazzoni; the Social-Democrats were Carnazza and the Duke of Cesarò. Of these Gentile, De Capitani and Carnazza subsequently became Fascists.
[33] Mussolini, *La Nuova Politica,* cited, Vol. II, p. 204.

numbering 356. The remaining 179 seats were to be distributed among other parties on the basis of proportional representation. The chief merit of this system, according to a Fascist writer, was "that the majority was compact and amenable to strict party discipline." [34] The opposition parties were unable to come to an understanding, and each went to the polls with its own list, while Fascist supporters and sympathizers presented a united front. Of the total vote, estimated at over seven and a half million, four and a half million votes were cast for the Fascist party (including the Nationalists), which received 375 seats in the Chamber, and nearly three million for opposition parties, which were assigned 160 seats. [35]

The Matteotti Affair

On May 30, 1924, the Socialist deputy Giacomo Matteotti made a speech in the new Chamber in which he contested the validity of the Fascist majority. He declared that the voters had not been given an opportunity to express their opinion freely, and that the government had prejudged the results of the elections by stating that, whatever the outcome, it would still remain in power. He described and denounced various violations of the electoral law, and closed his speech, which had been con-

[34] Villari, *The Fascist Experiment,* cited, p. 207.

[35] The seats assigned to the Fascist party included those given to so-called "philo-Fascists"—Liberals, Democrats and others who, while not members of the Fascist party, were in sympathy with its policy. The opposition seats were divided as follows: 25 followers of Giolitti and other small independent groups, 40 Popularists, 25 Unitary Socialists, 14 Maximalists, 19 Communists, 8 Republicans and 25 Democrats. For an account of this election from the anti-Fascist point of view, *cf.* Sturzo, *Italy and Fascismo,* cited; Salvemini, *The Fascist Dictatorship in Italy,* cited; Ferrari, *Le Régime Fasciste,* cited, pp. 55–56.

stantly interrupted, by demanding annulment of
of the elections.[36] Commenting on this speech, Mussolini's organ, *Popolo d'Italia,* said on June 1, 1924:
"The honorable Matteotti has made a monstrously
provocative speech which would merit something
more tangible than the epithet 'ruffian' [which had
been applied to him by a Fascist deputy]." Addressing the Chamber of Deputies on June 6, 1924,
Mussolini praised the example of Russia, "where
there are magnificent teachers. . . . We made a
mistake," he declared, "not to imitate them fully,
because at this hour you would no longer be here,
you would be in prison. . . . You would have had
lead in your back. But we have courage, and we
shall prove it to you." [37] On the following day, again
in the Chamber of Deputies, Mussolini declared that
he would make Parliament function, and invited
the opposition to give him "positive or negative
collaboration"; political indifference, he said, would
condemn the opposition to "perpetual exile from
history." [38]

Three days after this speech, on June 10, Matteotti suddenly disappeared. On June 12 Mussolini
attempted to reassure the Chamber of Deputies regarding the fate of Matteotti, and stated that the
police were making every effort to probe the mys-
tery. The disappearance, he said, had taken place
"in circumstances of time and place not yet ascertained but such as to arouse suspicion of a crime
which, if it had been committed, could but arouse
the indignation and emotion of Parliament." The

[36] Italy, *Atti del Parlamento Italiano, Camera dei Deputati,
XXVII Legislatura, Sessione 1924–25, Discussioni* (Rome, Printing Office of the Chamber of Deputies, 1925), Vol. I, p. 57 *et seq.*
[37] *Ibid.,* p. 206.
[38] *Ibid.,* p. 246.

Socialist deputy Gonzales cried: "Then Matteotti is dead!" In the midst of general commotion the Republican deputy Chiesa shouted: "Let the head of the government speak! He is silent! He is an accomplice!" [39] On June 13, when it became apparent that Matteotti had been murdered, Mussolini said in the Chamber of Deputies:

"If there is anyone here who has the right to be grieved and, I may add, exasperated, it is I. Only an enemy of mine, who for many a long night had meditated on some diabolic act against me could have committed this crime which today fills us with horror and draws from us a cry of indignation. The situation . . . is extremely delicate." [40]

On June 24, in the Senate, he quoted Talleyrand, and said of the Matteotti affair: "It is not only a crime but a blunder." Senator Albertini, an opponent of Fascism, made the following statement on that occasion:

"The apparent order which now reigns in Italy is founded not on the restoration of the authority of the Italian state but on the application, by irresponsible powers, of sanctions as humiliating for human dignity as they are terrible in their uncertainty against whoever disapproves too much of what takes place on the periphery or at the centre." [41]

Police investigation revealed that Matteotti had been kidnapped on June 10 by five Fascists, and had subsequently been murdered. The body was not recovered until two months later. The investigation implicated Finzi, Under-Secretary for the Interior,

[39] *Ibid.*, p. 323 *et seq.*
[40] Mussolini, *La Nuova Politica*, cited, Vol. III, pp. 172–173.
[41] Italy, *Atti Parlamentari della Camera dei Senatori, Legislatura XXVII, Discussioni, 1a Sessione 1924* (Rome, Senate Printing Office, 1924), p. 84.

and Cesare Rossi, chief of the Press Department. Fascist writers do not attempt to defend Finzi who, they claim, proved "a broken reed" when Mussolini, burdened by other duties, entrusted him with the bulk of the work in the Ministry of the Interior.[42] Finzi resigned but asked for an official inquiry into his conduct, which was refused. Yielding to public indignation, Mussolini placed Luigi Federzoni, formerly a Nationalist, in charge of the Ministry of the Interior. General De Bono, who had hitherto combined the duties of Director of Public Safety and Commander-General of the militia, was forced to resign the former office; subsequently he was appointed Governor of Tripoli, and is now Minister for the Colonies. Other prominent Fascists were involved in the affair, and it was even rumored that both Finzi and Rossi had implicated Mussolini in their confessions. Following preliminary examination of the case by a parliamentary committee, the five men accused of murdering Matteotti were brought to trial in 1926. The trial was held in the small town of Chieti in the Abruzzes, and Farinacci, Secretary-General of the Fascist party, acted as counsel for the defendants. Two of the defendants were acquitted, and the three others condemned to imprisonment; they were, however, released two months later, under the terms of an amnesty granted in 1925.[43] It is

[42] Villari, *The Fascist Experiment*, cited, p. 69.
[43] For details of this trial, *cf.* Salvemini, *The Fascist Dictatorship in Italy*, cited, and Villari, *The Fascist Experiment*, cited. For Matteotti's views on Fascism, *cf.* Matteotti, *The Fascisti Exposed*, cited. In addition to Matteotti, the Fascist government is charged by its opponents with the death of Giovanni Amendola, a Liberal deputy, and Piero Gobetti, a Liberal editor, both of whom died in exile, as a result, it is claimed, of maltreatment at the hands of Fascists.

believed, in Fascist circles, that Matteotti was murdered by extreme Fascists who wished to prevent
any possibility of further collaboration between the
government and the opposition.

The Opposition Withdraws from Parliament

The Matteotti affair aroused public opinion to an
extraordinary pitch. The government was attacked
in the Senate, and bitterly denounced by the press.
The Italian historian Guglielmo Ferrero described
the elections of 1924 as a "strangulation of the
country." [44] Mussolini himself, addressing the Grand
Council on July 22, 1924, acknowledged that the
murder of Matteotti had produced "a profound
moral oscillation in the Italian masses." [45] The Opposition parties, as a sign of protest, withdrew from
the Chamber of Deputies immediately following the
murder of Matteotti, and became known as the
Aventine.[46] The "elder statesmen"—Giolitti, Or-
lando and Salandra—who hitherto had sympathized
with the Fascist government while maintaining an
independent position in Parliament, now joined the
ranks of the opposition. It is the opinion of competent observers that at no time in its history was
the Fascist government in such grave danger of
downfall as in the summer and autumn of 1924.

Mussolini Inaugurates Policy of Intransigeance

The Opposition parties, however, failed to rally
the country against Fascism. The government, sup-

[44] Guglielmo Ferrero, La Democrazia in Italia (Milan, Edizioni
della Rassegna Internazionale, 1925).
[45] Mussolini, La Nuova Politica, cited, Vol. III, p. 209.
[46] This name was given the Opposition parties because their
secession resembled the withdrawal of the Roman plebs to the
Sacred Mount in 494 B.C. as a sign of protest against the exactions
of the patricians.

ported by the propertied classes, which desired the
maintenance of public order at any cost, and
strengthened by sympathizers in the ranks of
other parties, known as *fiancheggiatori* (flankers),
adopted a policy of repression and intransigeance.
On January 3, 1925, in a speech which inaugurated
a new era in the history of Fascism, Mussolini denied the existence of a Fascist *Cheka,* and challenged
the Chamber of Deputies to impeach him for the
murder of Matteotti. He declared that he accepted
full responsibility for the Matteotti affair.

"If Fascism has been nothing more than castor oil and
cudgels, and not a magnificent passion of the best youth
of Italy, the fault is mine. If Fascism has been a criminal association, well, I am its chief, and I am responsible! If all the acts of violence are the result of a
certain historical, political and moral atmosphere, the
responsibility for this is mine, for this historical, political
and moral atmosphere was created by me, by means of
propaganda which starts with Italian intervention in the
war and comes down to the present day." [47]

Mussolini's watchwords to the Fascists were: "Absolute intransigeance, theoretical and practical," and
"All power to all Fascism!" He reaffirmed his conviction that opposition is neither sacred nor un-
touchable. He denounced the *Aventine* as sedi-
tious and unconstitutional. The Opposition parties
replied by a manifesto which declared that the
Aventine was a "resolute and irrepressible protest
against the most atrocious crime of the régime."

The government, however, had gained the upper

[47] Mussolini, *Discorsi del 1925,* cited, pp. 13–14. Commenting
on this speech, Salvemini remarks that Mussolini accepted moral,
political and historical, but not penal, responsibility for the
Matteotti affair. *Cf.* Salvemini, *The Fascist Dictatorship in Italy,*
cited.

hand, and proceeded to strengthen its position in
1925 by a series of legislative measures known
as *leggi fascistissime* (most Fascist laws), dealing with the press, secret associations, the civil
service and public safety. These measures were
adopted with little discussion by the Chamber of
Deputies, now composed only of Fascists and Fascist
sympathizers. Various acts of violence committed
at this time against anti-Fascists were pardoned
under the terms of an amnesty granted by the King
on the twenty-fifth anniversary of his reign.

Collapse of the Opposition

Meanwhile, the Opposition parties, temporarily
united by the Matteotti affair, gradually drifted
apart, and after July 1925 the *Aventine* ceased to
exist except as a convenient phrase. Continued ab-
stention from parliamentary work robbed the opposition of the last vestiges of power, while the
government's legislation concerning the right of association and the press deprived them of all means of
action and expression. The government, for its part,
had no intention of parleying with the opposition.
When members of the Popular party attempted to
return to the Chamber of Deputies in January 1926,
Mussolini declared that the secessionists would be
"tolerated" only if they undertook to accept Fascism
unconditionally and to dissociate themselves from
anti-Fascist activities at home and abroad.[48] This
ultimatum marked the close of parliamentary government in Italy.

The task of examining various problems regarding
"the fundamental relations between the state and
the forces which it must contain and guarantee" had

[48] Mussolini, *Discorsi del 1926,* cited, pp. 10–11.

been entrusted by the government on January 31, 1925, to a commission of eighteen Senators, deputies and experts, headed by the philosopher Giovanni Gentile, formerly Minister of Education.[49] The Gentile Commission favored modernization of the *Statuto,* and elaborated a reform of the Chamber of Deputies which formed the basis of the law "on political representation of May 17, 1928." [50] This law was passed by the Chamber of Deputies acting, to use Mussolini's phrase, as a constituent assembly.

The Electoral Law of 1928

The law of May 17, 1928 established a single electoral district—the nation. Eight hundred candidates are to be designated by Fascist syndicates, and two hundred by "the legally constituted bodies and by associations, the scope of which is cultural, educational, charitable or propagandist, and which exist owing to the fact that they are of national importance." Candidates are assigned to the various organizations in accordance with the relative weight of the latter in the productive life of the country. The candidates must be men not only of recognized professional ability, but capable as well "of furthering the historical aims of the nation." That none but Fascists may expect to be selected was indicated by Mussolini when he said, in his farewell speech to the old Chamber of Deputies on December 8, 1928: "If the Chamber which is about to conclude its labors today has been, from the point of view of

[49] This commission took the place of a similar body of fifteen men appointed in 1924 by the Fascist party for the same purpose.

[50] *Gazzetta Ufficiale,* No. 118, May 21, 1928, p. 2150. Some of the recommendations of the Gentile commission were not finally embodied in the law of May 17, 1928.

numbers, eighty-five per cent Fascist, the Chamber
which will assemble for the first time on Saturday,
April 20 of Year VII (1929), will be a one hundred
per cent Fascist Chamber." [51]

Preparation of the National List

From the one thousand names presented by the
syndicates and other associations, the Grand Council selects a list of four hundred names, which is then
submitted to the voters for a "plebiscite." The right
to vote is conditioned on active participation in
national life, whether as producers or taxpayers.
All male Italian citizens who have reached the age
of twenty-one (or eighteen, if they are married and
have children), may vote if they pay syndicate contributions, or one hundred lire in taxes; if they
receive a pension from the state; or if they belong
to the clergy. The voters are asked only one question: "Do you approve of the list of deputies
designated by the National Grand Council?" and
their sole function consists in answering "yes" or
"no." In other words, the voters are invited to express their views, not regarding individual candidates, but regarding the program of the government as a whole. In the event the country should
reject the list prepared by the Grand Council, lists
of deputies shall be drawn up by all the associations,
and the voters shall be permitted to make a choice
among these lists. All candidates on the list which
obtains the greatest number of votes shall then be
declared elected and the seats reserved for the minority shall be distributed among the remaining

---

[51] *Corriere della Sera,* December 9, 1928. The year 1922 is
regarded as year I of the Fascist era, and all public documents
bear a double date, such as 1929 (A.VII).

lists. This provision, however, is viewed by Fascist spokesmen as of little importance, since rejection of the list prepared by the Grand Council is regarded as impossible.[52] Moreover, Mussolini declared in the Chamber of Deputies on December 8, 1928 that even a vote unfavorable to Fascism would not cause the overthrow of the government. "We are mathematically certain of continuance in power." [53]

The "Plebiscite" of 1929

The new electoral law was first put to the test in the "plebiscite" held on March 24, 1929. The confederations of employees and employers in each branch of national economy were assigned the same number of candidates. This apparent equality resulted actually in considerable inequality between the two groups. Thus the employers' and employees' confederations of industry each presented 80 candidates, although the former consisted of 71,459 and the latter of 1,300,000 members. Similarly, the employers' confederation of agriculture composed of 314,658 members named 96 candidates, the number assigned to the employees' confederation, representing 1,021,461.[54] Critics of this procedure claim further that it fails to give the various economic interests a representation commensurate

[52] "La Elezione dei Deputati," *Corriere della Sera,* February 1, 1929.
[53] *Corriere della Sera,* December 9, 1928. *Cf.* also speech by Achille Starace, vice-secretary of the Fascist party, April 23, 1929: "If the twelve million votes 'yes' should transform themselves into twenty-four million 'noes,' Mussolini would still remain at Palazzo Venezia and the revolution of the Black Shirts would not thereby have suffered any check." *Il Popolo d'Italia,* April 24, 1929, translated by Carmen Haider, *Capital and Labor under Fascism* (New York, Columbia University Press, 1930), p. 257.
[54] The distribution of the eight hundred candidates assigned

with their actual weight in the life of the country. Thus agriculture, which forms the occupation of more than fifty per cent of the population, is accorded less than one-fourth of the total number of candidates.[55]

The list prepared by the Grand Council and published on March 1, 1929, consisted entirely of Fascists selected, according to the official *communiqué,* on the basis of personal qualifications and length of service in the party. Of the 400 candidates, 55 had joined the Fascist organizations in 1919, 54 in 1920, 65 in 1921, 60 in 1922, 59 in 1923, 36 in 1924 and 30 in 1925.[56] The elections were preceded by a week of active propaganda. Deputies and members of the government designated for this purpose by the Grand Council were sent to the more important centres to deliver speeches illustrating the activities of the government in various fields.[57] Individuals and groups opposed to Fascism

to National Confederations of Fascist Syndicates was made as follows:

Agricultural Employers	96	(12%)
" Employees	96	(12%)
Industrial Employers	80	(10%)
" Employees	80	(10%)
Commercial Employers	48	(6%)
" Employees	48	(6%)
Maritime and Air Transportation Employers	40	(5%)
" " " " Employees	40	(5%)
Land Transportation and Inland Navigation Employers	32	(4%)
Land Transportation and Inland Navigation Employees	32	(4%)
Bank Employers	24	(3%)
" Employees	24	(3%)
Professional Men and Artists	160	(20%)
TOTAL	800	

[55] Haider, *Capital and Labor under Fascism,* cited, p. **255.**
[56] *Ibid.,* p. 256.
[57] *Corriere della Sera,* March 14, 1929.

were given no opportunity to advocate their views. The voters were warned by their respective syndicates, and frequently by their employers, that they might be deprived of various privileges, and even of their jobs, if they failed to appear at the polls or cast a negative vote. The president of the National Confederation of Fascist Syndicates of Industry issued a circular stating that "industrial workers must go to the polls perfectly organized, and demonstrate their acceptance of the régime." [58] The Catholic clergy, gratified by the conclusion of the Lateran accord on February 11, 1929,[59] urged their parishioners to vote for the government list.[60] The Federation of Catholic Men advised its members to vote "yes" in a plebiscite "by which the Italian people is called on to express its own thought regarding the government program." [61] Finally, the tenth anniversary of the *Fasci di Combattimento* was celebrated on March 23, the day preceding the elections, and was the occasion for public demonstrations of loyalty to the government.

Fascists Victorious at the Polls

Critics of Fascism assert that the vote was cast under conditions which made the voters' apparent freedom of choice completely illusory. The voting was not secret. The voters were offered the choice of two ballots: one was decorated with the Italian tricolor, which remained visible after the ballot had been folded, and was inscribed: "Do you approve of the list of deputies designated by the national

[58] *Ibid.,* March 23, 1929.
[59] *Cf.* V. M. Dean, "The Lateran Accord," Foreign Policy Association, *Information Service,* Vol. V, No. 9, July 10, 1929.
[60] *Corriere della Sera,* March 9, 1929.
[61] *Ibid.,* March 21, 1929.

Grand Council? Yes." The other was plain, and inscribed with the single word "No." Various subter-
fuges, it is claimed, were employed to intimidate
those voters who attempted to cast a negative ballot.[62] Of the 9,673,049 registered voters, 8,663,412
went to the polls, and 8,519,559 voted "yes," 135,761
voting "no." [63]

The new Chamber of Deputies, whose term ex-
pired in March 1934, was solemnly inaugurated by
the King on April 20, 1929. On April 9 the Grand
Council had declared that the Chamber, "corporative
in origin, is political in character and has political
functions." The Chamber, according to the Grand
Council, has a two-fold task: it is to control all
questions pertaining to the administration of the
state, especially by means of budgetary discussion;
and it is to collaborate in the preparation of bills
introduced by the government or by individual
deputies.[64] Expulsion or suspension from the Fascist
party automatically causes cessation or suspension
of the parliamentary mandate. The rules of the
Chamber, elaborated by Augusto Turati, then
Secretary-General of the Fascist party, state that
no questions which are not already on the agenda
can be discussed by the Chamber, except on proposal
of the head of the government. Furthermore, *a priori*
opposition to any proposed legislation is definitely
eliminated. In practice, bills are first submitted by
the head of the government to the Grand Council,

[62] Haider, *Capital and Labor under Fascism,* cited, pp. 259–
260; C. H. Abad, "Fascist Italy's Suppression of Free Thought,"
Current History, January 1931, p. 534.
    [63] Official *communiqué, Corriere della Sera,* March 31, 1929.
The *communiqué* stated that 8,092 ballots had been nullified or
contested.
    [64] *Communiqué* of the Press Office of the Fascist party,
Corriere della Sera, April 9, 1929.

examined by the Council of Ministers, and only then placed before the Chamber of Deputies. The Chamber may at that time "freely discuss the work of the government, not, of course, for the purpose of overthrowing it, but for the purpose of criticism and collaboration." [65]

Senate Opposition to the Electoral Law

The new electoral law met with strong opposition in the Senate. "It means going backward," said Senator Ruffini on May 12, 1928, "to take from the Italian people the right freely to choose their own representatives." [66] Senator Albertini went further and denounced the absolutism of the Fascist government:

"The existence of an elective chamber does not suffice to take the absolute character from a régime, when the country is not allowed openly to fight . . . a régime which defends the captured position by such means as are used by Fascism. . . . The calling of elections has only a relative value when the executive power paralyzes the legislative power and where a situation is created in which but a single opinion is tolerated and regarded as worthy of respect, that of the government, that is, of the head of the government." [67]

A resolution presented by Senator Ruffini and signed by forty-two Senators declared that the electoral law deprived the Italian people of the most essential of its rights, and one guaranteed by the constitution. This resolution was rejected by a vote

[65] Mussolini, speech in the Chamber of Deputies, December 8, 1928, *Corriere della Sera,* December 9, 1928.

[66] Italy, *Atti Parlamentari della Camera dei Senatori, Legislatura XXVII, 1a Sessione 1924–1928, Discussioni* (Rome, Senate Printing Office, 1928), Vol. IX, p. 10244.

[67] *Ibid.,* p. 10246.

of 161 to 46, and the law was finally adopted by the Senate.

Conflict Regarding the Chamber of Deputies

Opponents of Fascism assert that the Chamber of Deputies has lost all significance, since it is merely the creature of the Grand Council, which is, in turn, a party as well as a government organ, and since any deputies unfavorable to the régime may be removed by expulsion from the party. In their opinion, it would be more logical to abolish the Chamber altogether. The Fascist government has defended the 1928 electoral law on the ground that it eliminates agitation for personal or local advantages, and that the Chamber, which represents the "totality of the country's interests," is more truly "popular" than one elected by popular suffrage. Mussolini, however, declared on December 11, 1933 that the Chamber of Deputies, which had never "pleased" him, is "now anachronistic in its very name," and it is expected that it will be replaced in the near future by a body representing producers grouped in "corporations" or guilds.[68] The Chamber election held on March 25, 1934, in which the Fascist list received an overwhelming vote, is expected to be the last under Fascist rule.

THE SENATE

The Senate, according to the constitution, is composed of princes of the royal house, and an unlimited number of members nominated by the King from among twenty-one specified categories.[69] The age

[68] *Cf.* p. 112.

[69] These categories are as follows: (1) Archbishops and Bishops; (2) President of the Chamber of Deputies; (3) Deputies having served for six years or in three legislatures; (4) Ministers of State; (5) Ministers Secretaries of State; (6) Ambassa-

and social position of the men appointed to the Senate generally have tended to make this body conservative in character. Despite this fact, the most consistent and determined opposition to the Fascist government has come from a group of some forty liberal Senators. Mussolini has always appealed to the higher wisdom and sense of responsibility of the Senate, emphasizing the danger of public disturbance should Fascism be overthrown. Nevertheless, he has found the liberal Senators arrayed against him on such important measures as the electoral law, the law on the Grand Council and the Lateran accord. This opposition has been materially curtailed by the recent absence from the Senate of outstanding opponents of Fascism such as Senators Luigi Albertini and Benedetto Croce. Various proposals have been made for a reform of the Senate which, without displacing the present members, would transform the Senate into a body based on trade and professional affiliations and elected by corporations. No steps, however, have as yet been taken to effect this reform, and the wisdom of establishing a body which would duplicate the Chamber of Deputies is doubted in some quarters. The opposition encountered by Fascism in the Senate has had little practical effect

dors; (7) Envoys extraordinary having served three years; (8) First presidents and presidents of the Court of Cassation and the Court of Accounts; (9) First presidents of the Courts of Appeals; (10) The Attorney-General and Procurator-General; (11) Presidents of chambers of Courts of Appeals having served three years; (12) Counselors of the Court of Cassation and Court of Accounts; (13) Advocates and officials of public ministries (*fiscali generali*) having served five years; (14) Generals of army and navy; (15) Counselors of State having served five years; (16) Members of provincial councils; (17) Prefects; (18) Members of the Royal Academies; (19) Members of the Supreme Council of Public Instruction; (20) Those who, by their merits or services, have honored the fatherland; (21) Persons who, for three years, have paid three thousand lire in direct taxes

on legislation. The government is assured of a majority and could, in any case, obtain the necessary number of votes by appointing Fascist sympathizers to the Senate.

LOCAL GOVERNMENT

Centralization of power, which constitutes a basic policy of Fascism, has been applied to local government as well. By a law of April 3, 1926, the powers of the prefect were extended to all state activities within his province, with the exception of justice, war, marine and aëronautics. The prefect is regarded not merely as a civil servant, but as a collaborator of the Fascist government in the province,[70] and is charged with the task of preventing all demonstrations of opposition, especially in the press.[71] In the communes, which were formerly considered the cradle of local autonomy, and where Socialism had been strongly entrenched, the elective *syndic* (mayor) and municipal council have been replaced by a *podestà,* appointed by the government, and a council partly appointed by the prefect and partly elected by syndicates and other organizations. The *podestà* exercises both executive and legislative power, subject to strict control and surveillance on the part of the prefect and the provincial council. The functions of the municipal council are purely consultative.

Fascist spokesmen commend the reforms effected in provincial and municipal government on the ground that local party feuds and maladministration by elective officials have given way to unified, continuous and efficient administration. Opponents

[70] Corso, *Lo Stato Fascista,* cited, pp. 432–433.
[71] *Cf.* p. 96.

of Fascism deny that municipal government is either
more honest or more efficient than in the past, and
deplore the disappearance of autonomous communes which, in their opinion, offered the Italian
people an opportunity to acquire experience in self-
government.[72]

THE FASCIST STATE AND INDIVIDUAL LIBERTY

It has already been pointed out that Fascism regards individual liberty not as a right, but as a concession on the part of the state; the latter reserves
the right to impose what limitations it may see fit
whenever the exercise of liberty by individuals or
groups appears to threaten public order.[73] In accordance with this conception, the Fascist government has adopted a series of legislative measures
dealing with public safety, the right of association,
and the press.

The law of January 31, 1926, provides that a citizen
who commits abroad an act intended to disturb the
public order of Italy, or injurious to Italian interests
or prestige, shall lose his citizenship, even if the act
in question does not constitute a crime (*delitto*).
Loss of citizenship may be accompanied by seques-
tration or, in grave cases, confiscation of property.[74]
This law was applied in 1926 to seventeen noted
Italians then living abroad, including the historian
Gaetano Salvemini, the former Fascist deputy Mas-
simo Rocca and the Catholic-Democrat editor Giuseppe Donati.[75] No attempt has been made to apply

[72] *Cf.* Ferrari, *Le Régime Fasciste Italien,* cited, p. 299.
[73] Rocco, *The Political Doctrine of Fascism,* cited; Corso, *Lo
Stato Fascista,* cited, p. 435.
[74] *Gazzetta Ufficiale,* No. 28, February 4, 1926, p. 462.
[75] *Cf. ibid.,* No. 243, October 19, 1926, p. 4628 *et seq.,* for
decrees applying the law in each of these cases.

the law since that time. A law of November 25, 1926, however, punishes by imprisonment of from five to ten years those citizens who spread false rumors abroad concerning the internal situation of Italy, or engage in activities contrary to national interests.[76]

Legislation Regarding Public Safety

The decree of November 6, 1926,[77] which covers all aspects of the question of public safety, provides that every citizen must be in possession of a *carta d'identità*. No person may emigrate without the permission of police authorities, and anyone who attempts to leave the country for political motives without a passport is subject to both fine and imprisonment. Persons accused of crimes against the state, or described as "ill-famed" (*diffamata*),[78] and those regarded as dangerous to public order, may be "admonished" by an administrative commission, from whose verdict there is no appeal. "Admonished" persons must report all their movements to the police. The administrative commission may deport such persons, as well as those who have committed, or have "manifested a serious intention to commit," acts directed against the public order. Deportation for a period of from one to five years may be made to various points in Italy or to the colonies. Political prisoners must perform the tasks assigned to them, and must conduct themselves in a manner such as not "to give grounds for suspicion." [79]

[76] *Ibid.*, No. 281, December 6, 1926, p. 5314, Article 5.
[77] *Gazzetta Ufficiale*, No. 257, November 8, 1926, p. 4822.
[78] This description is also applied to ordinary criminals.
[79] These provisions of the decree of November 6, 1926, apply to ordinary criminals as well.

It is estimated that, by 1927, 1,541 persons had been listed as "ill-famed," 959 had been "admonished" and 698 had been deported, chiefly to the penal colony situated on the Lipari Islands, off the coast of Sicily.[80] The actual number of those affected by the law, however, is not definitely known, and opponents of Fascism claim that the government intentionally maintains uncertainty on this point in order to terrorize the population. On November 6, 1932, between 15,000 and 20,000 prisoners, including some anti-Fascists, were amnestied by the government, and a supplementary decree of November 16 pardoned leading political prisoners and persons in exile for political reasons. Following Italy's victory in Ethiopia, Mussolini freed 495 prisoners from the penal islands on May 19, 1936.

Persons who have spent a term on the islands of Lipari claim that the physical hardships of deportation are greatly increased by the moral ill-effects of imprisonment at the mercy of brutal police.[81] Even when released, the prisoners remain subject to police surveillance. The Fascist government justifies these measures on the ground that they constitute a "prophylactic treatment," necessary to remove diseased elements from the body politic.[82] In presenting the decree on the defense of the state to the Chamber of Deputies, Rocco, Minister of Justice, stated that the enemies of Fascism, defeated on the political field, had sought

[80] Ferrari, *Le Régime Fasciste Italien*, cited, p. 146. These figures were given by Mussolini on May 26, 1927, *Discorsi del 1927*, cited, p. 114.

[81] *Cf.* Francesco F. Nitti, *Escape* (New York, Putnam, 1930); Emilio Lussu, "Flight from Lipari," *Atlantic Monthly*, July 1930, p. 31.

[82] Mussolini, speech in Chamber of Deputies, May 26, 1927, *Discorsi del 1927*, cited, p. 118.

refuge in the sphere of crime, and must be fought in that sphere on their own terms.

The Law on Secret Associations

According to Fascist theory, no groups or organizations, whether political or economic, can exist outside the framework of the state. The law of November 26, 1925,[83] directed primarily against Freemasonry, therefore provides that all associations in Italy and the colonies must communicate to the police their charters, statutes and internal regulations, the list of their members and activities, and any other information which may be requested by the authorities in the interest of order and security. An association which fails to submit such a declaration, or which furnishes false or incomplete data, may be dissolved by the prefect. Civil and military employees are required to declare whether they have ever belonged in the past to associations of any kind. Judges, administrative officials, university professors, teachers in secondary schools and persons employed in the ministries of Foreign Affairs, the Interior and the Colonies cannot become members of professional organizations.[84] Students may not organize associations for the protection of their interests.[85] Finally, the reconstitution of parties or associations dissolved by the government is punishable by imprisonment of from three to ten years. Membership in such associations, and propaganda of their doctrines by any means whatsoever, is punishable as a crime.

The essential features of the law of November 26,

[83] *Gazzetta Ufficiale*, No. 277, November 28, 1925, p. 4714.
[84] Law of April 3, 1926.
[85] Law of July 1, 1926.

1925 on secret associations are reproduced in the
penal code adopted by the Fascist government in
1931, which provides various terms of imprisonment
for those who form associations prohibited by the
government, or attempt to spread their doctrines.
In addition, those who form an association "having
an international character" without the authoriza-
tion of the government, or join similar associations
abroad, are punishable by a fine or six months' imprisonment.

The law of November 26, 1925 was sharply attacked in the Senate by a minority which claimed
that it constituted a violation of the fundamental
rights of the Italian people. Several Senators, who
approved of the law in general, objected to the provision making it obligatory for civil employees to
declare whether they had previously participated
in secret societies. This provision, as a matter of
fact, was allowed to remain in abeyance after it
was discovered that its strict enforcement would im-
plicate a number of Fascists.

THE SPECIAL TRIBUNAL FOR THE DEFENSE
OF THE STATE

By the law of November 25, 1926,[86] certain political crimes, notably the reconstitution of parties
and associations dissolved by the government, were
removed from the jurisdiction of ordinary courts and
submitted to the newly created Special Tribunal for
the Defense of the State.[87] This tribunal is composed
of a president chosen from among officers of the
army, navy, air-force or militia, and five judges

[86] *Gazzetta Ufficiale,* No. 281, December 6, 1926, p. 5314.
[87] This law was supplemented by a decree of December 12,
1926.

selected from officers holding the rank of consul (colonel) in the militia. During the preliminaries of the trial, the president may forbid the inspection of documents, cognizance of which "may be detrimental to the public interest." The president, at the request of the public prosecutor, or if he thinks it necessary "in the public interest," may exclude non-military counsel. At the trial in October 1930 of a group of Slovenes accused of throwing a bomb on the premises of a Fascist newspaper in Trieste, counsel for the defense, who was appointed by the president of the court, declared that his clients "were in a terrible position, and that a death sentence would be the proper thing." [88] At the trial of the group known as *Alleanza Nazionale*" [89] on December 22, 1930, the president of the Special Tribunal interrupted the proceedings to denounce the defendants as "liars" and "worms" unworthy of mercy. Foreign correspondents are usually excluded from these trials, while Italian newspapers publish only *communiqués* issued by the government. No appeal can be taken from the verdict of the Special Tribunal, although the sentence may be reviewed if fresh evidence showing the innocence of the condemned has been collected in the meantime. The King, moreover, may exercise his prerogative of reprieve if the commander of the prison consents to forward the petition of the condemned. In the case of the Trieste Slovenes, the commander failed to do this, and the men were executed twenty-four hours following the close of the trial.

The Special Tribunal for the Defense of the State is unreservedly condemned by opponents of Fascism

---

[88] *Corriere della Sera,* September 6, 1930.
[89] *Cf.* p. 121.

as an organ of party, as contrasted with state, justice.[90] Fascist spokesmen, for their part, defend the tribunal as an institution essential for the preservation of public order; they claim that "the rapidity and rigor" of its procedure "give the most certain guarantee of the equity and, at the same time, rigor of the decisions." [91]

THE FASCIST GOVERNMENT AND THE PRESS

The sole function of the press in the Fascist state is that of collaboration with the government. After the March on Rome the Italian press, which had always served as the principal source of information on political subjects, was outspokenly critical of Fascism, and exercised considerable influence, especially in the industrial centres of the North. The "fourth estate" was denounced by Fascist spokesmen on the ground that it made irresponsible use of its undisputed powers. The Fascist press, however, lacked journalistic talent, and could not compete with liberal and socialist organs for the attention of the public.[92] Following the murder of Matteotti, the anti-Fascist press became virulent in its attacks on the government, and various restrictions were gradually imposed on it, culminating in the law of December 31, 1925, which brought the press under government control.[93] This law, supplemented by the regulations of March 4, 1926 and the decree of February 28, 1928, provides that a responsible director, approved by the government, must be in charge of all periodical publications. Only journalists whose names appear on a special register kept by regional

[90] Ferrari, *Le Régime Fasciste Italien,* cited, p. 130.
[91] *Ibid.,* p. 131.
[92] Villari, *The Fascist Experiment,* cited, p. 210.
[93] *Gazzetta Ufficiale,* No. 3, January 5, 1926, p. 22.

Fascist syndicates of journalists may contribute to newspapers or periodicals, and no persons who have engaged in "public activity contrary to the interest of the nation" can be so listed. Properly registered publications are thereafter subject to supervision by the prefect, who may sequestrate them at any time. After a certain number of sequestrations, the prefect may issue a "warning" (*diffida*), and two such "warnings" may be followed by suspension or even suppression of the offending newspaper. The law provides that an appeal from the decision of the prefect may be taken to the Ministry of Justice. Measures adopted against opposition newspapers, however, have generally not been followed by court proceedings.

The rigorous application of the press laws dealt a sharp blow to the circulation and, consequently, the finances of independent newspapers, which have been forced or persuaded, one by one, to sell out to Fascist interests. *Il Corriere della Sera* (Milan), formerly directed by Senator Albertini, retains the largest circulation, and is distinguished by the literary quality of its contributions. *Il Popolo d'Italia* (Milan), founded by Mussolini in 1914 as a Socialist organ, is now directed by his nephew, Vito Mussolini, and may be regarded as a mouthpiece of the government. For the most part Fascist editorials are simply variations on the theme of the day, as expressed by Mussolini. Intolerance of all but official opinion has reduced the Italian press to a uniform level of monotony. In view of the strict censorship, greater credence is often given by the population to rumor and gossip than to published news. Foreign correspondents are also subject to censorship. All cables and radio messages pass through the

Ministry of the Interior, and while messages may not always be deleted, their transmission is considerably delayed.[94]

THE FASCIST MILITIA

The maintenance of public order is entrusted by the Fascist government to the Voluntary Militia for National Security (*Milizia Voluntaria per la Sicurezza Nazionale*), organized on January 14, 1923. The militia was originally composed of the squads of Black Shirts which participated in the March on Rome, and one of the *quadrumvirs,* General De Bono, was appointed Commander-General.[95] It was expected that these irregular troops would be disbanded by the Fascist government once it had come to power. Mussolini, however, claimed that the disbandment of the Black Shirts would not only constitute an act of ingratitude to his followers, but might lead to violence and disorder, especially in regions remote from the capital. He decided, therefore, to regularize the status of the Black Shirts by creating the militia.

The "voluntary militia," which now numbers over 300,000 men, constitutes a part of the armed forces of the state, and is directly under the orders of the head of the government, who acts as its Commander-

---

[94] *Cf.* Ralph W. Barnes, special article on conditions in Italy, *New York Herald Tribune,* March 5, 1931; Herbert L. Matthews, *New York Times,* March 12, 1933.

[95] Estimates of the number of men enrolled in Fascist squads in October 1922 vary considerably. Villari estimates the total number at 300,000 (Villari, *The Fascist Experiment,* cited, p. 163). Mussolini has stated that 52,000 actually participated in the March on Rome, and entered the city. Salvemini questions the latter figure, and asserts that there were only 8,000 Black Shirts in Rome on October 28, 1922. Fascist supporters adopted the uniform worn by the *Arditi* (shock troops) toward the close of the war, which included a black shirt.

General. Following the excitement created by the Matteotti affair, it was decreed on August 4, 1924, that the militia should take an oath of loyalty to the King, and this was done on the second anniversary of the March on Rome, October 28, 1924. At first no restrictions were placed on the political affiliations of members of the militia. In October 1930, however, the Grand Council adopted a regulation which provided that all members of the militia must be enrolled in the Fascist party.[96] Service in the militia is voluntary; with the exception of the permanent general staff, the officers and men are paid only for days of actual service, and are not required to live in barracks. In case of mobilization, the members of the militia are to be incorporated in units of the armed forces. The organization of the militia is modeled on that of the Roman legions, and consists of legions, cohorts, centuries and maniples.

Functions of the Militia

The object of the militia, as set forth by the Grand Council on January 14, 1923, is "to safeguard the inevitable and inexorable development of the October [1922] revolution." Its duties are those of a political police. The militia is charged with the task of preventing "every disturbance of public order, every gesture or attempt at sedition against the Fascist government," thereby assuring "constant normalcy in the productive and social life of the na-

---

[96] *Corriere della Sera*, October 21, 1930. The regular (conscript) Italian army numbers 491,398 men. The militia is responsible for preparatory military training in accordance with the rules and regulations issued by the Ministry of War under the supervision of the latter and of the territorial military authorities.

tion." [97] Ordinary police activities and the repression of common delinquency are left to the police. The militia is assigned to railways, ports, postal and telegraph offices, and to duty in the colonies, notably in Libya. The cost of the militia, estimated at 40,000,-000 lire in 1929, is defrayed by the Ministry of the Interior. This sum, however, does not include the money expended on the militia of railways and ports, which is charged to the budget of the Ministry of Communications, nor the cost of the Libyan militia, borne by the Ministry for the Colonies.

Opponents of Fascism denounce the militia as a partisan body, designed to enforce Fascist rule by force, and demand either its abolition or its absorption into the regular army. The Fascist government, however, regards the militia as an instrument indispensable to the maintenance of public order.

In addition to the militia, the Fascist government has established a secret police, known as the O.V.R.A. (*Organizzazione Vigilanza Reati Anti-fascisti*),[98] directly under the orders of the Ministry of the Interior, which is headed by Mussolini. The activities of this police became known to the public for the first time in an official *communiqué* of December 4, 1930, which stated that the O.V.R.A. had disclosed the existence of three anti-Fascist organizations which had for some time been conducting criminal activities against the régime.[99]

[97] Partito Nazionale Fascista, *Il Gran Consiglio nei Primi Cinqui Anni dell' Era Fascista,* cited, p. 69.
[98] Organization for Surveillance of Anti-Fascist Crimes.
[99] *Corriere della Sera,* December 5, 1930. For the activities and trials of members of these organizations, *cf.* section on opposition to Fascism, p. 121.

CHAPTER IV

THE ITALIAN CORPORATIVE SYSTEM

INTRODUCTION

WHEN Premier Mussolini, at a meeting of Fascist corporations on March 23, 1936, announced his intention to effect sweeping constitutional and economic reforms in preparation for a war he regards as inevitable, he took one more step toward "co-ordination" of Italy's economic activities within the framework of the totalitarian state.[1] The government already holds a majority of shares in a number of key industries, controls banking and credit, directs foreign trade, supervises the establishment of new plants and the expansion of old ones, and has established a gold monopoly. Private economic interests are being rapidly subordinated to the paramount objectives of the Fascist state, which is girding the entire population for national expansion. This process was greatly accelerated in 1935-1936 by the Ethiopian campaign and the imposition of League sanctions, which forced Italy to husband its slender resources of capital and raw materials.

According to *Il Duce's* announcement, the "anachronistic" Chamber of Deputies, which had become a mere rubber stamp for government decisions, is to be discarded in favor of the National Council of Corporations, representing economic interests; many key industries working directly or indirectly for na-

[1] For text, cf. *Corriere della Sera,* March 24, 1936; The Association of Italian Corporations, *Business and Financial Report, A Monthly Survey of Italian Trade and Industry,* February-May 1936, Supplement.

tional defense—a term which daily becomes more inclusive—are to be nationalized; and a régime of "higher social justice" is to be inaugurated, under which workers will be regarded as collaborators of their employers, with equal rights and equal duties to the state. The government, for the present at least, does not plan to touch agriculture, internal trade or small and medium-sized industries which are to remain in private hands, subject to national "discipline."

These reforms are in harmony with Fascist theory, which distinguishes between uncontrolled capitalism and capital. While capitalism is regarded as a malignant growth on the body of modern society which must be ruthlessly destroyed, capital is viewed as the humble fruit of individual or family labors and is considered essential to Italy's economic development.

Fascism has its roots in the post-war history of Italy. When it came to power in 1922 it represented a reaction of the young generation against the defeatism of the Socialists, the impotence of parliament and the outcome of the World War, denounced by nationalists as a "mutilated victory." The middle class, from industrialists and landowners to small shopkeepers and white-collar workers, regarded Fascism at that time as a bulwark against the alleged menace of Communism.

For the pluralism of the modern democratic state, where the government is only one of several groups which claim the individual's allegiance, Fascism has substituted the totalitarian state, which embraces all the activities of individuals and subordinates them to national ends. The development of this state is governed by two basic factors which determine Fas-

cist policy at home and abroad: Italy's lack of
natural resources, and its desire, despite this handi-
cap, to recover the position it occupied in the heyday
of the Roman Empire. Fascism, essentially a dy-

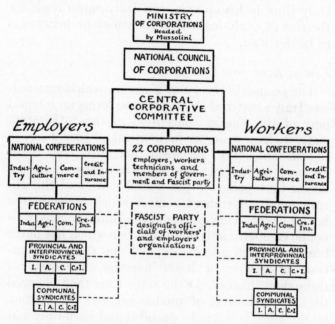

THE ITALIAN CORPORATIVE SYSTEM

namic movement, is hampered on all sides by basic
material limitations. Unlike Bolshevism, which has
Russia's natural wealth at its disposal, it can promise no tangible millennium. It undertakes the modest
and ungrateful task of so husbanding Italy's resources as to reduce its dependence on the outside
world and eventually achieve more equal distribution of wealth among the population. This task,

according to Mussolini, can be accomplished only by a high degree of self-discipline and self-sacrifice on the part of all classes, and by complete subordination of individual and class interests to those of the state, as determined by the Fascist party. Only thus, in his opinion, can Italy equip itself for the rôle of world-leadership for which he believes it to be destined.

Fascist Economic Theory

The economic theory of Fascism, which rationalizes Italy's material circumstances, forms an integral part of the Fascist conception of the totalitarian state. In economic, as in political, theory Fascism rejects democracy, socialism, liberalism and unrestrained capitalism. The Fascists oppose both the laissez-faire policy of the liberal state and the all-embracing government control which exists in the Soviet Union. They point out that untrammeled economic competition is an abstraction which has never been translated into reality, and that state intervention, in greater or lesser measure, has occurred throughout history. At the same time they believed that direct control of production and distribution by the state is not only wasteful and harmfully bureaucratic, but creates economic disorganization and widespread suffering.[2] Fascism contends that private initiative is the most valuable and efficient instrument for achieving the economic ends of the nation. Private interests, however, must be guided and harmonized by the state, in order that they may not conflict with the collective interests of society.

[2] Benito Mussolini, *New York American,* December 11, 1934; Arrigo Serpieri, *Problemi della Terra nell' Economia Corporativa* (Rome, Diritto del Lavoro, 1929), p. 28.

Fascist economy, according to Mussolini, "places the accent" not on individual profits, but on collective benefits.[3]

Fascism "absolutely" denies the individualism of the eighteenth century, "denies the individual as an element preceding the state and independent of it and his pretended natural rights, including that of property."[4] The *homo oeconomicus* of Fascism is not an individual competing with other individuals for his own particular ends, but a member of the state, to which he owes economic allegiance. Private initiative must be exercised within the state, for the good of the state, and subject to the discipline imposed by the state. This union of individual and collective interests is to be realized by the corporative system, which achieves "the interpenetration and absolute identification" of the individual's will and initiative with the supreme ends of the state.[5]

In the totalitarian state labor, both manual and intellectual, constitutes a social duty, and all forms of property—whether factory, land, or stocks and bonds—are vested with social obligations. Every owner of property must use it for national ends. If he fails to do so, the state must intervene to protect collective interests, up to and including expropriation. There can be no limits to state intervention except those dictated by national interests. The state has not only the right but the duty to intervene, "supervising, safeguarding, stimulating, or even supplanting the private owner." Such inter-

[3] Benito Mussolini, speech of October 6, 1934 at Milan, *Corriere della Sera,* October 7, 1934.

[4] Serpieri, *Problemi della Terra nell' Economia Corporativa,* cited, p. 58.

[5] Ugo Spirito, *La Critica della Economia Liberale* (Milan, Treves, 1930), p. 97 *et seq.*

vention is justified by the objectives of the state, which are not only political and economic, but spiritual. The individual, whose life span is limited, looks only to the present, and may sacrifice the interests of future generations to the more ample satisfaction of his own desires. "The state, which lives through countless generations of men," is guardian of the nation's interests; "it has among its essential tasks the duty to guarantee that the future is not sacrificed to the present."[6]

Intervention by the state, according to Fascism, does not necessarily imply coercion. Forcible interference will become superfluous when all individuals have developed a "corporative consciousness" and voluntarily collaborate for the good of the nation. "Corporative consciousness" is in reality sublimated nationalism; to Fascists it means "to feel that, in every act of our life as Italians, Italy is present; that every one of our acts is conditioned by the interests of the fatherland . . . because for an Italian there is only one way of being truly a man —to feel the interests of Italy as his own interests."[7]

The corporative system consists at present of separate Fascist organizations for workers and employers, linked by twenty-two corporations or guilds composed of workers, employers and technicians in particular categories of production appointed by their respective organizations subject to government approval, and headed by government and Fascist party officials representing the consumers. It is crowned by the National Council of Corporations, apparently destined to supplant the Chamber of

[6] Serpieri, *Problemi della Terra nell' Economia Corporativa*, cited, p. 27.
[7] *Ibid.*, p. 62.

Deputies, and by the Ministry of Corporations, of which Mussolini is head. The Fascists claim that this elaborate corporative structure assures self-government for Italian producers, and at the same time guarantees national interests against the effects of unregulated private competition. In practice the corporative system is controlled from top to bottom by the Fascist government. Workers and employers are prohibited from resorting to strikes or lockouts in defense of their interests. The state, through the Ministry of Corporations and the labor courts, acts as arbiter in conflicts between capital, labor and consumers, and dictates both the terms of collective contracts and the decisions of labor courts.

Critics of Fascism usually argue that the corporative system merely serves to regiment production along lines determined by the Fascist government, and perpetuates existing inequalities and maladjustments without offering a program of social and economic improvement. During the past two years Mussolini has attempted to meet these criticisms by declaring that the corporative system has two main objectives—to achieve "a higher social justice for all the Italian people" and to strengthen Italy "for expansion in the world."[8] He has defined social justice as "secure work, a fair salary, a decent home . . . and the possibility to develop and improve incessantly."[9] The workers, moreover, "must come ever more intimately to know the productive process and to participate in its necessary discipline."[10] If the nineteenth century "was the century of the power of capital, the twentieth century is that of the power

[8] Speech of November 10, 1934 inaugurating the twenty-two corporations. *Corriere della Sera*, November 11, 1934.
[9] Speech of October 6, 1934, cited.
[10] *Ibid.*

and the glory of labor." If the nineteenth century achieved the equality of men before the law, the twentieth must establish "the equality of men before labor, conceived as a duty and right, as a creative joy which must exalt and ennoble life, not mortify and depress it." Such basic equality, however, does not exclude, "in fact it demands" the clearest differentiation between groups, or hierarchies, not on the basis of wealth but on that of "functions, merit, responsibility."

Mussolini has not yet indicated how his concept of social justice is to be realized, beyond stating that the corporative state must solve the problem of distribution of wealth "in such a way that we should no longer witness the illogical, paradoxical, and at the same time cruel existence of misery in the midst of abundance." He has warned that miracles have no place in economics, and has rejected long-range economic planning, declaring that "the future cannot be fixed like an itinerary or a timetable." Italy, according to Mussolini, can solve its problems only by a gradual transition from existing forms of capitalism to a new corporative order. It is premature, in his opinion, to predict the effect which this order may have on production and distribution.[11] His ultimate aim, however, appears to be a form of state capitalism, under which the state will become "the supreme and sole proprietor and administrator of all the economy of the nation."[12] He has not yet divulged the formula by which he expects to reconcile state capitalism with private initiative and private property. It is conceivable, however, that if such a formula is evolved, it will

[11] Speech of November 10, 1934, cited.
[12] *New York American,* December 11, 1934.

reveal that Mussolini has not altogether abandoned the socialist ideas which he held before the World War.

FASCIST SYNDICAL ORGANIZATION

The growth of industry in Northern Italy in the first decade of the twentieth century was accompanied by the emergence of an industrial proletariat. The Italian workers, employed chiefly in small-scale industries, were for the most part poorly paid and inadequately organized. The Socialist party, which had at first drawn its strength from the small bourgeoisie and the intellectuals, sought to improve the lot of the workers by organizing them in Socialist labor unions, the most important of which was the General Confederation of Labor. A similar attempt to solve the social and economic problems created by industrialization was made by Catholic labor unions. Meanwhile the syndicalist movement, which had originated in France and had been elaborated into a philosophic system by Georges Sorel,[13] won many adherents among Italian Socialists.

The outcome of the World War, regarded in Italy as a Pyrrhic victory, and the establishment of the Soviet government in Russia strengthened the syndicalist elements in the Socialist party, which demanded the organization of a general strike and the overthrow of the government and inaugurated a period of industrial unrest. It is estimated that in 1920 there were 1,881 industrial strikes, in which 1,267,953 workers participated, and 189 agricultural strikes, involving 1,045,732 workers. When the metallurgical industrialists of Lombardy and Pied-

[13] Georges Sorel, *Réflexions sur la Violence* (Paris, Rivière, 5th edition, 1921).

mont refused in 1920 to raise wages and threatened a lockout, the workers first planned to declare a general strike, and then proceeded to occupy the factories. The government, adhering to the liberal policy of laissez-faire, made no attempt to interfere in these conflicts between workers and industrialists, which threatened to dislocate the economic life of the country, already impaired by the war. It was with the avowed purpose of re-establishing social order and assuring peaceful economic development that the Fascist party, formed in 1919 by Benito Mussolini, undertook a vigorous campaign against Socialists and Communists; and it was this objective which won for Fascism the support of the propertied classes—industrialists and landowners—irritated and alarmed by constant labor disturbances. By 1921, however, the workers' revolutionary impetus had spent itself. In 1922, on the eve of the March on Rome, only 89 industrial strikes occurred, supported by 79,298 workers, and 23 agricultural strikes, involving 25,146 workers.[14] Italy appeared to be reaching a stage of economic stabilization when, on October 29, 1922, King Victor Emmanuel summoned Mussolini to form a cabinet.

On assuming the office of Premier, Mussolini declared that the Fascist government would undertake the "guardianship" of all economic interests of the nation, would tolerate no conflicts between workers and employers resulting in an interruption of the country's productive life, and would not favor one

[14] Ivanoe Bonomi, *Dal Socialismo al Fascismo* (Rome, Formiggini, 1924); Carmen Haider, *Capital and Labor under Fascism* (New York, Columbia University Press, 1930), p. 25; Gaetano Salvemini, *The Fascist Dictatorship in Italy* (New York, Holt, 1927); Luigi Sturzo, *Italy and Fascismo* (London, Faber Gwyer, 1926).

group at the expense of the other.[15] The Fascist state, he said, rejected the laissez-faire policy of the "agnostic" liberal state, and would interfere whenever economic conflicts threatened to impair national interests.

The program of the Fascist party, adopted in 1922, provided for the establishment of syndicates and "corporations,"[16] which were intended to be an expression of national solidarity as well as a means of developing production. At that time Fascism favored syndicalism not as a means of improving the economic position of the workers, but as a method of organizing the labor elements within its own ranks.[17] Both in theory and practice Fascist syndicalism is the direct antithesis of the revolutionary syndicalism which exists in such countries as France and Spain. This antithesis has been clearly stated by a Fascist writer who points out that revolutionary syndicalism negates the nation-state exalted by Fascism; affirms the class struggle, while Fascism attempts to achieve the collaboration of all classes for the good of the state; envisages the general strike, which is prohibited by Fascism; and demands association on a class rather than on a political basis, in contrast to Fascism, which subordinates the interests of all classes to those of the Fascist party.[18]

The Fascist syndicates did not at first attract industrial workers, the majority of whom remained

[15] Speech in the Chamber of Deputies, November 16, 1922. Benito Mussolini, *Discorsi della Rivoluzione* (Milan, Imperia, 1923), p. 101-102.

[16] Until 1925 the Fascists used the term "corporation" to describe a national federation of syndicates.

[17] Haider, *Capital and Labor under Fascism*, cited, p. 57.

[18] C. Gangemi, as cited by François Perroux, *Contribution à l'Etude de l'Economie et des Finances de l'Italie depuis la Guerre* (Paris, Giard, 1929), p. 175, *et seq.*

affiliated with Socialist and Catholic labor unions. The government, having failed to reach an understanding with the General Confederation of Labor, proceeded to adopt a series of measures directed at the elimination of all but Fascist syndicates. At the invitation of Mussolini a meeting of Fascist workers' organizations and representatives of employers was held in Rome at Palazzo Vidoni on October 2, 1925, when the two groups concluded a pact by which the employers recognized Fascist syndicates as the workers' sole representatives. The General Confederation of Labor denounced this pact on the ground that it impaired the interests of the workers. On November 25, 1925, however, factory committees were declared illegal and their functions were entrusted to Fascist syndicates.[19] The system of syndicates was established by the law of April 3, 1926, supplemented by a decree of July 1, 1926, while the relations of workers and employers with each other and with the state were defined by the Charter of Labor, promulgated on April 21, 1927.

The Charter of Labor

The Charter of Labor[20] is regarded by Fascist spokesmen as the constitution of a new, corporative Italian society.[21] It declares that the nation is an organism having a life, ends and means superior to

[19] L. Rosenstock-Franck, *L'Economie Corporative Fasciste en Doctrine et en Fait* (Paris, Gamber, 1934), p. 39.

[20] For the text, cf. *Gazzetta Ufficiale del Regno d'Italia*, April 30, 1927, p. 1794.

[21] *L'Organisation Syndicale et Corporative Italienne* (Rome, Imprimerie de la Chambre des Députés de Charles Colombo, 1930), p. 25; Augusto Turati and Giuseppe Bottai, *La Carta del Lavoro* (Rome, Il Diritto del Lavoro, 1929); Giuseppe Bottai, *Esperienza Corporativa* (Rome, Il Diritto del Lavoro, 1929); Fausto Pitigliani, *The Italian Corporative State* (New York, Macmillan, 1934).

those of the separate individuals or groups which compose it. Labor in all forms, intellectual, technical and manual, is regarded as a social duty and, as such, is to be safeguarded by the state. The process of production is unitary from the national point of view, and its aims are the welfare of the producers and the growth of the nation's power.

The Charter of Labor regards private initiative in the field of production as the most useful and effective instrument for the achievement of national ends. Private organization of production, however, is a national function, and organizers of all enterprises are therefore responsible to the state. The latter intervenes in production only when private initiative is lacking or insufficient, or when political interests are at stake. Such intervention may assume the form of control, encouragement or direct management.

Professional or syndical organization is free; only those syndicates which are recognized and controlled by the state, however, have the right to represent the category of workers or employers for which they are established. The conflict of interests between workers and employers is recognized, but must be subordinated to the higher interests of production, and regulated by means of collective labor contracts.

In addition to this general statement, the Charter of Labor sets forth in detail the principles which are to govern the organization of syndicates, the conclusion of collective labor contracts, the establishment of employment agencies, and various measures for the education and insurance of workers.

The basic unit of the corporative system is the syndicate—a term by which the Fascists designate both associations of employers and unions of workers. The state recognizes only one syndicate for each territorial unit—commune, province or region. Syndicates of employers and workers must always be separate; mixed syndicates are not accorded recognition. A syndicate is recognized when it contains 10 per cent of the workers engaged in a given kind of work or, in the case of employers, when its members give work to at least 10 per cent of the workers engaged in that industry; when, in addition to economic activities, it undertakes the assistance, instruction, moral and political education of its members; and when its officials give a guarantee of ability, morality and strong patriotic convictions. The percentage of membership was set at a relatively low figure on the ground that Italian labor is as yet inadequately organized, especially in the agrarian South, and that the adoption of a higher percentage would have hampered the establishment of syndicates for certain categories of workers.[22] Membership in syndicates is open to all citizens who have reached the age of eighteen and have always given evidence of "good moral and political conduct from the national point of view."[23]

Recognition of a professional association is effected by royal decree, on proposal of the competent minister. Recognition is refused whenever it appears inopportune for reasons of a political, economic or social nature.[24] Under no circumstances is recognition accorded to associations in any way connected with international organizations—thus barring the existence of Socialist labor unions.

[22] *L'Organisation Syndicale et Corporative*, cited, p. 53.
[23] Law of April 3, 1926 regarding the legal regulation of collective relations of labor, *Gazzetta Ufficiale*, April 14, 1926, p. 1590; decree of July 1, 1926, *ibid.*, July 7, 1926, p. 2930, Article 1.
[24] Decree of July 1, 1926, Article 13.

Functions of the Syndicates

The recognized syndicate represents all persons in the category for which it is established, whether members or not. It has the right to conclude collective labor contracts, to charge syndical dues and discipline its own members, and to appear before labor courts on their behalf. Only regularly enrolled members, however, may participate in the activities of the syndicate. In addition to the recognized syndicates, the law permits the organization of *de facto* associations by various professions; no such associations actually exist.

The syndicates, following recognition, are subject to the control of the provincial prefect, if their activities are restricted to the boundaries of a single province, or to that of the Ministry of Corporations, if they cover two or more provinces. Ten per cent of the dues charged by each syndicate is set aside as its contribution to the expenses of the Ministry of Corporations.

The communal syndicates of workers and employers are grouped into provincial and inter-provincial syndicates, which in turn are grouped into federations. The federation holds plenary meetings only once every three years, its duties being performed in the interval by its council, executive committee, and president or secretary.[25] The federation is responsible for protecting the interests of the categories of production it represents. It "encourages

[25] The title "president" is applied to the chief officer of employers' organizations, and that of "secretary" to workers' organizations, "solely out of respect for tradition, since the chiefs of the syndical associations all occupy the same rank as regards dignity, responsibility and functions." Ministry of Corporations, *News Notes on Fascist Corporations* (Rome), August-September 1934, p. 10.

their technical and economic development in harmony with the interests of the nation" and frames collective contracts of more than local significance.[26] Both syndicates and federations are theoretically elective bodies, "in order that they may preserve their characteristic feature as the direct exponents of the views of the various groups of producers."[27] In practice all syndical officials are designated by the Fascist party, subject to ratification by the Ministry of Corporations, and may be removed whenever their work proves unsatisfactory to party leaders. This procedure is designed to assure "that no persons are summoned to fulfil any office within the syndical organization, unless they possess—in addition to such general qualifications of moral integrity and of capacity as are indispensable—that also of absolute political loyalty; and further unless their productive activities are in complete conformity with the principles of the Fascist corporative organization."[28]

The federations are organized into nine[29] national confederations, eight of which represent employers and workers respectively in industry, agriculture, commerce, credit and insurance, while the ninth represents professional men and artists. The confederation serves as a link between the syndicates and the government, and is regarded as semi-public in character. For that reason both the president and the

---

[26] *Ibid.*

[27] *Ibid.*

[28] *Ibid.*

[29] Until 1934, when the corporations were established, there had been four additional confederations, of employers and workers respectively, in maritime and aerial transportation, and land transportation and inland navigation. These four confederations have been abolished.

council of the confederation are appointed by the government.[30]

Critics of Fascism contend that designation of syndical officials by the Fascist party definitely discriminates against the workers. They declare that, while neither employers nor workers are free to elect their syndical leaders, the former are headed by officials who may be said to represent them in the sense that they are chosen from the employer class. By contrast, the workers' organizations are usually headed by men who are not selected from the ranks of the workers and consequently neither represent them nor have their interests at heart.

The Fascist syndicates, based on economic interests, were directly linked with governmental and party institutions by the electoral law of May 17, 1928, which provided that the syndicates were to designate eight hundred of the one thousand candidates for the Chamber of Deputies, the other two hundred being nominated by various "cultural, educational, charitable or propagandist" associations. From the one thousand names thus presented, the Fascist Grand Council selects a list of four hundred names, which is then submitted to the voters for a "plebiscite." This electoral law has been twice put to the test—in 1929 and 1934. Its operation has been criticized on the ground that the same number of candidates is assigned to employers' and workers' confederations, with resulting discrimination against the workers. Thus in 1934 the employers' confederation of agriculture, composed of 662,692 members, named 96 candidates, the number assigned to the workers' confederation, composed of 1,926,931 members. Critics of the electoral procedure also contend

[30] *News Notes on Fascist Corporations,* cited.

that it fails to give the various economic interests a representation corresponding to their actual weight in the life of the country. Thus agriculture, which forms the occupation of more than 50 per cent of the population, is accorded less than one-fourth of the total number of candidates.[31]

The National Council of Corporations

The law of April 1926 regarding syndical organization envisaged the eventual establishment of corporations (*corporazioni*),[32] which were to serve as liaison organs between employers' and workers' organizations in each category. No steps toward the creation of these corporations were taken at first, and the functions they were intended to perform were temporarily entrusted in 1931 to the National Council of Corporations which had been established the previous year.[33] This council, of which Mussolini is president, is composed of persons designated by syndical and other organizations, as well as members of the cabinet and secretaries of the Fascist party. It is designed to act as a coordinating and consultative body, charged with the task of achieving unity in national production, and ranks with the Fascist Grand Council and the Chamber of Deputies as a supreme organ of the state.[34] Actually, however, all important measures on economic, financial

[31] Haider, *Capital and Labor under Fascism,* cited, p. 255. For further details regarding Fascist electoral procedure, cf. V. M. Dean, "Fascist Rule in Italy," *New Governments in Europe* (New York, Thomas Nelson, 1934), p. 80 *et seq.*

[32] The Italian term *corporazione* can best be translated into English as guild.

[33] *Gazzetta Ufficiale,* March 28, 1930.

[34] Cf. "Il Consiglio delle Corporazioni," *Corriere della Sera,* September 25, 1929; Report of Giuseppe Bottai, then Minister of Corporations, regarding the law on the National Council of Corporations, *ibid.,* November 23, 1929.

and social matters have emanated from the political organs of the government—Premier Mussolini, the Ministry of Corporations, and the Fascist Grand Council—not from the National Council of Corporations, which frequently is not even consulted regarding such legislation. The Ministry of Corporations, headed by Mussolini, regulates and coordinates the work of the syndicates and supervises the development of national production, and has the final decision in labor disputes. The expenditures of this ministry are partly included in the state budget, and partly financed from a special fund consisting of syndical contributions.

The Corporations

With its parallel but separate organizations of employers and workers, topped by the National Council and Ministry of Corporations, the corporative system was like a structure composed of pillars and roof, but lacking all internal means of communication. On July 1, 1933 Mussolini announced his intention to complete the structure, and on November 13 he introduced a resolution in the National Council of Corporations providing for the establishment of "corporations of category" to be headed by the Council.[35] These corporations were defined as "the instrument which, under the aegis of the state, carries out the integral, organic and unitary discipline of productive forces, with a view to the development of the wealth, the political power and the welfare of the Italian people." Three principal functions were assigned to the corporations: they were to act as advisory bodies to the government, con-

[35] For the text of this speech, cf. *Corriere della Sera,* November 14, 1933.

ciliate disputes between capital and labor, and regulate wages and production costs within their respective categories, as well as relations between the several categories. The National Council of Corporations was to be charged with legislative authority in the economic field, while the Fascist Grand Council was entrusted with all decisions as to future developments of a political and constitutional nature which might arise from the practical operation of the corporative system.

The nature of these developments was indicated by Mussolini on November 14, 1933, when he told the National Council of Corporations that, as political liberalism had been buried in 1923 with the creation of the Fascist Grand Council, so "today we bury economic liberalism." "It is perfectly conceivable," he declared, "that a National Council of Corporations will supplant *in toto* the present Chamber of Deputies," which "has never pleased me," and is "alien to our mentality, to our Fascist passion."[36]

The resolution of November 13, 1933, which gave Mussolini, as president of the National Council of Corporations, full and direct control of the corporative system, was embodied in a law approved by the Grand Council on December 10, 1933, by an overwhelming majority of the Senate on January 13, 1934, and by the Chamber of Deputies on January 18. On May 9 Mussolini announced the formation of twenty-two corporations representing every phase of Italy's economic life, and grouped according to three main divisions of production—industry, agriculture, and activities productive of services, such as credit, insurance, professions and transportation. On

[36] For the text of this speech cf. *Corriere della Sera*, November 15, 1933.

November 10, in a solemn ceremony at the Campidoglio in the hall of Julius Caesar, who in the words of an Italian editorial "was also a great social reformer,"[37] *Il Duce* inaugurated the twenty-two corporations, whose representatives he greeted as "a revolutionary assembly." The purpose of the corporations, he said, is to achieve social justice at home and increase "the total strength of the nation for its expansion in the world." Reiterating that the world crisis is a crisis of the existing economic system, he declared that it is necessary "to advance courageously toward the creation of a new system," emphasizing that the corporations are a point of departure, not a point of arrival.[38]

The twenty-two corporations, each of which has Mussolini as president and members of either the government or the Fascist party among its officers, are composed of representatives of employers, workers and technicians in the following branches of production: cereals; fruits, vegetables and flowers; viticulture and wine; beets and sugar; edible oil; husbandry and fisheries; forestry, lumber and wood; textile fibers and products; metals and metallurgical engineering; chemical trades; water, gas and electricity; paper and printing; building trades; clothing trades; mining and quarrying; glass and pottery; credit and insurance; arts and professions; sea and air transport; inland communications; theatres and public entertainments; and hotels and restaurants, grouped into a corporation of public hospitality.[39] The members of these corporations, totaling 824, form the Central Corporative Committee which, ac-

[37] "Un Fatto Storico," *Corriere della Sera,* November 11, 1934.
[38] For the text of this speech, cf. *ibid.*
[39] For a detailed list of the members of each corporation, cf. *Corriere della Sera,* November 9, 1934.

cording to a remark made by Mussolini on November 10, may eventually usurp the place of the National Council of Corporations, and fall heir to the functions of the Chamber of Deputies. Five women—representing silk cocoon workers, dressmakers, glove factory employers, trained nurses, and midwives—are members of this committee, the first time in the history of Fascism that women have been admitted to a body of national importance.

Each corporation is vertical in organization, containing representatives of all stages of production in its particular category, from raw material to distribution of the finished product. Thus the corporation of textile fibers and products includes representatives of employers, workers and technicians in wool growing, woolen and worsted, silk breeding, cocoon raising, silk reeling and silk throwing, silk weaving, rayon mills, linen and hemp works, jute, textile dyeing and printing, carpet making, and wholesale and retail textile merchants, as well as technical experts representing agriculture, chemical trades, artists and designers, and cooperative cocoon drying plants.

Mussolini, as president, will submit to each corporation, through the appropriate government officials, the program of study he wants it to undertake.[40] The specific problems presented to the textile corporation, for example, include a study of means to increase silk exports, the changes necessary in the cotton industry to meet Japanese competition, and means of utilizing hemp and other Italian fibers as substitutes for imported raw materials.[41] Each corporation is to analyze the manufacturing costs of its

[40] *Ibid.*, November 10, 1934.
[41] For a detailed list of the questions presented to the corporations, cf. *ibid.*, November 11, 1934.

products, reduce them whenever possible by rationalization, and set a "fair price," which must assure a margin of profit for the employer and proper remuneration for the worker without overcharging the consumer, and at the same time permit Italian exports to compete successfully on world markets. It is expected that the proposals and suggestions made by the corporations, all composed of experts, will serve as the basis of legislation with respect to their particular categories of production. Critics of Fascism point out that the program of study presented to the corporations is limited to technical questions and contains no reference to the objectives of social justice proclaimed by Mussolini in October 1934—"secure work, a fair salary, a decent home."

While the establishment of the corporations marks the end of laissez-faire, which in Fascist opinion is inextricably associated with decadent capitalism and outworn democracy, the Fascist government denies that it implies the end of private initiative. Production, according to Mussolini, remains in the hands of self-governing groups of producers, both employers and workers.[42] Private initiative has been merely translated from the individual to the corporate plane. The state, as in the past, will intervene in economic activities only when the corporations have failed to harmonize conflicting economic interests, and will then act as the representative of the great unorganized mass of consumers—the collectivity of citizens. By its participation in the work of each corporation, however, the government will actually exercise a decisive influence on the regulation of prices, profits and wages. This stage in corporative development is regarded by Mussolini as experi-

[42] Speech of October 6, 1934, cited.

mental,[43] and he apparently anticipates further adjustments designed to assure a more equal distribution of wealth and closer participation by workers in the process of production.[44]

COLLECTIVE LABOR CONTRACTS

The effect which further developments in the corporative system may have on relations between capital and labor is not yet clear. At the present time these relations are regulated by collective labor contracts. The recognized syndicate alone has the right to conclude such contracts, which are applicable to all persons in the category it represents, whether members or not. These contracts are binding in all cases, except when the terms of a contract made by an individual with his employer are more favorable than those of a collective contract. The Charter of Labor provides that each collective contract must cover the subjects of labor discipline, period of probation, scale and payment of wages, hours of work, vacations, and conditions of dismissal. No minimum wage is established by the Charter, which declares that wages in all cases must be determined by collective contracts. The government undertakes to collect and publish statistical data on conditions of work and production, the situation of the financial market and variations in the standard of living of the workers, which may serve as a criterion for determination of wages.

Collective contracts must be made in writing, approved by the Ministry of Corporations and published; in the case of many contracts the entire text

[43] Speech of November 10, 1934, cited.
[44] Speech of October 6, 1934, cited.

has been drafted by the Ministry.[45] Workers and employers are legally responsible for fulfilment of the contracts, and may be punished by a fine in case of violation. It is estimated that 1,092 collective contracts of national and inter-provincial application and 9,164 provincial contracts have been concluded since 1927.[46] The largest number of contracts have been made in industry, which is more highly organized than other branches of production, notably agriculture.

Fascism, as has already been pointed out, repudiates the idea of the class struggle. Measures of class self-defense, such as strikes and lockouts, are strictly prohibited, and are subject to punishment by heavy fines. Should strikes and lockouts involve recourse to force, the participants may be condemned to imprisonment. Organizers of strikes and lockouts are in all cases subject to imprisonment for a period of from one to two years. Suspension of public services is regarded as a crime against the state.[47] So far as can be ascertained, no attempts have been made to organize large-scale strikes, although workers have occasionally suspended operations in protest against the failure of employers to apply collective labor contracts. The provincial courts have usually refused to regard such stoppages as strikes.[48] According to official Fascist information, only two lockouts

[45] "The Settlement of Labour Disputes in Italy," *The International Labour Review,* October 1934, p. 509.

[46] Ministry of Corporations, *News Notes on Fascist Corporations,* March 1934, p. 4.

[47] In addition to telephone, telegraph, railway, gas, water and other necessities of modern life, public services are made to include the work of physicians, lawyers, engineers, architects, land surveyors and agricultural experts. Decree of July 1, 1926, Article 98.

[48] L. Rosenstock-Franck, *L'Economie Corporative Fasciste en Doctrine et en Fait,* cited, p. 205-206.

and 153 strikes involving 7,750 workers occurred during the period 1926-1930, none of which had a political character.[49]

LABOR COURTS

Workers and employers are obliged to resort to the procedure of conciliation or to the courts for settlement of their conflicts. The Ministry of Corporations must in every case attempt to effect a reconciliation between the two groups. Only when this procedure has failed can the dispute be submitted to a special section of one of Italy's sixteen courts of appeals, acting as a labor court. This section is composed of three magistrates and two citizens acquainted with the technical aspects of labor and production.

The labor courts have jurisdiction over all collective, as distinguished from individual, conflicts between workers and employers. They are empowered to apply the rules of collective contracts and, in the absence of such contracts, to establish norms for the regulation of labor conditions. The Ministry of Corporations is always represented in the labor courts, and its opinion has a decisive influence on the verdicts. These verdicts are binding, and employers or workers who refuse to abide by them are subject to fine and imprisonment. Individual labor conflicts must be submitted to ordinary courts, assisted by two experts, one selected from the employers and one from the workers.[50]

During the period 1927-1933 the Ministry of Corporations examined 498 disputes involving collective

[49] Bruno Biagi, "La Disciplina del Lavoro in Regime Corporativo," *Corriere della Sera,* November 29, 1934.
[50] Decree of February 28, 1928 Regarding the Settlement of Individual Labor Conflicts.

labor contracts; 34 collective disputes were submitted to the labor courts; and 145,255 individual disputes came before the ordinary courts.[51] Of the disputes referred to the Ministry of Corporations two-thirds, or 347, concerned industry, 74 agriculture, 25 commerce, 21 land transportation, 18 banking, and 13 sea and air transportation. In 68 per cent of these disputes an agreement was reached at the ministry; 19 per cent was postponed for further consideration, of which many were subsequently resolved either by a settlement outside the ministry or by a voluntary agreement to abandon the dispute; and 13 per cent remained unsettled. The majority of the disputes involved the question of wages, especially wage and salary reductions effected during the depression. The settlement usually represented a compromise between the demands of workers and employers, and was drafted by the Ministry of Corporations, frequently after a detailed inquiry into the conditions of the industry concerned.

Of the 34 collective disputes brought before the labor courts, most of which are also concerned with wages and conditions of work, 14 had been decided by November 1933.[52] The decisions of the labor

[51] Ministry of Corporations, *News Notes on Fascist Corporations,* March 1934, p. 1; "The Settlement of Labour Disputes in Italy," cited, p. 509.

[52] The Rome Labor Court has rendered decisions in the following five cases: wages of rice weeders in the provinces of Pavia, Novara, Cremona and Vercelli (July 19, 1927); wages and other items in the remuneration of persons engaged in shipping and land transportation (February 18, 1928); wages of rice weeders in the provinces of Milan, Pavia, Vercelli, Alessandria and Crema (June 18, 1931); the method of cancelling contracts governed by collective agreements between deck officers and the Italia and Cosulich shipping companies (July 25, 1932); and the establishment of new conditions of employment for workers in the silk industry (June 5, 1933). Two decisions have been rendered by the Naples Labor Court; the establishment of new conditions of employment for manual workers and salaried employees of the Naples Aque-

courts have usually been more favorable to the workers than the proposals made by employers, but have nevertheless involved heavy sacrifices by the former. Thus, when the officials of the rice weeders' syndicate protested in 1931 against a 35 per cent reduction in wages proposed by agriculturists and suggested a 20 per cent cut, the Rome Labor Court fixed the wage reduction at 28 per cent. Like the Ministry of Corporations, the labor courts seek to effect a compromise on the basis of a study of cost and methods of production, cost of living, and other factors. In 1930 the Trieste Labor Court fixed the cost of living index number which was to serve as a basis for wage reduction. The Venice Labor Court decided in 1931 that the total remuneration for work performed in the course of a year "must not be less than the minimum needed for the normal requirements of life." It failed to specify this minimum, however, stating only that "it must represent the lowest limit below which wages cannot be allowed to fall." Critics of Fascism admit that the labor courts have on the whole been distinctly more favorable to workers than to employers, but argue

duct Company (November 30, 1931) and conditions of employment of workers in the food-preserving industry, as regards both material and moral conditions (May 31, 1932). The Milan Labor Court has taken one decision regarding three sets of collective regulations of wages for textile workers in the provinces of Como, Varese and Milan (July 21, 1933). The Turin Labor Court has fixed the wages of auxiliary workers in the rice fields of the province of Vercelli (April 27, 1933). The Bari Labor Court has passed on legal interpretation of collective labor contracts (August 13, 1930 and July 2, 1931). The Trieste Labor Court has fixed the cost of living index number which was to serve as a basis for wage reduction (February 15, 1930); the Catanzaro Labor Court has defined the legal character of trade associations and corporations (February 3, 1931); and the Venice Labor Court has ruled on total remuneration for work performed in the course of a year (December 24, 1931). "The Settlement of Labour Disputes in Italy," cited, p. 518-519.

that the judges are not in a position to ascertain the real cost of production or fix a "fair wage," and that their verdicts inevitably represent a compromise dictated by political, not economic, considerations.[53]

Of the 145,255 individual disputes submitted to labor magistrates, 29,144 were settled during the preliminary conciliation proceedings; 86,505 were settled by the courts; 9,449 are still pending; and 20,191 were either abandoned by the parties or settled by amicable agreement.[54] The delays in settling individual disputes have been criticized by Fascist labor leaders, who have demanded that the procedure be made more rapid and flexible and less expensive.[55] The procedure was reformed on May 21, 1934 by a decree which laid down definitive rules for the settlement of individual labor disputes.[56]

Criticism of Fascist Labor Policy

The two main criticisms directed against the syndical and corporative organization of Fascism are, first, that the free association of workers for the defense of their legitimate interests has been replaced by a highly bureaucratized system subject to the control of the state which is ruled by a single political party; and, second, that workers' syndicates have been used by the government and the employers chiefly to impose wage cuts on the workers. Anti-Fascists assert that the practical exclusion of all but legally recognized syndicates from participation in

[53] Rosenstock-Franck, *L'Economie Corporative Fasciste en Doctrine et en Fait,* cited, p. 181, 202.

[54] "The Settlement of Labour Disputes in Italy," cited, p. 520.

[55] *Lavoro Fascista,* December 8, 1932.

[56] For a summary of this decree, cf. *News Notes on Fascist Corporations,* October 1934, cited, p. 4.

the economic life of the country forces the workers to join these syndicates, irrespective of their views regarding Fascism. Collective labor contracts, they argue, tend to perpetuate, rather than improve, existing conditions of work, and to reduce the status of all workers, whatever their ability, to the same economic level. Critics of Fascism claim, moreover, that the labor courts in no sense achieve the practical results formerly attained by means of labor agitation and strikes, since their verdicts are dictated by Fascist interests, which do not necessarily coincide with those of the workers. Finally, it is claimed that the Fascist syndical organization, highly centralized and subject to close supervision by government organs, prevents the development of leadership and initiative on the part of the workers, and thus places them at a disadvantage in the class struggle which may eventually take place.[57]

To this the Fascists reply that no organizations, economic or political, can exist outside the state, and that only syndicates and corporations committed to Fascist ideals should be permitted to participate in the regulation of production. Fascism prides itself on having transformed the syndical association, "critical and polemical in character," into a public institution devoted to national ends.[58] The interests of workers and employers, according to Fascism, must never threaten the economic equilibrium of the state, and syndical organization is justified on the ground that it maintains a balance between the two groups. Fascism does not deny the existence

[57] Cf. Haider, *Capital and Labor under Fascism,* cited; Rosenstock-Franck, *L'Economie Corporative Fasciste en Doctrine et en Fait,* cited.

[58] *L'Organisation Syndicale et Corporative Italienne,* cited, p. 159.

of conflicts between workers and employers. It believes, however, that such conflicts may cause in-
calculable injury to the state, and must in all cases
be settled by resort not to violence but to conciliation and judicial procedure. The class struggle, according to Mussolini, is a luxury which a poor
country like Italy cannot afford. He believes that
only a long period of social peace will enable Italy
to overcome its inferiority in natural resources and
assume in world affairs the place to which it is entitled by its glorious past.[59] If Italy can recapture
the rôle of world leadership by peaceful means, the
Italian people will be ready "to adorn the barrels of
their guns with olive branches."[60] If not, then the
corporative system will prepare the entire nation for
waging a successful war by coordinating and dis-
ciplining its economic forces in time of peace.[61]

CONCLUSION

It may be seen from the foregoing analysis that
Fascism has preserved the forms and methods of
capitalist production and distribution, but has subjected them to the control of an all-powerful political dictatorship personified by Mussolini, who believes that only strict economic discipline can equip
Italy for the tasks of both peace and war. *Il Duce*
has indicated that state capitalism is his ultimate
goal, but has not revealed how this goal is to be
achieved without sacrificing private initiative, which
Fascism has hitherto considered the mainspring of
economic activity. Both employers and workers have

[59] Speech of December 20, 1923. *La Nuova Politica dell' Italia*
(Milan, Imperia, 1924), Vol. II, p. 136.
[60] Mussolini, speech of October 6, 1934, cited.
[61] "Nazione Guerriera e Stato Corporativo," *Corriere della Sera*,
December 14, 1934.

been regimented in syndical organizations whose leaders are designated by the Fascist party, and have been prohibited from staging strikes or lockouts in defense of their interests, which are subordinated to those of the nation as defined by the Fascist party. Neither group may be said to enjoy economic self-government. The employers, however, have in practice exercised greater influence than the workers, both on their own organizations and on the country's economic life. The two groups have been linked by twenty-two corporations, which Fascists regard as a revolutionary step on the road from capitalism to a new corporative order. These corporations have not yet been entrusted with authority over economic and social matters, which are directly controlled by the political organs of the government, and have been given only technical functions similar to those exercised by economic councils in non-Fascist countries.

American critics of both right and left have compared the New Deal with the Italian corporative system, arguing that the Roosevelt administration, like Mussolini, has sought to group industries along corporative lines and has undertaken to control or regulate industry, agriculture, credit and other branches of economic activity. Supporters of the New Deal admit that its economic framework bears a certain outward resemblance to Fascism. They declare, however, that unlike Fascism, it does not seek to set up a political dictatorship but, on the contrary, attempts to introduce economic democracy, which political democracy of the pre-Roosevelt era had failed to achieve. In support of this thesis it may be pointed out that, in contrast to Fascism, the Roosevelt administration, while assuming extraordinary emergency powers, has not deprived repre-

sentative assemblies of their authority; has not in-
terfered with the freedom of the press; has not
abolished labor organizations; and has not prohibited strikes and lockouts, although it has sought
to prevent them by urging capital and labor to resort
to arbitration and conciliation.

One of the best-informed and bitterest critics of
Fascism has commented as follows on relations between labor and capital in Italy: "For the time
being one may gladly admit that Fascism has solved
the problem of the relations between capital and
labor by suppressing the laissez-faire of labor. To
forbid strikes, to outlaw autonomous unions and
create nation-wide 'company unions'—this is such
a brilliant solution of the problem, that one wonders
why it is not adopted in every country. It has the
powerful logic of that commandment which, according to Anatole France, would forbid both rich and
poor to steal bread or to sleep in the open air. But
is this really a solution? Italian big business men
would of course answer in the affirmative. He who
would think with his own brain, and not with that of
the big business men, has more than one reason for
affirming that the Fascist experiment indicates how
the problem must *not* be solved, not only out of an
elementary respect for human dignity, but because
it is no solution at all."[59]

CHAPTER V

OPPOSITION TO FASCISM

THE opponents of Fascism in Italy—Liberals,
Democratic Catholics, Socialists, Communists, Free-

[59] Gaetano Salvemini, *Under the Axe of Fascism* (New York,
Viking Press, 1936), p. 392.

masons—have been effectively silenced by their
exclusion from Parliament and by the restrictions
imposed on the right of association and the freedom
of the press. Any attempt to reconstitute the old
political parties or create new ones is subject to
severe punishment. "No tolerance, no indulgence,"
said Arpinati, Under-Secretary of the Interior on
March 3, 1931, "will be conceded to those who, after
nine years of the régime and after the titanic work
accomplished by *Il Duce*, insist on regarding the
Fascist revolution as a transitional episode." [1]

The Fascist press, which is uniformly laudatory,
gives the impression that the entire population en-
dorses the Fascist program without reservations or
qualifications. Nevertheless, from time to time, official *communiqués* reveal the existence of some anti-
Fascist plot, and indicate that the culprits will be
tried by the Special Tribunal for the Defense of
the State. The most spectacular of these plots, un-
covered by the secret police (O.V.R.A.), concerned
the National Alliance (*Alleanza Nazionale*). The
latter had been founded in June 1930 by a young
writer, Lauro De Bosis, formerly associated with the
Casa Italiana in New York; its leading members
were his mother, Signora De Bosis, an American by
birth, and two prominent journalists, Mario Vinciguerra and Renzo Rendi. This group circulated a
bulletin, for the most part written by Lauro De
Bosis, who resided abroad. These bulletins were
mimeographed by Signora De Bosis, and mailed to a
list of persons, each of whom was requested to type
six copies, and send them to six persons, always the
same, at least two of whom were to be Fascists. The
articles published in this bulletin invited patriotic

[1] *Il Giornale d'Italia,* March 4, 1931.

Italians to unite against Fascism under the leadership of the monarchy and the Church, and thus prevent monopolization of anti-Fascist opposition by the Communists. "Today," said the bulletin of July 15, 1930, "the National Alliance includes men of all non-subversive parties and can have only one enemy, Fascism." [2]

At the trial of the *Alleanza Nazionale* on December 22, 1930, the prosecutor accused its members of having represented the Church and the monarchy as antagonistic to the régime. Vinciguerra admitted that the bulletins were critical of Fascism, but denied that they advocated recourse to violence. The president of the tribunal interrupted him at this point and described the articles in the bulletins as "lies." Signora De Bosis, who had written Mussolini a letter from prison expressing penitence for her action and admiration for the Fascist government, was pardoned, while Vinciguerra and Rendi were condemned to fifteen years' imprisonment.[3]

ANTI-FASCIST TENDENCIES IN ITALY

It is the opinion of competent observers that there is little prospect at the present time of a violent overthrow of the Fascist government. Dissatisfaction with the government is found chiefly among industrialists and professional men. The industrialists, forced to maintain a prescribed scale of wages in the face of economic depression, accuse Fascism of undue leniency towards the workers. In general,

[2] *Alleanza Nazionale* (Paris, Imprimerie Vendôme, 1931). Nine bulletins were published by the *Alleanza Nazionale* between June 1 and November 1, 1930, when its members were arrested by the police.

[3] For an account of the trial, *cf. Corriere della Sera,* December 23, 1930.

however, the propertied classes, which welcomed
Fascism in 1922 in the hope that it would restore
public order, fear that the only alternative today
would be a return to revolutionary Socialism. Intellectuals and professional men oppose restrictions
on the liberty of association and of the press, and
complain of Italy's intellectual stagnation under
Fascism. Here again, however, there seem to be
no signs of concerted action. The workers, on the
whole, appear to have benefited by recent social
reforms, and with the exception of the Communists
have not openly attacked Fascism. Finally, the opposition of the Church, which might have proved a
serious obstacle, was in large part removed by the
conclusion of the Lateran accord in 1929. Nevertheless, the Pope has occasionally criticized Fascism
for the liberty accorded to Protestant sects, and the
Osservatore Romano, now published on Vatican territory, is the only Italian newspaper which takes
issue with the government.

MUSSOLINI'S PERSONAL INFLUENCE

The absence of any widespread active opposition
may be attributed, in part, to the political indifference of the population. In larger measure, however,
it appears to be due to the admiration with which
Mussolini is regarded in many circles otherwise opposed to Fascism. The fact that Mussolini enjoys so
great a degree of personal prestige has caused considerable speculation concerning the effects which
may be produced by his disappearance. The Fascist
party has been frequently divided on major questions of policy, the older, conservative elements advocating closer coöperation with capitalism, and the
former Socialists demanding radical reforms for the

benefit of the workers. Until now Mussolini has succeeded in preserving the unity of the party, with the result that the inner cleavage has not been reflected in the government's policy. It is as yet too early to say whether, in the absence of Mussolini, Fascism could be maintained indefinitely in its present form.

ANTI-FASCIST ACTIVITIES ABROAD

The anti-Fascist irreconcilables have for the most part transferred their activities abroad, and have established their headquarters in Brussels and Paris. The émigrés are divided into three main schools of political thought—Communists, Democratic Republicans and Democratic Monarchists. The Communists, rather numerous among the workers, have a widespread press which, according to their opponents among the émigrés, is subsidized by the Soviet government and by Italian *agents provocateurs*. The majority of the bourgeois émigrés are Democratic Republicans, but are further split into Right and Left Wing Socialists and Republicans. The Right Wing Socialists and Republicans form the so-called Anti-Fascist Concentration (*Concentrazione Antifascista*), which publishes a newspaper *Libertà* and, until 1932, issued a bulletin, *Italia*, both in Paris. In addition, the Concentration published a satirical paper, *Becco Giallo* (Yellow Beak), printed on very thin paper and smuggled every fortnight into Italy at the rate of some 7,500 copies. The Concentration has had among its leaders Professor Gaetano Salvemini and the late Filipo Turati, editor of *Italia*. Finally, the Democratic Monarchists, including Count Carlo Sforza, former Minister of Foreign Affairs, and ex-Premier Nitti, favor retention of the House of Savoy; in all other respects, they appear to agree, and actually collaborate, with the Democratic Republicans. The Fascist government professes nothing but contempt for the émigrés. On March 3, 1931, Arpinati, Under-Secretary of the Interior, described them as "people who make politics their profession, and who live on anti-Fascism as they once lived on subversive doctrines, people who have lost all notion of time and all sense of reality." [4]

SUMMARY

The émigrés charge the Fascists with the suppression of parliamentary government at a time when the latter not only had shown no signs of decadence, but was susceptible of further successful development. The Fascist government, they claim, has completely destroyed the spirit of the Italian constitution, while preserving a semblance of legality. The restrictions placed by Fascism on individual liberty, they argue, may have had some justification during a transitional period of political readjustment; subsequently, however, the government should have returned to normalcy—that is, apparently, restored the conditions which it set out to remove. The émigrés admit that such "normalization" would involve the disappearance of Fascism, but believe that this eventuality would redound to the benefit of the country. The anti-Fascists contend that at the present time the country's economic development is hampered by the control exercised by the state over production. They believe that, if order has been restored, it has only been at the expense of individual liberty, and that the govern-

[4] *Il Giornale d'Italia,* March 4, 1931.

ment has signally failed to solve the country's economic problems. Finally, they assert that the government has pursued an aggressive foreign policy which has injured Italy's prestige and credit abroad.

The Fascists, for their part, claim that parliamentary government was not an indigenous product, had never taken root in Italy, and had become completely impotent during the post-war years. They believe that a highly centralized government is alone capable of regulating the economic life of a country like Italy, poor in natural resources, and of insuring a just distribution of material goods among a rapidly growing population. The Fascists do not deny the suppression of individual liberty, but contend that they have introduced higher ethical values into Italian life by imposing on all groups of the population a discipline dictated by national, as contrasted with personal, interests. They assert that, as a result of this discipline, the Italian people have applied themselves with a new energy to the task of production, and that Italy's prestige among nations has thereby been restored and enhanced.

THE THIRD REICH

CHAPTER I

THE RISE OF GERMAN NATIONALISM

THE Hitler Third Reich is now an accomplished fact. Both democratic forms and terroristic methods have been used to destroy the Weimar Republic and set up a Nazi dictatorship. The National Socialist German Workers' party rules supreme in Germany. Hitler and his lieutenants have dissolved or "co-ordinated" all other political parties; Germany has been completely unified; all opposition has been ruthlessly suppressed; and the ground has thus been cleared for the practical application of Nazi principles.

At the Reichstag election on March 5, 1933, more than 17 million Germans—comprising 44 per cent of the electorate—cast their votes for the National Socialist party, thus giving expression to an unparalleled unanimity of opinion in a country noted for particularist sentiment. These 17 million voters were drawn primarily from three sources: the youth of Germany who have come of age since the war, former supporters of the numerous conservative small bourgeois parties, and previous non-voters who were roused from political lethargy by economic disaster and National Socialist propaganda.

Despite the thoroughness and effectiveness of Nazi agitation, the success of the movement can only be explained by the psychological, physical and material suffering which the German people have undergone during the past two decades. The ideology and philosophy of the movement, however, have their roots far in the past. It is not only a mass protest against the hardships endured during and since the war, it is also a form of self-vindication for a people which, although trained and educated in a militarized state, were defeated in a great war. It is at the same time a national attempt to escape from the harsh realities of the present by resurrecting many of the attributes of the past which to a suffering people seems glorious in retrospect, and by introducing an undefined "socialism" which shall solve present-day economic and social problems.

In considering the present resurgence of German nationalism, it must be remembered that the Germans were the last great people to achieve national unity, and that the centuries-long history of the small kingdoms and principalities which made up the so-called "Germanies" was the record not of a united people but of Prussians, Saxons, Bavarians, and others. Even after Bismarck had founded the Empire in 1871, local patriotism was still predominant. The self-conscious nationalism which marked imperial Germany in the decades before the World War must be regarded as the manifestation of a people politically united but not sufficiently unified to take its national patriotism for granted.

The "Mission" of the German People

The movement for German political unity which finally bore fruit in 1871, had been profoundly influenced by German intellectuals—historians, philosophers and writers. The poetry of the Romanticists and the theories of the state expounded by Kant and Hegel had had a large share in developing that spirit of patriotic nationalism which finally won the battle of Leipzig in 1813 and liberated Prussia. Furthermore, the philosopher Fichte, in his *Reden an die deutsche Nation,* had set forth an exalted conception of the character and mission of the Germans, and put forward the idea of a geographically isolated and economically self-sufficient community as the ideal nation. Hegel particularly had glorified the state, declaring that "the State is God on Earth!" [1] He pictured mankind as progressing through the ages, steadily but unconsciously, toward the Germanic perfection of the nineteenth century. The German historians, meanwhile, developed the doctrine of the great "mission" of the German people and became leaders of nationalist thought. Histories lauding the Hohenzollerns, the glories of the German medieval period, German prowess in the crusades, and the deeds of the Teutonic knights contributed to nationalist fervor and did much to convince the Germans that Prussia and the Hohenzollerns were charged with a special "mission." The founding of the University of Berlin gave impetus to the development of glorious national history—past, present and future—supported by the Hegelian theory of the state. Most Prussian historians [2] shared Hegel's belief that civilization is spread only by war, and that the triumph of civiliza-

[1] Hegel, *Grundlinien der Philosophie des Rechts,* Vols. VIII–IX, sec. 258, p. 313.

[2] Duncker, Droysen, Leopold von Ranke, von Treitschke, von Sybel and Mommsen were the leading historians of this persuasion.

tion demanded the suppression of races less capable of or less advanced in culture by nations of a higher order. War and the doctrine of force thus became the embodiment of progress to many Germans.[3]

In addition to this glorification of the state and of force, a new "science" of race aided German nationalists in explaining the superiority of the German race over all others. The publication in 1854, of a work by a Frenchman, Count Joseph Arthur de Gobineau, entitled *Essai sur l'inégalité des races humaines,* did much to strengthen the cause of nationalism in Germany. The theories of Gobineau, moreover, furnish the "scientific" background for the anti-Semitism which forms a part of the intense Nazi nationalism. According to Gobineau, racial questions overshadow all other problems of history and hold the key to them. The inequality of races from whose fusion a people is formed explains the whole course of human destiny, Gobineau argued; and, further asserting the inherent superiority of the "Aryan" race, he held that racial degeneration was the inevitable result of the mixture of Aryans with inferior races.[4] This mystical glorification of Aryanism decisively influenced the growth of race vanity in Germany and the increasingly evident spirit of imperialism manifested after 1890.[5] Gobineau paved the way for the work of an Englishman,

[3] Mildred S. Wertheimer, *The Pan-German League, 1890–1914* (New York, Longmans Green, 1924), p. 13 *et seq.*

[4] Gobineau, *Essai sur l'inégalité des races humaines* (Paris, 1884, 2 vols., translated by Adrian Collins, New York, 1915, p. xiv, 33); *cf.* also Wertheimer, *The Pan-German League, 1890–1914,* cited; Frank H. Hankins, *The Racial Basis of Civilization, A Critique of the Nordic Doctrine* (New York, Knopf, 1931), p. 33 *et seq.*

[5] Hankins, *The Racial Basis of Civilization,* cited, p. 51.

Houston Stewart Chamberlain, whose *Grundlagen des neunzehnten Jahrhunderts* appeared in 1899. Chamberlain's main thesis was the assertion of the superiority of the Teuton family over all the other races of the world. "The awakening of the Teutonic peoples," he wrote, "to the consciousness of their all-important vocation and culture forms the turning point [in the history of Europe]." [6] Chamberlain's book was widely read and discussed in Germany; it became a best-seller and was popular with the Kaiser, who is said to have financed the distribution of thousands of copies.

It is impossible to estimate the extent to which such works as those of Gobineau and Chamberlain actually influenced historical events, but they were doubtless of considerable importance in nourishing German national egotism. [7] Mystical, abstract principles have always appealed to the German mind and have played a considerable rôle in German political life, as evidenced by the fact that all German parties in their official platforms outlined the broad philosophical bases of party dogma rather than policies on specific questions. Whether or not these theories had great influence on the German people before 1914, they established a most convenient foundation for Allied propaganda during the war

[6] H. S. Chamberlain, *The Foundations of the Nineteenth Century* (English translation by John Lees, London and New York, J. Lane, 1911), p. xv.

[7] Professor John Dewey has made the pertinent statement that "the philosopher sees movements, which might have passed away with change of circumstance as casually as they arose, acquire persistence and dignity because thought has taken cognizance of them and given them intellectual names. The witness of history is that to think in general and abstract terms is dangerous; it elevates ideas beyond situations in which they were born and charges them with we know not what menace for the future." (John Dewey, *German Philosophy and Politics*, New York, Holt, 1915, p. 12.)

and provided moral justification for the Versailles Treaty, particularly the "war guilt" article.

EVOLUTION OF THE NATIONAL SOCIALIST PARTY

It will be recalled, that the first post-war years in Germany were marked by the blackest disillusionment and discouragement. The Allied blockade, which was not lifted until after the signature of the peace treaty, increased the suffering of a people already starving and in the grip of revolution. The former German rulers had abdicated and the Kaiser had fled to Holland; the untried Social Democratic leaders, who had taken over the government, were faced with the necessity not only of saving the country from Bolshevism, but of setting up a new democratic state. Added to this was the dislocation entailed by the demobilization of the German army. It was only with the aid of former officers of the imperial army that this demobilization was carried through and the Left revolution was crushed, while officials of the old régime stuck to their posts and carried on the administration of the country. As a result, the Republic incurred a large debt to these officials and officers, despite the fact that many of them paid only lip-service to the new régime and, as time went on, became openly antagonistic.[8] The seeds of counter-revolution were thus being planted even before the legal establishment of the Republic at Weimar on August 11, 1919. The new Republic also received a staggering blow in the Versailles Treaty. The German people, expecting a peace settlement based on Wilson's Fourteen Points, were

[8] Walter Gerhart, *Um des Reiches Zukunft* (Freiburg i/Br., Herder, 1932), p. 46 *et seq.*; Edgar Ansell Mowrer, *Germany Puts the Clock Back* (New York, Morrow, 1933), p. 17 *et seq.*

thunderstruck by the terms of a treaty which imposed huge reparation demands, losses of German
territory, occupation of the Rhineland and unilateral
disarmament of the Reich. The moral condemnation expressed in Article 231 of the treaty, which
was interpreted as placing the entire responsibility
for the war on Germany and its allies, the Reich's
loss of its colonies on the ground of German maladministration, and the demand that the so-called
war criminals be turned over to the Allies for trial
all seemed incomprehensible to the German people
who had believed Wilson's pronouncements. As a
result, the Weimar Republic was inextricably associated in popular opinion with the humiliation and
disappointment engendered by the Versailles Treaty.
The "stab-in-the-back legend" [9] so carefully nurtured by the Nazis—according to which the Weimar
coalition of Social Democrats, Catholic Centrists
and Democrats which founded the Republic was
held responsible for the German defeat—was thus
strengthened.

During the years 1919–1923, while the struggling
young Republic was endeavoring to consolidate its
position and pull the Reich out of the chaos caused
by war and revolution, its major task lay in the field
of foreign affairs, and was concerned primarily with
the reparation problem. This was the period of Allied ultimata, rejection of German counter-proposals,
Allied sanctions in the form of occupation of more
German cities, increasingly strict customs control
and recurring abortive reparation conferences.
Meanwhile the German mark sank deeper in the
mire of inflation. In January 1923, the French and
Belgians occupied the Ruhr, Germany countered
with measures of passive resistance, and by autumn

[9] *Dolchstoss Legende.*

of that year the value of the mark had sunk to zero
and the life savings of the German lower middle
class were wiped out. Furthermore, the Rhineland
separatist movement—supported by the French [10]—
seemed for a time to threaten the very unity of
the Reich.

Under these circumstances it was all too easy to
win support for an extreme nationalist movement
of protest. This was particularly true in Bavaria
which, after the murder of Kurt Eisner in Munich
in February 1919 and the relatively short-lived
Soviet interregnum which followed, had become the
headquarters of German monarchist and militarist
reaction. The brief Bavarian revolutionary episode
had burned itself into the memory of the bourgeoisie; anti-Semitism has been strong in Bavaria
ever since, for the conservatives blame all their
troubles on the fact that Eisner and other revolutionaries were Jews. During the first post-war years,
moreover, Germany was a veritable camp of so-
called volunteer corps (*Freikorps*), composed of unemployed former officers and soldiers,[11] many of
which had their headquarters in Bavaria. These
groups were extra-legal, and although ostensibly organized only for defense purposes, were most reactionary in character. Their influence may be
traced through the Kapp *Putsch* in 1920, the murders of Erzberger and Rathenau, as well as the
many other political murders which marked the
early years of the Republic.[12]

It was in such troublous times that the National

[10] G. E. R. Gedye, *The Revolver Republic* (London, Arrow-
smith, 1930), *passim*.
[11] The Ehrhardt Brigade, the Baltic Defense Corps, the Bavarian *Einwohnerwehr*, the Black *Reichswehr*, etc.
[12] Mildred S. Wertheimer, "The Hitler Movement in Germany," Foreign Policy Association, *Information Service*, January 21, 1931.

Socialist party had its obscure birth. The party grew out of a group of six men who met during 1919, in a small back room of a Munich café. Adolf Hitler joined the group as its seventh member and almost immediately became its leading personality. In the autumn of 1919, these men founded the National Socialist German Workers' party in Munich. Among the earliest members were some of the leaders of the volunteer corps, notably General von Epp and Captain Röhm. The latter, who had close connections with the Reichswehr, brought into the party many of his friends, both officers and men, with the result that up to 1923, these army men were apparently the backbone of the movement.[13] Röhm is also reported to have been an important liaison officer between the volunteer corps and the militarist clubs and groups (*Wehrverbände*), which apparently furnished many recruits for the Reichswehr as well as for the Nazis. Meanwhile, Hitler by tireless speechmaking gained further supporters, and by the end of 1920, his party had 3,000 members; by November 1923, there were 5,000 paying members of the National Socialist party.[14]

Hitler's Beer-Hall Putsch

Hitler and his party first came into the limelight in 1923. By that time Hitler had attracted the attention of General Ludendorff and the latter's

[13] Konrad Heiden, *Geschichte des Nationalsozialismus* (Berlin, Rowohlt, 1932), p. 12 *et seq.*

[14] *Ibid.*, pp. 44, 143. A comprehensive description of the *Freikorps* movement in Bavaria is contained in Ernst Röhm, *Die Geschichte eines Hochverräters* (Munich, Eher Verlag, 1933). The late Captain Röhm, former Chief of Staff of the Nazi Storm Troops and Minister without Portfolio in the Reich government, was an important figure in the *Freikorps* movement. According to his own account, he acted as liaison between these illegal *Freikorps* and the German *Reichswehr* in which he was an officer.

nationalist followers. The crisis caused by the occupation of the Ruhr and the attendant growth of ultra-nationalist sentiment in Germany seemed to offer the psychological moment for Hitler's *Putsch*. On November 9, 1923, the combined forces of Hitler and Ludendorff attempted a coup d'état in Munich under Hitler's leadership, but it missed fire entirely. The attempt has gone down in history as the Beer-Hall *Putsch*.

As a result of this attempted coup, Hitler was arrested and on April 1, 1924, was sentenced to five years' imprisonment for treason. During his imprisonment, his followers had, against his will, joined forces with another extremist group—the German People's Freedom party (*Deutsch-Völkische Freiheitspartei*)—which managed to elect 32 members of the Reichstag at the general election on May 4, 1924. Hitler was released at the end of 1924 and at once renewed his political activity. In February 1925, he reorganized the National Socialist party, and assumed leadership over both this party and the German People's Freedom party.

After the stabilization of the mark, Germany enjoyed a period of comparative recovery and prosperity from 1924 to 1928, although even then there was considerable unemployment.[15] It was during this period that the great influx of foreign loans to Germany took place. Furthermore, this was the era of improved international relations, the Dawes Plan, Locarno, of Germany's entrance into the League of

[15] In January 1924 there were 1,900,000 unemployed in Germany; in January 1926, 2,221,000 were out of work. Even in the boom year 1928, there were 1,862,000 unemployed in January. (Institut für Konjunkturforschung, *Kurven und Zahlen in Deutschland*, Berlin, Reimer Hobbing, 1932, p. 8; also Mildred S. Wertheimer, "The Financial Crisis in Germany," *Foreign Policy Reports*, March 2, 1932.)

Nations, and the partial evacuation of the Rhine-land. The domestic political situation was reflected in the results of the 1928 Reichstag election, when the moderate Social Democratic party made large gains, the middle bourgeois groups held their own fairly well, and the Communists showed only a small though steady growth. The Nationalists, however, lost 30 seats and the Nazis, who in the December 1924 election had dropped from 32 to 14, elected only 12 deputies in 1928.[16]

These four years of comparatively prosperous times proved to be merely a lull before the storm. German economic improvement, which was part of prevailing world prosperity had, however, been made possible largely by the great amounts of foreign capital, much of it borrowed at short-term, which had not only helped create an illusion of prosperity, but made it possible for the Reich to meet and transfer its reparation obligations. Nevertheless, Germany's reparation creditors, meeting in Paris early in 1929, drafted the Young Plan which replaced the Dawes Plan of 1924. The new arrange-ment was predicated on the continuation and expansion of world prosperity, which alone could assure the Reich a favorable trade balance sufficient to meet its obligations under the Young Plan. The world depression, which began even before the Young Plan had gone into effect, nullified the financial advantages which the Reich expected to derive from the plan, and eventually caused its demise for all practical purposes. German accept-ance of the Young Plan, however, had freed the Rhineland from foreign occupation five years before the date stipulated in the Versailles Treaty. But

[16] *Statistisches Jahrbuch für das deutsche Reich, 1931,* p. 545.

when the evacuation of the Rhineland took place in June 1930, Germany was already in the grip of the depression. As a result, the salutary effects expected from the Rhineland liberation were not realized. On the contrary, the Hitler movement, of which little had been heard during the preceding years of relative prosperity, suddenly came once more into the limelight.

Hitler had coöperated with the Nationalist leader, Hugenberg, in the plebiscite on the Young Plan which was held late in 1929. On November 25, at the first poll, 4,135,300 votes were cast by Nazis and Nationalists, or only .02 per cent more than the 10 per cent of qualified voters necessary to force the Reichstag to introduce a bill against the Young Plan. The Reichstag rejected this bill on November 29 by an overwhelming majority and, when the actual plebiscite took place on December 22, only 5,825,082 votes, or less than one-third of the number necessary to prevent acceptance of the Young Plan, were cast by the combined forces of Hitler and Hugenberg.[17]

Economic Depression Fosters National Socialism

The fact that the Nazis and Nationalists together polled less than six million votes at the end of 1929, makes the success of Hitler at the Reichstag election on September 14, 1930, the more striking. Less than a year after the Young Plan plebiscite, the Nazis alone rolled up 6,401,210 votes and elected 107 members of the Reichstag. The Hugenberg Na-

---

[17] *Cf.* Cuno Horkenbach, *Das deutsche Reich von 1918 bis Heute* (Berlin, Verlag für Presse, Wirtschaft und Politik, 1930), p. 292 *et seq.* The popular vote polled by the Hugenberg Nationalists in May 1928, the last election before the plebiscite, was 4,380,200. The Nazis had polled only 809,000 at that election.

tionalists received only 2,458,497 votes, or slightly more than half of their 1928 following. The Nazi landslide had begun.

There were three principal causes for the tremendous Nazi increase. In the first place, the deepening depression had already thrown three million people out of work by September 1930.[18] Second, the inner political difficulties in the Reich created an increasing distrust and antipathy for the Republic and parliamentary government. The Reichstag, with its multiplicity of parties, seemed incapable of coping with the complex economic and financial problems confronting the country,[19] while the situation of the German people grew progressively worse. Both of these factors contributed to the third cause of Nazi growth—the success of the untiring agitation of the Hitlerites themselves. Between the autumn of 1929 and September 1930, the National Socialists staged meeting after meeting; [20] during the fortnight before the September elections, the *Völkische Beobachter*, official organ of the party, listed some 3,300 meetings; [21] many of these were held in small out-of-the-way villages, where few if any political gatherings had been held before. Hitler's stalwarts, clad in their brown uniforms, toured the countryside in trucks, unceasingly addressing the peasants and farm workers. In many small villages these meetings, well advertised beforehand, were much like a traveling circus to the inhabitants. The stage

[18] *Statistisches Jahrbuch für das deutsche Reich, 1931*, Graph VII.
[19] Mildred S. Wertheimer, "The Significance of the German Elections," *Foreign Policy Association Information Service*, September 3, 1930.
[20] Heiden, *Geschichte des Nationalsozialismus*, cited, p. 277 et seq.
[21] *Völkische Beobachter*, September 1–13, 1930, inclusive.

management of all Nazi gatherings was dramatic in the extreme. Flags, bands, the marching of uniformed men appealed to a people which reacted *en masse* to the spectacular, especially in a Republic singularly devoid of colorful ceremonies which had succeeded an Empire with all its pomp and circumstance of kings, princes, courts and army.

CHAPTER II

THE NATIONAL SOCIALIST PROGRAM

THE Nazi agitation, from first to last, was based on denunciation of the Versailles "dictate," the Republic, its leaders, the Jews, the "Marxists," and the so-called "System." It followed Hitler's theories, expressed in his autobiography, that in propaganda the end justifies the means, and that all agitation should be directed solely to influence the masses. "Propaganda is not science," wrote Hitler, and while attempting to prove certain facts to the masses, "the appeal must be directed to the emotions and only in a very qualified manner to so-called intelligence." [1] The program of the party was sufficiently vague to allow Hitlerite orators to promise help to everyone, adjusting their remarks to suit their audiences. The Third Reich, which the Nazis told their followers would replace the hated Republic, appeared to many harassed Germans like the promised land, and Hitler himself became the Messiah of this new order.

[1] Adolf Hitler, *Mein Kampf* (Munich, Eher Verlag, 1930), p. 195 *et seq.* This was first published in 1924. At present German libraries are compelled to have several copies of this book on their shelves.

Negative propaganda was the cornerstone of all Nazi agitation. It denounced the Republic, its "liberalistic" governments and its "pusillanimous foreign policy." On the more positive side stood the vague and contradictory official program of the party which contains twenty-five points. It was written by Gottfried Feder[2] in February 1920, and is prefaced by the following statement: "The program of the party is a program dedicated to the present (*Zeit-programm*)." After the aims set forth in the present program have been achieved, "the leaders decline to set themselves new goals which can only serve to make possible the continuation of the party by means of artificially heightened dissatisfaction among the masses." The official commentary published in the 1932 edition of the program contained the following further statement:

"We refuse to act as other parties do and, for reasons of opportunism, adapt our program to meet so-called conditions. We will on the contrary adapt conditions to square with our program in that we will master these conditions."[3]

THE TWENTY-FIVE POINTS

The Twenty-five Points, which were thus declared unalterable, are as follows:

I. We demand the union of all Germans by the right of self-determination of peoples, in one great Germany.

[2] Herr Feder was appointed Under-Secretary in the Reich Ministry of Economics on June 29, 1932. *New York Times,* June 30, 1933.

[3] This statement and the Twenty-five Points, as well as the following analysis of the program, are taken from the party's official program: Gottfried Feder, *Das Programm der N.S.D.A.P. und seine Weltanschaulichen Grundgedanken* (Munich, Verlag Frz. Eher Nachf. G.m.b.H., 1932).

II. We demand the equality of the German people with all other nations and the abrogation of the treaties of Versailles and St. Germain.

III. We demand land and territory (colonies) sufficient for the feeding of our people and for settlement by our surplus population.

IV. Only a member of our own people (*Volksgenosse*) may be a citizen (*Staatsbürger*). Our own people are *only* those of German blood without reference to confession. Therefore, no Jew may be a member of our people.

V. He who is not a citizen may live in Germany only as a guest and must be governed by laws regulating foreigners.

VI. Only citizens may decide on the leadership and laws of the State. Therefore, we demand that every public office, no matter of what sort, whether in the Reich, the States or the Communes, shall be filled only by citizens.

We fight against the corrupting parliamentary system which fills positions with people chosen only for their party politics without reference to character or ability.

VII. We demand that the State be obliged to provide working and living possibilities for its citizens. If it is not possible to feed the entire population of the State, all members of foreign nations (non-citizens) must be expelled from the Reich at once.

VIII. All further immigration of non-Germans must be stopped. We demand that all non-Germans who have immigrated to Germany since August 2, 1914, shall be ousted from the Reich.

IX. All citizens must have the same rights and duties.

X. It must be the primary duty of every citizen to engage in productive work, whether in physical or intellectual fields. The activities of individuals must not be such as to conflict with the general interest but, on the contrary, must be for the common good.

THEREFORE WE DEMAND:

XI. Abolition of all income acquired without work or trouble; DESTRUCTION OF THE SLAVERY TO INTEREST (ZINSKNECHTSCHAFT).

XII. Because of the tremendous sacrifice in goods and blood which every war demands of the people, personal enrichment through war must be branded as a crime against the people. We demand, therefore, complete confiscation of all war profits.

XIII. We demand the nationalization of all trusts.

XIV. We demand distribution of the profits of large industries.

XV. We demand an increase on a large scale in care for the aged.

XVI. We demand the building-up of a healthy middle class and its preservation; we demand immediate communalization of large department stores and further, that they be rented at moderate prices to small shopkeepers; the strictest control of all shopkeepers in their sales to the Reich, the States and the Communes.

XVII. We demand agrarian reform consistent with our national needs; the passage of a law to expropriate without compensation land which is to be used for common purposes; the abolition of interest on land debts (*Bodenzinsen*) and of all speculation in land values.[4]

XVIII. We demand a ruthless fight against those people who through their activities harm the common welfare. Dangerous criminals, usurers, profiteers, etc.,

[4] An "explanation" of this section of the program was added by Hitler on April 13, 1928, as follows: "In reply to the lying expositions of Point XVII of the program of the National Socialist party which our opponents have made, the following declaration is necessary. Since the National Socialist party stands firmly for the principle of private property, it is self-evident that the passage 'to expropriate without compensation' can only apply to the creation of laws concerning land which has been illegally acquired or which has not been administered according to the common good and which, therefore, should be expropriated when necessary. Such action is directed in the first place against Jewish companies engaged in land speculation."

must be punished with death without regard to religion or race.

XIX. We demand a German common law as a substitute for the Roman law which serves the materialistic world-order.

XX. To make it possible for every hard-working and capable German to secure a higher education and therefore the opportunity of attaining a leading position, the State has the responsibility of providing for a fundamental extension of our common educational system. The plans of instruction of all institutions of learning must correspond to the demands of practical life. An understanding of the theory of the State must be taught to the children at the earliest possible age. We demand special education at State expense of gifted children of poor parents, without regard to their profession or position.

XXI. The State must care for the improvement of the health of the people by protection of mother and child, by forbidding child labor, by making laws for the development of sport and gymnastics in order to build up the bodies of its citizens and by the most generous support of all clubs which work toward building up the bodies of the youth of the nation.

XXII. We demand the abolition of the mercenary army and the development of a people's army.

XXIII. We demand a legal (*gesetzlich*) battle against the conscious political lies and their propagation in the press. In order to make possible the creation of a German press, we demand that:

a. All editors and workers on newspapers which appear in the German language must be citizens.

b. Non-German newspapers require the specific permission of the State for publication. They may not be printed in the German language.

c. Any financial participation or influence in a German newspaper is to be forbidden by law and punished by confiscation of the paper as well as by the immediate expulsion from the Reich of the non-German in question.

Newspapers which work against the common good are to be prohibited.

We demand laws against tendencies in art and literature which have a bad influence on our life as a people, and the closing of institutions which conflict with this demand.

XXIV. We demand freedom for all religious sects in the State in so far as they do not endanger the State or work against the customs and morals of the German race. The party as such represents the point of view of a positive Christianity without binding itself to any particular confession. It fights the spirit of Jewish materialism in us and outside us and is convinced that a lasting convalescence of our people can only take place from the inner conviction that "common welfare comes before individual welfare."

XXV. In order to carry out all of this program, we demand the creation of a strong central authority in the Reich; unqualified authority of the political central parliament over the entire Reich and its organizations; the creation of professional chambers [like Soviets] to carry out the laws promulgated by the Reich in the several Federal States.

The leaders of the party promise to work ruthlessly for the fulfillment of the above [Twenty-five] Points even, if necessary, to the extent of staking their lives for the program.

OFFICIAL NAZI INTERPRETATION

The official commentary on the Twenty-five Points gives some further indication of the meaning of the program, declaring that the most important tenets in the Nazi program are those specifying that "the common welfare comes before individual welfare," and that "slavery to interest" must be abolished. The Nazi racial theories and anti-Semitism, however, form a connecting link between these apparently unrelated demands and the entire Nazi program as well. Thus the aim of the Hitlerites is said to be the creation of order out of the chaos caused by "a government fighting against the people, party against party, parliament against government, worker against employer, consumer against producer," with resulting "impoverishment, graft and betrayal." The cause of this state of affairs is the shattered and false spiritual foundations of society brought about by Marxists, capitalists, industrialists and public leaders, all of whom are motivated by the same individualist philosophy: personal individual aggrandizement. The Jews are the world enemy, responsible not only for Marxism but for large capitalism, for they hold the whip hand over the people in the form of interest on capital. Therefore, the Nazis contend, the "slavery to interest" must be broken, although the means by which this policy is to be carried out are not indicated.

Of primary importance in overcoming both "individualistic materialism" and "interest slavery" is the settlement of the Jewish question which is described as "the emotional foundation of the National Socialist movement." According to Nazi ideology, the Jewish "materialistic spirit" is the root of all evil. The Nazis envisage the struggle against this spirit as a battle between two philosophies: "the elemental, creative, productive spirit of the Aryans, firmly rooted in the earth; and the ravaging, rootless, self-seeking spirit of the Jews." Germany, say the Hitlerites, must be the home of the Germans and not the abiding place of "Jews, Russians (Communists), and Social Democrats who recognize no fatherland." In this statement is contained

Nazi foreign policy, the demand for political freedom of the Reich, all racial-political demands and
citizenship requirements.

Main Principles of Nazi Foreign Policy

The primary object of Nazi foreign policy is to
liberate Germany from "political and economic
slavery." [5] Some indication of the measures by
which this is to be achieved is given in Hitler's autobiography. Germany, he declared, must strengthen
its position as a Continental power; this it can do
only through alliances with Great Britain and Italy.
France is the arch-enemy of Germany, and it is
primarily against the French that Germany must
fight. In his book Hitler envisages two wars with
the aid of Great Britain and Italy—one against
France and one against Russia. The fact that England does not seem particularly anxious to ally itself
with Germany, Hitler ascribes to the influence of
"international Jews," stating that in this "freest democracy [England] the Jews today dictate by the
roundabout method of influencing public opinion, in
a fashion which is practically unlimited. There is in
England, almost uninterrupted coöperation between
the representatives of the British state and the
pioneer workers for a Jewish world-dictatorship." [6]
As for Russia, Hitler contends that Germany needs
territory on which its surplus population can settle;
that territory is available only in the East, and
therefore Germany must make war on Russia to
obtain land.

[5] *Nationalsozialistisches Jahrbuch, 1931.* Hrsg. unter Mit-
wirkung der Reichsleitung der N.S.D.A.P., 5th year (Munich,
Frz. Eher Nachf., 1931), p. 29.

[6] Hitler, *Mein Kampf,* cited, p. 721; for his foreign policy,
cf. pp. 687–758.

Further light on Nazi aims in foreign policy is shed
by the writings of Alfred Rosenberg, now head of
the Foreign Affairs Bureau of the National Socialist
party. Rosenberg proclaims that the Nazis desire
"no *Mitteleuropa* without racial and national
differences such as Naumann dreamed of, no Franco-
Jewish Pan-Europa. A Nordic Europe is the solution of the future, together with a German *Mitteleuropa*. Germany as a racial and national state from
Strassburg to Memel, from Eupen to Prague and
Laibach, as the central power of the continent, as a
guarantee for the South and Southeast. The Scandinavian states and Finland as a second alliance to
guarantee the Northeast; and Great Britain as a
guarantee in the West and overseas necessary in the
interest of the Nordic race." [7]

The program commentary also contains further
illuminating remarks regarding Nazi foreign policy.
Thus in demanding "a self-sufficient national state
comprising all Germans," Herr Feder, the official
commentator, states that "all people of German
blood, whether they live under Danish, Polish,
Czech, Italian or French rule, must be united in a
German Reich." And he adds: "We will not renounce a single German in Sudeten,[8] in Alsace-
Lorraine, in Poland, in the League of Nations' colony
Austria, or in the Succession States of old Austria."
Moreover, in foreign policy in general, the Nazis demand that the "dust of the Foreign Office must be

[7] Alfred Rosenberg, *Der Mythus des 20 Jahrhunderts, Eine
Wertung der seelisch-geistigen Gestaltenkämpfe unserer Zeit*
(Munich, Hoheneichen-Verlag, 1930), p. 602. In a speech at
Münster on May 13, 1933, Vice Chancellor von Papen attacked
pacificism and declared that "the battlefield is for a man what
motherhood is for a woman." *New York Times*, May 14, 1933.

[8] A mountain district in Prussia, Saxony, Silesia and Czechoslovakia.

swept out with an iron broom. There must be an end to the toadying of the Erzbergers and Stresemanns to foreigners and we shall soon see how a strong representation of German interests abroad will receive proper respect, and how German wishes will gain respect and consideration instead of kicks and blows."

NAZI RACIAL POLICIES

At home, however, the German Reich, comprising all Germans, is to be purely Teutonic. Nazi anti-Semitism is a racial and not a religious matter. It is based on the theory that no Jew is a German, regardless of how many centuries he and his ancestors may have lived in the Reich. Therefore, according to the Nazis, no Jew may be a German citizen. As a corollary, all Jews must be excluded from responsible positions in German public life. The official program commentary states in this connection:

"This demand is so much a matter of course to us Nazis that it requires no amplification. A person who regards Jews as 'German citizens of Jewish faith' and not as a foreign race, a strictly exclusive people of decidedly parasitic character, cannot understand the essentials of our demands."

Hitler himself may be listed as the primary source of Nazi anti-Semitism, and his autobiography is illuminating on this point. According to his own account, when he went from his childhood home in Linz to Vienna as a young man, he had already become an ardent nationalist, hating the Austro-Hungarian Empire because it was an empire of nationalities and not a national empire.[9] In Vienna he appears eventually to have found a job in the building trades, and finally to have become a draughtsman. He was asked to join the Social Democratic party but refused. After listening to his fellow workers for a time, he argued with them and finally appears to have opposed them so hotly that he was forced to leave his job. This happened several times and, as a result, Hitler lived in great poverty for a number of years. This may explain in part his intense anti-Marxian feeling as well as his anti-Semitism.[10] Since some of the Socialist leaders were Jews, to Hitler the whole Socialist movement was, and is, a plot of the "international Jews" to gain control of the workers.

During the last decade of the nineteenth and the first years of the twentieth century, Austria-Hungary was a hotbed of anti-Semitism. Although by the time Hitler reached Vienna the movement, which had been largely political, was on the wane, the prestige of the pan-German leader, Ritter von Schoenerer, and of the notoriously anti-Semitic Mayor of Vienna, Karl Lueger, was still great.[11] Hitler was influenced by the views of both Schoenerer and Lueger,[12] although he apparently did not always agree with their political tactics. It was during his Vienna days, also, that Hitler for the first time saw a Galician Jew in caftan and side curls. His reactions, written many years later, are significant. He noted:

[9] *Mein Kampf*, p. 8 *et seq. Nationalitätenstaat* as opposed to *Nationalstaat.*
[10] *Ibid.*, p. 40 *et seq.*
[11] Lucien Wolf, "Anti-Semitism," *Encyclopedia Britannica* (11th Ed., New York, 1910), p. 141 *et seq.*
[12] *Mein Kampf*, cited, p. 105 *et seq.*

"Once while I was going through the inner city I came suddenly upon an apparition in a long caftan with black curls. Is this also a Jew? was my first thought. Jews in Linz had not looked like that. I observed the man, furtive and stealthy, and the longer I stared at this foreign face and regarded it feature by feature, the more the question crystallized itself in my mind in another form: Is this a German as well?" [13]

Thus, even before the war, Hitler was a confirmed anti-Semite. After the war, when the National Socialist party was already active in Munich, Hitler met Alfred Rosenberg, the present head of the Nazi Foreign Affairs Bureau. It was apparently Rosenberg's influence which gave Hitler's anti-Semitism its "Black Hundred" [14] characteristics so evident since the Nazi accession to power, for Rosenberg, although of German ancestry, was born in Reval (Estonia); he spent the war years in Russia as a student and, like many other Russian emigrés, fled to Munich in 1919. [15]

BASES OF GERMAN ANTI-SEMITISM

It cannot be denied, however, that there had been considerable anti-Semitism in Germany even before Hitler's advent, and on several occasions feeling against the Jews reached large proportions. This was particularly the case during the last three decades of the nineteenth century. Anti-Semitism was started by a series of financial scandals involving prominent Jews as well as important Gentile aristocrats after the panic of 1873, which had resulted from wild speculation due to the rapid payment of the large French war indemnity. The publication at

[13] *Ibid.,* p. 59.
[14] The most reactionary elements in Tsarist Russia.
[15] Heiden, *Geschichte des Nationalsozialismus,* cited, p. 47.

this time of a pamphlet entitled *Der Sieg des Judentums über das Germanentum* by an obscure journalist, Wilhelm Marr, fell on fertile soil. Marr was imbued with Hegel's theory of nationality—namely, that the nation should be a unit comprising individuals speaking the same language and of the same racial origin, and demanding the elimination of all elements which could not be reduced to the so-called national type. The Jews, according to Marr, were of course an element incapable of such standardization. The exigencies of German party politics added to the financial difficulties of the time, fed the flame of this new pseudo-scientific anti-Semitism which was based not on religious but on racial grounds. Bismarck's breach with the National Liberal party in 1879 was followed by a tremendous growth of feeling against the Jews, which led to the formation of a definitely anti-Semitic political group —the Christian Socialist party—under the leadership of Adolf Stöcker, the court preacher. While Stöcker's so-called Christian Socialism had appealed to German conservative elements, a more popular leader named Ahlwardt, whose name was connected with many unsavory scandals, had gained a considerable hold on the masses as an anti-Semitic agitator. Ahlwardt's propaganda was apparently "wild, unscrupulous and full-blooded," and a prosecution and conviction for libel only seemed to increase his influence. Although eventually all this agitation died down, there can be no doubt that the wave of anti-Semitism left its mark on the German people.[16]

The anti-Semitic sections of the National Socialist

---

[16] For a summary of anti-Semitism in Germany, *cf.* Wolf, "Anti-Semitism," cited, p. 135 *et seq.*

program were thus not an entirely new thing in German politics. Furthermore, Nazi anti-Semitism offered the German people a welcome scapegoat on which to blame all their hardships since the war. Moreover, German youth, which today forms so important a section of Hitler's followers, was subjected to intense anti-Semitic propaganda almost from the beginning of its political consciousness.

COMPOSITION OF THE NATIONAL SOCIALIST MOVEMENT

The National Socialist movement is to a large extent a youth movement. The German birth rate during the fifteen years before the war was particularly high [17] and the children born during that period, now adults between the ages of 20 and 30, have undergone the severest hardships. First the war, with its attendant lack of proper food, lax discipline at school and at home, and overwrought emotional state; then the uncertainty of the Revolution and hunger intensified by the blockade. Later, at the time when youth should have been learning the value of money, came the inflation. Finally, when they were grown and ready to work, no jobs were available. As a result, these young people became completely disillusioned, and lost all hope regarding their future. Those young people who had any international sentiments became Communists; the large majority, attracted by the pomp and circumstance with which the Hitler movement surrounded itself, became National Socialists. Hotheaded and impulsive, these young Germans are tremendously idealistic. Since they had nothing to do with the war, they feel intensely that there is no

[17] *Statistisches Jahrbuch für das deutsche Reich, 1931*, p. ii.

reason why they themselves, and their children and grandchildren after them, should pay for it, and they have been told unceasingly that their Fatherland was humiliated by the Treaty of Versailles and betrayed into signing it. They have lost faith in their elders who, they believe, have made a complete failure of life: now it is their turn to set the world right and Hitler is their prophet.[18]

Among the older generation, the Nazi followers have come very largely from the ranks of the bourgeoisie. Many small white-collar people whose businesses have been completely disrupted by the depression, but who felt that it would degrade them to vote for one of the Left parties, turned National Socialist. This tendency was apparent also among farmers and agricultural workers, where Nazi propaganda was especially active. Finally, many people belonging to what has been called in the Reich the "non-voters' party"—people who had never voted before—went to the polls in the four Reichstag elections between 1930 and 1933 and voted for Hitler. Aroused by the Nazi propaganda, and utterly disillusioned with the older parties which apparently had been unable to help them out of their difficulties, these people also saw in Hitler their last hope.

Support of Hitler by the bourgeoisie and the younger generation caused a steady decline in all parties of the German Right except the Nazis, whose gains were correspondingly large. The Catholic parties managed to hold their own fairly well, while on the Left, the moderate Social Democrats declined somewhat, losing some supporters to the

[18] Hanns Heinz Ewers, *Horst Wessel* (Berlin, J. G. Cotta'sche Buchhandlung Nachf., 1933). This biography of the young Nazi "martyr," sympathetically written, attempts to portray the idealism and "pure patriotic feeling" of Hitler's young storm troopers.

Communists and failing to attract their proportion of the young workers who would normally have filled the Socialist ranks. The age distribution of the Social Democratic, Communist and Nazi deputies elected to the 1930 Reichstag as shown in the following table illustrates this situation: [19]

Age	Social Democrats	Nazis	Communists
Over 70	1	....	1
50–70	73	12	1
40–50	49	21	20
30–40	20	63	47
Under 30	...	9	8

The discipline of the older German workers, however, even at the elections on March 5, 1933, was demonstrated by the fact that at that poll, despite terror and suppression, the Socialists elected 120 Reichstag deputies, as compared with 121 at the previous election, while the Communists dropped from 100 to 81.

Paradoxically, the political discipline of the German workers during the whole period of the Republic proved of ultimate advantage to the Nazis: many important German industrialists and landowners saw in Hitler a means by which to crush organized German labor and the power of the trade unions, and thus free themselves from the expensive social insurances, fixed wage scales and compulsory labor arbitration. These magnates regarded the Nazis as the best bulwark against Socialism and Communism, despite the vague socialistic theories of the Hitlerites which they did not take seriously. As a result, many big industrialists gave the Nazis

[19] *Cf.* Sigmund Neumann, *Die deutschen Parteien* (Berlin, Junker and Dünnhaupt, 1932), p. 134. By 1933 this age distribution was even more marked.

financial assistance,[20] and the latter w
not only to carry on expensive propa
paigns, but also to support their increas
ful private army, the Storm Troops
teilung-S.A.) and the picked men wh
so-called *Schutzstaffel-S.S.*, a sort of part
bodyguard of the Nazi leaders.[21] For more than
two years there was virtual civil war in the Reich,
the Nazi private army striving for "control of the
streets" against the Republican *Reichsbanner* and
the Communists.[22]

CHAPTER III

HITLER AND THE GERMAN POLITICAL CRISIS

DEEPENING economic depression and increasing
inability of the German political system to cope
with the crisis provided a fertile field for the Hitler
movement with its elaborate, all-inclusive organization. The Treaty of Versailles, furthermore, gave
the Nazis a popular basis for their agitation which
carried out the following sentiments of Hitler:
"What a means to an end this instrument of un-

[20] Heiden, *Geschichte des Nationalsozialismus,* cited, p. 144
et seq.; Richard Lewinson (Morus), *Das Geld in der Politik*
(Berlin, Fischer Verlag, 1930), p. 146 *et seq.;* Mowrer, *Germany
Puts the Clock Back,* cited, p. 142 *et seq.*

[21] It has been estimated that by the beginning of 1933, when
Hitler came to power, the Nazi private army comprised between
five and six hundred thousand men.

[22] The Nazi S.A. also had frequent encounters with the Nationalist *Stahlhelm,* the veteran's association, although the main riots
were between the S.A. and the Communists.

limited oppression and shameful degradation [the Treaty of Versailles] could become," he wrote in his autobiography, *Mein Kampf*,[1] "in the hands of a government which desires to whip up national passions to the boiling point. . . ." As a result, millions of Germans rallied to the Nazis. This swing to the extreme Right, however, was made at the expense of the more moderate bourgeois parties of the Right and the Middle. The two Republican Catholic parties of the Middle nevertheless managed to maintain their strength practically unchanged, while within the proletarian Left there was a large shift with the continued growth of the extreme Communist party which drew away supporters from the more moderate Social Democrats. Thus, as the accompanying chart indicates, there was a marked trend toward extremism on both the Right and the Left during the fourteen years of the German Republic. The economic depression which broke in 1931 rapidly accelerated this movement.

THE POLITICAL SITUATION, APRIL TO JULY, 1932

The tide of Hitlerism had apparently reached a peak in the summer of 1932. In the four major elections held between March 10 and July 31, 1932, the movement registered heavy gains although in a slightly reduced tempo. Thus, in the first presidential poll on March 10, Field Marshal von Hindenburg received 18,654,244 votes to Hitler's 11,341,119.[2] In the "run-off" election on April 10, the presi-

[1] Adolf Hitler, *Mein Kampf* (Munich, Eher Verlag, 1930), p. 714.

[2] *Der Heimatdienst*, XIIth year, No. 6, 2nd Märzheft 1932. There were three other candidates also running.

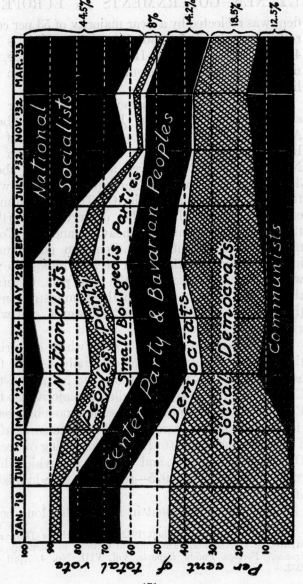

CHANGES IN PARTY POWER IN GERMANY [4]

JAN. '19   JUNE '20   MAY '24   DEC. '24   MAY '28   SEPT. '30   JULY '32   NOV. '32   MAR. '33

Per cent of total vote

National Socialists — 44.5%

Nationalists

Peoples Party

Small Bourgeois Parties — 8%

Center Party & Bavarian Peoples

Democrats — 14.2%

Social Democrats — 18.5%

Communists — 12.5%

[4] Based on graph published in *Die Tat* (Jena, Eugen Diederichs Verlag), September 1932

dent was reëlected by a clear majority of 53 per cent, rolling up a total of 19,361,229 votes to Hitler's 13,-418,676.[3] President von Hindenburg, therefore, remained the one stable element in the German political situation.

This fact became even more apparent after the state elections in Prussia, Bavaria, Württemberg, Anhalt and Hamburg—comprising five-sixths of the Reich—which took place on April 24. Although the National Socialists received an average of about 35 per cent of the votes in these polls, nowhere were they able to obtain a majority. The Nazis almost entirely absorbed the smaller conservative parties, the Social Democrats lost heavily, and the Communists made slight gains. Coalition government in large sections of the Reich became impossible; it was therefore necessary, for the most part, to retain the old Cabinets to carry on the administration of the government. These cabinets, however, met with ever greater difficulties.

The situation in Prussia, a state which comprises three-fifths of Germany, was especially serious, for, as a result of the April elections, the Nazis and the Catholic Center party controlled a majority in the Prussian Diet, and negotiations for a possible coalition between these two parties were unsuccessful. The government of Otto Braun—consisting of Social Democrats, Centrists and Democrats, which had ruled Prussia since 1925—remained to administer affairs.

The Braun government in Prussia had long been

[3] *Ibid.*, No. 8, 2nd Aprilheft 1932. Vera Micheles Dean and Mildred S. Wertheimer, "The Political Outlook in Germany and France," *Foreign Policy Reports,* Vol. VIII, No. 4, April 27, 1932.

regarded by German moderates as one of the three principal pillars of the Reich; President von Hindenburg, impelled by his stern sense of duty to maintain his oath to uphold the Constitution, was the second; the third was the Reich government of Chancellor Heinrich Brüning who, although governing entirely by means of drastic decrees issued under Article 48 of the Weimar Constitution, had at least preserved the forms of that Constitution by securing indirect parliamentary assent to his measures. This was possible only through Social Democratic toleration of the Brüning government in which that party was not represented. The National Socialists were in noisy opposition and Dr. Brüning made no attempt to force them into the responsibilities of office, probably because of his desire to retain foreign confidence. Brüning managed to steer Germany through the 1931 financial crisis,[5] although only at the expense of drastic currency deflation which further increased misery in the Reich. Meanwhile, he hoped that a major success in foreign affairs would strengthen his hand and that international economic action would pull Germany out of the financial mire and deflate the Nazi movement.

Dr. Brüning's hopes were not realized. The Lausanne Reparation Conference, first scheduled to convene in January 1932, was postponed until June; the Disarmament Conference dragged on in Geneva and made no move toward recognizing the German claim for equality.[6]

[5] *Cf.* Mildred S. Wertheimer, "The Financial Crisis in Germany," *Foreign Policy Reports,* Vol. VII, No. 26, March 2, 1932.

[6] *Cf.* Mildred S. Wertheimer, "The Lausanne Reparation Settlement," *Foreign Policy Reports,* Vol. VIII, No. 19, November 23, 1932; also William T. Stone, "The World Disarmament Conference: Second Stage," *Foreign Policy Reports,* Vol. VIII, No. 23, January 18, 1933.

Meanwhile political tension and bitterness in the Reich had greatly increased. Despite Hitler's defeat in the presidential poll, the state elections in the spring of 1932 registered the continued growth of the National Socialist movement. More and more voices were raised against the "Brüning system"— the all-embracing epithet of the Hitlerites for everything against which their agitation was directed. Political riots and bloodshed increased, and there was latent civil war. In an attempt to restore order, General Groener, Minister of Defense and of the Interior in the Brüning Cabinet, decreed the dissolution of Hitler's private army on April 13.

On May 12 the Reichstag defeated a motion of non-confidence in the Brüning government by a margin of 30 votes, but on the same day General Groener resigned as Defense Minister—although he remained as Minister of the Interior. It was evident that Groener had been forced out because he had lost the confidence of the Reichswehr Ministry, particularly General Kurt von Schleicher, the permanent chief [7] of that Ministry.[8] On May 30 the storm broke and Chancellor Brüning and his entire Cabinet resigned.

Brüning fell, not because of the withdrawal of Reichstag confidence, but due to the increased pressure which was brought to bear on President von Hindenburg. The immediate reason for the President's refusal, on the eve of the Lausanne Conference, to accord his Chancellor a free hand in directing German policy was von Hindenburg's opposition to a projected emergency decree. This

[7] *Chef des Ministeramtes.*

[8] *Cf. Der deutsche Volkswirt,* May 20, 1932; also Kurt Caro and Walter Oehme, *Schleicher's Aufstieg* (Berlin, Rowohlt, 1933), p. 222 *et seq.*

measure undertook to secure small land allotments
for the unemployed by dividing up many large,
bankrupt East Prussian estates. The underlying
reason for Brüning's dismissal, however, was the
President's conviction, reinforced by the arguments
of influential conservative advisers,[9] that the Brüning government no longer represented the German
people. Dr. Brüning, at the urgent request of von
Hindenburg, had taken office in March 1930 as a
conservatively inclined chancellor.[10] The course of
events during the next two years, however, particularly the rising tide of Hitlerism, had forced him
to rely increasingly on the Socialists and the Catholic Center for support. In May 1932, President von
Hindenburg was persuaded that the time had come
to part with Brüning, despite the fact that the latter was primarily responsible for Hindenburg's re-
election to the presidency, and without regard for
the Reichstag's recent vote of confidence in the
Chancellor. The German conservatives felt that by
harnessing the Nazis to governmental responsibility
the Reich might secure a strong and stable national
government,[11] which alone, they were convinced,
could win concessions abroad and keep order at
home. Furthermore, it seemed apparent that the
Reichswehr no longer had confidence in the
Brüning government, a factor which no doubt especially disturbed the old Field Marshal.

[9] The President's son, Major Oscar von Hindenburg, his Chef
du Cabinet, Dr. Otto Meissner, and General von Schleicher
were apparently the real actors in the drama, although behind
the scenes. Cf. Caro and Oehme, *Schleicher's Aufstieg,* cited.

[10] Cf. Mildred S. Wertheimer "The Significance of the German
Elections," Foreign Policy Association, *Information Service,*
Vol. VI, No. 13, September 13, 1930.

[11] Cf. *Frankfurter Zeitung,* May 29, 30, 31, June 1, 2, 1932;
Der deutsche Volkswirt, June 3, 10, 1932.

Papen-Schleicher Government

As a result, after conversations with most of the parliamentary leaders—a proceeding which somewhat preserved constitutional forms—President von Hindenburg on May 31 asked Colonel Franz von Papen, then a right wing Centrist, to form a government of "national concentration," apparently hoping to assure the toleration of the Catholic Center party for the new Ministry.[12] The Center, however, smarting under the dismissal of its leader, Dr. Brüning, went into opposition and von Papen resigned from the party.

The Papen-Schleicher government took office with little or no apparent parliamentary support. It was designated as a presidial Ministry responsible to the President alone, and was entirely satisfactory to the Reichswehr. The new Cabinet, which for the most part consisted of non-party aristocrats of the class which before the war ruled Germany, was announced on June 2, as follows: [13]

Chancellor:	Colonel von Papen
Interior:	Baron von Gayl
Foreign:	Baron von Neurath
Finance:	Count Schwerin von Krosigk
Commerce:	Professor Warmbold
Defense:	General von Schleicher
Justice:	Dr. Gürtner
Agriculture:	Baron von Braun
Transportation:	Baron von Eltz-Rübenach
Labor:	Dr. Schaeffer

[12] It was evidently hoped to secure the services of Dr. Brüning at the forthcoming Lausanne Conference; however, he refused the offer of the Foreign Ministry in the Papen Cabinet. Cf. *Frankfurter Zeitung,* May 31, 1932.

[13] *Frankfurter Zeitung,* June 3, 7, 1932. The Papen government was often called the Cabinet of Barons.

The Nazis, it will be noted, were not represented. It was reported, however, that a gentlemen's agreement had been reached between Hitler and the new rulers of the Reich, to the effect that in return for certain concessions the Nazis would not oppose the government. These concessions were said to be dissolution of the Reichstag and new elections—which could not fail to result in greatly increased Nazi representation in the new Parliament—and the removal of the ban on the Hitler Storm Troops.[14]

Events bore out the report that an effort would be made to propitiate the Nazis. On June 4, President von Hindenburg dissolved the Reichstag, which was not in session, on the ground that state elections during the past months had shown that the Parliament no longer represented the will of the people, and new Reichstag elections were announced for July 31.[15] The Papen-Schleicher government had not dared to risk its official life by facing the Reichstag, in which, under the circumstances, it could have counted on the support of less than one-tenth of the deputies.

Nevertheless, the Reich government, despite pressing political and financial tasks, had at once taken steps to break the Prussian deadlock. This action not only aroused opposition and resentment in Catholic and Social Democratic circles in Prussia, but was viewed with particular alarm in South Germany. On June 7, Chancellor von Papen attempted to bring financial pressure to bear on Prussia, and also requested the Nazi president of the Prussian Diet to convene that body as soon as possible.

[14] *Cf.* p. 163. *New York Herald Tribune,* June 4, 1932; *Frankfurter Zeitung,* June 7, 1932.
[15] *Frankfurter Zeitung,* June 4, 7, 1932.

Papen's move was ostensibly based on the need for a responsible Prussian government with which financial questions could be settled, but rumors at once began to circulate that the Chancellor was actually seeking to provoke open conflict as an excuse for installing a Reich Commissioner. Such a development, from the point of view of the Papen-Schleicher régime would have had the advantage of removing the liberal Braun government from office and placing the powerful Prussian police in the hands of the Reich. It was intimated, moreover, that a clarification of the situation in Prussia might be looked on with favor by Hitler.[16]

It should be noted that plans to abolish the dual régime by bringing the Prussian administration under the Reich authorities had long been discussed.[17] In fact, the relations of the Reich and its component states had always been recognized as a major German problem. Its solution, however, was envisaged as possible only by democratic methods, with due consideration of local feeling in all parts of the Reich. The energetic moves of the Papen government in the matter of Prussia at once inflamed particularist sentiment in South Germany. The situation was further aggravated on June 16 by the government's action in lifting the ban on the Hitler Storm Troops—the second major concession of the Reich government to the Nazis. Disturbances and riots, with many casualties, immediately increased throughout the Reich. The South German states, jealous of their authority and genuinely concerned with the difficulty of maintaining order within their

[16] *Frankfurter Zeitung,* June 8, 9, 10, 1932.
[17] *Cf.* particularly H. Höpker-Aschoff, "Reichsreform," *Der deutsche Volkswirt,* August 21, 1931; also *ibid.,* August 28, 1931.

borders, met the situation by renewing the ban on political uniforms within their territories.[18] On June 22, at a conference between the Reich Minister of the Interior, von Gayl, and the Interior Ministers of the states, von Gayl "urgently requested the states to adapt their political legal measures to those of the Reich." [19] Two days later, however, Bavaria took even stronger measures to preserve order. Finally, on June 28, the Reich government issued a second emergency decree "to protect public order," providing similar legal measures for the entire Reich and abrogating state decrees which were not consistent with this action. State officials, however, were given the right to prohibit political meetings "in case of unquestionable danger to public safety." [20]

Thus, during its first month in office, the Papen government succeeded in stirring up South German particularism without either propitiating the Nazis or clarifying the Prussian situation. Political bitterness had increased and the campaign preparatory to the July 31 elections was marked by a mounting casualty list. The most serious riot took place on July 17, in Altona, where a National Socialist parade through the Communist section of the city caused severe fighting in which 15 were killed and 70 wounded.[21] As a result, the Reich government on July 18 decreed a ban on demonstrations throughout the Reich, forbidding all open-air meetings and parades, and imposing severe punishments for offenses against the decree.

[18] *Frankfurter Zeitung*, June 23, 1932; *Der deutsche Volkswirt*, June 24, 1932.
[19] *Cf. Frankfurter Zeitung*, June 23, 1932.
[20] *Ibid.*, June 30, 1932.
[21] *Ibid.*, July 19, 20, 1932.

The Prussian Coup D'État

An even more important result of the Altona riots was von Papen's action in ousting the Braun government and installing a Reich Commissioner in Prussia. This move was as radical as it was sudden. Without warning, Chancellor von Papen issued on July 20 an emergency decree under Article 48, paragraphs 1 and 2, naming himself Reich Commissioner and Prussian Minister of the Interior, and appointing Dr. Bracht, the chief mayor of Essen, as his permanent representative to administer these offices. Simultaneously, the Reich government dismissed from office Minister President Otto Braun [22] and Minister of the Interior Severing—both Socialists—and placed Berlin and the province of Brandenburg under martial law. Herr Severing refused to desert his post and was temporarily arrested by a Reichswehr lieutenant and two men. At the same time, the Socialist police president of Berlin, Grzesinski, the Commandant of the Berlin police, Colonel Heimannsberg, and the Socialist vice-president of the Berlin police, Dr. Weiss, were forced out of office. These officials refused to submit and were promptly arrested by Lieutenant-General Rundstedt who, under the martial law decree, was in command of Berlin and Brandenburg, and who appeared at Police Headquarters with fifteen soldiers armed with hand grenades. The deposed officials were released after some hours and filed suits with the Reich Supreme Court against the government.

The reason given by the Reich government for its drastic action was the alleged inability of the Prus-

---

[22] Herr Braun was absent from Berlin on sick leave, and Dr. Hirtsiefer, a Centrist, was Acting Minister President of Prussia.

sian authorities to cope with the so-called Communist menace which, von Papen declared, had been responsible for the terror and latent civil war of the past weeks.[23] It was, however, generally admitted by impartial observers that before the ban on the Hitler Storm Troops had been lifted the Prussian police had had no difficulty in keeping order. Other motives seem to have actuated the events of July 20.

The attitude of the Papen government in the Prussian question had been considered vacillating by both the Nazis and the Hugenberg Nationalists, who were bending every effort to gain control of that all-important state. In a speech on July 18, Geheimrat Hugenberg had brought pressure on Papen by stating:

"We [the German Nationalist People's party] expect the Reich government at this moment to make an immediate end of the Marxist scum in Prussia and to install a Reich Commissioner armed with all necessary powers. We Nationalists have no responsibility toward the Papen government, but we will be willing to support it in anything which would lead to the ending of the present impossible situation in Prussia."

The Hitlerites, for their part, also demanded the appointment of a Reich Commissioner, and the Nazi president of the Prussian Landtag, Kerrl, wrote an open letter to von Papen on July 18, blaming the Socialists and the Communists for the Prussian deadlock, and stating that the existing situation was fostering an increase in Marxian propaganda which threatened to undermine the very foundations of the state.[24] This pressure evidently stiffened

[23] Cf. radio speech of von Papen on July 20. Text in *Frankfurter Zeitung*, July 21, 1932.
[24] *Frankfurter Zeitung*, July 20, 1932.

the determination of the Papen-Schleicher régime.

From the government's point of view, the coup d'état of July 20, in addition to being a bid for Nazi and Nationalist support, had many advantages. The powerful Prussian police was removed from Socialist control and placed in the hands of the Reich. It could now be relied on, it was felt, as a reserve for the Reichswehr in case of serious internal disorders. The government's position was thus consolidated by concentrating power in its hands. Furthermore, the Prussian deadlock had been broken and the dualism between the Reich and Prussia abolished, clearing the way for the abrogation of much administrative duplication.

The first general reaction to the coup d'état was stunned amazement. The Hitlerites, however, were jubilant, many of their leaders stating publicly that the government's move was the direct result of Nazi pressure; in their eyes, the first decisive step against the "November traitors" [25] had been taken. The Social Democrats and the Catholic Center party were of course not only incensed but gravely apprehensive over the consequences of the events of July 20. Nevertheless, with great self-control, the leaders confined themselves to strongly worded resolutions of protest, while exhorting their followers to maintain discipline and avoid disorder. Word went out to concentrate all efforts on demonstrating to the Papen-Schleicher government, through a peaceful revolution at the polls on July 31, that German democracy could not be trampled on.

In non-Prussian Germany there was not only bit-

[25] A Nazi term of opprobrium for the Socialists, whom they accuse of betraying the Fatherland in the November 1918 revolution.

terness against the government, but great uneasiness. As in Prussia, the particularistic, democratic South German states were administered by provisional "business governments" because the parliamentary deadlock had made it impossible to form new ministries. These states, furthermore, had already crossed swords with the Papen government in the matter of the prohibition of the Nazi Storm Troops. They therefore saw in the events of July 20 a possible precedent for action against themselves and were correspondingly alarmed despite the Reich government's denial of any such intention.

Meanwhile, the deposed Prussian Ministers had appealed to the Reich Supreme Court in Leipzig for a temporary injunction to restrain further removals of Prussian officials from office, and to restrict von Papen as Reich Commissioner for Prussia in the internal administration of the state. The Court handed down an interim decision on July 25, declining to grant this request. The real issue as to the constitutional right of the Reich government to intervene in the affairs of a state was not settled, however, the Court stating that a decision on this important point would be given later after a full investigation.[26] The legal aspects of the Papen government's action in Prussia remained completely obscure, and relations between the Reich and the state governments were greatly aggravated.

THE POLITICAL DEADLOCK, JULY TO NOVEMBER, 1932

The German people went to the polls on July 31 with passions roused to fever pitch.[27] The only party

[26] *Frankfurter Zeitung,* July 26, 1932.
[27] *Der deutsche Volkswirt,* August 5, 1932.

backing the Cabinet—the Hugenberg Nationalists
—suffered a loss of four seats.[28] The National Socialist vote amounted to something more than one-
third of the electorate. While it showed an immense
increase compared with that cast in the 1930 Reichstag election, it was only slightly larger than the
vote polled by the party in the April 1932 state and
presidential elections. Many observers believed that
the movement had now reached its peak, and later
events seemed to justify this opinion. The Hitlerites
were not only unsuccessful in massing a majority of
the German people under their banner, but lacked
a majority even with the coöperation of the other
Right parties, although the latter groups had gained
strength. The combined Middle parties, on the other
hand, remained exactly the same size. There were,
however, shifts within the group, the democratic
State party dwindling almost to nothing, while the
two Catholic parties showed gains. On the Left,
also, there was practically no change in the total
proletarian vote. The Communists, however, made
large gains at Socialist expense.

The large Communist vote was, in fact, the chief
surprise of the election, for in previous polls during 1932, it had fallen off considerably. The success
of the Communists on July 31 has been directly attributed to the lukewarm resistance of the Social
Democrats to the action of the Papen Ministry in
deposing the Prussian government. The Social Democrats had been faced with the difficult choice of resisting the Reich government through the proclamation of a general strike in coöperation with the
Communists, or accepting a *fait accompli.* In March
1920, at the time of the Kapp *Putsch,* a general

[28] *Cf.* p. 192 for table of 1930–1932 Reichstag election returns.

strike had defeated the attempted *coup.* In 1932, however, with more than five million unemployed in the Reich, the moderate Social Democrats felt that they dared not risk throwing the country into further economic chaos by provoking civil war. As a result, many of these erstwhile supporters lost patience with this attitude, and apparently turned to the Communists.[29]

The Nazis and Governmental Responsibility

The problem of inducing the Nazis to accept governmental responsibility reappeared in even more pressing form after the elections. The only possibility for coalition government appeared to be through Nazi-Center coöperation, for these two groups together commanded a bare majority in the new Reichstag. The Centrists were apparently willing to enter such a combination in the hope of reestablishing constitutional government. Back-stage negotiations between the two parties were carried on early in August, but it soon became apparent that Hitler would accept nothing less than the Chancellorship. Meanwhile, despite von Hindenburg's proclamation of a political truce, a veritable reign of terror, involving murders, bomb outrages and riots, had broken out. In view of the dangerously disturbed situation, Hitler's aspirations for sole power seemed incongruous to many Germans.

On August 9 the Reich government finally took drastic action to restore public safety and order. After several warnings, emergency decrees were promulgated extending the ban on demonstrations until August 31, 1932, and setting severe penalties for its infraction, including sentence of death for political

[29] *Cf. Der deutsche Volkswirt,* August 5, 1932.

murders, arson, destruction of property by explosives, or the endangering of railway traffic. Imprisonment of not less than ten years for slightly less extreme cases was decreed, and even for minor offenses the penalties were severe. Special courts were set up to administer these laws.

On the night the new decrees came into force, a gang of Nazis shot and killed a Communist in Beuthen, Upper Silesia, and brutally mistreated the body. One of the new special courts promptly tried those concerned in the affair and sentenced five Nazis to death. The verdict was the occasion for a mob demonstration against the liberal newspapers and Jewish department stores in Beuthen. The Nazi press took up the cause of the condemned men and Hitler himself telegraphed them: "From this moment your freedom is a question of our honor and a fight against the government under which this sentence has been possible is our duty." Strong Nazi protests were sent to the President and von Papen urging immediate pardon, but the government insisted that impartial justice must be done.[30]

Meanwhile, with public feeling aroused to the highest pitch by the terror and general uncertainty, negotiations to bring Hitler into the government were continued. Apparently the Catholic parties, under certain conditions, were willing to enter a coalition with the Nazis—even with Hitler as Chancellor; the Hitlerites, however, would not accept these conditions. On August 10 President von Hindenburg is reported to have expressed himself

---

[30] The sentence was eventually commuted to life imprisonment, on the ground that the new decrees had gone into force only 90 minutes before the murder was committed.

as opposed to allowing Hitler to become Chancellor.[31]

On August 13 the long-awaited interview between the President and the Nazi leader took place in Berlin. It lasted fifteen minutes. President von Hindenburg asked Hitler whether he and his followers were ready to enter the Papen Cabinet. Hitler refused the proffered Vice-Chancellorship, demanding leadership of the Reich government and entire power. In reply the President stated that his conscience and his duty to the Fatherland would not allow him to give complete power to the National Socialist movement, and expressed regret that Herr Hitler did not find it possible to support the national government as he had promised before the Reichstag elections. The interview closed with the earnest appeal of the President that Hitler carry out his announced opposition to the government in a chivalrous manner and realize his (Hitler's) responsibility to the Fatherland and to the German people.[32]

Thus despite the gentlemen's agreement,[33] the attempt to induce the Nazis to coöperate positively with the government had failed again. Hitler, backed—or forced—by his advisers, demanded "all or nothing."

Dissolution of the Reichstag

As a result, the Papen-Schleicher Cabinet had no opportunity to secure the confidence or toleration of the Reichstag which was to convene on August 30, and the government therefore announced that it would dissolve the Reichstag and call new elections. The Reichstag, nevertheless, met on schedule, and

[31] *Frankfurter Zeitung*, August 11, 1932.
[32] *Ibid.*, August 14, 1932, official communiqué.
[33] *Cf.* p. 166.

elected as its president the National Socialist deputy, Captain Hermann Goering. The session was surprisingly orderly, and the shadow of impending dissolution led the Nazis—traditional foes of constitutional government—to become the champion of a parliamentary régime, protesting that the Reichstag was capable of "constructive" work and should not be excluded from its share in governing the Reich. The parliament then adjourned until September 12, hoping to be able to convince President von Hindenburg in the interval that there was no need for dissolution.

This, however, proved impossible. Continued negotiations between the Center and the Nazis were unsuccessful. The Reichstag reconvened on September 12 and, after a stormy session during which there was great confusion in regard to constitutional procedure and rules of order, was dissolved by the government before the Chancellor had presented his program. A Communist motion of non-confidence, however, was unexpectedly brought to a vote and passed by the huge poll of 512 to 42, only the Hugenberg Nationalists and the People's party supporting the Cabinet. Although the motion was later declared null and void, having been enacted by an already dissolved parliament, it nevertheless gave striking evidence of the unpopularity of the Papen régime.

Thus, by the use of rather questionable constitutional methods, a government with the support of less than one-tenth of the German electorate remained in office. The Cabinet's official reason for dissolving the Reichstag and calling new elections, which were later fixed for November 6, was its conviction that the newly announced economic program had to be put into effect and that the Papen Ministry, therefore, must remain to carry out the task.

The government's economic program as promulgated in the emergency decree of September 5, provided for indirect credit inflation by the issue of tax credit certificates acceptable from 1934 to 1938 for the partial payment of all except income taxes. These certificates were to be used to refund part of the taxes paid by industrialists which had been regarded as especially crippling to industry. The decree further provided bonuses in the form of tax credit certificates for employers who hired additional workers. Provision was made for large appropriations for public works and virtually full power was given the Reich government to revise the social insurance legislation and the collective wage agreements, as well as the compulsory wage arbitration system.[34] The decree also envisaged the introduction of agricultural import contingents.

The reception of this decree was mixed. Industrialists were strongly in favor of it, since its provisions were undoubtedly to their advantage. Nevertheless, they entertained grave doubts regarding its promise to introduce agricultural contingents. The workers, on the other hand, were highly skeptical as to its success, and fearful that it would be the means of nullifying most, if not all, of their hard-won privileges—notably the social insurances, the fixed wage system and the arbitration of labor disputes.[35] The decree also proved unacceptable to the Nazis, either from the point of view of social welfare or from pique against the Cabinet.

[34] Text of the September 5, 1932, decree in *Frankfurter Zeitung*, September 6, 1932.
[35] *Cf. Frankfurter Zeitung*, September 9, 1932.

The serious differences of opinion regarding the
Papen government's energetic action in the economic field were paralleled by the general reaction
to statements by various Cabinet members fore-
casting extensive constitutional and social reforms.
The parliamentary impasse which had furnished the
raison d'être for the introduction of presidential government emphasized the need for constitutional
reforms; however, the depth of German political
passions—both cause and effect of the deadlock—
made it equally difficult, if not impossible, to institute the necessary changes. Thus, in his first Ministerial Declaration on June 4, von Papen immediately antagonized and embittered the Left as well
as part of the Middle parties by stating that German financial difficulties were due mainly to mounting social costs. Despite the partial truth of this
statement, his further remark that the Reich had
become a "charity state"[36] and that the moral
forces of the nation had been weakened by steadily
increasing state socialism did not enhance his
prestige except in the eyes of big industry and
agriculture. Von Papen's forcible removal of the
Socialist Ministers in Prussia on July 20 seemed
further evidence of anti-labor tendencies, and the
government's economic program reinforced this impression. The unpopularity of the "Cabinet of
Barons" was further increased by the speech of
Minister of the Interior von Gayl on August 11, the
anniversary of the signing of the Weimar Constitution, in which he indicated the amendments to that
instrument which the Cabinet felt were essential.
The suggested changes were designed to increase the
power of the Executive, and strengthen the federal
government *vis-à-vis* the states. Many of these re-

[36] *Wohlfahrtsstaat.*

forms had been thoroughly studied and discussed in the Reich, and for years had been considered necessary. The fear that they would be summarily forced on the people by decree, however, motivated the unfavorable reception which they were generally accorded. The events of July 20 in Prussia, moreover, seemed to many, particularly in South and Southwest Germany and among the workers, to be symptomatic of the Cabinet's intentions in other matters.

The position of the Papen government was further weakened by a final decision of the Supreme Court of the Reich in the Prussian question, handed down on October 25.[37] The Court ruled that the suspension of the Prussian government and appointment of a Reich Commissioner for Prussia were constitutional under Article 48, since, in its opinion, law and order in Prussia had been endangered on July 20. The Court held, however, that the suspension of the Prussian Cabinet was constitutionally valid only as a temporary measure; and, further, that the suspension deprived the Prussian Ministers of their administrative functions only. The Cabinet's right to represent Prussia in the Reichsrat (Federal Council) and in Prussia's relations with the other German states could not be abrogated. The Braun Ministry, therefore, remained the constitutional Prussian government while the acts of the Reich Commissioner for Prussia and his deputy were deemed valid only in the field of administration. In general, both sides were able to claim the decision as a victory and it contributed little to an immediate clarification of the situation.[38] Moreover, von Pap-

[37] *Cf.* p. 169.
[38] *Cf. Preussen contra Reich vor dem Staatsgerichtshof* (Berlin,

en's action in replacing Social Democratic Prussian officials with more conservative men indicated that the Reich government did not regard the existing order in Prussia as temporary despite the decision of the Supreme Court.

NOVEMBER 6 ELECTIONS FAIL TO BREAK DEADLOCK

Although markedly unpopular throughout the Reich because of its domestic policies, the Papen Ministry hoped that its strong stand in foreign affairs would serve to win it support at the polls on November 6. Von Papen's undoubted success at the Lausanne Conference, which had virtually wiped out German reparation,[39] and the government's renewed and energetic demands for equality in armaments [40] were calculated, from the internal political point of view, further to steal Hitler's thunder and add to the prestige and strength of the Papen Ministry. The latter, however, had been formed as a non-party government, and was definitely backed by only one party—the Hugenberg Nationalists. In order to register support of the Papen policies at the polls, it was therefore necessary to vote for the Nationalists, a conservative Protestant party which appealed, for the most part, only to large agricultural and industrial interests. Thus, in a sense, the election of November 6 was fought in a vacuum without either clearly defined issues or sharply drawn fronts.

J. H. W. Dietz Nachf. Verlag, 1933). This volume contains the complete stenographic report of the hearings before the Court from October 10 to 14 and on October 17, 1932, as well as full text of the decision and an explanatory foreword by Dr. Arnold Brecht, counsel for Prussia in the proceedings.

[39] Wertheimer, "The Lausanne Reparation Settlement," cited.

[40] *Cf. Stone,* "The World Disarmament Conference: Second Stage," cited.

While the poll on November 6 did not serve to break the parliamentary deadlock, it reflected two major shifts in German public sentiment: the Nazis lost 34 seats, and the Communists gained 11. At the same time, the Nationalists regained 14 mandates, apparently at Hitler's expense. The terror which obtained immediately after the July 31 elections and Hitler's defense of the Storm Troopers convicted in the Beuthen murder case had evidently frightened and alienated many of the Nazi leader's former supporters. Furthermore, Hitler's refusal to accept the proffered post of Reich Vice-Chancellor on August 13, 1932[41] and his subsequent critical remarks about President von Hindenburg had made a bad impression. Finally, there had been considerable dissatisfaction among the younger and more radical Hitler followers, who were impatient with his "legal tactics." Recognizing that some of their relatively moderate bourgeois supporters were returning to the government camp and hoping to prevent further defections among the younger radicals, the Nazis had appealed primarily to the workers during the campaign. A transit strike in Berlin on the election day week-end, put through under combined Nazi and Communist leadership, was an example of their tactics.

Despite the election agitation of the Hitlerites, however, the Nazi losses on November 6 do not seem to have accrued to the Communists. On the contrary, the latter's gain of 11 seats was apparently made at the expense of the Social Democrats who lost 12 mandates. Beside the changes in the Nazi, Social Democratic and Communist camps, the No-

[41] *Cf.* p. 176.

vember 6 election showed a continued shrinkage in the representation of the smaller parties.[42]

The election had shown conclusively that the great majority of the German people were opposed to the Papen government; the feeling against the Ministry and in particular against the Chancellor was unmistakable. As a result, von Papen felt it necessary after the election to state that the way was now clear for the formation of a "real government of national concentration," and that for his part the question of personalities would not be allowed to block such development. President von Hindenburg on November 10, therefore, charged von Papen to sound out the various party leaders with a view to ascertaining which groups were ready to support the government's political and economic program. These conversations brought out the fact that only the Hugenberg Nationalists and the People's party were willing to back von Papen; the Catholic parties withheld their support, while the Social Democrats refused even to negotiate. The Nazis, however, declared themselves willing, under certain circumstances, to engage in written negotiations with the Chancellor. Realizing the hopelessness of its position, the Papen Cabinet resigned on November 17.

The Schleicher Government

President von Hindenburg thereupon took over the task of setting up a government. On November 19 the President received Adolf Hitler, who assured him that he could form a government acceptable to the Reichstag. On November 21, at a

[42] *Cf.* table, p. 192 for results of July 31 and November 6 elections.

second meeting, von Hindenburg charged Hitler, "as the leader of the largest German party," to determine whether and under what conditions he could be sure of a "secure, positive majority for a strong, unified program." On the same day the President laid down in writing several conditions which he considered a *sine qua non* for the formation of such a Ministry. These included the formulation of a workable economic program, no attempt to return to the former dual relationship between the Reich and Prussia, and no tampering with Article 48 of the Constitution. Furthermore, in the matter of personnel, the President insisted that he must have the final decision regarding the list of Ministers, and reserved the right to appoint the Foreign Minister and the Minister of Defense as consistent with his legal position as head of the Reich and Commander-in-Chief of the army. Following this communication, there was a further exchange of letters between Hitler and the President's Secretary of State, Dr. Meissner, regarding the definition of presidial government, in which it was stated that von Hindenburg could not appoint as Chancellor, in a government responsible to the President alone, the leader of a party which demanded sole power for itself. Despite this statement, Hitler wrote von Hindenburg on November 23 requesting the latter to commission him to form a presidial Ministry with full powers. The President flatly refused this demand on November 24, stating that he could not reconcile it with his oath of office or his conscience.[43] A second direct attempt to bring

[43] Text of the Hindenburg-Hitler exchange of notes in *Frankfurter Zeitung*, November 25, 1932; *cf.* also *ibid.*, November 12 to 24, 1932; *Der Zeitspiegel*, 1st year, No. 23, December 3, 1932.

the Nazis into the government had failed; Hitler still insisted on "all power or nothing."

After thus rebuffing Hitler, President von Hindenburg on December 2 named General von Schleicher Chancellor, although the old Field Marshal had apparently endeavored to reappoint von Papen in whom he still had the highest confidence. It is reported that the declaration of several important Ministers [44] that they would not serve in a new Papen Cabinet, added to von Papen's earnest request to the President to release him from responsibility, finally forced von Hindenburg to appoint von Schleicher.

The new presidial Cabinet, as finally constituted, had the following membership: [45]

Chancellor, Minister of Defense, and Reich Commissioner for Prussia, General von Schleicher;
Interior, Dr. Bracht;
Labor, Dr. Syrup;
Foreign Affairs, Baron von Neurath;
Finance, Count Schwerin von Krosigk;
Justice, Dr. Gürtner;
Posts, Baron von Eltz-Rübenach;
Reëmployment, Dr. Gereke;
Agriculture, Baron von Braun;
Commerce, Professor Warmbold;
Without Portfolio, Dr. Popitz.

The composition of the new government showed that consideration had been given to the factors

---

[44] The Ministers were: Baron von Neurath, Foreign Minister; Dr. Bracht, deputy Reich Commissioner for Prussia and member of the Reich government without portfolio; the Finance Minister, Count von Krosigk; and Dr. Popitz, a financial expert and also Minister without portfolio. *Cf. Der Zeitspiegel,* 1st year, No. 24, December 17, 1932; *Frankfurter Zeitung,* November 29 to December 3, 1932; also *Der deutsche Volkswirt,* December 9, 1932.

[45] *Frankfurter Zeitung,* December 4, 5, 1932.

which had discredited von Papen's régime; namely, its outspoken anti-labor tendencies, which had resulted in many strikes and contributed to the increase in the Communist vote; the introduction of agricultural import contingents designed to benefit the bankrupt East Elbian landowners, which jeopardized Germany's already precarious foreign trade with the threat of serious retaliation; and the government's attempts to establish a strongly centralized state and to reform the constitution, which aroused animosity throughout South Germany and Prussia. The von Schleicher Cabinet attempted to remedy the situation by appointing a Minister of Labor more sympathetic to the workers; dropping the system of import contingents; and replacing the former Minister of the Interior, Baron von Gayl, with a man less conspicuously associated with schemes for constitutional reform.

Von Schleicher was reputed to be more conciliatory than his predecessor and slightly more acceptable to labor. The Ministerial Declaration of the new government, announced in a radio speech by the Chancellor on December 15, bore out this prediction. In this statement the new government's policy was summarized in one outstanding point: creation of work.

For the rest, von Schleicher both by omission and commission, attempted to allay the fears of the German people. He declared himself opposed to a military dictatorship, saying that one cannot "sit comfortably on bayonet points"; expressed himself in favor of increased settlement of unemployed on the land; and stated that he was neither a "capitalist nor a socialist." The Ministerial Declaration, moreover, contained nothing in regard to "authoritative government," there was no mention of "abolishing the state as a charity organization," and no word about reforming the constitution or the "divine and historical misson" of the government.[46]

As an earnest of its conciliatory intentions, the government indicated to the trade unions immediately upon taking office that it would not be unwilling to renounce the blanket powers for revision of the social insurances which had formed a part of von Papen's September 5 emergency decree.[47] The Reichstag, which met from December 6 to 9, repealed this section of the decree and reinstituted the system of wage agreements.[48]

During the first month after von Schleicher assumed office, there was apparent a noticeable relaxation throughout Germany. Political passions appeared to have somewhat subsided; there were a few visible signs of improvement in the economic situation; the year-end summaries of conditions were relatively optimistic; [49] the German people seemed to yearn for peace and stability after the financial and political crises of the past two years.

[46] Text of Ministerial Declaration in *Hamburger Fremdenblatt*, December 16, 1932.

[47] *Cf.* p. 178.

[48] *Der deutsche Volkswirt*, December 16, 1932.

[49] *Cf. Der deutsche Volkswirt*, December 23, 1932; *Frankfurter Zeitung*, December 31, 1932; *Berliner Handelsgesellschaft*, confidential reports, Berlin, December 23, 30, 1932; Deutsche Bank und Disconto Gesellschaft, *Wirtschaftliche Mitteilungen*, January 14, 1933; *Vierteljahreshefte zur Konjunkturforschung*, Hrsg. vom Institut für Konjunkturforschung, 7th year, Heft 3, Berlin, December 1932, Parts A and B. Cf. also an important work, J. W. Wheeler-Bennett, *Wooden Titan: Hindenburg in Twenty Years of German History, 1914-1934* (New York, Morrow, 1936).

CHAPTER IV

THE NATIONAL REVOLUTION

SUDDENLY, on January 28, 1933, the Schleicher government resigned when President von Hindenburg refused it power to dissolve a hostile Reichstag. On January 30 a new Cabinet took office, with Hitler as Chancellor and von Papen as Vice-Chancellor and Reich Commissioner for Prussia.

Von Schleicher's endeavors to gain the confidence of both Right and Left had been unsuccessful. He had not only failed to induce the Nazis to accept governmental responsibilities, but his flirtation with the trade unions—although it strengthened his position to a certain extent—completely alienated the big industrialists and the Junkers. The Schleicher government, therefore, would have faced the Reichstag without the support of a single party. The President's refusal to retain von Schleicher might appear to have been a logical step toward reintroduction of parliamentary government.

For some weeks backstage negotiations between industrialists and Nazis had been in progress to induce Hitler to depart from his uncompromising position of "all power or nothing." The reported indebtedness of the National Socialist party to its industrialist friends, estimated at some twelve million marks, was probably a factor in the situation. Moreover, the large East Elbian landed interests had found it increasingly difficult to extract concessions from the Schleicher government, and the discovery by a Reichstag committee of financial graft in the administration of the *Osthilfe* fund [1] added to the Junkers' grievances against von Schleicher. News had leaked out of a meeting in Cologne, January 4 between Hitler and von Papen, at which a government of "national concentration" was admittedly discussed, although the participants flatly denied that they were trying to undermine von Schleicher's position. Von Papen's easy access to President von Hindenburg undoubtedly made it possible for him to persuade the aged Field Marshal of the necessity for a change of government, and to convince him of Hitler's qualifications.

His efforts evidently met with complete success: not only was von Schleicher forced out, but the new government represented the most conservative elements in the Reich. The Cabinet, in addition to Hitler and Papen, was composed as follows:

> Hermann Goering (Nazi), Aviation and Acting Prussian Minister of the Interior
> Wilhelm Frick (Nazi), Interior
> Alfred Hugenberg (Nationalist), Agriculture and Commerce
> Franz Seldte (Nationalist), Labor
> General von Blomberg, Defense
> Count von Eltz-Rübenach, Posts and Communications
> Dr. Gereke, Commissioner for Reëmployment
> Baron von Neurath, Foreign Affairs
> Count Schwerin von Krosigk, Finance

The outstanding feature of the Cabinet was its balance of Nazi and Nationalist Ministers, although

[1] The money appropriated to assist bankrupt eastern agriculturists at Reich expense. *Cf. Der deutsche Volkswirt*, January 27, 1933.

the non-party Ministers were known to be close to the Nationalist party.

Since the new government could count definitely on only 247 votes in the Reichstag, and, even with the aid of the smaller Right groups, lacked a majority by a margin of at least 25 votes, the support or toleration of the Catholic parties was indispensable. Negotiations between Hitler and Monsignor Kaas, the Centrist leader, were initiated on January 31. The next day, the Center party addressed a series of questions to Hitler to ascertain the government's intentions regarding observance of the constitution; assistance to industry; possible reactionary social measures; and sound currency. Without replying to these inquiries, Hitler suddenly broke off negotiations and on February 1 the government announced the dissolution of the Reichstag, with new elections on March 5. Elections for the Prussian Diet—which was summarily dissolved on February 6 after President von Hindenburg had appointed von Papen head of the state government, apparently in direct violation of the constitutional principles defined by the Reich Supreme Court on October 25 [2]—were also scheduled for March 5.

Hitler's accession to power on January 30, 1933, as Chancellor of Germany marked the beginning of the so-called National Revolution. Despite the fact that the new government was supposedly a coalition of Hitlerites and Nationalists, containing only three Nazi Ministers, it soon became apparent that the latter were the driving force in the Cabinet. Backed by a party organization which covered every phase of German life and in reality constituted a

[2] *Cf.* p. 180.

state within a state,[3] and uninhibited by scruples of any sort, the Nazis were able to dominate the government completely and put through the revolution. Their task was facilitated not only by Hitler's Chancellorship but also by the fact that his lieutenants, Frick and Goering, were respectively Reich and Prussian Ministers of the Interior, and thus controlled the police in the entire country. Furthermore, the non-Nazi members of the Hitler government were apparently willing that the major share of the election campaign preparatory to the March 5 Reichstag poll should be carried on by the Nazis, who were universally recognized as excelling in propaganda of this sort. The Nationalists hoped thus to consolidate their own position and ride to power, as it were, on the shoulders of the Hitlerites.

The campaign as directed by the Nazis was used to stir up an immense Communist scare in the Reich, culminating in the burning of the Reichstag building on the night of February 27 by alleged Communists. This incident gave the Nazis an opportunity to effect complete suppression of Socialist and Communist election meetings and press, to arrest the Communist leaders, to institute a drastic censorship, and to abolish all forms of personal liberty in general. A decree proclaimed by President von Hindenburg on February 28, 1933, rescinded until further notice all the articles of the Weimar constitution providing for liberty of the person; freedom of opinion, including freedom of the press; right of assembly; secrecy of postal, telegraphic and telephonic communication; inviolability of dwellings; and sanctity of private property. Furthermore, under this decree the Reich government was given

[3] *Cf.* p. 155.

the right to enforce its provisions in the federal
states, and the penalties for infraction were made
very severe. The death sentence, life or long imprisonment were specified for particular crimes including high treason, poisoning, arson, conspiracy
against the life of the Reich President, the members
of the Reich government or Reich Commissioners.
The execution of the decree was placed entirely in
the hands of the police, with no appeal.[4] As a result
of this decree and of Nazi terrorism, the opposition
was prevented from carrying on its campaign. The
actual election, however, apparently took place without incident, although the atmosphere throughout
the Reich was tense in the extreme. The following
table gives the results of the voting on March 5,

Parties	Mar. 5, 1933 Seats	Nov. 6, 1932 Seats	July 31, 1932 Seats	Sept. 14, 1930 Seats
National Socialist	288	196	230	107
German National People's *	52	51	37	41
German People's.	2	11	7	30
Economic	...	1	2	23
Other Parties ...	7	12	9	55
Catholic Center .	74	70	75	68
Bavarian People's	18	20	22	19
State	5	2	4	14
Social Democratic	120	121	133	143
Communist	81	100	89	77
Totals	647	584	608	577

* The German National People's party fought the March 1933
election under the designation *Schwarz-Weiss-Rote-Front*—Black-
White-Red Front.

[4] For English text of the decree, *cf.* J. K. Pollock and H. J.
Heneman, *The Hitler Decrees* (Ann Arbor, George Wahr, 1934),
p. 10. German texts in Werner Hoche, *Die Gesetzgebung des
Kabinetts Hitler: Die Gesetze in Reich und Preussen seit dem
30 Januar 1933*, vol. I, p. 236 *et seq.; Reichsgesetzblatt I*, p. 83
(1933). The articles of the Constitution which have been
rescinded are: 114, 115, 117, 118, 123, 124 and 153. For texts of
the articles, *cf.* p. 259 *et seq.*

as well as the returns in the three previous elections, thus presenting a complete picture of the rise of the Nazis.[5]

THE BROWN TERROR

Thus the Nazis, with 44 per cent of the total vote, and their Nationalist colleagues in the government, who polled 8 per cent, achieved a working majority of the German electorate on March 5. The so-called National Revolution must be characterized, however, as the consolidation of complete Nazi control of the Reich.

Following the example of Soviet Russia and Fascist Italy, the accession of the Nazis to power—known as the "National Revolution"—was accompanied by a reign of terror. Responsible Ministers in the Hitler Cabinet repeatedly stated that no revolution was ever consummated with less bloodshed. This contention may be accurate, since the Nazis came to power originally by constitutional means and not by an actual coup d'état; nevertheless, the consolidation of their rule, after the manner of most revolutions, was accomplished by suppressing constitutional guarantees and by systematic action against persons whom the Nazis considered enemies of the "new Germany," including all "Marxists," such as Communists and Socialists; all "internationalists," including liberals and pacifists; and all Jews. More recently Catholics and even Nationalists have not been exempted.[6]

As early as February 24, Nazi Storm Troopers and

[5] *Der Zeitspiegel,* March 19, 1933; *Der Heimatdienst,* Jahrgang XII, No. 16, August 2, 1932; *Frankfurter Zeitung,* August 16, 1932; *Reichstagshandbuch V. Wahlperiode, 1930,* Hrsg. vom Bureau des Reichstags (Berlin, Reichsdruckerei, 1930).

[6] *Cf.* p. 226.

some members of the Steel Helmet veterans' organization had been inducted into the police as auxiliaries[7] and the control of law and order throughout the Reich was therefore virtually in the hands of the Nazis. Even before the election on March 5, many terrorist acts had been perpetrated by Nazis. A well-informed foreign observer stated on March 1: "The last few weeks have looked very much like a cold-blooded, long-drawn-out, diluted St. Bartholomew's Eve."[8] The election itself passed off without disturbances, but in the succeeding weeks more and more acts of violence by uniformed Nazi Storm Troopers against Jews and "Marxists" were reported abroad. In the Reich the Nationalist *Deutsche Allgemeine Zeitung* ventured to say on March 13:

"Certain sections of the population in the large towns have been in a state of panic and terror. . . . Whoever is guilty today of breaking into houses, of kidnapping, of threats, or of any other crimes and offenses punishable by law must immediately be handed over to the police.

"The houses where 'political prisoners' are supposed to have been locked up by private individuals must, if the police do not know of them already, be immediately indicated to the police authorities. . . . Private revenge in blood must no longer be taken."[9]

The occasion for this statement in the *Deutsche Allgemeine Zeitung* was an appeal issued by Hitler

[7] *The Times* (London), February 25, 1933.

[8] *Ibid.*, March 2, 1933.

[9] *Deutsche Allgemeine Zeitung,* March 13, 1933. This paper, supported by the heavy industries, was eventually banned on May 30 for three months; but was permitted to re-appear on June 16 after the editor, Dr. Fritz Klein, had been forced to resign. *Cf. New York Times,* June 17, 1933; *The Times* (London), March 14, 1933; and *Manchester Guardian Weekly,* March 17, 1933.

on March 10 to his followers to refrain from molesting individuals and disturbing business. On the same day Captain Goering [10] declared, in a speech rejecting the idea of using the police to protect Jewish stores: "We have been saying to the people for years that they might settle accounts with the traitors. We stand by our word: accounts are being settled." [11] Hitler's command to the Storm Troopers to cease acts of political terror, however, was broadcast over the government radio on March 12.[12] It was immediately stated in Berlin that the Storm Troops had been restrained by Hitler's action, although reports of outrages against Jews and "Marxists" continued. The government attempted to convince the world that such terrorization as had occurred was perpetrated by "Communist impostors clad in Nazi uniform." In many statements government officials denied even the existence of a terror,[13] despite the virtual admission contained in Hitler's order to the Storm Troops and the fully authenticated accounts sent out by all responsible foreign journalists. In response to strong American protests. Secretary of State Hull asked the American diplomatic and consular agents in Germany for a full report and, in an official statement issued on March 26, declared that "a reply has now been received indicating that whereas there was for a short time considerable mistreatment of Jews, this phase may be considered virtually terminated.

[10] At that time Deputy Minister of the Interior for Prussia, Federal Commissioner of Aviation and Minister without Portfolio in the Reich Cabinet. On April 11 Hitler appointed Goering to the post of Prussian Premier responsible only to the Regent (*Staathalter*) for Prussia, a post held by Hitler.

[11] *The Times* (London), March 13, 1933.

[12] *New York Times*, March 13, 1933.

[13] *The Times* (London), March 27, 1933.

There was some picketing of Jewish merchandising stores and instances of professional discrimination. These manifestations were viewed with serious concern by the German government." [14]

Reports of terrorization and further "preventive arrests" continued, the Nazis having set up concentration camps for political prisoners before the end of March.[15] Goering's promised action against the Jews apparently made a deeper impression at home and abroad than Hitler's appeals to his Storm Troopers. Large meetings protesting Nazi persecution of the Jews were held in the United States and elsewhere, at which both Jewish and non-Jewish leaders voiced their condemnation of Nazi actions. Within the Reich, the Nazis retaliated by using German Jews as hostages to force the cessation of anti-Nazi protests abroad. On March 27, it was officially announced that the "National Socialist movement will now take the most drastic legal counter-measures aimed against the intellectual authors and exploiters of this treasonable agitation which is mainly conducted abroad by Jews formerly resident in Germany." The same official statement announced the formation of Nazi "Committees of Action" to take measures against atrocity reports abroad by organizing a boycott of Jewish business men in Germany, and forecast the introduction of a *numerus clausus* for Jewish doctors and lawyers.[16]

The Jewish Boycott

National Socialist party headquarters issued a manifesto on the night of March 28, proclaiming a

---

[14] Department of State, *Press Releases*, April 1, 1933.
[15] *The Times* (London), March 25, 1933.
[16] *Frankfurter Zeitung,* March 28, 1933.

national boycott of Jewish goods and Jews in the professions to start on April 1, as a counter-action to the "lies and defamations of absolutely shocking perversity which have been let loose about Germany." This official declaration stated categorically that "Communist and Marxist criminals and their Jewish-intellectual instigators, who managed in good time to escape abroad with their money, are now conducting a conscienceless, treasonable propaganda campaign against the German people . . . from the capitals of the former Entente countries." [17] The manifesto was accompanied by an official order organizing the boycott as follows: [18]

(1) "In every local branch and unit of the N.S.D.A.P.,[19] Committees of Action must be appointed immediately to carry out a systematically planned boycott of Jewish businesses, Jewish doctors and Jewish lawyers . . .

(2) "The Committees of Action are responsible for the most careful protection of all foreigners without regard to confession, origin or race. The boycott is a purely defensive measure which is directed solely against German Jewry.

(3) "The Committees of Action must immediately popularize the boycott by propaganda and enlightenment. Its keynote is that no German shall buy from a Jew. . . . The boycott must be all inclusive. It shall be undertaken by the whole people and must strike Jewry in its most sensitive spot.

(4) "In doubtful cases, boycotting of the concerns in question may be dispensed with until the Central Committee in Munich can make a definite decision.

---

[17] *Ibid.*, March 29, 1933.

[18] Translated from the *Frankfurter Zeitung,* March 29, 1933.

[19] *National Sozialistische Deutsche Arbeiter Partei* (National Socialist German Workers' party).

Party Comrade Streicher [20] is appointed chairman of the boycott committee.

(5) "The Committees of Action must watch the newspapers closely and observe how strongly they participate in the campaign of enlightenment of the German people against Jewish atrocity agitation abroad. Papers which do not participate or do so only to a limited extent are to be immediately removed from every German home. No German and no German business shall give advertising to such papers. They must be ruined by public contempt and may be written only for their Jewish racial comrades but not for the German people.

(6) "The Committees of Action in cooperation with the Work Cells organization of the party, must carry enlightenment into the factories as to the consequences of the Jewish atrocity agitation to German work and therefore to German workers. In particular, the workers must be enlightened as to the necessity for a national boycott as a defensive measure to protect German work.

(7) "The Committees of Action must penetrate into the smallest villages in order particularly to strike at Jewish traders in the country. It must always be explained that this action has been forced upon us as a defensive measure.

(8) "The boycott is not to start in a scattered fashion but must begin at one stroke and all preparations are now to be toward this end. Orders will be issued to the Storm Troops to stand guard, beginning the

[20] Julius Streicher had been a school teacher in Nuremberg. In 1920 he became known as an agitator for a small group calling itself "German Socialists" and strongly agrarian in sympathy. He was particularly notorious as an anti-Semite and as publisher of *Der Stürmer,* a sheet with a large circulation devoted primarily to so-called Jewish scandals, treated in a fashion bordering on the pornographic. Streicher in the earlier years of the so-called *Voelkische* movement in Germany was a bitter enemy of Hitler, always striving to attain leadership in the movement. *Cf.* Konrad Heiden, *Geschichte des Nationalsozialismus* (Berlin, Rowohlt. 1932), pp. 29, 53–55, 122, 178.

second at which the boycott starts, in order to warn the people from entering Jewish businesses. The start of the boycott will be announced by placards, by the press, by handbills, etc. The boycott will begin at one stroke on Saturday, April 1, at 10 A.M. sharp. It will continue until an order of the party executive decrees its end.

(9) "The Committees of Action shall immediately organize tens of thousands of mass meetings which shall reach into the tiniest hamlets and which shall demand the introduction of a quota system for Jews in all professions. . . . In order to intensify the effect of this action, these demands shall be confined for the present to the following three categories: (a) Attendance at German middle and higher schools (colleges); (b) Doctors; and (c) Lawyers.

(10) "The Committees of Action have the further task of seeing to it that every German who has any connections whatsoever in foreign countries shall make use of them to spread the truth in letters, telegrams and telephone messages: that peace and order prevail in Germany, that the German people has no more ardent wish than to live in peace with the rest of the world and that it is conducting its struggle against Jewish atrocity agitation as a purely defensive battle.

(11) "The Committees of Action are responsible that the entire struggle be conducted in complete peace and strictest discipline. Not a hair on any Jewish head shall be touched. We will cope with this agitation only by means of the decisive pressure of these measures."

As a result of this order, individuals and organizations in the United States and abroad having contacts with Germans were flooded with denials of the existence of a terror in the Reich and assured that German Jews could and did go about their affairs as usual. Nevertheless, foreign protests and reports of atrocities did not cease. The Hitler government, through the medium of the strictly censored German press, announced on March 31, that the "foreign atrocity agitation" was waning and therefore the boycott would be put into effect for one day only—April 1. It threatened to resume the boycott on April 5, if by that date the "foreign agitation" had not entirely ceased.[21]

Thus the boycott, originally proclaimed by the National Socialist party as distinct from the Hitler government, was actually carried out by the latter. On April 1, all Jewish concerns, with the exception of banks and newspapers, were placed under guard by Storm Troopers from ten o'clock in the morning until midnight. The Storm Troopers not only tried to keep out the few who attempted to enter boycotted establishments, but pasted up signs announcing that "no German buys from Jews," smeared windows with the word "Jew" in large red or white letters, and similarly decorated the name plates of doctors and attorneys. In Berlin the regular police were apparently inactive, and "groups of Nazis with heavy, weighted riding-crops strode about . . ." [22] Besides boycotting Jewish places of business, Storm Troop pickets kept Jewish judges, lawyers and jurymen out of the courthouses, admittance to the grounds of the University of Berlin was denied to Jewish students, and the Prussian State Library refused to admit Jewish readers.[23]

While the Jewish boycott was a strictly official matter, the terror which existed in the Reich during March was apparently due in large part to individual actions by Storm Troopers. This is evident from the contradictory statements made during March by

[21] *Frankfurter Zeitung,* April 1, 1933.
[22] *The Times* (London), April 2, 1933.
[23] *New York Times,* April 2, 1933.

Hitler in attempting to restrain his private army, and by Goering who, while exhorting the Storm Troopers to preserve discipline, openly incited them to fresh violence against the Jews. In the early stages of the Revolution, the Storm Troopers were kept busy for a time hoisting the red, black and white Imperial flag and the Nazi swastika on all public buildings in place of the black, red and gold Republican colors.[24] This relatively harmless task did not satisfy the Storm Troopers, whose leaders had promised them for a decade that once Hitler came to power they could revenge themselves on all their enemies, particularly the Jews. Thus the anti-Jewish boycott was an earnest of the government's intentions to put into effect the Nazi program, of which anti-Semitism forms such an important part,[25] and also provided an occupation for the Storm Troops. The Nazis, in consolidating their power, had met with little or no opposition. Their opponents collapsing like a house of cards, the Nazis found themselves within a short time in complete control, and concentrated much of their fury and surplus energy on the Jews—who offered a convenient scapegoat. By placing the responsibility for spreading so-called atrocity stories on the Jews, the Nazis hoped to convince the German people that the reports of excesses perpetrated by Storm Troopers were false, and thus to clear themselves. By making German Jews hostages for the "good behavior" of the world, the Nazis apparently expected to control public opinion abroad as they controlled it within the Reich.

[24] The flag was officially changed on March 12 by a decree of President von Hindenburg. *New York Times,* March 13, 1933.
[25] *Cf.* pp. 140–144.

Revolution or Staatsstreich?

Although Hitler's consolidation of power was generally called a revolution by the Nazis themselves, some doubt may be expressed of the technical accuracy of the term as applied to German developments during the early months of 1933. Furthermore, while the Nazi leaders on the one hand protested that never in history had so bloodless a revolution been achieved, they strove, on the other hand, to give the impression that this revolution had been carried out by constitutional methods—obviously a contradiction in terms. Hitler, moreover, on taking office on January 30, 1933, had solemnly sworn to uphold the constitution and defend the law and, since the Nazis laid great stress on the so-called "old German virtue" of fidelity, the bad psychological impression involved in a purported breach of his oath was doubtless a factor in the situation.

It would probably be more accurate to term the establishment of the Third Reich a *Staatsstreich,* or coup d'état. The Nazis did not achieve power by fighting as in an out-and-out revolution, but instead Hitler took office in a constitutional manner. Once in control of the government, however, the Nazis consolidated their power and set up the Third Reich by effecting changes which appear to have been in violation of existing constitutional law. The principal instrument under which these changes were made was the Enabling Act, and the question of the authority of the rump Reichstag which accepted that Act is therefore of importance. This question, however, was never settled by recourse to a competent court.

THE ENABLING ACT

The Reichstag elected on March 5, 1933, held a solemn opening session on March 21, at the Garrison Church in Potsdam, which was marked by a ceremony at the tomb of Frederick the Great, participated in by President von Hindenburg and Chancellor Hitler. The Potsdam meeting was followed by an organization session in Berlin on the afternoon of the same day, when Minister Goering was reëlected President of the Reichstag. On March 23, the parliament assembled once more and listened to a speech by Chancellor Hitler in which he outlined the policy of the government and introduced an Enabling Act which was promptly passed by a vote of 441 to 94, only the Social Democrats opposing the bill.

The Enabling Act, officially entitled "Law to Combat the Misery of People and Reich," went into force on March 24, 1933. It concentrated practically complete power in the hands of the Reich government through the following provisions:

"The Reichstag has enacted the following law which, with the consent of the Reichsrat[26] and after determining that the requirement for laws changing the constitution have been complied with, is hereby promulgated:

ARTICLE 1

"National laws can be enacted by the Reich cabinet as well as in accordance with the procedure established in the constitution. This applies also to the laws referred to in article 85, paragraph 2,[27] and in article 87[28] of the constitution.

[26] The Reichsrat met immediately after the adjournment of the Reichstag session and adopted the Enabling Act on the same day, March 23, 1933. Medicus, "Programm der Reichsregierung und Ermächtigungsgesetz," cited, p. 14.

[27] *Cf.* p. 272.

[28] *Ibid.*

ARTICLE 2

"The Reich laws enacted by the Reich cabinet may deviate from the constitution in so far as they do not affect the position of the Reichstag and the Reichsrat. The powers of the President remain undisturbed.

ARTICLE 3

"The Reich laws enacted by the Reich cabinet are prepared by the Chancellor and published in the *Reichsgesetzblatt*. They come into effect, unless otherwise specified, upon the day following their publication. Articles 68 to 77[29] of the constitution do not apply to the laws promulgated by the Reich government.

ARTICLE 4

"Treaties of the Reich with foreign states which concern matters of national legislation do not require the consent of the bodies participating in legislation. The Reich cabinet is empowered to issue the necessary provisions for the execution of these treaties.

ARTICLE 5

"This law becomes effective on the day of its publication. It becomes invalid on April 1, 1937; it further becomes invalid when the present Reich cabinet is replaced by another.[30]

"Berlin, March 24, 1933.

> The Reich President
> von Hindenburg
> The Reich Chancellor
> Adolf Hitler
> The Reich Minister of the Interior
> Frick
> The Reich Minister of Foreign Affairs
> Freiherr von Neurath
> The Reich Minister of Finance
> Graf Schwerin von Krosigk"[31]

[29] For text of these articles, *cf.* pp. 269-274. Article 77 was not abolished.

[30] The following analysis of the Enabling Act is based on the official commentary published in *Das Recht der nationalen Revolution* No. 1, Medicus, "Programm der Reichsregierung und Ermächtigungsgesetz," cited.

[31] English text in J. K. Pollock and H. J. Heneman, *The Hitler Decrees* (Ann Arbor, George Wahr, 1934). German texts: Medicus, "Programm der Reichsregierung und Ermächtigungsgesetze," cited; *Die Gesetzgebung des Kabinetts Hitler: Die Gesetze in Reich und Preussen seit dem 30 Januar 1933,* Hrsg. von Dr. Werner Hoche, Vol. 1 (Berlin, Vahlen Verlag, 1933), p. 23 *et seq.; Reichsgesetzblatt,* I (1933), p. 141.

With the aid of this law the cabinet carried through a rapid transformation of the Reich's governmental machinery. Germany became a completely unified and centralized state, offering a great contrast to the federal character of the old Empire and the Republic. A law promulgated on March 31, 1933[32] empowered state cabinets to enact state laws in the same manner as the Reich government acting under the terms of the Enabling Act. It also dissolved state and other local legislatures and diets—with the exception of the Prussian Diet which was elected on March 5, 1933—and reconstituted them "according to the number of votes, which, in the election to the German Reichstag on March 5, 1933, were cast within each state for each party list." No seats were apportioned to the Communists. A second law promulgated on April 7, 1933 placed the states under the control of governors appointed by Hitler,[33] thus eliminating all possibility of political opposition or even of individual policy on the part of a state government. The dissolution of the Reichstag on October 14, 1933 was accompanied by dissolution of all state diets, but since no new elections were decreed for the state legislatures, these automatically passed out of existence. A law promptly voted by the Reichstag and Reichsrat on January 30, 1934 formally abolished the popular representations of the states, transferred the sovereign rights of the states to the Reich and completely subordinated their governments to Berlin.[34] German "federalism" had ceased to be. The German states had become little more than administrative units ruled by the *Statthalter* as agents of the central government.

[32] *Reichsgesetzblatt,* Part I, 1933, p. 153.
[33] *Ibid.,* p. 173, 225, 293.
[34] *Ibid.,* Part I, 1934, p. 75.

REFORM OF THE CIVIL SERVICE

In considering the rapidity with which the Hitler régime was able to transform the Reich into a totalitarian state, one important factor must not be overlooked: the civil service. In the 1918 Revolution, the victorious Republican forces had never undertaken a thorough weeding-out of the reactionary elements from the civil service,[35] an omission which seriously weakened the Republic from its inception. The Nazis, however, made no such mistake. One of the first important measures promulgated by the Hitler government under the terms of the Enabling Act was a law for the restoration of the civil service, which formed the basis for most of the subsequent restrictive action of the Nazis against the Jews, liberals, pacifists, Socialists, Communists and others regarded by the Hitlerites as "enemies of the state."

The Civil Service Law was promulgated on April 7, 1933, and went into force on the following day.[36] The Ministers of Finance and the Interior subsequently issued several decrees designed to carry out the law and defining its provisions exactly.[37] The law

[35] *Cf.* p. 131.

[36] *Gesetz zur Wiederherstellung des Berufsbeamtentums.* This law was promulgated directly by the Reich government under the authority of the Enabling Act of March 24, 1933, which vested full legislative power in that government for a period of four years. Published on April 7, 1933, in the *Reichsgesetzblatt*, I, p. 175.

[37] The following summary of the provisions of the Civil Service Law, and excerpts from the official commentary on it are taken from Hanns Seel, "Erneuerung des Berufsbeamtentums," no. IV in *Das Recht der nationalen Revolution* (Schriftenreihe Hrsg. von Dr. Georg Kaisenberg und Dr. Franz Albrecht Medicus; Berlin, Carl Heymanns Verlag, 1933). This series on the law of the National Revolution is the official publication concerning the new laws, etc., promulgated by the Hitler government. The amplifying decrees are dated April 11, 1933 (*Reichsgesetzblatt*, I,

and the supplementary decrees, were applied, even when they conflicted with previously existing laws, to all officials of the Reich, the states and the municipalities, including not only the regular civil servants but also employees in semi-public enterprises and undertakings in which the government had a 50 per cent or larger financial interest. It applied as well to employees in the social services having the rights and duties of officials, while the Reichsbank and the German Railway Company were empowered to enforce its provisions. Furthermore, the following persons were included in the German civil service: judges; all court officials; notaries; teachers in schools, including teachers and instructors in scientific universities (*Hochschulen*); all professors; officials of the old and new army (*Wehrmacht*); members of the police forces of the states, not including officers, army doctors or veterinarians; elected municipal officials; and office employees and workers in public enterprises.[38]

RESTRICTIONS IMPOSED BY CIVIL SERVICE LAW

The Civil Service Law provided that "officials who are of non-Aryan descent must be retired; in so far as concerns honorary officials, the latter must be dismissed from their positions." A "non-Aryan" was then defined as "a person descended from non-Aryan, particularly Jewish, parents or grandparents.[39] It suffices if one parent or grandparent is

p. 195); May 4, 1933 (*ibid.*, I, p. 233); May 6, 1933 (*ibid.*, I, p. 245).

[38] *Frankfurter Zeitung*, June 30, 1933.

[39] In the decree of April 11, 1933. A decree of September 16 provides that any official can be regarded as "non-Aryan" whose great-grandfather belonged to the Jewish faith, even if he were baptized in the Christian church. *New York Times*, September 17, 1933.

a non-Aryan. This applies especially if one parent or grandparent has professed the Jewish religion." Every official was required to fill out a detailed questionnaire giving information as to the names, professions, addresses, places and dates of birth, religion, and places and dates of death and marriage of himself, his wife, and their respective parents and grandparents. Proof had to be offered by presentation of such documents as birth and marriage certificates of parents or military papers. If Aryan descent was questionable, a ruling must be secured from the "expert on racial research" attached to the Ministry of the Interior. Moreover, if the official was an Aryan married to a "non-Aryan," he rated as "non-Aryan" himself and was dismissed.[40] All officials whose Aryan antecedents were in doubt had to swear to the following statement:

"I herewith testify on oath that: despite careful examination, no circumstances are known to me which could justify the supposition that I am not of Aryan descent or that one of my parents or grandparents at any time professed the Jewish religion. I am aware that I am liable to legal prosecution and dismissal from service if this declaration does not contain the truth."[41]

The "Aryan paragraph" of the Civil Service Law contained provisions exempting certain "non-Aryan" officials from dismissal. Thus the law did not apply to persons "who held office on or before August 1, 1914, or who fought in the World War at the front for the German Reich or its allies, or whose fathers or sons fell in the war." Army service during the war was defined as

[40] *Frankfurter Zeitung*, July 4, 1933.
[41] *Reichsbesoldungsblatt*, Reichsfinanzministerium, June 12, 1933, p. 31.

"participation with a fighting troop in a battle, a fight, a struggle for position or a siege. It does not suffice if the military service during the war was performed without having actually met the enemy, if, for instance, the person was merely in the war zone on official business or in the service at home or behind the lines. The promotion lists (*Rangliste*) and war service records (*Kriegsstammrollen*) are the only valid documentary proofs in determining whether the individual in question was actually a front-line soldier. A person possessing a wound certificate is always to be regarded as a front-line soldier without further proof.

"Participation in the fighting in the Baltic, in Upper Silesia, against the Sparticists and Separatists, as well as against the enemies of the national resurgence, counts equally with participation in the World War."

These exemptions, however, were terminated by decree of November 14, 1935.[42]

Besides stipulating immediate dismissal of "non-Aryan" officials, the Civil Service Law contained other far-reaching provisions. Thus "officials may be dismissed from service who because of their previous political activities do not offer surety that they will at all times act unreservedly for the national state." "Previous political activities" were further defined as membership in the Communist party or in its affiliated organizations; moreover, officials who have been connected with the so-called "*Schwarze Front*"—the extreme "National Bolshevist" wing of the Nazis—were dismissed as "unsuitable." It was further provided that every official must report to the proper authorities the parties to which he had belonged, and "parties" were

[42] *Reichsgesetzblatt,* Part I, p. 1333.

defined for the purpose of the law as including the republican Reichsbanner Black-Red-Gold, the Union of Republican Judges, the League for the Defense of the Rights of Man, the Union of Republican Officials, and the Iron Front.[43] Furthermore, political unreliability was stated to be present "particularly when an official in word, writing or other conduct has come out in an odious fashion against the national movement [Nazi], has insulted its leaders or has misused his official position to persecute, to slight or otherwise injure nationally-minded officials. In such case, the fact that the person in question has joined since January 30, 1933, a party or organization supporting the government of national resurgence will not suffice to clear him."

The Civil Service Law further provided that officials who lacked requisite education and training might be dismissed, and that an official might be transferred to a post lower in rank and salary—which allowed the Nazis to demote "non-Aryan" and other officials who, because of war services, etc., could not be dismissed. Officials who were dismissed or retired might be prosecuted and punished for any dereliction of duty during their tenure of office. Persons dismissed on the grounds of insufficient training, "non-Aryan" descent or political unreliability were liable to be sued until April 7, 1934.

Finally, the new law contained detailed provisions concerning pensions. Officials dismissed on grounds of insufficient education and training did not receive pensions save in exceptional cases of destitution. Those ousted because of previous political activities

[43] The latter organization was one of the principal supporters of President von Hindenburg at the last presidential election in 1932.

were entitled to three months' salary and thereafter, provided they had held office for at least ten years, to three-fourths of their normal legal pensions,[44] while a proportionate allowance was to accrue to their families after death. The same regulations applied to ousted Jewish officials except that they were to receive full pension.

As a result of these measures, any civil servant in whom the Nazis lacked confidence, against whom they bore a grudge, or whose position some member of the party coveted might be dismissed on the ground that his politics in the past showed he could not be trusted as an official of Nazi Germany. In order to comprehend the radical changes effected by the new Civil Service Law, it is necessary to recall that in Germany under both the Empire and the Republic, officials held a specially favored position and the public administration always enjoyed an enviable reputation for integrity, efficiency and stability. Before the war, in practice if not in law, higher officials were recruited from the upper classes of society and few Jews were admitted. Under the democratic Republic, however, the Weimar constitution laid down the principle that "citizens without discrimination shall be eligible for public office in accordance with the laws and their capacities and merits."[45] It stated that "officials shall be appointed for life except as otherwise provided by law," and specified the rights and protective measures applying to them.[46] The Weimar instrument declared that "officials are servants of the whole community and

[44] After only ten years' service, however, salaries are small; the pension allowance is also small, since it is based on the last actual salary received.

[45] Article 128.

[46] Article 129.

not of a party," and granted them "freedom of political opinion and freedom of association."[47]

The new Civil Service Law offered a great contrast to previous legislative and constitutional regulations concerning the German civil service. In explanation, the official commentary on the new law declared that the

"government of national resurgence, in fulfillment of its tasks, requires above all the strength of the German civil service. The latter, however, once so highly respected throughout the entire world, has not remained unaffected by the influence and consequences of the revolution of 1918. With an eye to party politics, numerous members of the November parties[48] were allowed to enter the public administration without the required education and preparation. These people in many instances have not only displaced professional civil servants but through their incompetence, self-interest and, in fact, criminal acts have terribly damaged the prestige of the German civil service.

"Only by cleansing the civil service of these elements, part of which are of an alien race, can a national civil service be created which will not be primarily interested in material advantages but, as formerly, will recognize that its highest goal is uncompromising fulfillment of duty and will prove worthy of the national honor which is placed in its hands."

The commentary stressed the special importance of the "Aryan paragraph" and pointed out that this created a "completely new law which was a conscious antithesis to the previous law." Specifically this paragraph and the regulations connected with it

[47] Article 130. For a discussion of the question of rights, duties, privileges and status of officials in Republican Germany, cf. F. F. Blachly and M. E. Oatman, *The Government and Administration of Germany* (Baltimore, Johns Hopkins, 1928), p. 371 *et seq.*

[48] The Social Democratic, Catholic Center and Democratic parties.

became the model for a series of other laws such as those for the admission of lawyers to the bar, the decree dealing with admission of doctors to practice under the social insurance laws and the law directed against the overcrowding of German universities [*Hochschulen*] and schools.[49] The commentary added that these radical measures were essential for the welfare of the state and declared that they were not conceived in a spirit of hate but had become necessary because of the increasingly dangerous alienization (*Ueberfremdung*) of the German people.

FORMATION OF A ONE-PARTY NATION

Meanwhile, before the complete constitutional reorganization of the Reich was completed, the Hitler government had effected absolute political consolidation of its power by abolishing all the German parties except the National Socialist. The Communist party was banned on March 31, 1933, by the provisional law for the coördination of the states with the Reich[50] which voided the Communist mandates in the Reichstag and Prussian Diet elected on March 5. Actually, however, no Communists had attended the sessions of the Reichstag held before the law of March 31 was promulgated by the government, for a large portion of the Communist deputies were in prison or refugees abroad.[51] The

[49] Many doctors and lawyers and all professors have the status of officials in Germany.

[50] *Cf.* p. 216. According to Article 10 of this law.

[51] All property and funds of the Communist party and its affiliated organizations were seized by the state under a law of May 26, 1933. *Reichsgesetzblatt,* I (1933) p. 293; Werner Hoche, *Die Gesetzgebung des Kabinetts Hitler: Die Gesetze in Reich und Preussen seit dem 30 Januar, 1933,* cited. Vol. 2, p. 224, *et seq.;* Vol. 3, p. 374 *et seq.*

Social Democrats were the next to come under the Nazi axe; 94 of the 120 Socialist deputies elected to the Reichstag on March 5 had been present and had voted against the Enabling Act on March 23. The party received its death-blow, however, when on May 2 the Nazis seized control of the German trade unions, occupied the buildings and offices of the unions, arrested their principal leaders, seized the labor banks and coöperatives and impounded the funds of leaders and unions. A government decree of July 7, 1933, abolishing the Socialist mandates in the Reichstag and the Prussian Diet,[52] and in all state and local organizations as well, legally terminated the existence of the once powerful Social Democratic party, which had already been officially banned on June 22, by an order issued by Reich Minister of the Interior Frick.[53] The smaller State party (*Staatspartei*), which had been allied with the Socialists for the March 5 elections, was also wiped out[54] by the July 7 decree. The grounds for the abolition of all these Left and Liberal groups were given by the Nazis as "high treason."

The dissolution of the less radical German parties which occurred during the same period was on a slightly different basis: the Right and Middle political groups may be said to have committed suicide under pressure. During June 1933, repressive measures against the Nationalist *Stahlhelm* were reported in different parts of Germany, many of the *Stahlhelm* leaders were arrested and local units of the

[52] *Reichsgesetzblatt,* I (1933) p. 462; Werner Hoche, *Die Gesetzgebung des Kabinetts Hitler: Die Gesetze in Reich und Preussen seit dem 30 Januar, 1933,* cited, vol. 3, p. 49 *et seq.*
[53] *Der Zeitspiegel,* July 2, 1933.
[54] *Das Recht der nationalen Revolution,* no. 1; Medicus, "Programm der Reichsregierung und Ermächtigungsgesetz," cited.

226 NEW GOVERNMENTS IN EUROPE

organization dissolved. On June 21 the independent existence of the entire Nationalist veterans' association (the *Stahlhelm*) was terminated and it was placed under Hitler's command. At the same time Nationalist organizations were dissolved by the Nazis because of "absolute proof that the Communists and other enemies of the state had joined these groups in large numbers."[55] Finally, on June 27, the Nationalist leader, Dr. Hugenberg, resigned from his post as Reich and Prussian Minister of Agriculture and Economics and on the same day the German National Front, which had taken the place of the Nationalist party soon after Hitler's accession to power, declared itself dissolved. The act of dissolution was stated to have been taken "in full understanding with the Reich Chancellor and in recognition of the fact that the state based on political parties is no longer in existence."

The end of the other important German political parties followed almost immediately. The Nazis had already taken repressive action against the Catholic parties—the Center and the Bavarian People's party. Catholic organizations had been dissolved by the secret police, meetings had been disrupted and some of the Catholic leaders had been taken into custody. Finally on July 4, the Bavarian People's party voted to dissolve itself, and on the following day the important Catholic Center party, which had held the balance of power in almost every Republican ministry and had played a great rôle under the Empire, followed suit. The German People's party, once led by Dr. Stresemann, also terminated its life on July 4.[56]

[55] *Der Zeitspiegel,* July 2, 1933.
[56] *Der Zeitspiegel,* July 23, 1933.

As a result of the Nazi dissolution of the Communist, Social Democratic and State parties and of the suicide of the other political groups in the Reich, the law promulgated by the Hitler government on July 14, 1933, which prohibited the formation of new political parties merely recorded an already accomplished fact. This law provides as follows:[57]

Law Prohibiting the Formation of New Political Parties

1

"The National Socialist German Workers' party is the only political party in Germany.

2

"Whoever undertakes to maintain the organization of another political party, or to form a new political party, is to be punished with imprisonment in a penitentiary up to three years or with confinement in a jail from six months to three years unless the act is punishable by a higher penalty under other provisions."

Thus the Nazi party, to all intents and purposes, obtained a monopoly of political power only six months after the beginning of the Hitler régime. In the Reichstag election of November 12, 1933 there was but one list of candidates: the National Socialist. Several of the former Nationalist leaders were allowed to run, but they were included in the Nazi list. In the poll, 92 per cent of the qualified voters backed the government. Three million of the ballots cast were invalid—the only way in which opposition to the Hitler policies could be expressed.

With the elimination of all other parties the National Socialist influence in the government was greatly strengthened. The number of party members in the cabinet rapidly increased. In March

[57] English text in Pollock and Heneman, *The Hitler Decrees,* cited p. 34; German texts: *Reichsgesetzblatt,* I (1933) p. 479; Werner Hoche, *Die Gesetzgebung des Kabinetts Hitler: Die Gesetze in Reich und Preussen,* cited, vol. 3, p. 66 *et seq.*

1933, Dr. Gereke was arrested on charges of embezzlement and removed from his ministerial post. Dr. Joseph Goebbels was made Reich Minister for Propaganda and Popular Enlightenment in the same month. Hugenberg, who had believed himself capable of controlling the Nazis, was compelled to resign on June 29, 1933. In the Ministry of Economics he was succeeded by a recent party recruit, Dr. Kurt Schmitt, and the latter in turn gave way on August 2, 1934, to Dr. Hjalmar Schacht, the President of the Reichsbank, who, although not a party member, had for some time been one of Hitler's close advisers. Dr. R. Walther Darré, a party veteran, took over the Ministry of Agriculture. In December 1933, Rudolf Hess, deputy leader of the party, and Ernst Röhm, chief of the S.A., were appointed ministers without portfolio. About six months later the Prussian Minister of Justice, Dr. Hans Kerrl, was also added to the cabinet after his ministry had been . taken over by the Reich. In July 1934, Franz von Papen resigned his post as Vice-Chancellor and was demoted to the post of special minister in Vienna. A National Socialist, Dr. Bernhard Rust, was named to head the newly created Reich Ministry for Education in December 1934. Finally at the beginning of the following year, Dr. Hans Frank, hitherto Bavarian Minister of Justice, became Reich Minister without Portfolio. The National Socialist party thus obtained almost all the posts in the cabinet. Non-party members remained only at the discretion of the Leader.

The Blood Purge of June 1934

The dissolution of all opposition parties, the coordination of the press, the purge of the civil service, the ruthless treatment of political opponents—all these did not suffice to stamp out all signs of dissent. This fact was dramatically revealed by the events of June 1934. For some time there had been increasing criticism and grumbling about the régime by both radicals and conservatives. Within the party itself dissatisfaction was rife in the S.A. Many members of the Storm Troops felt they had not obtained a just share of the spoils of victory. They saw "reactionaries" and "conservatives" still entrenched everywhere—in the army, in business, the civil service and in the Church. Discontented with their lot, they longed for a "second revolution." The spokesman of these "radicals" was Captain Ernst Röhm, chief of the S.A. Röhm's ambition to become a powerful force in the Third Reich had been thwarted. In the S.A. he had created a huge private army, increasing its size to about three million by admitting numerous former Communists and Socialists. He made no secret of his conviction that the S.A. should be the dominating power in the state. His goal was to fuse this private army with the Reichswehr and become the leader of their amalgamated forces. Many conservatives were also critical of the régime. Industrialists, junkers and Reichswehr generals became increasingly alarmed about "radical" trends in the National Socialist party. The Right deplored the gradual elimination of "decent" elements from positions of influence. General von Schleicher, displaced by Hitler, hoped for revenge on the "scoundrels and criminals" governing Germany. In a speech at Marburg on June 17, Vice Chancellor von Papen sharply and frankly condemned Nazi extremists in the name of conservatives.

In this atmosphere, National Socialist leaders

claim, a conspiracy to unseat the government was hatched. The alleged plot linked Röhm, von Schleicher and Strasser, and it was even hinted that the French ambassador in Berlin had cognizance of it. Whatever be the truth about the conspiracy, no convincing and documentary proof was ever brought out in support of its existence.[58] According to Hitler and Göring, the plot was thwarted in the nick of time on June 30, 1934. Hitler in Munich, Göring in Berlin ordered the arrest and summary execution of the "conspirators." How many met their death on June 30 and succeeding days will probably never be known. In a speech before the Reichstag on July 13, Hitler put the total at 77, but foreign estimates have ranged as high as a thousand and over.[59] The opportunity appears to have been seized to square many old accounts. The party leadership struck indiscriminately at opponents on both Right and Left. Aside from von Schleicher, Röhm and Strasser, many men of prominence were killed. Old S.A. veterans such as Ernst, Heines, von Heydebreck, Schneidhuber and von Krausner were shot. Among conservatives, von Papen escaped, but his friend, Edgar Jung, and his chief of staff, von Bose, did not. Adelbert Probst, leader of the Catholic Youth, Dr. Erich Klausener, head of the Catholic Action, and General von Bredow were among the many other victims.

This unprecedented purge undoubtedly consolidated the régime both by intimidating the opposition and by ruthlessly eliminating possible leaders about whom opposition could crystallize. It was fol-

[58] Cf. Frederick L. Schuman, The Nazi Dictatorship (2nd revised edition, New York, Knopf, 1936), p. 423 et seq.; also Konrad Heiden, Hitler (New York, Knopf, 1936), Chapter V.
[59] Schuman, The Nazi Dictatorship, cited, p. 443.

lowed shortly by removal of the last obstacle to the perpetuation of complete National Socialist hegemony. The only one still theoretically empowered to dismiss Hitler—President Paul von Hindenburg —died on August 2, 1934. The day before, the cabinet had already approved a law uniting the office of Reich President with that of Chancellor and conferring the powers of both on the "Leader and Reich Chancellor Adolf Hitler."[60] This law was submitted to the people for approval in a plebiscite on August 19, and overwhelmingly ratified by about 84 per cent of the eligible voters. Hitler was confirmed as the supreme, omnipotent dictator of the Reich.

CHAPTER V

THE GERMAN PEOPLE AND THE JEWS

WHAT is the new Third Reich that has been created on the ruins of the Weimar Republic? It may be said to rest on three pillars—people, party and state.[1] The German people or the German racial community (*Volkstum*) constitutes both the foundation and the goal of the entire system. It is the foundation inasmuch as the Third Reich is supposed to be based on popular sovereignty. Although the Reich has been reorganized along authoritarian and totalitarian lines, its leaders still boast that as the "most enobled form of a modern European democracy,"[2] it depends in the last analysis on the will of the people. The German people are not permitted

[60] *Reichsgesetzblatt*, Part I, 1934, p. 747.
[1] Fritz Morstein Marx, *Government in the Third Reich* (New York, McGraw-Hill, 1936), p. 67.
[2] *Ibid.*, p. 63.

to legislate, but they are asked from time to time to confirm the leadership of Hitler and the National Socialist party through the machinery of plebiscites. The national community is the purpose and aim of the régime in so far as the idea of service to the German people is supposed to motivate every action of party and state. The German community has become a mystical entity. The state is dedicated to the preservation and improvement of its racial purity, to the promotion of its material and spiritual welfare, and to the advancement of its place in the world.

According to National Socialist theory and practice, the Jews have no place in this national community. German race, German culture, German political life must be kept pure and "undefiled" by Jewish race and Jewish influence. The Jews or "non-Aryans" have therefore been excluded from the German community. They have become social, political and racial outcasts. Gradually, but inexorably they are even being deprived of means of livelihood.

According to the last German census for which figures are available, June 16, 1925, the total population of the Reich was 62,410,619, of which 564,379 were Jews,[3] who thus comprised nine-tenths of one per cent.[4] The anti-Jewish measures of the Nazis, however, affected not only those listed as Jews, but also a newly created class of "non-Aryans."[5] Although no official figures are available, it has been estimated that this "non-Aryan" category comprised approximately two million Germans,[6] making a total

[3] *Statistisches Jahrbuch für das deutsche Reich, 1931* (Berlin, Reimer Hobbing, 1931), p. 15 *et seq.*

[4] *Ibid.*, p. 15. The above percentage is calculated on the same territorial basis as that for 1925.

[5] Persons one of whose parents or grandparents were Jewish. *Cf.* p. 179.

[6] *Jewish Daily Bulletin,* July 18, 1933.

of 2½ million persons in the Reich who, according to Nazi standards, were classified as Jews. In analyzing the rôle of the Jews both under the Empire and the Republic, the available data concerns only those officially listed as Jews.

In Imperial Germany almost no Jews held posts as officials in the civil service, the army or the navy. As a result of their position, the largest number of Jews turned to commerce, industry and banking.[7] Those Jews desirous of entering professional life became for the most part doctors or lawyers, the two branches most readily open to them, which accounts in part for the relatively greater percentage of Jews in the liberal professions. During the war 96,327 Jews, or 17.3 per cent of the Jewish population, served in the German army and navy. The percentage of Germans with the colors was slightly higher, 18.73 per cent, but the fact that the Jewish birth rate had been falling steadily[8] for some time was apparently responsible for the existence of fewer Jewish than non-Jewish males of military age. Of the 96,000 enlisted Jewish soldiers and sailors, approximately 12,000 were killed, 78 per cent were at the front, and 12 per cent of those with the colors were volunteers. These figures are particularly important in view of the Nazi contention that most of the Jews who fought in the war held soft posts.[9]

The establishment of the Weimar Republic undoubtedly improved the status of the Jews. The

---

[7] Heinrich Silbergleit, *Die Bevölkerungs- und Berufs- Verhältnisse der Juden im deutschen Reich* (Berlin, Akademie Verlag, 1930), Vol. I, p. 89.*

[8] The Jewish birth rate fell from 32.26 per thousand in 1880 to 16.55 in 1910. The total birth rate for the same period fell from 41.05 per thousand to 33.05. *Ibid.*, p. 14.

[9] Jakob Segall, *Die deutschen Juden als Soldaten im Kriege, 1914-1918* (Berlin, Philo-Verlag, 1922), p. 11 *et seq.*

largest proportion still found its way into commerce and industry, although many more than formerly entered the public administration. There are no reliable figures available for the occupational distribution of the Jews in the entire Reich. For Prussia, however—a state comprising three-fifths of Germany—statistics compiled from official sources give a full picture of the situation: of the Jews in Germany in 1925, 71.6 per cent lived in Prussia, where they formed 1.5 per cent of the population as compared with nine-tenths of one per cent in the Reich as a whole.

According to the 1925 census, on which the following data is primarily based, the working population in Prussia totaled 21,267,033, of which 225,523 were Jews, or 1.06 per cent.[10] Of the Jews gainfully employed, 71.7 per cent were engaged in commerce and industry, as compared with 51.7 per cent of the gainfully employed non-Jews. Only seven-tenths of one per cent of Jews gainfully employed found their way into public administration, in contrast to 2.3 per cent of the gainfully employed non-Jews. The other professions, however, accounted for 10 per cent of the gainfully employed Jews, and 6.8 per cent of the gainfully employed non-Jews. The occupational distribution of both Jews and non-Jews is shown in the table on page 235.

The percentage of Jews in commerce and in the liberal professions was higher than their relation to the total population. They comprised, however, only 3.4 per cent of all persons engaged in commerce and business in Prussia, and 2.3 per cent of the profes-

[10] It must be stated again, however, that the latter figure comprises only the Jews, and not the so-called "non-Aryan" class created by the Nazis.

OCCUPATIONAL DISTRIBUTION OF JEWS AND NON-JEWS
GAINFULLY EMPLOYED IN PRUSSIA

	Jewish workers	Non-Jewish workers	Total workers	Per-centage of Jews
Commerce and transportation	112,188	3,135,957	3,248,145	3.4
Industry	49,318	7,722,481	7,771,799	0.63
Professional class[1]	9,761	422,572	432,333	2.3
Health, medicine and charity[2]	8,297	348,119	356,416	2.3
Domestic service	6,338	1,085,097	1,091,435	0.58
Agriculture, truck farming, forestry, fishing	3,324	5,589,820	5,593,144	0.06
Public administration, officials of the law, army and navy[3]	1,563	487,152	488,715	0.32
Without profession[4]	34,734	2,250,312	2,285,046	1.08
Totals and average percentage....	225,523	21,041,510	21,267,033	1.06

[1] This group included:
    a. All clerics, workers in religious institutions and associations with religious aims. b. All teachers, professors, etc., in universities, colleges, private and public schools, scientific institutes and art centers. c. Lawyers and legal trustees. d. Artists, scholars, editors, writers, persons connected with theaters, opera houses, music centers, cinemas, radio. e. Persons in physical training centers.

[2] This group included:
    a. All doctors and dentists. b. All persons connected with hospitals, clinics, asylums, public and private. c. All persons connected with bathing and swimming pools, masseurs, barbers. d. All persons connected with life-saving and first aid stations, ambulance service. e. Veterinarians, meat inspectors. f. Disinfection service. g. Street cleaning, canalization, garbage collection and comfort stations. h. Undertakers. i. Druggists. j. Social services.

[3] This group included:
    a. Diplomacy. b. All officials of the Reich, states and municipalities. c. All court officials in so far as they have civil service rank. d. Army and navy, and military and naval administration, including military hospitals.

[4] This group included:
    a. Persons living from private fortunes, *rentiers* and persons living on pensions. b. Persons living from outside support (inmates of poorhouses, etc.). c. Inmates of insane asylums. d. Students not living with their families. e. Persons serving prison sentences.

sional classes. The Jews in public administration and government, on which the Nazis have laid so much emphasis, comprised only .32 of one per cent of all officials in Prussia.

In their anti-Semitic agitation the Nazis continually stressed the fact that great numbers of Eastern Jews (*Ostjuden*) entered Germany during and since the war and, in a period of severe economic crisis, secured good jobs which should have gone to deserving Germans. Whether or not this Nazi charge can be substantiated, undoubtedly a large number of Jewish emigrants came into the Reich after the war, many if not most of them coming from territory which had formerly been German. Thus between 1910 and 1925 the number of Jews in Prussia increased by 37,093[11] despite the war, the economic difficulties and a continually falling Jewish birth rate. There were, in 1925, 601,779 non-citizens in Prussia; of this number 76,387[12] were Jewish. According to figures prepared by the Nazis, 12,500 Eastern Jews became citizens in Prussia between 1919 and 1931.[13]

THE "COLD POGROM"

Despite the relatively small percentage of Jews in the Reich, Hitler told his followers for ten years and more that the Jews were responsible for all German difficulties, and promised that once in power he would eliminate "Jewish influence" from all phases of German life. The first step toward achieving this end was the Jewish boycott on April 1, 1933. The second was the promulgation of the Civil Service Law which, as has been stated, formed the basis for all subsequent anti-Semitic action as well as action against Socialists, liberals, etc. The effects of this law must now be considered.

Lawyers

At the time of the general boycott, Jewish judges and lawyers were excluded from the courts although the procedure adopted varied in different sections

[11] Silbergleit, *Die Bevölkerungs- und Berufs- Verhältnisse der Juden im deutschen Reich,* cited, p. 37* *et seq.* The figures are: 1910—366,876; 1925—403,969. These compilations were made on the territorial basis of 1925.

[12] This figure is included in the 564,397 Jews in the Reich.

[13] *Frankfurter Zeitung,* August 12, 1933.

of the Reich.[14] In Prussia, Nazi Commissioner of Justice Kerrl issued instructions that all Jewish judges were to be granted immediate leave of absence and that the powers of Jewish court officials were to be cancelled at once. The declaration added: "Any Jewish judge refusing to apply for leave shall be forbidden to enter the court building on the basis of the law of trespass." Jewish commercial arbitrators, jurors, etc., were no longer to be appointed, Jewish states' attorneys and other officials were to be granted leave of absence, and only certain Jewish lawyers, not to exceed in numbers the percentage of the Jewish population to the total population, were to be allowed to enter the courts.[15] On April 7[16] matters were regularized by the promulgation of a law concerning the admission of lawyers to the bar,[17] which provided that all "non-Aryan"[18] lawyers might be disbarred up to September 30, 1933. The exceptions to this ruling were the same as those stipulated in the Civil Service Law: no "non-Aryans" might be admitted to the bar; lawyers who had been engaged in Communist activities must be disbarred immediately; and disbarment was recognized as a basis for cancelling contracts already made with the persons in question.

As a result of the exemptions for front-line soldiers and pre-1914 appointments, however, a large number of "non-Aryan" lawyers were eligible to practice and Nazi lawyers, especially in Berlin, were

[14] Calvin B. Hoover, *Germany Enters the Third Reich* (New York, Macmillan, 1933), p. 128.
[15] *Frankfurter Zeitung,* April 1, 1933.
[16] The date on which the Civil Service Law was promulgated.
[17] *Reichsgesetzblatt* No. 86, April 10, 1933, p. 188.
[18] According to the Civil Service Law definition.

incensed. On May 13, therefore, the Prussian Ministry of Justice published statistics concerning the situation as it then stood: before the "cleansing" of the bar there had been 11,814 lawyers in Prussia, of whom 3,515 were Jews and 8,299 "Aryan." Of the 3,515 Jewish lawyers, 1,383 had been admitted to the bar before 1914 and 735 had been at the front during the war. Nine hundred and twenty-three Jews and 118 Communists were ousted and in future, 2,158 Jewish lawyers were to have the right to practice in Prussia, the number of Jewish lawyers allowed to practice in Berlin being 1,203.[19]

The situation of the Jewish lawyers in Prussia and throughout the Reich was far different from what these figures might imply. Early in July the Berlin Federation of Lawyers issued an order prohibiting Aryan lawyers from entering into partnership or sharing offices with Jewish lawyers, and dissolving partnerships of Aryans and Jews entered into since September 1930, even though the Jewish partner was entitled to exemption because of war service.[20] The press continued to report the dismissal of large numbers of notaries and lawyers.[21] Equally serious was the fact that an actual boycott was enforced against Jewish lawyers who theoretically were eligible to practice. Early in June the Berlin section of the Association of National Socialist Lawyers sent a protest to the presidents of all Berlin courts against the appointment of Jewish lawyers as attorneys for the poor, official defendants,

[19] *Frankfurter Zeitung*, May 13, 1933.
[20] *The Times* (London), July 5, 1933.
[21] A further list of 214 dismissed notaries was published on July 8 by the Prussian Ministry of Justice, and on the same day an order was issued ousting 150 lawyers. *Le Temps,* July 13, 1933.

trustees and executors. These appointments, it was stated, were acts of sabotage against the measures enacted by the national government to restore German law, and gave proof that the judges who made such appointments were not ruthlessly enforcing the provisions of the Civil Service Law.[22]

Doctors and Dentists

The situation in regard to the medical profession was similar to that of the legal profession, since the Jews had been especially prominent in both fields. Most German medical men derived 80 to 90 per cent of their income from membership in the so-called panels of the health insurance offices. "Non-Aryan" panel doctors were directly affected by the provisions of the Civil Service Law and even though many were exempt because of war service, etc., their position became rapidly worse. A special law of June 2, 1933, excluded dentists and dental technicians from panel practice on the basis of the Civil Service Law,[23] and in the social insurance clinics and offices patients could refuse to be examined by a "non-Aryan" physician.[24] It was reported that 1,500 Jewish physicians were expelled from the health insurance clinics in Berlin alone, and that at least 6,000 were ousted in Prussia,[25] while practically all "non-Aryan" doctors in private health insurance institutions were dismissed.[26]

The situation in private practice was just as serious. The medical association issued a regulation according to which German and "non-Aryan" doc-

[22] *Frankfurter Zeitung*, June 8, 1933.
[23] *Reichsgesetzblatt*, June 10, 1933, p. 350.
[24] *Frankfurter Zeitung*, June 28, 1933.
[25] *Le Temps*, July 11, 1933.
[26] *Frankfurter Zeitung*, July 9, 1933.

tors were forbidden to substitute for one another; German doctors might not send patients to "non-Aryan" physicians or call "non-Aryans" into consultation.[27] Furthermore, partnerships with "non-Aryan" doctors were forbidden.[28] As a result of these prohibitions, plus the tacit boycott to which doctors as well as lawyers were subjected, large numbers of "non-Aryan" physicians and dentists faced a black future and many emigrated from Germany.

Professors and Students

The measures enacted by the Nazis against "non-Aryan" lawyers and doctors had far-reaching effects on the status of law and medicine in the Reich, but the real foundations of the Third Reich were laid in the realm of education. Not only is the rising generation taught by "pure" Aryans, but there is no possibility for German youth to become tainted by exposure to the hated doctrines of liberalism and democracy. Instruction is given in racial question; great emphasis is laid on the glorious history of Germany and the "shame" of the years 1919 to 1932; *Wehrsport, i.e.,* military sports, have a prominent place in the curriculum for both students and teachers; and youth is imbued with real fighting spirit and extreme nationalism as the primary object of education.[29] Fact-finding, painstaking research is no more; the Nazis "must think with their blood."

To put these theories into practice, German professors, instructors and teachers, including many of

[27] *Ibid.*, August 15, 1933.
[28] *New York Times,* August 20, 1933.
[29] Prospectus of *Hochschule für Politik, 1933-1934.*

the most eminent, were ousted from their positions. The Civil Service Law applied to them directly and, in cases where the "non-Aryan" paragraph was not applicable, the provisions in regard to "political unreliability" were often used. "Non-Aryan" professors who might have been exempt as war veterans or who had been appointed before 1914 were forced to resign by Nazi students who organized demonstrations against them and made their positions untenable.[30]

While professors and teachers, theoretically at least, were regulated by the Civil Service Law, students were selected under the terms of a law promulgated on April 25, 1933, "against the overcrowding of the German universities."[31] This measure was designed, it was officially stated, to rebuild German education along the lines of the German heritage, by molding the youth through discipline and comradeship. The new laws introduced a complete educational reformation, which "is worthy of the desire and the struggle of the German people during the past decades for inner unity and strength."

To achieve these ends, liberal hypotheses have been replaced by popular national (*voelkische*) hypotheses. As a first step, admission of students was based on entirely different standards from heretofore. According to the new law, students were admitted only in numbers consistent with the oppor-

---

[30] Hoover, *Germany Enters the Third Reich*, cited.

[31] "Gesetz gegen die Ueberfüllung der deutschen Schulen und Hochschulen," April 25, 1933, *Reichsgesetzblatt*, April 26, 1933, I, p. 225. The text of the law, as well as the texts of the various orders issued by Rust, the Prussian Minister of Science, Art and Popular Education, are given with official commentaries in Joachim Haupt. "Neuordnung im Schulwesen und Hochschulwesen," No. V in *Das Recht der nationalen Revolution*, cited.

tunities in the professions for which they wish to prepare themselves. New applicants of "non-Aryan"[32] descent were admitted according to a *numerus clausus* which limited the total of such newly entered students in any school and any faculty of a school to the proportion of "non-Aryans" in the total population of the Reich. A decree issued simultaneously with the School Law placed this proportion at 1½ per cent of the students in a given institution of learning. If the percentage of "non-Aryan" students already enrolled exceeds 5 per cent of the total, it must be lowered to that percentage by dismissal of "non-Aryans." The law did not apply to students whose fathers fought at the front during the war or to children one of whose parents or both of whose grandparents were "Aryans," if the marriage took place before the promulgation of this law. Obviously, the full effect of these regulations will not be felt for several years. Further regulations for candidates for the general *Abitur* examination, which must be passed before entrance to any German university, made possible the exclusion of candidates for alleged political heresy. All "Marxist" and "anti-National" students were ousted from Prussian universities.[33]

Once admitted to a college or university, the students were officially organized in a National Socialist Association recognized by the government.[34] Only students of "German descent and mother tongue" may belong to this organization which rep-

[32] In accordance with the definition of the Civil Service Law.

[33] Decree issued August 9, 1933, by Rust, Prussian Minister of Education. *New York Herald Tribune*, August 10, 1933.

[34] According to a law of April 22, 1933, *Reichsgesetzblatt*, I, p. 215. Included in *Das Recht der nationalen Revolution*, No. V, cited.

resents the student body and has as its purpose "the fulfillment by the students of their duty to people, state and university." A decree issued in Prussia on April 12, 1933, by the Ministry of Education defined "German descent" according to the standard Civil Service Law terms. This decree also stressed the Nazi principle of "leadership," and declared that one of the purposes of the students' association is "the education of the students for military service and for coöperation with the German people as a whole by means of military and labor service and physical exercises," a provision obviously contrary to the terms of the Versailles Treaty. "Non-Aryans" are not admitted to the inner student life of the university, while German-speaking students from Austria and those countries which have German minorities are to be received into the fold. Two major planks of the Nazi program are here in process of fulfillment.[35]

Nazi Cultural Activities

The cultural aspects of the Nazi revolution were exemplified by the *auto-do-fé* held on May 10, 1933, when books by Jewish authors, pacifists, so-called "Marxists" etc., were publicly burned by students.[36] An even more illuminating example is found in the "Theses" posted prominently on the bulletin boards of German universities, which stated:[37]

"Our most dangerous enemy is the Jew and everyone connected with him. The Jew can only think Jewish. If he writes German, he lies. The German who writes Ger-

[35] Wertheimer, "Forces Underlying the Nazi Revolution," cited.

[36] A fairly complete list of the books banned is to be found in the *Essener Volks-Zeitung*, May 18, 1933.

[37] *The Times* (London), August 15, 1933.

man but thinks un-German is a traitor. We censor Jewish works. We wish German students to destroy Jewish intellectualism. We demand that students and professors should be chosen from Germans and that the German spirit should be thus safeguarded."

A further indication of this "safeguarding" of the German spirit is to be found in the law ousting all Jewish actors, directors, producers, cameramen, authors and conductors from the German film industry[38] and the German theatre. Most "non-Aryans" were expelled from orchestras,[39] both as conductors and as musicians, and in principle no "non-Aryan" soloists may appear in concerts or on the radio;[40] so-called Jewish influence was thus removed from music, literature and art. In the field of journalism, many eminent writers have been dismissed because of their race, and the confiscation of the entire Socialist and Communist press has thrown large numbers out of work. Furthermore, during the process of "coördinating" the non-Nazi press, numerous "non-Aryans" have been ousted.[41]

Commerce and Industry

Nazi opposition to Jewish "intelligence" was apparent in these measures which not only made it practically impossible for Jews in the liberal professions to earn a living, but also limited the possibilities, especially in higher education, for "non-

[38] *New York Times,* July 1, 1933.
[39] *Ibid.,* July 5, 1933.
[40] The "Aryan" paragraph of the Civil Service Law is the definition used.
[41] The National Press Law promulgated by the Hitler government on October 5 provided that every working newspaper man in Germany is to be regarded as a servant of the state, and will be held morally and legally responsible for his professional activities. The "Aryan" provisions of the Civil Service Code are incorporated in the press law.

Aryan" youth to acquire training and knowledge. The fear and hatred of the Hitlerites for so-called Jewish business acumen was undoubtedly just as great, as indicated by their constant references to "Jewish materialism."[42] The thoroughness with which the Nazis acted in economic life was perhaps not quite so marked as in the professions, where definite laws were promulgated regulating Jewish participation. While the measures taken in regard to business were far-reaching, there were some indications that concern over the grave economic situation tempered Nazi ardor to "cleanse" business.

The effects of the boycott of April 1 on commerce, however, outlasted the one day to which it was officially limited. This was reported to be especially the case in small towns and cities, for on June 30, 1933, the city of Dortmund staged a private anti-Jewish boycott of its own which was declared a great success;[43] a week or so later the local *Dortmunder Generalanzeiger* warned all members of the National Socialist party and related organizations not to enter Jewish business premises.[44] Instances of persecution can be multiplied many times. On July 20 in Nuremberg 300 Jews, chiefly shop-keepers but including several well-known lawyers and doctors, were arrested. Their houses were searched and they were made to march through the streets in a procession, flanked on either side by Storm Troopers, treated with derision and brutality, and finally interned in a large public barracks.[45] In Berlin the municipal authorities excluded Jewish merchants from the pub-

[42] Wertheimer, "Forces Underlying the Nazi Revolution," cited.
[43] *The Times* (London), July 11, 1933.
[44] *Ibid.*, July 20, 1933.
[45] *Ibid.*, July 21, August 1, 1933.

lic market;[46] in Munich the municipal council decreed that no Jewish merchants may be permitted in the auction room of the city pawnshop or allowed to participate in the October Fairs;[47] in Hamburg no "non-Aryans" may have public telephone booths in their shops.[48] The National Association of German Shoe Merchants demanded the exclusion of "non-Aryans" from the shoe trade, and that shoe shops owned by Jews shall be closed on Saturday as well as Sunday.[49] A final instance was the announcement that the government on September 30, 1933, would rescind all permits to trade on the Stock Exchange. Only those persons who fulfilled the necessary "moral" and "technical" requirements were readmitted.[50] While these were scattered incidents, they showed clearly the temper of the Nazi rank and file.

During the first weeks of the Nazi revolution, many Jewish members of boards of directors and managements of important firms were forced out in the general coördination, or *Gleichschaltung*, of every aspect of German life. Even the powerful Association of German Industry[51] was "coördinated" early in March 1933, and the coördination of all other trade associations, large and small, wholesale and retail, followed.[52] Nazi commissars were installed in almost all firms and zealously worked to purify business. As the first flush of the Revolution passed, many of the Nazi leaders apparently began

[46] *Le Temps*, July 15-16, 1933.
[47] *Frankfurter Zeitung*, August 13, 1933.
[48] *Ibid.*, p. 19.
[49] *Le Temps*, July 20, 1933.
[50] *Voelkischer Beobachter*, July 6, 1933.
[51] *Reichsverband der deutschen Industrie*.
[52] Hoover, *Germany Enters the Third Reich*, cited, p. 137 *et seq.*

to realize that business and industry in the Reich was being harmed by these tactics, with consequent detriment to employment. In July, in a series of speeches by Hitler and other Nazis, it was announced that the revolution was over, that there would be no second revolution, and Nazi followers were exhorted to refrain from meddling in industry. Hitler, on July 7, went so far as to say that "an industrial leader cannot be removed if he is a good business man merely because he is not yet a National Socialist, especially if the National Socialist being put in his place knows nothing about industry."[53] In a decision of July 14, 1933, the Cabinet laid down a policy in regard to government contracts to be awarded "non-Aryan" firms. If bids made by German firms equal bids by firms whose owners or directors are "non-Aryan," the German firm is to be preferred.[54] On September 27, however, Dr. Kurt Schmitt, Minister of Economics, declared that discrimination between Aryan and non-Aryan business establishments would hamper economic recovery, and should therefore be discountenanced. Furthermore, many similar statements were made subsequently as it became evident that complete exclusion of Jews from German economic and financial life would seriously hamper economic recovery.

The situation of Jewish industrial and office workers was also difficult and uncertain. All labor, including the white-collar class, had been organized in the so-called "German Labor Front," and "non-Aryans"[55] were excluded from this organization.[56] There were reports that only members of the Labor

[53] *New York Herald Tribune,* July 8, 1933.
[54] *Frankfurter Zeitung,* August 4, 1933.
[55] According to the civil service definition.
[56] *Frankfurter Zeitung,* July 7, 13, 1933.

Front would be able to secure jobs. The situation was greatly complicated by the fact that a large proportion of German workers were "Marxists," against whom the Nazis have been as violent in their repressive measures as against the Jews. On October 2 the Hitler government promulgated the Hereditary Homestead Law creating a "peasant aristocracy," which consists of "Germans, Aryan and honorable." Under this law. "Aryans" are those whose families have been free of Jewish blood since 1800.[57] While very few Jews in the Reich were engaged in agriculture,[58] this was nevertheless a significant move.

Race Defilement

To keep the German race free from the contamination of Jewish blood, the Reichstag approved on September 15 a Law for the Protection of German Blood and German Honor.[59] This statute and an executive decree of November 14, 1935[60] forbade all marriages between Jews and people of German or related race (*Blut*). Individuals with two Jewish grandparents need the consent of the authorities before they can marry Germans, while those only one-quarter Jewish may be wed only to Germans, presumably so that they may have their blood "purified." Extra-marital relations between Jews and Germans are likewise prohibited, and in order to reinforce this provision Jewish households are forbidden to employ any German women under forty-five years of age. By means of these statutes and with the aid of laws providing for the sterilization of

[57] *New York Herald Tribune,* October 3, 1933.
[58] *Cf.* table, p. 235.
[59] *Reichsgesetzblatt,* Part I, 1935, p. 1146.
[60] *Ibid.,* p. 1334

physical and mental defectives and the fulfillment of certain health requirements before marriage, the German race is to be ennobled.

Deprivation of Political Rights

Exclusion of the Jews from the German community was made final in 1935 when they were deprived of political rights. The National Socialist program had demanded the elimination of the Jews from political life in the following terms: "Only a member of our own people (*Volksgenosse*) may be a citizen (*Staatsbürger*). Our own people are only those of German blood without reference to confession. Therefore no Jews may be a member of our people. . . . Only citizens may decide on the leadership and laws of the state." As a first step toward carrying out this platform the Reich cabinet decided, on July 14, 1933, to withdraw German citizenship at its discretion from "undesirables" naturalized within the last fifteen years—between November 9, 1918, and January 30, 1933. The National Defense Law of May 21, 1935[61] excluded all Jews from active military service and stipulated that only persons of Aryan descent could become officers. Jews capable of military service were placed in the second replacement reserves of the army. Finally, on September 15, 1935 the Reichstag approved a law, complemented by a decree on November 14, depriving all Jews[62]

[61] *Reichsgesetzblatt*, Part I, 1935, p. 609.

[62] Within the meaning of the statute, Jews are those (1) descended from at least three completely Jewish grandparents, (2) descended from two completely Jewish grandparents or belonging to a Jewish religious community, (3) one of whose parents in turn had three Jewish grandparents and married after September 15, 1935, (4) born out of wedlock after July 31, 1936 and one of whose parents was descended from at least three Jewish grandparents.

of citizenship and relegating them to the status of members of the state (*Staatsangehörige*). Only persons of German or related race can now be citizens of the Reich and exercise political rights such as the right to vote and hold office. Jewish officeholders previously excepted from dismissal were retired from service at the end of 1935, although their salary and pension rights were safeguarded. To complete the humiliation of the Jews, the Law for the Protection of German Blood and German Honor forbade them to fly the Reich flag or show the German national colors. In this way the National Socialist ideal of a Germany reserved to those of German blood and race has been realized.

CHAPTER VI

THE NATIONAL SOCIALIST PARTY

The National Socialist party, second pillar of the Third Reich, today has the monopoly of political power in Germany. After dissolution of the old parties and the general prohibition against the formation of new ones, it remains the only political organization in the country. The party is defined as a "corporation of public law" by a statute which went into effect on December 2, 1933:

Law for Safeguarding the Unity of Party and State[1]

1

"(1) After the victory of the National Socialist Revolution the National Socialist German Workers' party has become the

[1] English text in Pollock and Heneman, *The Hitler Decrees,* cited, p. 34 *et seq.*; German texts: *Reichsgesetzblatt,* I (1933) p. 1016; Werner Hoche, *Die Gesetzgebung des Kabinetts Hitler: Die Gesetze in Reich und Preussen seit dem 30 Januar,* cited, vol. 5, p. 60 *et seq.*

keystone (*Trägerin*) of the government and is inseparably connected with the state.

"(2) It is a corporation of public law. Its constitution is determined by the leader (*der Führer*).

2

"To secure the closest cooperation of services of the party with the public authorities, the assistant of the leader[2] is a member of the Reich cabinet.[3]

3

"(1) Members of the National Socialist German Workers' party and of the Storm Troops (including affiliated organizations) have, as the leading and moving power of the National Socialist state, increased duties toward the people and the state.

"(2) For violation or neglect of these duties the members are subject to special party and Storm Troop jurisdiction.

"(3) The leader may extend these regulations to the members of other organizations.

4

"Violations or neglect of duty may mean any action or neglect which may attack or endanger the stability of the organization, or the authority of the National Socialist German Workers' party, and in case of members of the Storm Troops (including affiliated organizations), any violation against discipline and order.

5

"Besides the customary disciplinary measures, arrest and imprisonment may be decreed (*verhängt*).

6

"Public authorities must, within their power, give assistance to party and Storm Troop officials who are vested with party and Storm Troop jurisdiction in rendering justice and legal redress.

7

"The law governing penal authority over members of the Storm Troops (S.A.) and Special Guards (S.S.) of April 28, 1933, is declared inoperative.[4]

8

"The Reich Chancellor, as leader of the National Socialist German Workers' party and as supreme chief of the Storm Troops, issues orders and regulations necessary for the execution and

[2] Rudolf Hess.
[3] Amendment of July 3, 1934, *Reichsgesetzblatt*, Part I, 1934, p. 529.
[4] Text of this law in Werner Hoche, *Die Gesetzgebung des Kabinetts Hitler: Die Gesetze in Reich und Preussen seit dem 30 Januar,* cited, vol. II, p. 38.

extension of this law, especially regulations concerning the formation and procedure of the party's and Storm Troops' jurisdiction.
He determines the date on which the regulations concerning this
jurisdiction are to become effective."

Like the state, the party is organized on the leadership principle. Its constitution, its officials and its
principles are determined by the Supreme Leader,
Adolf Hitler. Many of his duties he delegates, however, to his assistant or deputy, Rudolf Hess. A
party cabinet consisting of nineteen men, each of
whom heads a major bureau or division, also assists
the Leader. This cabinet is composed as follows:[5]

Rudolf Hess, Assistant to the Leader in all questions
of party leadership.

Martin Bormann, Chief of Staff to Rudolf Hess.

Viktor Lutze, Chief of Staff of the Storm Troops.

Heinrich Himmler, Reich leader of the *Schutzstaffel*
(Protective Corps or Party Guard).

Franz Xaver Schwarz, Reich Treasurer of the party.

Philipp Bouhler, Chief of the Leader's Chancery and
chairman of party examination commission for the protection of National Socialist literature.

Walter Buch, Chairman of the Party Supreme Court
(*Oberstes Parteigericht*).

Wilhelm Grimm, Chairman of the Second Chamber
of the Party Supreme Court.

Dr. Robert Ley, Director of the Reich Organization
Division.

Dr. R. Walther Darré, Director of the Bureau for
Agricultural Policy.

Dr. Joseph Goebbels, Reich Propaganda Director.

Dr. Hans Frank II, Director of the Legal Department.

Dr. Otto Dietrich, Reich Press Chief.

Max Amann, Director of the Press Bureau.

Alfred Rosenberg, Director of the Foreign Policy

[5] *Nationalsozialistisches Jahrbuch 1936* (Munich, Eher Verlag,
1935), pp. 131-33.

Bureau and specially entrusted by the Leader with the spiritual and philosophical education of the N.S.D.A.P.

Baldur von Schirach, Reich Youth Leader.

Franz Ritter von Epp, Director of the Colonial Policy Bureau.

Karl Fiehler, Secretary of the N.S.D.A.P.

Dr. Wilhelm Frick, Leader of the Reichstag Delegation of the Party.

Each of these bureaus or divisions has a complete organization under it which is responsible for various phases of German life. The Reich Organization Division, for instance, has within its jurisdiction education, labor organization, corporate organization, local government, public health, charity, women's activities and student groups. It supervises all National Socialist organizations and associations in these fields. The other divisions are less far-reaching in scope but all together form a network which penetrates into every corner of German life.

Besides this all-inclusive organization of the party from the top, the Reich is divided in sections or *Gaue*, each of which is under the command of a so-called *Gauleiter* who is the party leader in that part of the country. There are 31 of these *Gaue* in Germany proper, one for the Free City of Danzig and one for National Socialists in other countries.[6]

Integral parts of the National Socialist party are the brown-shirted *Sturm Abteilung* or S.A., the black-uniformed *Schutzstaffel* or S.S., the National Socialist Motor Corps, the Hitler Youth, the National Socialist Student League and the National Socialist Women's Organization.[7] The S.A. and S.S.

[6] *Ibid.*, p. 150-52.

[7] *Cf.* decree of March 29, 1935, *Reichsgesetzblatt*, Part I, 1935, p. 502.

constitute the party police and are organized along military lines. After the "purge" of June 1934, the S.A. suffered a temporary eclipse, but at the Nuremberg party Congress in September 1936 its strength was again placed at 2,000,000 men.[8] The S.S., well-drilled and to a large extent armed, are the elite troops of the party, the praetorian guard of the Leader. They are commanded by Heinrich Himmler, who is also Chief of the Reich police, and number between 260,000 and 270,000.[9] The Hitler Youth is of particular importance, not only because it forms the chief instrument through which German youth is trained in the National Socialist faith, but also because new party members are today exclusively recruited from its ranks. This youth organization, headed by Baldur von Schirach, includes both boys and girls. Boys from ten to fourteen years old form the *Deutsches Jungvolk*, while those from fourteen to eighteen constitute the *Hitlerjugend* proper. Similarly, younger girls are organized as *Jungmädel* while the older ones make up the *Bund Deutscher Mädel*.

Aside from the integral organizations of the party there exist a number of affiliated groups. These include the National Socialist Leagues of doctors, jurists, teachers, civil servants and engineers, the Labor Front, the National Socialist Welfare Organization and the National Socialist Organization of Disabled Veterans. They have their own corporate existence but are subject to party supervision. Their leaders, too, are appointed, not elected.

As a privileged corporation, the party enjoys far-reaching tax exemptions. This is true also of its integral formations and many of the affiliated or-

[8] *New York Herald Tribune,* September 14, 1936.
[9] *Ibid.*

ganizations. The party is specially empowered to penalize and discipline its own members and those of its organizations. For this purpose a comprehensive system of party courts culminating in a supreme court at Munich has been set up.

The Party as Propagator of the Faith

The primary function of the party is to keep alive and propagate the National Socialist ideology. Popular enthusiasm must constantly be rekindled through meetings, parades and other demonstrations. In September of each year a spectacular party congress is held at Nuremberg where the leaders review and laud the achievements of the past and outline the course for the future. The party campaigns in defense of the government and mobilizes the people in support of its policies. It educates and develops the leaders of the future. As the guardian of National Socialist ideas, it maintains a special office to examine in advance of publication all literature claiming to expound the party's philosophy. The "spiritual and philosophical" education of the party membership itself has been specially entrusted to Alfred Rosenberg, author of *Der Mythus des 20. Jahrhunderts*.

Party and State

In reality the party may be said to be above the state, for it determines the constitution of the state and guides its policies. The law defines the party as the *Trägerin des deutschen Staatsgedanken* which may be roughly translated as the "pillar of the German philosophy of state." The party must see that every action of the state and government is inspired by, or consistent with, National Socialist doctrine. It exercises a continuous vigilance over the public and private acts of all officials. A special *Verbin-dungstab* coordinates the action of party and state. The two are, in fact, to a large extent identical. Adolf Hitler, as Leader of the party, is at the same time Leader and Chancellor of the Reich, and his party deputy sits in the cabinet. A preponderant majority of the members of the government are National Socialists, and Goebbels and Darré, Ministers of Propaganda and Agriculture respectively, head similar functional divisions in the party cabinet. With the exception of Prussia and Bavaria, Nazi district leaders or *Gauleiter* function as Governors (*Statthalter*) in the various German states. In the cities of the Reich, special party "delegates" share in the appointment of the chief functionaries.

The law specifically charges Rudolf Hess in his dual rôle of cabinet member and assistant to the Leader in party affairs with the task of securing close coöperation between party agencies and government officials. Accordingly he must be consulted on all proposed legislation even before it is submitted to the Reich cabinet. He is also the chief "patronage" officer of the party. All administrative appointments and promotions made by Hitler first go through his hands.[10] He tests and rewards loyalty to party principles.

CHAPTER VII

THE NEW STATE

THEORETICALLY the Weimar constitution still forms the legal basis of the German state. It sur-

[10] Marx, *Government in the Third Reich*, cited, p. 85.

vives, however, as but an empty shell. The Chancellorship and Presidency have been merged into a single omnipotent office. No division between executive, legislative and judicial powers remains. Individual liberties have largely disappeared. The federal structure has been swept away. Germany has become an authoritarian, unified state.

The extent of the transformation is fully realized when the chief provisions of the Weimar constitution are briefly reviewed.

The German constitution, drawn up by the Weimar Assembly, was described as the most democratic in the world. Article I stated that "The German Reich is a Republic. The political power emanates from the people." A Reichstag, elected by universal suffrage, according to the principles of proportional representation, was the chief legislative body of the Republic. A second chamber, the Reichsrat, representing the component states or *Länder* of the Reich, had subordinate legislative powers. The executive was composed of a President, elected for seven years by popular vote, and a cabinet of ministers appointed by the President and responsible to the Reichstag. Under the Empire, the power of Prussia had been supreme; the Weimar constitution limited Prussia's votes in the Reichsrat —the successor of the old Bundesrat—to two-fifths of the total votes. The powers of the Reichsrat were also greatly reduced.

The Weimar constitution thus established parliamentary government on a broad democratic basis and introduced some interesting experiments. Committees of investigation and permanent committees of the Reichstag watched over the government when the Reichstag was not in session. The constitution provided for the initiative and referendum; it made possible the recall of the President and provided as well that all his acts had to be countersigned by a responsible minister. In the field of socialization, the constitution had several novel provisions, chief among them having been an important attempt to establish an advisory body of representatives of occupations. Factory Workers' Councils, District Workers' Councils and a Workers' Council for the Reich were provided for, the original intention having been to give labor an actual participation in the control of industry and government, although a subsequent law gave these bodies only advisory power. The Councils, however, were empowered to name one or two members to the boards of directors of industrial enterprises, and under some circumstances they also had access to the books of such concerns. The constitution further provided for the representation of economic interests in an advisory capacity in political matters. Drafts of bills of a political-social nature which were of fundamental significance had to be submitted to the Economic Council of the Reich for consideration before they were introduced into the Reichstag. This Council included representatives of all important economic groups and had power also to initiate bills.

The constitution contained far-reaching and very liberal provisions for the protection of the rights of individuals;[1] the State church was done away with; the constitution provided for a school system and all schools were placed under governmental control; private preparatory schools were abolished.

The constitution greatly altered the relations of the various provinces of Germany to the Reich. It

[1] For text of these articles, *cf.* p. 269 *et seq.*

no longer spoke of them as states, but as territories (*Länder*), and the powers which might be exercised solely by the central government were greatly increased. The intense jealousy of the south German states, particularly Bavaria and Württemberg, toward Prussia made the drafting of the constitution exceptionally difficult and complicated domestic politics in Germany during the entire republican era.

The constitution was finally adopted on July 31, 1919, and came into force on August 11. The Weimar constitution provided that each of the German states must have a republican constitution, and as a result the units of the German Reich all had constitutions modeled largely on the Weimar instrument itself.[2]

Although, as has been pointed out, the Weimar constitution was one of the most democratic in the world, ironically enough the German republican governments felt forced by stress of circumstances to make increasing use of one of its least democratic provisions—Article 48. This article provided:

"If a state fails to carry out the duties imposed upon it by the national constitution or national laws, the President of the Reich may compel performance with the aid of armed force.

"If public safety and order be seriously disturbed or threatened within the German Reich, the President of the Reich may take the necessary measures to restore public safety and order; if necessary, with the aid of armed force. For this purpose he may temporarily suspend in whole or in part the fundamental rights enumerated in Articles 114, 115, 117, 118, 123, 124 and 153.[3]

"The President of the Reich must immediately communicate to the Reichstag all measures taken by virtue of Paragraph 1 or Paragraph 2 of this Article. On demand of the Reichstag these measures must be abrogated.

"Detailed regulations shall be prescribed by a national law."[4]

From October 1919, through September 1932, no

[2] *Cf.* Gerhard Anschütz, *Die Verfassung des Deutschen Reichs von 11 August 1919* (4th edition, Berlin, Stilke, 1933).
[3] *Cf.* pp. 272-74.
[4] This law was never passed.

less than 233 emergency decrees were issued under
Article 48. During the troubled early years of the
Republic from 1919 to 1925, there were 135 such
decrees promulgated. In contrast, only 16 emergency
decrees were issued between 1925 and 1931, no recourse to Article 48 having been necessary during
the year 1929. By the beginning of 1931, however,
the deepening economic depression, with the attendant growth of the National Socialist and Communist parties, made it increasingly difficult for the
Reich governments to put necessary legislation
through the Reichstag directly, and Article 48 was invoked more and more frequently. Thus in 1931 the
proportion between emergency decrees and regular
laws passed by the Reichstag was 42 to 35; in 1932
there were only 5 laws as compared with 59 emergency decrees.[5] Nevertheless, the Reichstag, which
was incapable of legislating directly because the
deputies felt unable to accept the political onus involved, did not refuse its assent to the emergency
decrees as provided in Article 48.

The increasing reliance placed on Article 48 by
governments of the Weimar Republic as the political deadlock continued provided a convenient precedent for the Nazis after the formation of the Hitler
ministry on January 30, 1933. Hitler merely substituted out-and-out dictatorship based on dubious
constitutional changes for an indirect dictatorship
under Article 48.[6]

[5] For list of emergency decrees promulgated between October 1919 and the end of September 1932, cf. Lindsay Rogers and
others, "German Political Institutions II: Article 48," in *Political
Science Quarterly*, December 1932. The proportion of laws to
decrees is given in Dr. Franz Albrecht Medicus, "Programm der
Reichsregierung und Ermächtigungsgesetz," No. 1 of *Das Recht
der nationalen Revolution* (Berlin, Carl Heymanns Verlag, 1933).

[6] *Cf.* Chapter "Hitler and the German Political Crisis," p. 169.

A Leadership State

Possessing the powers of both President and Chancellor, Adolf Hitler is the undisputed chief of the National Socialist State. His tenure is for life and he can determine his own substitute. Members of the cabinet are not his colleagues, but his subordinates. They, as well as all government officials and the personnel of the army and navy, are bound to him by an unqualified oath of obedience and loyalty. He is chief of the defense forces and directly or indirectly appoints all officials of the central government and constituent states of the Reich. As he demonstrated in the purge of June 1934, he has absolute control over the lives and liberty of German citizens.

In the Reich cabinet, headed by Hitler, are concentrated complete legislative as well as executive powers. Under the Enabling Act[7] laws may even deviate from the constitution so long as they do not affect the position of the Reichstag and the powers of the President whose office has since been fused with that of Chancellor. The Statute Concerning the New Structure of the Reich, approved by the Reichstag on January 30, 1934, further empowers the Reich government to determine new constitutional law. Up to the present the authority under this law has not been employed to draw up a wholly new constitution for the Reich.

There are apparently no limitations on the government's power of legislating by decree under the Enabling Act except that the Act is to remain in force for a period of four years only. During that time, the government may do anything that it sees

[7] *Cf.* pp. 214-15.

fit in order "to combat the misery of people and Reich." Despite the provision in the Act that it will become invalid when the present national cabinet is replaced by another, the resignation of Dr. Hugenberg from the Ministries of Economics and Agriculture on June 27, 1933, in no way changed the status of the Hitler government. The German Nationalists maintained at the time of Dr. Hugenberg's resignation that this action voided the Enabling Act but their protests were disregarded. Moreover, on March 13, the government had created a new Ministry of Propaganda and Public Enlightenment headed by Dr. Goebbels, who was given a seat in the Reich cabinet. On December 1, two more Nazis—Captain Roehm and Rudolf Hess—were appointed Ministers without Portfolio in the Reich government. The official commentary explains at some length that it would minimize the strength and importance of the government of national concentration to consider that the resignation of one or another minister might invalidate the Enabling Act. Apparently the same interpretation applies to the appointment of new Ministers.

In financial matters, the Enabling Act sets aside the provision of the constitution which states that "the budget shall be adopted by law before the beginning of the fiscal year,"[8] the official commentary pointing out in this connection that the budget law was only law in "form" but in reality merely an administrative measure. The same interpretation is applied to the borrowing power of the state,[9] which the Enabling Act also places in the hands of the gov-

[8] Article 85, paragraph 2. For text, cf. p. 272.
[9] Article 87. For text, cf. p. 272.

ernment. Thus the entire control of the elected legislature over finances has been abolished.

In the same way, the authority of the Reichstag in foreign affairs over ratification of treaties was abrogated by the Enabling Act.[10] According to the official commentary, the further question of putting treaties with foreign states into effect by legislative action was left open in Article I of the Enabling Act. If the carrying out of treaties between states requires the passage of legislation by the Reichstag or the Reichsrat, according to Article 4, paragraph 2 of the Enabling Act, this function may now be undertaken by the Reich government.

There is no mention made in the official commentary of the important second paragraph of Article 45 of the Weimar constitution—"Declaration of war and conclusion of peace shall be made by national law." Doubtless, the Reich government has the supreme power here also, although since the Reichstag, as at present constituted,[11] consists almost entirely of members of the National Socialist party, its consent would be a foregone conclusion. Moreover, fusion of the offices of President and Chancellor rendered nugatory the constitutional requirement that all the President's orders and decrees be countersigned by the Chancellor or by the competent national minister. The Enabling Act had already empowered the Chancellor to promulgate laws without any counter-signature. The official commentary pointed out, however, that "nevertheless, the Reich government evidently intends to follow the former procedure of counter-signature by the responsible minister or ministers concerned."

[10] *Cf.* Article 4 of the Enabling Act.
[11] *Cf.* p. 264.

"Parliamentarism," so often condemned by the National Socialists, has disappeared under the Third Reich. The Reichstag is the only elected assembly that survives, and it has delegated away its authority to legislate and its all-important power over the purse. Its consent is no longer needed for legislation, although laws are from time to time still submitted for its approval. In general the government employs it only as a sounding board for its policies. True, the Enabling Act expires on April 1, 1937 after which the Reichstag can in theory recover its full powers. In fact, it will not be difficult for the government to obtain a renewal of its mandate, for the Reichstag is completely dominated by the National Socialist party. In elections to this body the party draws up one list of candidates. All other candidates are barred, and the electorate can only approve or reject the single list. So sure is the government of success that no provision has been made for the contingency of rejection.

If Parliament no longer constitutes a check on the government, neither does the judiciary. Since judges are no longer guaranteed security of tenure, the courts have ceased to be independent. Political reliability is essential for appointment to, or retention of, judicial posts. The Leader can interfere in the administration of justice through his power to intercept criminal trials or investigations[12] and his unrestricted right of pardon. Moreover, the Leader's word is practically law for the courts and the latter must at any rate interpret the law in accordance with the program and principles of the National Socialist party.

[12] Marx, *Government in the Third Reich,* cited, p. 73.

Centralization

In the Third Reich the German states have become mere administrative subdivisions of the central government. The unification of Germany has at last been completed. Separate state citizenship has ceased to exist,[13] the various state "embassies" in Berlin have been abolished, and the Reichsrat, the upper house of Parliament consisting of state representatives, has been swept away.[14] The special privileges retained by certain states such as Bavaria under the Weimar constitution have disappeared. All this has been accomplished in an effort to unify the German people and wipe out the distinction between Bavarians, Prussians, Saxons, etc.

The states are under the direct control of Reich Governors whose powers have been defined by a law of January 30, 1935.[15] Appointment and dismissal of the Governors is reserved to the Leader and Chancellor. Adolf Hitler himself is the Governor of Prussia, although he has delegated the duties of this office to the Prussian Minister President, Hermann Göring. The governor is the permanent representative of the central government and has the special task of ensuring that the lines of policy laid down by the Leader are carried out in his territory. He drafts and promulgates state laws after securing the consent of the Reich government. He nominates, and Hitler appoints, the members of state cabinets. The governor himself may be asked to form a cabinet. He may be given jurisdiction over more than one state. All state officials are subject to appointment

[13] Decree of February 5, 1934, *Reichsgesetzblatt,* Part I, 1934. p. 85.
[14] Decree of February 14, 1934, *Ibid.,* p. 89.
[15] *Reichsgesetzblatt,* Part I, 1935, p. 65.

and dismissal by the Leader, although he may delegate his powers to the governor and ministers of the Reich cabinet. In practice, higher state officials are appointed by Hitler on the nomination of Reich ministers, while others are designated by cabinet members who have in turn assigned some of their powers to state governors. In Prussia Göring nominates or appoints all officials.[16] The *Reichsstatthalter*, as the governors are known in German, are under the administrative supervision of the Reich Minister of Interior, Dr. Frick. Other national ministers may also issue direct instructions to the *Statthalter* in their respective fields.

Except where it has been specifically restricted, the scope of the state's activities and jurisdiction remains as large as before. In at least four respects, however, this jurisdiction has been considerably curtailed. The states have been deprived of all authority over municipal government. The administration of justice, formerly largely reserved to the states, has been completely nationalized by a series of decrees culminating in an act of January 24, 1935.[17] Under this law, the Reich took over, on April 1, some 65,000 judicial officials and 2,000 government offices. A single Ministry of Justice now functions for all the states as well as the Reich. All police forces within Germany have also been unified under a single head directly responsible to the Minister of Interior for the Reich and Prussia.[18] Finally, Church affairs have passed under the jurisdiction of the Reich. A national ministry was created for this purpose on July

---

[16] *Cf.* R. H. Wells, "The Liquidation of the German Länder," *American Political Science Review*, April 1936.
[17] *Reichsgesetzblatt*, Part I, 1935, p. 68.
[18] Cf. decree published on June 18, 1936, *National-Zeitung*, June 18, 1936.

16, 1935,[19] and a special court has been established to decide legal questions pertaining to the Evangelical Church.

Prussia, with three-fifths of the area and population of Germany, is even more closely controlled by the central government than the other states. The heads or *Oberpräsidenten* of the twelve Prussian provinces have been made direct representatives of the Reich,[20] so that they now occupy practically the same position as *Statthalter*. The provinces have thus become administrative areas of the Reich.[21] The central and Prussian governments have also been intimately linked through "interlocking" directorates. By the end of June 1934, all Prussian ministries except that of finance were headed by the same persons who directed similar Reich departments. Since that time outright fusion has combined the ministries of interior, justice, economics, labor, transportation, agriculture and education.[22] The Ministry of Interior, for instance, is now known as the Reich *and* Prussian Ministry of Interior. For the Ministry of Justice even that dual designation has been dropped.

In one respect Reich reform is not yet complete. Numerous projects have been advanced to eliminate the old German states and divide Germany into uniform administrative districts. Toward the end of 1934, the Minister of Interior announced that twenty such districts would soon be created, but the reform has so far not materialized. No territorial

[19] Cf. *Reichsgesetzblatt*, Part I, 1935, p. 1029.
[20] Decree of November 27, 1934, *Reichsgesetzblatt*, Part I, 1934, p. 1190.
[21] Cf. Albert Lepawsky, "The Nazis Reform the Reich," *The American Political Science Review*, April 1936.
[22] R. H. Wells, "The Liquidation of the German Länder," cited.

changes have taken place except for the union of Mecklenburg-Swerin and Mecklenburg-Strelitz on January 1, 1934. Prussia and its ambitious Minister President, Hermann Göring, are apparently the chief obstacles to the consummation of the reform.

Municipal Government

The government of German rural and urban communities has been unified and revised under the direct control of the Reich by the Municipal Ordinance of January 30, 1935.[23] A party delegate is appointed for each municipality by Deputy Leader Hess. This delegate, however, has no administrative work. That task remains entrusted to the burgomaster or chief burgomaster who is designated by the Reich Minister of Interior from three names selected in turn by the party delegate from a list of qualified experts in administration after consultation with members of the municipal council. Other executive officers are nominated in a similar way, although with the advice of the burgomaster. Full-time, paid burgomasters serve for twelve years, others for six. Except in the first year, they may be removed only for certain disciplinary offenses. In accordance with the leadership principle, full administrative responsibility is vested in the burgomaster. Before the enactment of ordinances and adoption of the budget he must obtain the advice of the council. The advice is not binding, however, and members of the council are not permitted to vote on any projects submitted to them. They are appointed by the party delegate in agreement with the mayor for a term of six years.

[23] *Reichsgesetzblatt,* Part I, 1935, p. 49; cf. also R. H. Wells, "Municipal Government in National Socialist Germany," *The American Political Science Review,* August 1935.

The scope of municipal government has not been greatly restricted, but the new system can hardly be said, as its authors claim, to carry on "the true spirit of Baron von Stein, the creator of municipal self-administration.[24] Like each individual community, the various leagues of local authorities have been "coordinated." They have been dissolved and re-united in a *Deutscher Gemeindetag* whose chairman, executive president, board of directors and expert commissions are all appointed by, and subject to the control of, the Minister of the Interior.

APPENDIX

PERTINENT ARTICLES OF THE WEIMAR CONSTITUTION

Article 45: The President of the Reich represents the Reich in international relations. In the name of the Reich he makes alliances and other treaties with foreign powers. He accredits and receives diplomatic representatives.

Declarations of war and conclusion of peace shall be made by national law.

Alliances and treaties with foreign states which relate to subjects of national legislation require the consent of the Reichstag.

Article 68: Bills shall be introduced by the National Ministry, or by members of the Reichstag. National laws shall be enacted by the Reichstag.

Article 69: The initiation of a bill by the National Ministry shall require the consent of the Reichsrat. If the National Ministry and the Reichsrat fail to agree, the National Ministry may, nevertheless, in-

---

[24] The city of Berlin enjoys a special though not dissimilar régime defined by Prussian state law and supervised by a state commissioner.

troduce the bill but must present therewith the dissenting opinion of the Reichsrat.

If the Reichsrat passes a bill to which the National Ministry fails to assent, the Ministry must introduce such bill in the Reichstag accompanied by an expression of its views.

Article 70: The President of the Reich shall proclaim the laws constitutionally enacted, and shall publish them within a month in the *Reichsgesetzblatt.*

Article 71: National laws, unless otherwise provided, shall be effective on the fourteenth day after the day of publication in the *Reichsgesetzblatt* in the capital of the Reich.

Article 72: Publication of a national law shall be deferred for two months on request of one-third of the members of the Reichstag. Laws which the Reichstag and the Reichsrat declare to be urgent may be published by the President of the Reich regardless of this request.

Article 73: A law passed by the Reichstag shall, before its publication, be subject to a referendum, if the President of the Reich, within a month so decides.

A law, the publication of which has been deferred on the request of one-third of the members of the Reichstag, shall be subject to a referendum upon the request of one-twentieth of the qualified voters.

A referendum shall also take place, if one-tenth of the qualified voters petition for the submission of a proposed law. Such petition must be based on a fully elaborated bill. The bill shall be submitted to the Reichstag accompanied by an expression of its views. The referendum shall not take place if the bill petitioned for is accepted by the Reichstag without amendment.

Only the President of the Reich may order a referendum concerning the budget, tax laws, and salary regulations.

Detailed regulations in respect to the referendum and initiative shall be prescribed by a national law.

Article 74: Laws enacted by the Reichstag shall be subject to veto by the Reichsrat.

The veto must be communicated to the National Ministry within two weeks after the final vote in the Reichstag, and within two additional weeks must be supported by reasons.

In case of veto the law must be presented to the Reichstag for reconsideration. If no agreement upon the matter is reached between the Reichstag and the Reichsrat, the President of the Reich may within three months submit the matter in dispute to a referendum. If the President fails to exercise this right, the law shall be considered as of no effect. If the Reichstag overrules the veto of the Reichsrat by a two-thirds majority vote, the President shall within three months publish the law in the form adopted by the Reichstag or shall order a referendum.

Article 75: A resolution of the Reichstag shall not be annulled unless a majority of the qualified voters participate in the election.

Article 76: The constitution may be amended by legislative action. However, resolutions of the Reichstag for amendment of the constitution are valid only if two-thirds of the legal members are present and if two-thirds of those present give their assent. Moreover, resolutions of the Reichsrat for amendment of the constitution require a two-thirds majority of all the votes cast. If by popular petition a constitutional amendment is to be submitted to a referendum, it must be approved by a majority of the qualified voters.

If the Reichstag adopts a constitutional amendment over the veto of the Reichsrat, the President of the Reich shall not publish this law if the Reichsrat within two weeks demands a referendum.

Article 85, paragraph 2: The budget shall be adopted by law before the beginning of the fiscal year.

Article 87: Funds may be procured on credit only for extraordinary needs and as a rule only for expenditures for productive works. Such a procurement as well as the assumption of any liability by the Reich may be undertaken only by authority of a national law.

Article 114: Liberty of the person is inviolable. A restriction upon, or deprivation of, personal liberty, may not be imposed by public authority except by law.

Persons who have been deprived of their liberty must be informed no later than the following day by what authority, and upon what grounds, the deprivation of liberty was ordered; without delay they shall have the opportunity to lodge objections against such deprivation of liberty.

Article 115: The dwelling of every German is his sanctuary and is inviolable. Exceptions may be imposed only by authority of law.

Article 117: Secrecy of postal, telegraphic, and telephonic communication is inviolable. Exceptions may be permitted only by a national law.

Article 118: Every German has the right within the limits of the general laws, to express his opinion orally, in writing, in print, pictorially, or in any other way. No circumstance arising out of his work or employment shall hinder him in the exercise of this right, and no one shall discriminate against him if he makes use of such right.

No censorship shall be established, but exceptional provisions may be made by law for cinematographs. Moreover, legal measures are permissible for the suppression of indecent and obscene literature, as well as for the protection of youth at public plays and exhibitions.

Article 123: All Germans have the right to assemble peaceably and unarmed without notice or special permission.

By national law notice may be required for meetings in the open air, and they may be prohibited in case of immediate danger to the public safety.

Article 124: All Germans have the right to form societies or associations for purposes not prohibited by the criminal code. This right may not be limited by preventive regulations. The same provision applies to religious societies and associations.

Every association has the right to incorporate according to the provisions of the civil code. Such right may not be denied to an association on the ground that its purpose is political, social, or religious.

Article 153: Property shall be guaranteed by the constitution. Its nature and limits shall be prescribed by law.

Expropriation shall take place only for the general good and only on the basis of law. It shall be accompanied by payment of just compensation unless otherwise provided by national law. In case of dispute over the amount of compensation, recourse to the ordinary courts shall be permitted, unless otherwise provided by national law. Expropriation by the Reich over against the states, municipalities, and associations serving the public welfare may take place only upon the payment of compensation.

Property imposes obligations. Its use by its owner shall at the same time serve the public good.

CHAPTER VIII

ORGANIZATION OF INDUSTRY, TRADE AND AGRICULTURE

THE Third Reich is totalitarian in scope, penetrating into every aspect of German life. Business therefore has been unable to escape governmental regimentation. As the National Socialist program foreshadowed, industry, trade and agriculture have been organized into estates or corporations and enlisted in the service of the state. Here, too, the leadership principle has prevailed and an attempt has been made to submerge as far as possible the old conflict of classes and economic interests. Union of the German people in accordance with National Socialist ideals has been the aim. Divergent interests between labor and capital, and between industry and agriculture are either ignored or subjected to compulsory arbitration by the government.

Estate of Industry and Trade

The organization of industry and trade has been carried out under the Law for the Preparation of the Organic Construction of German Business which was enacted on February 27, 1934,[1] and by a number

[1] *Reichsgesetzblatt*, Part I, 1934, p. 185.

of executive decrees the most important of which is that of November 27, 1934.[2] The resulting Estate of Industry and Trade was modified and simplified by a decree of the Minister of Economics issued on July 7, 1936.[3]

The Estate has been built up on the basis of the former trade associations. Membership in it is compulsory for all enterprises and employers, and precludes participation in other associations. It is organized along functional and regional lines. Functionally the Estate is divided into six National Branches (*Reichsgruppen*) comprising industry, trade, handicraft, banks, insurance and the power-producing industry. Each Branch includes a number of Main Groups (*Hauptgruppen*) which are again divided into Economic Groups (*Wirtschaftsgruppen*. The latter constitute the most important units. They are made up of sections (*Fachgruppen*) and sub-sections (*Fachuntergruppen*). Thus Industry, the most important National Branch, has six Main Groups. One of these is composed of six Economic Groups—steel and iron construction, machine construction, vehicles, aircraft industry, electrotechnical industry, and precision, instrumental and optical industry.

Regionally German business enterprise has been organized into eighteen Boards of Industry (*Wirtschaftskammern*). These comprise in three departments the district membership of the National Branches Industry and Trade and the old Chambers of Commerce which have been reorganized on the leadership principle and represent local trade and

[2] *Ibid.*, p. 1194.
[3] *Cf.* Akademischer Austauschdienst, *News in Brief,* July 31, 1936, pp. 176-79.

industry. The other National Branches have not yet obtained representation in these district Boards, but it is apparently intended to include them at a later stage.

German Handicrafts are organized in a somewhat different way. The functional division is into fifty Reich Guild Associations (*Reichsinnungsverbände*) to which are attached all the Handicraft Workers Guilds (*Handwerkerinnungen*). Territorially, however, the Handicrafts form a separate Estate (*Reichstand des deutschen Handwerks*). The Reich is divided into 750 regions in each of which functions a Regional Guild Association (*Kreishandwerkschaft*), including all the guilds within the area. More important regional groupings are the sixty-one Chambers of Handicraft (*Handwerkskammern*) which establish the guilds and issue their statutes. They are in turn federated as the Reich Association of Chambers of Handicraft (*Deutscher Handwerks-und Gewerbekammertag*). Both the Estate and the functional organization culminating in the National Branch of Handicrafts are headed by a single Grand Master of Handicrafts (*Reichshandwerkmeister*).

All the functional and regional formations of the Estate of Industry and Trade are included in a supreme body called the Reich Economic Chamber (*Reichswirtschaftskammer*). Its statutes are framed by the Minister of Economics who also appoints its director and his deputies. The director has at his side an Advisory Council consisting of the directors of National Branches and Main Groups, the directors of Industrial Boards, representatives of Transport, the Agricultural Estate and Municipalities, and a number of industrialists designated by the Minister of Economics.

The whole organization is supposed to represent a system of self-administration for business. The directors, however, are all appointed, either directly by the Minister of Economics, or on the recommendation of the head of a higher formation by the latter's superior. The budget of each formation must also be approved by the one superior to it. The directors, who function primarily through business managers (*Geschäftsführer*), are usually assisted by advisory councils, but these, too, have either an *ex officio* or a purely appointive membership. The directors and managers are enjoined, however, to keep in close touch with the members. The latter must be convened at least once a year in assembly and informed of the activities and financial condition of the formation. If they vote a resolution of non-confidence in their director, the head of the next higher group must consider his recall. The organization is financed by contributions which are assessed exclusively by the Economic Groups.

The Estate was originally not permitted to concern itself with the regulation of prices and markets or with labor questions. On November 14, 1936, however, the Minister of Economics issued a decree instructing the group organizations of the Estate to investigate and rationalize markets and regulate cartel prices. This duty is to be carried out in conjunction with the Four Year Plan for the production of German raw materials which was launched by Hitler in September 1936 and with which the Estate has been ordered to cooperate.[4] Aside from the specific tasks entrusted to it from time to time, the Estate's competence covers such subjects as general economic and trade policies, foreign exchange con-

[4] *New York Times,* November 15, 1936.

trol, finance and credit, advertising and promotion. In general the functional groups confine their attention to matters of particular concern to a specific branch of trade or industry, while the regional formations handle questions of common concern and act as conciliators of divergent interests. The whole organization exists primarily to maintain close contact between government and industry. Its chief function is not so much to make the wants of business known to the government, as to carry out the latter's instructions. For the state it represents a means of regimenting business and enforcing responsibility for the execution of governmental policies pertaining to trade and industry.

It should be remarked, in parenthesis, that transportation has been given an organization of its own, because 80 per sent of transport enterprises are public property.[5] The Minister of Transport is the supreme head of the organization. There are seven functional Central Transport Groups (*Reichsverkehrsgruppen*) divided into sections and sub-sections. Each group is organized regionally in district formations (*Bezirksgruppen*) and local formations (*Bezirksuntergruppen*). District Transport Councils, federating the various regional groups, are also provided for. The entire organization is capped by a Reich Transport Council composed of representatives of both carriers and transport users.[6]

The Agricultural Estate

All those engaged in the production, processing and distribution of agricultural commodities have

[5] E. C. Donaldson Rawlins, *Economic Conditions in Germany to March 1936* (London, His Majesty's Stationery Office, 1936), p. 181.

[6] *Cf.* Decree of September 25, 1935, *Reichsgesetzblatt*, Part I, 1935, p. 1169.

been organized, on a compulsory basis, in the Reich Agricultural Estate (*Reichsnährstand*) under a law of September 13, 1933[7] and subsequent executive decrees. Jurisdiction of this Estate extends to forestry, fisheries, viticulture and game as well as to farming proper. The smallest regional groups are the local units (*Ortsbauernschaften*) which lead up successively to 520 district associations and 20 regional associations.[8] The whole is headed by a Farm Leader who at present is also Minister of Agriculture. With the aid of a deputy and a large staff he directs the central office of the Estate. Although in accordance with the leadership principle his authority is absolutely supreme, he has an Advisory Council of about one hundred members appointed by himself. There is also a Farm Committee (*Reichsbauernthing*) composed of local, district and regional directors selected by the Farm Leader and entrusted with preparations for the annual Farm Congress.

The central office of the Estate comprises a Department of Policy and an Administrative Department. The first includes seven sections dealing respectively with economic, legal, racial, press, propaganda, international questions, and with tradition and development. The second has three main sections. One deals with "The Worker" and as such is in charge of agricultural labor, its political and social education, questions of insurance and the like. Another whose jurisdiction covers "The Farm" is responsible for farm management and improvement in production technique. The last covers "The Market" and supervises the management of agricultural sales and prices through marketing associations. The Ad-

[7] *Ibid.*, Part I, 1933, p. 626.
[8] Rawlins, *Economic Conditions in Germany to March 1936*, cited, pp. 41-42.

ministrative Department is duplicated in the regional and local farmers' groups, but the Policy Department is confined to the central office.

The functions of the Agricultural Estate are generally much more important than those of the corresponding organization for industry. One of its chief tasks is to stimulate domestic production in order to decrease Germany's dependence on foreign sources of supply. It studies and fosters the utilization of more efficient methods of cultivation, promotes rationalization and improvement of production, develops better animal breeds and strains, and encourages the growing of certain crops which Germany particularly needs. Unlike the Estate for Industry, the primary function of the corporate organization for agriculture is to regulate the marketing of its products. The Market Section of the Estate's Administrative Department comprises nine Central Marketing Associations dealing with grain, cattle and meat, milk and other dairy products, potatoes, eggs, market garden produce, the brewing industry, sugar and fish.[9] These, divided again into regional associations, are self-governing bodies controlling the distribution of farm commodities from the prime producer to the ultimate consumer. Although not alike in all respects, they generally fix production quotas, determine standards of grading and quality, and enforce minimum and maximum prices through all or most stages of marketing. The regulation of imports and exports, however, is reserved to Reich offices directly under control of the Minister of Agriculture.

[9] Rawlins, *Economic Conditions in Germany to March 1936,* cited, p. 43.

The Organization of Labor

Labor is not represented in the estates for industry and agriculture. In repudiation of the "Marxist" concept of the class struggle, all labor unions and the corresponding employers' associations have been dissolved. A Labor Front including both workers and employers was set up in May 1933. Membership, which is closed to Jews, is in theory voluntary, but in practice it "pays" to belong. It may be individual or corporate. Thus the industrial and agricultural estates are corporative members. The organization is affiliated with the National Socialist party and directed by Dr. Ley, the party's Reich Leader of Political Organizations. All its leaders must belong to the party. The smallest unit of the Labor Front is constituted by the members in a single firm (*Betriebsgemeinschaft*). These are gathered in 14,744 local groups (*Ortsverwaltungen*). The superior territorial organization consists of 821 district and 32 regional groups. The Labor Front is also organized along vocational lines in 18 divisions. Needless to say, the leadership principle is applied everywhere.

The Labor Front is not an agency for collective bargaining between labor and capital. Its work is primarily social and educational. It must reconcile and create a community of spirit between employers and employees. This is evident from the organization and functions of its central administration. Its organization office includes a press section which publishes a number of political and technical periodicals and supervises others, a political schooling section which trains labor leaders, a social section which deals with social insurance and relief, and an economic section controlling the Front's insurance companies, building societies and bank. Still other sections are devoted to propaganda, health, vocational training, legal advice, youth, education, women's work, housing, labor research, and self-administration. Undoubtedly the most important part of the Labor Front is the Strength through Joy association (*Kraft durch Freude*). It provides members with low-cost trips and excursions, sports and other forms of recreation, and looks to the improvement of factory ventilation, rest rooms, sanitation and the general aesthetic appearance of industrial plants.

The actual relations between labor and capital are determined by the Law for the Regulation of National Labor which was enacted on January 20, 1934.[10] Under the system established by this law strikes and lockouts are forbidden. The manager or employer of each enterprise, called the Leader, is held responsible for labor conditions in his enterprise. He draws up and promulgates works-regulations (*Betriebsordnungen*) covering such questions as working hours, wages and salaries, factory discipline and the like. He must, however, consult in advance the Mutual Trust Council or *Vertrauenrat* which exists in every concern employing more than twenty people. This Council consists of the Leader and from two to ten members of his personnel who are designated as his "followers." In electing members of the Council for one-year terms the employees have only a choice of approving or rejecting a single list of candidates drawn up by the Leader in conjunction with the head of the National Socialist party cell which has been formed in every establishment. If the list is rejected, the Labor Trustee, a

[10] *Reichsgesetzblatt,* Part I, 1934, p. 45.

government official, appoints the members. The Council acts in a purely advisory capacity. Its chief functions are to strengthen the bonds between workers and employer, discuss measures to increase the efficiency of the plant, give advice in the drafting of works-regulations and settle disputes about the application and interpretation of its provisions.

The whole set-up is supervised by fourteen Labor Trustees appointed by the Reich government. The Labor Trustee for each district superintends the constitution and acts of Mutual Trust Councils. He lays down general rules for the drafting of works-regulations and individual contracts of employment. Although the leader of the concern may depart from these rules when he deems them harmful to his business or employees, wilful violations are punishable. The Trustee also has sweeping powers regarding wages and dismissals. He may issue new wage schedules for enterprises when necessary to protect workers or keep the concern going and has, in fact, made frequent use of that power.[11] His approval is necessary for collective dismissals by employers of over ten per cent of the staff. In reality, therefore, the determination of working conditions has been taken largely out of the hands of both employers and employees and entrusted to officials of the Reich. These officials fall under the jurisdiction of the Minister of Labor to whom they regularly report on their activities and from whom they receive their instructions.

To advise him, each Labor Trustee has a permanent Council of Experts of not over sixteen members

[11] During 1934 and 1935 the Labor Trustees issued 1700 wage-schedules and sets of rules. *Cf.* Rawlins, *Economic Conditions in Germany to March 1936,* cited, p. 217.

who must represent all the industries in his district. Three-fourths are chosen by the Trustee from lists submitted by the Labor Front which must include five employers and five Mutual Trust Council members from every industry. The remaining members he may appoint at his discretion. In addition, the Trustee is advised in special cases, particularly in determining wage-schedules, by temporary Expert Committees composed of not more than eight members and drawn equally from workers and employers.

The National Socialists hold that labor and capital are bound to collaborate by a sense of honor and duty. For this reason they have established Courts of Social Honor—one for each of fourteen labor districts—to punish certain offenses. Each court consists of a judge and two assessors, one employer and one member of a Mutual Trust Council selected by the presiding judge from lists drawn up by the Labor Front. Cases can be submitted to the court only by the Labor Trustee, to whom complaints may be addressed in writing by any member of a business enterprise. Employers may be found guilty of an offense against "social honor" if they abuse their power, exploit their workers or insult their honor. Offenses by workers include malicious incitement of fellow-employees, deliberate disturbance of the *esprit de corps* in the plant, and exercise of undue rights of interference in the management of the business. The repeated dispatch to the Labor Trustee of frivolous and unfounded complaints may also be punished. The courts may issue warnings or reprimands, levy fines up to 10,000 marks and deprive employers of their right to "lead" the firm and thus determine conditions of labor. They may also dismiss workers and members of Mutual Trust Councils from their posts. The Labor Trustee may always appeal—and the accused under certain conditions —to a Supreme Court of Social Honor.

The Linking of Labor and Industry

After the Estate for Industry and Trade and the labor organization had been created, need was felt for cooperation between the two in order to prevent possible conflict. Accordingly, Dr. Schacht and Dr. Ley reached an agreement at Leipzig in March 1935 providing for the establishment of a Joint Self-Administration of Labor and Industry (*Selbstverwaltungsgemeinschaft von Arbeit und Wirtschaft*).[12] This agreement linked the Advisory Councils of the central Reich Economic Chamber and the regional Industrial Boards with the newly-created national and regional Chambers of Labor of the Labor Front. A Reich Council of Labor and Industry has been created, consisting of the Advisory Council of the Reich Economic Chamber and the Chamber of Labor. The latter, in turn, consists of national and regional heads of the Labor Front and specially appointed members. The function of the Reich Council is to discuss "common questions of business and social policy, creation of loyal cooperation of all divisions of the Labor Front, and acting on communications of the Government and of the leaders of the Labor Front." The same tasks are entrusted to regional councils which include the advisory body of the district Industrial Board and the membership of the regional Chambers of Labor. In addition, local Labor Committees of no more than twelve members have been set up. They represent a single branch

[12] For the text of the agreement, *cf.* Deutscher Akademischer Austauschdienst, *News in Brief*, First April Issue, 1935.

of industry in each locality and are composed half of employers, half of employees. One half of the membership must be taken from the expert committee which advises the Labor Trustee on that particular industry. The Committees are not permitted to make decisions, but may discuss matters of common interest to labor and capital, such as wage rates, measures preventing accidents and occupational diseases, and labor welfare, and submit recommendations to the Labor Trustee. Lowest in this organizational hierarchy are the Mutual Trust Councils for each enterprise.

The entire organization of German economic life is still in a fluid state. New bodies are constantly being established and old ones dissolved. Moreover, much of this complicated and rather bureaucratic corporate structure remains largely on paper. The functions of many of the constituent organizations are ill-defined and tend to overlap. Nevertheless, the system as a whole seems firmly established. Whatever its usefulness to business and labor, the government finds it an effective means of controlling and directing economic activity in the Third Reich.

CHAPTER IX

CULTURE AND RELIGION IN THE THIRD REICH

By its very nature the Third Reich was bound to insist upon the "coordination" of the cultural and religious life of the German people as well as upon the regimentation of German economic activity. Culture and religion and the organs dedicated to their propagation had to be fitted into the National Socialist mold. In National Socialist opinion culture is not something neutral, but the expression of race and fundamental philosophies of life (*Weltanschauungen*) which are inevitably tainted by political views. Thus the task of the state and the party which supports it is to free German Kultur from alien influences and keep it in conformity with Nazi racial and political thought. In religion the same conformity is essential. Here, however, the issue goes deeper. Historically there has often been conflict between Church and State, with the people divided in their allegiance. The totalitarian state cannot tolerate such divided loyalties. It insists on monopolizing the allegiance of its citizens.

The Chamber of Culture

On the basis of a law enacted on September 22, 1933[1] the government has established a Reich Chamber of Culture to bring under state control the various manifestations of cultural life. It is appropriately directed by the Minister for Popular Enlightenment and Propaganda. The Chamber is organized along professional lines into seven corporate entities. These include the Chambers of Press, Radio, Authorship, Theatre, Music, Plastic Arts and Painting, and Motion Picture Films. The presidents of the constituent chambers are all appointed by the Propaganda Minister. They constitute an Advisory Council to assist the head of the entire Chamber. The same function is performed by a Congress of Culture established in 1935 and including persons prominent in German cultural life.

The functional and regional organization of the

[1] *Reichsgesetzblatt,* Part I, 1933, p. 661.

Chambers has not yet been fully completed. Ultimately there will be district groups for each Chamber supervised by the regional directors of the propaganda ministry. More detailed functional classification is also being carried out.

As in the agricultural and industrial estates, membership in the Chamber of Culture is obligatory. It is not confined to "creative" workers, but includes all those engaged in the production, processing, marketing and custody of cultural products. Thus it comprises book publishers and dealers as well as authors; art galleries as well as painters. The president of each Chamber, however, may refuse membership to "unreliable" and "unsuitable" persons. By this means Jews have been excluded from the press, and the publishing and bookselling trades.

The general object of the organization is to promote German culture as the National Socialists conceive it. The Chamber largely determines what reaches the German people in the way of literature, music and art. It is also entrusted with the regulation of economic and social questions relating to each of the constituent professions.

State vs. Church

The coordination of cultural groups in the Reich was carried out with relatively little resistance. With the Church it has been different. Here the Third Reich has had to contend with its most formidable opposition. Even today the ultimate issue is not entirely sure. In the realm of religion the state has had to deal with organizations that have been long and powerfully entrenched, with convictions that are deeply rooted.

From the very beginning a clash between the National Socialist state and organized religion seemed inevitable. With the consolidation of Nazi power it became clear that National Socialism is an ideology or *Weltanschauung* which must itself be regarded as a religion. In its propagation of extreme national-ism—as expressed by the Nazi conceptions of blood (race), soil and honor and its glorification of the state—National Socialism is considered by leading theologians, both in Germany and abroad, as funda-mentally irreconcilable with the tenets of Chris-tianity, either Catholic or Protestant. Thus the present struggle is in essence a conflict between op-posing faiths—political and religious.

The major religious affiliations of the German peo-ple since the Reformation have been Evangelical (Lutheran-Reformed) and Roman Catholic, the former predominating in the north of Germany and the latter in the south and west. According to the 1925 census, 40 million Germans professed Lutheran-ism and 20 million, Roman Catholicism.[2] Before the revolution of 1918, the Lutheran churches had been state institutions under control of the separate Ger-man kings, princes and dukes. Even after the uni-fication of Germany in 1871 there was no Reich church and little change in church administration.[3] The reorganization of the Lutheran church which followed establishment of the Weimar Republic did not radically alter its form. The church had derived its governing power from the state, and continued to do so under the Weimar constitution. That instru-

[2] *Statistisches Jahrbuch für das deutsche Reich 1933,* Statis-tisches Reichsamt (Berlin, Reimar Hobbing, 1933), p. 18.
[3] *Die Religion in Geschichte und Gegenwart (Handwörter-buch für Theologie und Religionswissenschaft),* 2nd ed. (Mohr Verlag, Tübingen, 1928), Vol. I, p. 1888; Paul B. Means, *Things That Are Caesar's, The Genesis of the German Church Conflict* (New York, The Round Table Press, 1935), p. 5 *et seq.*

ment,[4] however, recognized the separation of church and state, providing that "there is no state church." Nevertheless, a complete divorce of church and state did not take place, although there was less state supervision and for the first time the church was independent of political interference. In administrative matters the church remained essentially decentralized along territorial lines. In 1922 the 28 territorial churches organized a union—the German Evangelical Church Federation—which somewhat unified them. The emphasis, however, remained on autonomy of these territorial districts, which continued to be the basic units of church government.

Lutheranism has always been essentially passive so far as its relations with the state and the development of political and social ideals are concerned. Respect for authority—spiritual, temporal and family—is its very essence.[5] Luther, moreover, made a distinction between private and public morality and regarded the state as "the divinely appointed authority based on reason, whose business it is to execute all the tasks which affect public order and the common weal; by this very fact the State is distinct from the Church, which is dependent solely upon spiritual influence and vital personal fellowship." War, too, is justified by this reasoning.[6-7] The economic thought of Lutheranism was as conservative and authoritarian as its political theories. The masses were discouraged from rising above their "stations in life," for existing conditions were regarded as part of an unchanging divine order.

[4] Articles 135-141.
[5] Ernst Troeltsch. *The Social Teachings of the Christian Churches,* translated from the German, 2 volumes (New York, Macmillan, 1931). Vol. II, p. 540 *et seq.*
[6-7] *Ibid.,* p. 550.

Although the temporal influence of Lutheranism was apparently in large part responsible for the failure of democratic principles to attain a secure foothold in Germany, the purely spiritual aspects of Lutheran doctrine make it impossible for the Evangelical church to accept National Socialism as a philosophy of life (*Weltanschauung*). For the Lutheran is taught that he must submit to the existing order except when commanded to deny the faith which Luther charged him to confess. It then becomes his duty to resist.[8]

THE RELIGION OF NATIONAL SOCIALISM

The official Nazi program declares (Point XXIV) that the party stands for "positive Christianity without binding itself to any particular confession."[9] In his Reichstag speech on March 23, 1933, Chancellor Hitler reiterated the Nazi avowal of "positive Christianity" and promised that the rights of the church would remain unchanged, declaring that the relations of church and state need undergo no alteration. During the intervening years, moreover, the Leader has repeatedly affirmed "positive Christianity." Alfred Rosenberg the supreme overseer of Nazi ideology, further defined the meaning of this phrase in his official commentary on the Nazi program. Rosenberg declares that "the idea which alone is capable of uniting all classes and confessions in the German people is the new and yet ancient *völkisch*[10]

[8] *Ibid.*, p. 540.
[9] Alfred Rosenberg, *Wesen, Grundsätze und Ziele der NSDAP: Das Programm der Bewegung erweitert durch das Agrarprogramm* (Munich, Volksverlag, 1934).
[10] The German word *völkisch* is an untranslatable mystical expression connoting the entire national, racial heritage of Germanism.

ideology, founded on the spirit of the German community which has only [temporarily] been frustrated. This ideology today is National Socialism."[11]

Rosenberg's philosophy—or religion—is expounded in his treatise, *The Myth of the Twentieth Century*[12] which, although officially characterized as an expression of the author's personal views, has nevertheless been made required reading for Nazis. In this book Rosenberg sets forth a "religion of blood,"[13] whose fundamental doctrine is the Nordic myth and, above all, the supremacy of Germanic man. He consequently insists that Christianity must be purged of every trace of Jewish influence. "The so-called Old Testament must once and for all be done away with as a religious book. By this act, the unsuccessful attempts during the past 1,500 years to transform us spiritually into Jews will fall to the ground."[14] "The Old Testament stories of immorality and cattle trading will be replaced by the Nordic Sagas and fairy tales, at first simply related, then understood as symbols. Not the dreams of hate and murdering Messiahs but the dream of honor and freedom is what must be kindled by the Nordic, Germanic Sagas. . . . The longing of the Nordic racial soul to give the folkic myths [*Volksmythus*] form as the German church, that is the greatest task of our century."[15] All "Jewish influence and interpretation" in the New Testament, moreover, must be eradicated.

Rosenberg, however, apparently does not wish to

[11] Rosenberg, *Wesen, Grundsätze und Ziele der NSDAP,* cited, p. 45.
[12] *Der Mythus des zwanzigsten Jahrhunderts* (Munich, Hoheneichen Verlag, 1930).
[13] *Ibid.,* p. 243.
[14] *Ibid.,* p. 566.
[15] *Ibid.,* pp. 575-76.

discard Christianity entirely but to re-evaluate it in terms of the so-called German race-soul.[16] Thus he rejects the conception of Christ as the "Lamb of God"[17] on the ground that it is Jewish, and denounces the Christian teaching of humility as a gigantic falsification. He declares:

"the prior hypothesis of all German education is recognition of the fact that it was not Christianity which brought morality to us [Germans] but that Christianity owes its lasting values to the German character. . . . The German character values therefore are the absolutes which regulate everything else."[18]

In the heroes of the World War Rosenberg sees the martyrs and saints of a new religious faith, because these men died for the myth of the blood. This myth is as heroic as that of 2000 years ago.

"The God whom we honor would not exist if our souls and our blood did not exist . . . therefore the task of our religion, of our law, of our State is everything which protects, strengthens, purifies the honor and freedom of this soul."[19]

Much the same ideas are being inculcated in German youth, organized under the leadership of Baldur von Schirach in the *Hitler Jugend* and *Bund deutscher Mädel* (Hitler Youth, and Federation of German Girls). Von Schirach's views were expressed in a recent speech[20] to the *Hitler Jugend*:

"Just as today a youth group is assembled in this spot which is neither Catholic nor Evangelical but simply

[16] *Cf.* Paul F. Douglass, *God Among the Germans* (Philadelphia, University of Pennsylvania Press, 1935), p. 39 *et seq.*
[17] Rosenberg, *Der Mythus des zwanzigsten Jahrhunderts,* cited, p. 577 *et seq.*
[18] *Ibid.,* p. 595.
[19] *Ibid.,* p. 656 *et seq.*
[20] Text of speech in *Junge Kirche* (Göttingen), November 2, 1935, p. 933 *et seq.*

German, so will an entire people eventually stand together; a people which is no longer divided into confessions but is united in belief in its leader and its holy mother earth. It is said that such a goal signifies cutting loose from all religion and we are accused of being Godless, enemies of Divine Providence. . . . All of us who stand together in this movement know that we are not here to fight against God, but on the contrary because we believe that we are fulfilling the will of God. . . . God has commanded us, that we feel to be an eternal truth: Stand together, fight for Adolf Hitler, fight for our German Fatherland. And if you do this, then you are fulfilling God's will."

The so-called *völkisch* ideas of religion—deification of Germanism and of race—of which National Socialism is in part at least an outgrowth, existed long before the Nazi revolution. Hitler's accession to power, however, brought them to the fore. Among the movements striving for advancement of a German faith[21] was the Tannenberg *Bund* (Federation), inspired by General Ludendorff and his wife, which attacked Christianity on the charge that the Bible is not original and that important elements of Christian doctrine are merely borrowed from Indian sources, while the Gospels are full of elements destructive of culture. Intensely anti-Semitic and anti-Catholic, the *Bund* stressed the importance of race and folkic Germanism. Another group advocating much the same theories was the Hermann Wirth Society, which spread the cult of supremacy of the Nordic race, believing that the origin of all true culture is not the Orient but the North. The same views were shared to some extent by the German Faith Movement—probably the most important of

[21] For a detailed account of these movements, *cf.* Douglass, *God Among the Germans,* cited, p. 47 *et seq.*

these groups—led by Professor William Hauer. Professor Ernst Bergmann, one of the foremost advocates of the new religion and closely associated with this movement, summarized the German creed as follows:

"I believe in the God of the German religion who is at work in nature, in the noble Spirit of Man, and in the strength of my people. I believe in the helper-in-need, Christ, who fights for the nobility of man, and in Germany, where the new humanity is being created."[22]

These groups differed from one another in the vehemence with which they denounced various aspects of Christianity, but all deified Germanism.

The year before the Nazi revolution a group calling itself the Religious Movement of German Christians was organized under the leadership of Pastor Hossenfelder of Berlin, a man almost unknown in Evangelical circles. This movement developed rapidly under the protection of the Nazis, and early in 1933 Hossenfelder was recognized by Hitler as the official leader of the German Christians. Although less radical than the out-and-out *völkisch* sects, their aim is to achieve Hitler's "positive Christianity" and eliminate from Evangelical Christianity anything incompatible with Naziism.[23] Their goal is "one people, one leader, one faith," and they believe that

"no German [*deutscher Volksgenosse*] in the Third Reich who pledges himself to a living Christianity can believe otherwise than that the achievement of such a unity of faith is the shining religious goal toward which the German soul is striving."[24]

[22] *Ibid.*, p. 67.

[23] Means, *Things That Are Caesar's,* cited, p. 218 *et seq.*; Douglas Reed, "The German Church Conflict," *Foreign Affairs,* April 1935.

[24] Dr. Christian Kinder, *Volk vor Gott* (Hamburg, Hanseatische Verlagsanstalt, 1935), p. 19.

Although maintaining that "the eternal foundations of our church are the revelations of God as found in Christ's history," the German Christians declare that the Nazi revolution also has brought to the German people new perceptions which are valuable in the life of the church:

> "Besides knowledge of the conjunction of race and culture, of race and politics, the conjunction of race and religion has been disclosed to us. With one accord we now see how we are tied in our own life and being to the ancient fundamentals of the beliefs of our fathers."[25]

The Jewish problem is regarded as a racial and not a religious question which must be solved in relation to existing conditions. The German Christians declare that "the [anti-Jewish] measures taken by the state and the people naturally apply in the regulation of our church."[26]

EFFORTS TO COORDINATE EVANGELICAL CHURCH

After the Hitler revolution, the initial move in pressing coordination of the Evangelical church with National Socialism came from the German Christians, backed by powerful Nazi political leaders. The revolution had been hailed at first by many important Evangelical leaders who, strongly nationalist and conservative in outlook, thought that Hitler had saved Germany from Communism. They believed, too, that godlessness—associated in their minds with Marxism—would now be vigorously suppressed and public morals reformed. For, due to the war, the post-war crisis, and what appeared to many Germans as failure of the church to meet the challenge of a changing world, real religious devotion

[25] *Ibid.,* pp. 27-28.
[26] *Ibid.,* pp. 34-35.

and church attendance had fallen off among both Catholics and Protestants. Many young people were disillusioned and uninterested in organized religion, despite various religious reform movements.[27]

At a conference held in Berlin on April 3, 1933, the German Christians demanded that the church take a firm stand for the sacredness of race and the limited value of the Old Testament; they pledged themselves in their constitution to war against "atheistic Marxism and ultramontanism."[28] Pastor Hossenfelder publicly insisted that the Evangelical church must become a single national organization and the existing administration dissolved at once, while the Nazi leader in the Prussian Diet, Kube, backed up Hossenfelder and threatened force if the demands of the German Christians were not instantly complied with.

Thus the first phase of the church conflict seemed primarily concerned with organization: the establishment of a unified Evangelical Reich church under a single leader, paralleling the political unification and centralization of the Reich. The 28 self-governing independent Evangelical churches, partly Lutheran and partly "Reformed" (Calvinist), apparently had nothing against unification as such.[29] The Church Federation[30] therefore directed Dr. Kapler, its lay president, and two eminent theologians to draft a constitution for a unified church.[31] On April 26, 1933 Chancellor Hitler announced the appointment of Military Chaplain Ludwig Müller—previ-

[27] Cf. Means, Things That Are Caesar's, cited.
[28] George N. Shuster, Like A Mighty Army (New York, Appleton-Century, 1935), p. 99 et seq.
[29] Reed, "The German Church Conflict," cited, p. 486.
[30] Cf. p. 290.
[31] For text of the Church Federation's statement, cf. Means, Things That Are Caesar's, cited, p. 222.

ously little known in church circles—as his representative in all matters affecting the Protestant church. It soon developed that Müller, who suddenly received the full backing of Hitler, was the Nazi choice for Reichbishop. At the end of April he met with the three Evangelical delegates at Loccum in Hanover to assist in drawing up a church constitution.

On May 26, 1933 the Loccum conference announced that the drafting was making progress, that there would be no interference with church doctrine and that a Reichbishop would be elected. The same day, the Church Federation announced that Dr. Friedrich von Bodelschwingh—administrator of the well-known Bethel Inner Mission—was their candidate for the national bishopric.

Immediately a battle began between the church and the German Christians, the latter supported by the Nazi authorities. Müller made a speech over the state-controlled radio, in which he declared that the church leaders had not listened to the "call of the hour"; that the German people wanted a fighter in the struggle for German freedom; that the Storm Troops must hear the Gospel preached in words which left no doubt that Christianity was "an heroic faith."[32] Use of radio and press was open only to the German Christians, and the disorganized opposition thus experienced great difficulty in supporting Dr. von Bodelschwingh.[33] Nevertheless, resistance to Müller stiffened, despite arrests and dismissals.[34] Dr. Rust, Nazi Minister of Education in Prussia, who had previously assured the church of his neu-

---

[32] Reed, "The German Church Conflict," cited, p. 488.
[33] Means, *Things That Are Caesar's,* cited, p. 227.
[34] Reed, "The German Church Conflict," cited, p. 487.

trality in the conflict, suddenly announced dismissal of the Evangelical expert in his department, who was succeeded by Dr. August Jaeger, a Nazi lawyer. On June 24 Rust made Jaeger commissioner of all the Evangelical churches in Prussia. These moves constituted open interference by the state in the administrative affairs of the church. Jaeger's appointment was hailed by the German Christians, and one of his first acts was to dissolve important church governing bodies in Prussia. This was followed by the resignation of Dr. von Bodelschwingh on the ground that the installation of Jaeger made continuation of his work impossible. German Protestantism was shaken to its depths by these events, and on June 30, 1933 President von Hindenburg intervened, requesting Hitler to attempt settlement of the conflict. The Leader commissioned Reich Minister of the Interior Frick to undertake negotiations to this end. Meanwhile, Müller and Jaeger had turned out of office practically the whole personnel of the church administration in Prussia.

Frick established a joint commission representing both parties to the dispute, which actually announced the terms of a new constitution on July 11. The document was officially approved and signed on July 14, and went into force the following day. Its provisions were relatively moderate and did not conform with extreme German Christian demands.[35] The preamble declared that the German Evangelical churches had unified themselves in the hour "when Almighty God has permitted our German nation to undergo a great historical transformation" and that

[35] For text of the constitution, cf. Werner Hoche, *Die Gesetzgebung des Kabinetts Hitler* (Berlin, Vahlen Verlag, 1933), Vol. III, p. 698 *et seq.*

these bodies now formed a German Evangelical Church. Section I, Article 1, however, proclaimed that the inviolable foundation of this church is the "Gospel of Jesus Christ as it has been revealed to us in the Holy Scriptures and newly confirmed in the confessions of the Reformation. Herein the powers which the church requires to fulfill its mission are determined and defined."

Although the constitution does not tamper with religious doctrine, it provides that "at the head of the church stands a Lutheran Reichbishop." In accordance with the Nazi leadership principle, this functionary is "summoned" by the National Synod. He is assisted in his duties by a Religious Ministerial Council—a sort of cabinet—the members of which are appointed by the Reichbishop. The National Synod, on the other hand, is formed of 20 members appointed by the German Evangelical Church "from among those who have distinguished themselves by service in the church," and 40 delegates from the synods and councils of the provincial churches. The latter are made up of "persons chosen by the church members." The Synod must meet once a year but its powers are nominal.

Elections to the synods were announced for July 23, 1933, and the powerful Nazi party machine backed the German Christian candidates. On the eve of the poll Hitler broadcast a speech which made it clear that a vote against the German Christians was equivalent to a vote against himself. The actual polling took place in an atmosphere of intimidation and terror[36] and the outcome was a foregone con-

[36] Reed, "The German Church Conflict," cited, p. 490; Shuster, *Like A Mighty Army*, cited, p. 106; Means, *Things That Are Caesar's*, cited, p. 237 *et seq.*

clusion, the German Christians obtaining a two-thirds majority in most of the local, district and national synods. In Prussia, as a result, the Synod of the Old Prussian Union Church (Evangelical) immediately chose Müller as State Bishop of Prussia, and the latter appointed Hossenfelder, leader of the German Christians, Bishop of Brandenburg. The 75 members of the Synod who were not German Christians were proclaimed "traitors" by Bishop Müller and threatened with imprisonment in a concentration camp. The Prussian Synod, moreover, enacted a law excluding from the clergy and from church office all persons who were not "politically reliable" or had Jewish antecedents within two generations. When the National Synod met on September 27, Müller was unanimously chosen Reichbishop.

Meanwhile, the cleavage within the church was growing more pronounced and the opposition was organizing. The situation of those pastors not belonging to the German Christian movement was complicated by the fact that most of them sincerely believed Hitler had saved Germany from Communism, awakened the people and restored German national honor. These men also had faith in Hitler's earlier pledge not to interfere in church affairs and consequently thought that attempts to Nazify the church had been undertaken without his knowledge. As time went on, however, these hopes proved unfounded and more and more Christian pastors joined the ranks of the church opposition, although always declaring that they were not hostile to the new state or National Socialism as a political movement. The opposition at first organized a group called "Gospel and Church," which by September 1933 comprised more than 2000 pastors. Their task was seriously

hampered by Nazi terror and censorship. In spite of
these obstacles, the opposition expanded its organization in October 1933 and renamed it "Pastors'
Emergency League." The 3000 members[37] were
pledged to defy the authority of Müller and resist
government interference with the ministry, especially application of the Aryan paragraph which
they contended was contrary to Holy Gospel.[38] The
Pastors' Emergency League declared that it "stood
unequivocally on the basis of the Holy Scriptures,
the Old and New Testaments, as the only law and
rule of conduct for our faith and our lives. . . ."[39]

The opposition group was of necessity loosely organized, and its task was made more difficult by the
fact that it had no way of convoking its entire membership. Nevertheless, it put up stiff resistance, aided
to some extent by outspoken protests and denuncia-
tions of Nazi church policy from foreign Protestants.
It was evident that the basis of the conflict had
shifted from church organization and administration,
and relation between church and state, to the more
fundamental problem of religious conviction. This
fact was underlined by publication of a series of
pamphlets written by Karl Barth, acting on behalf
of the Reformed (Calvinist) churches. Professor
Barth, recognized as one of the outstanding theologians in Central Europe whose words carried great
weight, condemned introduction of the so-called
leadership principle in the church, and unequivocally
rejected the doctrines of the German Christians,
maintaining that the "Evangelical Church ought

[37] *Kreuzzeitung,* November 19, 1933, quoted in *Der Zeitspiegel,*
December 3, 1933.

[38] Mildred S. Wertheimer, "The Jews in the Third Reich,"
Foreign Policy Reports, October 11, 1933.

[39] Manifesto of the Pastors' Emergency League, November 19
1933. Quoted in *Der Zeitspiegel,* December 3, 1933.

rather to elect to be thinned down till it be a tiny group and go into the catacombs than to make a compact even covertly with this doctrine."[40]

Despite Barth's influence and the stiffening of organized resistance to Müller and the German Christians, the latter seemed to have achieved fairly complete control of the church. On November 13, 1933 a huge German Christian meeting was held in the Berlin *Sportpalast* commemorating the 450th anniversary of Luther's death. The principal speaker was Dr. Krause, leader of the Berlin German Christian group, who delivered an impassioned address, demanding that church, divine service and doctrine be cleansed of everything "unGerman"—i.e. Jewish —and that the Old Testament with its "Jewish materialism" be eliminated together with the "superstitious portions" of the New Testament. These include the teachings of human brotherhood and humility which must be replaced by a return to "Jesus the hero." Therefore the crucifix, too, must be abolished. "As leaders, we do not need a God enthroned in the dim distance but only a fighter. . . . Worship of heroes must become the worship of God."[41]

Krause's speech aroused consternation throughout the Reich, and as a result Müller was forced to dismiss him from all church offices, publicly stating on November 15 that "such opinions and demands were nothing more than an insupportable attack on the doctrine of the church."[42] The speech, however, was believed to have embodied the real aims of the Nazis, and membership in the Pastors'

[40] Karl Barth, *Theological Existence Today; A Plea for Theological Freedom* (translated by R. B. Hoyle; London, Hodder and Stoughton, 1933), p. 45 *et seq.*
[41] *Der Zeitspiegel*, December 3, 1933.
[42] For text of Müller's declaration, cf. *ibid.*

Emergency League increased to almost 7000. The League demanded that Müller dismiss Hossenfelder, revoke the anti-Jewish church law and repudiate the German Christian heresies "including the doctrine that nationhood [*Volkstum*], history and contemporary developments should rank with Holy Scripture as a second source of revelation."[43]

Müller, temporarily on the defensive, dropped Hossenfelder and for the time being withdrew his support from the German Christians, but he no longer possessed authority. The Prussian opposition in the Pastors' League was reinforced by adherence of the Lutheran bishops of Bavaria, Baden, Hanover, Hesse and Württemberg. Müller, however, announced that opposition to his administration would be met by immediate suspension, and installed German Christian bishops widely throughout the country. Instead of uniting the church, Müller's methods and measures seemed to increase dissension. On December 8 he declared that the Evangelical youth groups were to be incorporated in the Hitler Youth. This important step placed a large section of German youth under the tutelage of Baldur von Schirach, whose deification of Germanism and repudiation—since retracted—of Christianity have alienated many German parents.

The German Christians, meanwhile, had split up into warring factions as a result of the *Sportpalast* meeting, some of them professing frankly anti-Christian views. The radicals had much in common with the Hauer-Bergmann-Reventlow group, which calls itself the Third Confession, and the doctrines of Rosenberg and von Schirach.[44]

[43] Reed, "The German Church Conflict," cited, p. 492.
[44] *Cf.* pp. 295-96.

Despite lack of unity within the German Christian and anti-Christian movements, there seemed no doubt that the Nazi régime was determined to support Müller and coordinate the church. Realizing this, the opposition pastors converted their Emergency League into a "Confessional Synod of the German Evangelical Church," which claimed to be the rightful church and which has since led the struggle against Nazification. Meeting at Barmen on May 30, 1934, this group agreed on six "evangelical principles" in refutation of what it regarded as heretical ideas:

"1. Jesus Christ, as He is revealed to us in the Holy Gospel, is the only word of God. . . . The heresy is refuted that the Church can and must recognize in addition to this one word, other events and powers, figures and truths as the revelation of God.

"2. God, through Jesus Christ, claims our whole life. The heresy is refuted that there can be spheres of life in which we do not belong to Him, but to other masters.

"3. The Christian Church is a community of brethren and belongs solely to Christ. The heresy is refuted that the Church can do with its mission and its organization as it likes and surrender it to the vagaries of temporarily prevailing philosophical and political convictions.

"4. The offices of the Church are not there to give one man dominion over another. . . . The heresy is refuted that the Church can and should give itself, or allow itself to be given, leaders endowed with ruling powers.

"5. The Gospel tells us that the State has the divine task of looking after law and order in a world not yet delivered. . . . The heresy is refuted that the State, over and above its special task, should and can become the single and total regulator of human life and thus also fulfill the vocation of the Church. The heresy is also refuted that the Church, above and beyond its own special task, should assume State characteristics, State tasks, and State dignities and thereby itself become an organ of the State.

"6. The mission of the Church . . . consists in the preaching to all people . . . the message of God. The heresy is refuted that the Church can place the word and works of the Lord at the service of any arbitrarily chosen wishes, aims and plans."[45]

This declaration removed any remaining doubts as to the character of the church struggle.

During the summer of 1934 Müller continued his attempted unification. The National Synod (elected in 1933) met for the first time in August and legalized all of Müller's measures, abolished the church flag, completely merged all formerly independent churches with the Reich church, and obliged all pastors and church officials to swear an oath of loyalty jointly to Hitler and the Reichbishop's administration. This oath, confusing spiritual with worldly issues, presented the opposition with a grave problem, for most of these pastors were politically loyal to Hitler. They took up the challenge, however, and the Brotherhood Council (*Bruderrat*)—the executive of the Confessional Synod—immediately issued a strong protest, stating that "obedience to this [Müller's] church government is disobedience to God." Despite the danger involved—only a few weeks earlier the bloody purge of June 30 had taken place—the manifesto was read in many churches.

Outwardly, however, the church administration had been unified except for the heads of the Bavarian and Württemberg Protestant churches. On September 23, 1934—14 months after his election—

[45] For text, *cf.* Henry Smith Leiper. *The Church-State Struggle in Germany* (London, Friends of Europe), No. 21, January 1935, p. 10 *et seq.*

Müller was solemnly consecrated as Reichbishop in the presence of all the bishops he had appointed.

Meanwhile, the struggle continued and for a time the strongest opposition came from South Germany. Bishops Meiser of Bavaria and Wurm of Württemberg refused to recognize incorporation of their churches with the Reich church: as a result Wurm was suspended, there were strong protest meetings in South Germany, more pastors were suspended and the salaries of others stopped, and Wurm was put under house arrest. Dr. Jaeger, appeared in Bavaria and, assisted by secret police, retired Bishop Meiser by force. Public indignation among church congregations in Bavaria, however, was so strong against these coercive methods that Jaeger and Müller were forced to back down. Hitler received the protesting bishops on October 30, and is reported to have told them that the Nazi state was not interested in settling problems outside its domain and "would not attempt to arrive at a solution by force."[46]

There followed a period of relative calm during which Reich Minister of the Interior Frick—to whose office Hitler had meanwhile transferred the task of "supervising the church conflict"—attempted to effect a settlement. By April 1935, however, Dr. Frick intimated that no harmony or union was apparent in the Evangelical churches and that the government might have to renounce its position of neutrality. This threat was given reality by the Reich Cabinet's promulgation of a law on June 26, establishing a department or committee (*Beschlussstelle*) for settlement of legal disputes arising out of the church conflict. This body was authorized to

[46] Shuster, *Like A Mighty Army*, cited, p. 160.

decide "whether the measures taken in the Evangelical church since May 1, 1933 are legal or illegal." Its establishment revealed the confusion in the Evangelical church administration, where as a result of the staunch resistance put up by the opposition there have been two church governments. Many of the suspended pastors and church officials, moreover, had sued for damages in the German courts and often won their cases, a fact which embarrassed the Nazi authorities. A semi-official commentary on the new *Beschlussstelle* stated that in its decisions this body is not strictly bound by church regulations or church law precedents. "Formal justice does not need to be recognized at all costs when its application would have absurd consequences."[47]

On July 18, 1935 Hitler appointed Hans Kerrl Reich Minister for Church Affairs with complete authority over both Protestant and Catholic churches, thus in effect dropping Müller despite his continued refusal to resign. The establishment of a special church department with dictatorial powers in the Reich cabinet signified that the Nazi government had decided to bring order out of the chaos in the Evangelical church which had resulted from the Müller régime. Despite numerous pronouncements indicating that a coordinated church would be permitted religious freedom, other actions of the government showed that the Nazis had not abandoned their determination, once succinctly expressed by Reichbishop Müller, of not resting "until only National Socialists stood in the pulpits and only National Socialists sat in the pews."[48]

On September 24 the Hitler government promul-

---

[47] *Frankfurter Zeitung,* September 29, 1935.
[48] Reed, "The German Church Conflict," cited p. 494.

gated a law stating that "the Reich Minister for
Church Affairs is empowered to issue decrees which
have the force of law, in order to restore order in
the German Evangelical church and in the Evangelical territorial churches (*Landeskirchen*)."[49] This
measure was supplemented on October 3 by a decree
providing for appointment by Kerrl of a church directorate to assist him. This body was to direct and
represent the German Evangelical church, issue decrees regulating internal church affairs, and lay down
fundamental principles for church administration.
The directorate, in agreement with the Reich Church
Minister, appoints and dismisses the officials of the
German Evangelical church.[50] Similar directorates
were provided for the various territorial churches.

Appointment of the eight members of the Reich
Church Directorate was announced on October 14,
seven of them being opponents of Müller and the
German Christians, and only one representing the
latter group. Three of the seven were spokesmen of
the Confessional church, three others sympathized
with the opposition but had not taken a definite
stand, and the seventh was reported to be a neutral
who, however, had not supported Nazi church policies. Nevertheless, the Confessional Synod made it
clear that its attitude was distinctly reserved, while
the Prussian Synod—the largest territorial group in
the opposition movement—refused to have anything
to do with the directorate, rejecting the state control
thus implied and maintaining that the government
had no right to appoint such a body.[51]

The fundamental conflict of views persisted, and

[49] *Reichsgesetzblatt,* I, September 28, 1935, p. 1178.
[50] Text in *Junge Kirche,* October 19, 1935, pp. 976-77.
[51] *New York Times,* October 15, 1935.

this fact was underlined by a proclamation of the directorate, issued on October 17, which affirmed the "National Socialist nation—a creation on the basis of race, blood and soil." On the other hand, it proclaimed Christ as the "Messiah and Savior of all nations and races" and His Gospel as "the inviolable foundation of the German Evangelical church." The purpose of the manifesto, according to Kerrl, was to "establish a clear separation between the fields of politics and religion and still leave to each its rights."[52] Its publication, however, did not reassure those sections of the opposition which had tended to regard Kerrl's conciliatory moves with sympathy.

The friendly motives of the Reich government were further called into question when, during the first week of November, the Nazi secret police closed two new independent theological seminaries organized by the Confessional Synods, expelled professors and students, and sealed the buildings.[53] Thus the church conflict flared up anew and Kerrl openly resorted to extreme dictatorial measures. The Confessional leaders had refused cooperation with him until German Christians were removed and banned from influential positions in the church. Due to this opposition, Kerrl abandoned his previous attitude of benevolent neutrality, and on November 29 the secret police searched the Berlin headquarters of the Confessional Brotherhood and confiscated the funds of the Confessional churches and synods, consisting of voluntary contributions from Protestants throughout the Reich. These moneys were quite separate from the regular church funds, and the action

[52] *Ibid.*, October 18, 1935.
[53] *Ibid.*, November 3, 7, 1935.

of the secret police—i.e., the government—seems to have had no legal foundation.[54]

Following the government's moves, the Confessional leaders, some of whom had recently favored compromising with the Nazis, were once more reunited in strong opposition. On Sunday, December 1, declarations were read in the churches charging the government with aiding and abetting the introduction of heresy into the teachings of the German Protestant church. The following day, Kerrl issued a decree designed to extirpate the Confessional Synod root and branch. The measure prohibits "church associations or groups" from exercising executive or administrative functions, and forbids them to appoint pastors and other spiritual officeholders, to examine and ordain theological candidates, to make parish inspections, to issue instructions for announcement from the pulpit, to levy and administer church taxes and other moneys, to issue instructions for collections in connection with parish gatherings, and to summon synods. Groups or organizations which continue to exercise these functions may be dissolved. Freedom of preaching in the church and promotion of religious companionship in church associations or groups are declared to be unaffected.[55]

Met by open defiance on the part of the Confessional groups, the government did not completely enforce this decree. Instead, Minister Kerrl gave a conciliatory statement to the press on January 20, 1936 in which he denied any attempt to interfere with religious convictions and claimed that the state only desired to unify contending groups within the

[54] *Ibid.*, November 29, 30, 1935.
[55] *Reichsgesetzblatt*, Part I, 1935, December 2, 1935.

Evangelical Church.[56] His action left no doubt of an intention to alienate the moderate from the more radical faction in the Confessional Movement. He put moderates in control of the appointed provincial church committees and generally left the German Christians in a minority. Although Reichbishop Müller was not dismissed or compelled to resign, he was deprived of all power and funds for representation. These conciliatory tactics were increasingly successful in winning over the more conservative Confessional leaders such as Bishop Marahrens of Hanover. The radicals, headed by Niemoeller and Jacobi, denounced the compromise party. In the Reich Confessional Synod which closed its session on February 22, 1936, they succeeded in ousting the so-called Provisional Church Administration presided over by Bishop Marahrens and in appointing an executive council composed of three members belonging to the Niemoeller faction. In addition, they secured a categorical reaffirmation of the refusal to recognize any church committees appointed by the government.[57]

The February Synod brought about a serious split in the Confessional ranks. With the approval and support of Minister Kerrl the moderates organized in March 1936 an independent Council of the Evangelical Lutheran Church of Germany to which adhered the most important territorial churches, including those of Bavaria, Württemberg, Hanover, Saxony and Mecklenburg.[58] In theory the Council has remained part of the Confessional Church and claims to differ from the radicals only as to meth-

[56] Deutscher Akademischer Austauschdienst, *News in Brief,* First February Issue, 1936, pp. 35-36.
[57] *New York Herald Tribune,* February 24, 1936.
[58] *New York Times,* March 22, 1936.

ods. According to its head, Dr. Marahrens, "the attitude of the Lutheran Church Council is that we must give some support to the official committees, some appointed by the government and some in conjunction with the government, in order to find the proper relationship between the church and the government."[59] Meanwhile, the more radical faction, which remains strong in the old United Church of Prussia, has continued an uncompromising struggle against state interference. In a vigorously worded letter addressed to Hitler in May or June 1936, they denounced the anti-Christian spirit fostered by the National Socialist movement and the denial of religious principles in public life;[60] and in a pastoral letter, read in all Confessional Churches on August 23, they once more declared that "the right of existence of the Church of Jesus Christ in this world is at stake."[61] Nevertheless, the division in the Confessional Movement has strengthened the government's hand and enabled it to proceed with greater vigor against the opposition. Thus in July 1936 the Reich Church Ministry ordered all government authorities to break off relations with the administration of the Confessional Church and to entertain no more complaints from that quarter.[62] Dismissals and arrests of Confessional pastors have continued.

HITLER AND THE CATHOLIC CHURCH

National Socialism is in the long run even more irreconcilable with Catholicism than with Protestantism. For the Catholic church represents to its communicants a system of absolute authority which

[59] *Ibid.*, September 29, 1936.
[60] For the text, *cf. New York Herald Tribune*, July 28, 1936.
[61] *Ibid.*, August 23, 1936.
[62] *New York Times*, July 23, 1936.

must of necessity conflict with the Nazi goal of a totalitarian state claiming equally absolute authority.[63] Apparently recognizing the inherent strength of the German Catholic church backed by the Holy See in Rome, the Nazis have not attempted the impossible task of reorganizing the Catholic church in the Third Reich. They have, however, persecuted many individual Catholic leaders—both priests and laymen, killing several prominent Catholics in the June 30 purge—and have tried to discredit the church with the German masses, while doing everything possible to gain control of Catholic youth.

The first round in the Catholic-Nazi struggle was won by the Nazis with the dissolution of the Catholic Center party on July 4, 1933.[64] Although the political influence of the church was exercised through the Center party, the Vatican—apparently considering it expedient to establish a *modus vivendi* with the new Nazi state—consented to a Concordat with the Reich. This document was virtually completed on July 3, 1933—the day before the demise of the Center party—but was not signed until July 20 and did not go into force until September 10.[65] The Concordat sanctioned dissolution of the Center party by forbidding Catholic churchmen to speak or act politically and conceding the right of the state to destroy all Catholic organizations having even a semi-political program. The Hitler government, for its part, pledged itself to establish uniform educa-

[63] For an illuminating discussion of both Protestantism and Catholicism in relation to the Nazi state, *cf.* Paul Tillich, "The Totalitarian State," *Social Research* (New York), November 1934.

[64] Mildred S. Wertheimer, "Political Structure of the Third Reich," *Foreign Policy Reports,* June 20, 1934.

[65] For text of Concordat, *cf.* Hoche, *Die Gesetzgebung des Kabinetts Hitler,* cited, Vol. IV, p. 515 *et seq.*

tional laws throughout the Reich and to permit
confessional schools even in districts where they had
been forbidden. The Vatican, moreover, secured direct control of university theological professorships,
although the state was given the right to question
future appointments to episcopal sees. Catholic organizations having a religious objective were recognized as legitimate.

Despite the Concordat, many Catholics were victims of the Nazi terror during the summer of 1933,[66]
and as time went on the struggle between the state
and the Evangelical church brought out the fundamental issues at stake for all organized religions.
Catholic realization of this fact was strongly shown
in 1933 by the Advent sermons of Cardinal Faulhaber of Munich, which attracted wide attention
both in Germany and abroad. The Cardinal—a recognized authority on the Old Testament—demonstrated that the church is unalterably committed to
acknowledging the Old Testament as a revelation,
and that Christianity is not conceivable apart from
Judaism.[67]

Meanwhile, despite the Concordat, the recognized
Catholic organizations, especially the youth groups,
were experiencing grave difficulties, and Catholic
publications were censored and suppressed by the
Nazis. With the incorporation of the Evangelical
youth organizations in the *Hitler Jugend* at the end
of 1933, moreover, the Catholic youth organizations
were the only ones outside that official association.
Members of the Catholic groups were constantly
molested by the *Hitler Jugend*, and their activities

[66] Shuster, *Like A Mighty Army*, cited, p. 153 *et seq.*
[67] Cardinal Faulhaber, *Judaism, Christianity and Germany*
(translated by G. D. Smith; New York, Macmillan, 1934).

were curtailed; priests criticizing the Hitler Youth were jailed; by July 1935 Catholic youth organizations were officially forbidden to engage in sport, social or educational activities.[68] The Hitler Youth, moreover, had become more outspokenly anti-Christian, and reports concerning ancient pagan rites at their convocations had become more frequent.[69]

The appointment of Rosenberg as cultural arbiter of the Reich had seriously disturbed the Catholics, and the Pope placed his *Myth of the Twentieth Century* on the index of forbidden books. During 1934 Catholic theologians published comprehensive analysis of the Rosenberg *opus*, demonstrating the fallacies in his historical research and setting forth their conceptions of the true origin of the Bible.[70] Rosenberg answered in a vitriolic pamphlet, defending his work and taking the opportunity further to attack and revile the Catholic church as based on a tissue of lies taken from "Asiatic" and "African" traditions wholly incompatible with nordic German values.[71]

The Catholic conflict with Rosenberg reached a serious stage early in July 1935, when the Bishop of Münster in a pastoral letter protested strongly to the highest Nazi authorities that a forthcoming address to be delivered by Rosenberg in Münster would

[68] *New York Times*, July 27, 1935.

[69] *Ibid.*, December 23, 1935.

[70] *Studien zum Mythus des XX Jahrhunderts,* published as an official supplement to the Amtsblatt des Bischöflichen Ordinariats (Berlin, 1934); *Der Apostel Paul und das Urchristentum, Nachtrag zu den Studien zum Mythus des XX Jahrhunderts,* published as official supplement to the Kirchliches Amtsblatt für die Diozese Münster. More than 70 publications denouncing Rosenberg have appeared in Germany.

[71] Alfred Rosenberg, *An die Dunkelmänner unserer Zeit, Eine Antwort auf die Angriffe gegen den Mythus des XX Jahrhunderts* (Munich, Hoheneichen Verlag, 1935).

be an "unbearable provocation" to the Catholic public[72] and an insult to their "most sacred religious convictions." Despite this protest, Rosenberg spoke in Münster and bitterly attacked the bishop, declaring that his letter was tantamount to an attempt to arouse the Catholics against the government. On the following day Minister of the Interior Frick also spoke in Münster and officially repeated Rosenberg's statements. As spokesman of the Reich government, he declared that according to the Concordat of 1933 Catholics must consider as binding on them all Reich laws, such as the sterilization measure and foreign exchange regulations. He added that Catholic occupational and youth organizations do not fit into present-day life and are "often active in fields which the Nazi state must reserve for itself." On July 9 Dr. Frick issued a decree providing that any one opposing enforcement of the sterilization law would be prosecuted.[73] The Vatican entered the controversy on July 16, when it dispatched a note to Berlin protesting against alleged violations of the 1933 Concordat, and charging that—contrary to the terms of this Concordat—sterilization measures were being applied to Catholics, there was interference with Catholic lay organizations, and the freedom of the Catholic press in Germany was being attacked.

Despite these protests, Frick issued another decree on July 17 providing "severe punishment for persons spreading propaganda against compulsory sterilization." Then on July 18 General Goering promulgated a far-reaching measure which, he announced, had been sanctioned by Chancellor Hitler. The Goering decree charged the authorities "to em-

[72] Münster is the heart of Catholic Westphalia.
[73] *Current History*, September 1935, p. 649.

ploy all their legal weapons against members of the Catholic clergy who falsely employ the authority of their spiritual position for political purposes," and accused the priests of openly denouncing state institutions and measures from the pulpit. While stating that the Nazis "allow the Catholic as well as the Protestant church complete liberty in faith and teaching," the decree reiterated that "politically only one idea of the state exists and is possible in Germany—namely, the National Socialist idea.[74] Herr Kerrl's appointment as Minister for Church Affairs with power over Catholics and Protestants was also announced on July 18.[75]

Although the Concordat guarantees the right to confessional schools, Church and State have been in almost continuous conflict on this issue. The government and the National Socialist party have not concealed their hostility toward confessional schools, which, they feel, have prevented the complete "coordination" of education under unified state control. Again and again they have brought pressure to bear on Catholic parents to place their children in public schools. How successful they have been is illustrated by the fact that in February 1936 only 34.89 per cent of the children in Munich and Nuremberg were registered for Catholic schools, as compared with 65.45 per cent the year before.[76] On October 13, 1936 the Bavarian Department of Education dealt another blow to confessional schools by ousting 600 out of a total of 1,676 nuns teaching in such institutions. Moreover, it ordered the dismissal, on January 1, 1937 of all nuns and members of reli-

[74] *New York Times,* July 17, 18, 19, 1935; *Frankfurter Zeitung,* July 28, 1935.
[75] *Cf.* p. 300.
[76] *Völkischer Beobachter,* February 3, 1936.

gious orders employed in state-supported Catholic schools.[77] Repeated and vigorous protests by the Catholic hierarchy have been ignored.

The campaign against the Catholic Church has been greatly aided by a series of charges brought against priests and members of religious orders. In 1935 the state prosecuted numerous priests, monks and nuns for smuggling foreign exchange out of the Reich. Prison sentences were in many cases meted out to those convicted, and heavy fines imposed on Catholic charitable and monastic orders. In 1936 there was another wave of trials, this time on charges of immorality. In Koblenz alone 276 members of a Franciscan order were prosecuted[78] and many were found guilty. The National Socialist press gave wide publicity to these trials and made use of them to discredit Catholicism with the masses. Thus the Hitler government seems determined to do all in its power to undermine the influence of the Catholic church in Germany. Its determination to abolish Catholic youth, sport and workingmen's societies is at present hampered by the Concordat. Double membership in the Hitler youth and Catholic societies, however, is forbidden. This conflict over control of youth organizations will doubtless be further sharpened by the law promulgated on December 1, 1936, which requires the enlistment of all German boys and girls in the Hitler Youth under the leadership of Baldur von Schirach.[79] Civil servants had long been virtually forced to enroll their children in the Hitler Youth.[80] Workers must belong to the

[77] *New York Times,* October 14, 1936.
[78] *New York Times,* May 27, 1936.
[79] *Ibid.,* January 5, 1936.
[80] *Cf. The Times* (London), November 19, 1935 for court action upholding this principle.

Labor Front in order to secure or keep their jobs, while Catholic workingmen's groups are denied membership in the Labor Front.[81] Catholic youth organizations are continually harassed. Thus in February 1936 the leader and about 100 other officials of the Reich Union of Catholic Youth Associated were suddenly arrested and kept in prison for four months on charges of conspiring with Communists.[82]

The Church, for its part, is fighting to retain control of the education of Catholic youth through confessional schools and the youth organizations; for the right of the clergy to discuss questions of collective ethical import, such as sterilization; and, finally, for immunity of the clergy in the pulpit. It is clear that all of these aims may be—and are—construed by the Nazis as having political implications and furnishing a means of potential opposition to the Third Reich. The Catholics maintain, however, that they merely wish to live to themselves while rendering unto Caesar the things that are Caesar's without mixing in active politics.[83] The situation of the Catholics is perhaps not as dramatic as that of the Protestants, but it is equally serious. The Catholics are absolutely opposed to Nazi sterilization and race laws; the prosecution for the alleged violation of foreign exchange decrees, moreover, virtually constitutes state warfare against the Catholic orders in Germany. And the neo-pagan influence on the Hitler Youth, the difficulties of Catholic schools in Bavaria, besides the virtual suppression of Catholic youth organizations, are regarded not only as a

[81] *New York Times,* December 1, 1935.
[82] *Cf. New York Times,* February 12 and May 19, 1936.
[83] Pr. J. Muenzer, "Ce que Veulent les Catholiques," *Revu des Vivants,* October 1935, p. 1507 *et seq.*

violation of the Concordat but as a dangerous threat to the church.

Conclusion

While the final outcome of the struggle for control of the German conscience remains uncertain, the National Socialists appear to have made considerable progress in the Evangelical Church. There they have profited from division in opposition ranks to consolidate their hold on church government and minimize the influence of the more radical, uncompromising pastors. True, their success has been obtained only by a policy of greater moderation. They have had to sacrifice, at least temporarily, the German Christians who seem to have disintegrated into numerous factions ranging from out-and-out anti-Christians to moderates who still believe that Christianity and National Socialism can be reconciled by divorcing the former from Judaism. The Catholic Church, on the other hand, persists in united opposition to state control and impairment of its traditional rights. It is doubtful that this opposition can in the end deter the Hitler government from attaining its objective. That goal appears to be one people, one Reich, one faith—based on the doctrine of blood, race, soil and deification of the state.

THE
POLITICAL STRUCTURE OF
THE SOVIET STATE

INTRODUCTION

In 1936, nineteen years after the Bolshevik *coup d'état*, the Soviet Union is still in the throes of a profound economic and social revolution. In the face of innumerable handicaps the Soviet government has unremittingly pursued the gigantic task of socialization and industrialization. It has had to rely almost exclusively on the country's own resources of capital and raw materials. It has had to employ on giant undertakings labor which lacks the technical experience and discipline of Western labor. It has had to combat and suppress the hostility of important groups of the population, most formidable of which has been the passive resistance of the peasants. Much of the work accomplished under these circumstances has inevitably been hasty, crude, ill-devised; much has been of high quality, and has revealed at their best the imagination, resourcefulness and selfless zeal of Soviet leaders.

No generalization can adequately encompass the maelstrom of new ideas, new experiences, new aspirations in the midst of which the Russian people is working out its destiny. The state, far from "withering away" as predicted by Marxist doctrine, has daily encroached more and more on the individual. The abolition of class distinctions based on wealth, and the drastic social leveling intended to pave the way for the classless society of the future have failed to prevent class differentiations based on control of power. The suppression of organized religion, regarded as synonymous with ignorance and superstition, has been accompanied by an almost religious worship of the machine and the material benefits it is expected to produce.

The pace set by the Five-Year Plan has been feverish, has created serious tension between workers and peasants, has strained the nerves of even the iron young generation, has resulted in startling contradictions. Side by side with enthusiasm and unlimited faith in human progress which surpasses that of the Victorians, one finds depression and that kind of apathy which can be more dangerous than active opposition. Side by side with sincere concern for the improvement of living conditions, care of mother and child, a new humanitarian spirit, one finds readiness to sacrifice human lives to the achievement of plans dictated from above. Side by side with a materialistic conception of life, constant emphasis on scientific method, deprecation of sentimentality, one finds a mystic exaltation of socialism and its prophet Lenin, embalmed for posterity not unlike the saints exposed to public ridicule in anti-religious museums. The Soviet Union is still in a state of profound ferment and it would be hazardous to predict the ultimate outcome of its manifold undertakings. One thing can be said with assurance: state socialism—state control over industry, trade, transportation, banking and, ultimately, agriculture—is firmly established. Whatever changes may be effected in the near future will be directed not at the overthrow of the existing system, but at its consolidation and further adaptation to the needs of the U.S.S.R. It is therefore particularly important to examine the political structure of a state which, for the first time in world history, has undertaken to control and direct both production and distribution in accordance with a clearly defined program of social readjustment.

The autocratic rule of the Romanov dynasty established in 1613 remained unchallenged until the Napoleonic wars, which brought the Russian armies in contact with the theories of nationalism and constitutionalism then ripening in Western Europe. The spiritual ferment created by this glimpse of a new world of political thought found an outlet in the abortive Decembrist revolution of 1825, organized by a handful of nobles and army officers. Far from heeding this warning, however, Nicholas I sought to crush social unrest by a policy of severe repression. The weakness of his method, which stifled political initiative without uprooting opposition, was dramatically revealed by Russia's defeat in the Crimean war, which convinced the government that the country's prestige as a great power could be restored only by internal reforms. The reign of Alexander II, who succeeded Nicholas I in 1856, was consequently marked by a series of measures designed to improve agriculture, develop industry and establish the rudiments of civil liberty.[1]

[1] For the history of Russia, 1825–1917, cf. the following works: R. Beazley, N. Forbes and G. A. Birkett, *Russia from the Varangians to the Bolsheviks* (Oxford, Clarendon Press, 1918); Michael Karpovich, *Imperial Russia, 1801–1917* (New York, Holt, 1932); V. O. Kluchevsky, *A History of Russia* (four volumes, New York, Dutton, 1911–1926); Bernard Pares, *A History of Russia* (second edition, New York, Knopf, 1926); *Idem., Russia and Reform* (London, Constable, 1907); George Vernadsky, *A History of Russia* (revised edition, New Haven, Yale University Press, 1930); M. N. Pokrovsky, *Russkaya Istoriya s Drevneischich Vremen* (Russian History since the Most Ancient Times), fifth edition, Moscow, State Publishing House, 1923. For additional works on this period, cf. the bibliographies contained in the above volumes.

The first step toward agrarian reform was taken in 1861 with the promulgation of the Emancipation Edict, by the terms of which twenty million household and peasant serfs received personal freedom without compensation to their former masters. The distribution of land which accompanied emancipation, however, proved unsatisfactory to the peasants, who for the most part received smaller allotments than those they had previously leased from the landowners and had to purchase land at a price usually in excess of its actual value. The ownership of land, moreover, was vested not in individual farmers, as in Western Europe, but in the village community (*mir*), which the peasants could leave only with the greatest difficulty. The peasants consequently developed little or no sense of private property and, with the exception of a small group of *kulaks*—rich peasants who had succeeded in buying land other than that assigned to the *mir*—suffered from "land-hunger," intensified by the steady growth of the agricultural population. They regarded the Emancipation settlement as essentially unjust, and believed that the government should correct this injustice by dividing among them the estates of the gentry and the nobility.[2]

Despite these grievances, which constituted a potential danger to the established order, the peasants, who were for the most part illiterate, remained politically passive. Their principal spokesmen were drawn not from the village, but from the educated classes—gentry and intelligentsia—which advocated

[2] For a detailed analysis of the agrarian problem before the Bolshevik revolution, *cf.* G. T. Robinson, *Rural Russia under the Old Régime* (New York, Longmans, Green, 1932); Vera M. Dean, "Russia's Agrarian Problem," Foreign Policy Association, *Information Service,* Vol. VI, No. 10, July 23, 1930.

recognition of the peasants' right to land and civil liberty. This group of idealistic men and women, inspired by romantic devotion to the peasants and by a desire to go "to the people," formed the nucleus of the Social Revolutionary party organized about 1900. The Social Revolutionaries regarded the peasants as the keystone of the Russian state, and sought to arouse them by education and propaganda to revolt against autocracy.[3]

THE RISE OF THE PROLETARIAT

Beginning with the nineties, however, the activities of the Social Revolutionaries were overshadowed by the rise of a class-conscious proletariat. Industrialization, which had made a modest start under Peter the Great, received fresh impetus after the Crimean war, when the government not only encouraged, but frequently subsidized, the construction of factories and railways and the exploitation of natural resources. Like all undeveloped countries, Russia had to finance its industry with foreign capital, imported chiefly from France, which after the conclusion of the Franco-Russian alliance in 1893 invested heavily in strategic railways, mines and other enterprises.

Russia's industrialization was fraught with far-reaching political and social consequences. The growth of industry hastened the emergence of an educated middle class, roughly divided into two groups—the "big" bourgeoisie, composed of bankers and industrialists, and the "small" bourgeoisie and

---

[3] *Cf.* Katerina Breshkovskaia, *Hidden Springs of the Russian Revolution* (Stanford University, Stanford University Press, 1931), the memoirs of one of the leading figures in the Social Revolutionary party, and Vera Figner, *Memoirs of a Revolutionist* (New York, International Publishers, 1927).

intelligentsia, recruited from merchants, technical experts and the liberal professions. The "big" bourgeoisie, which enjoyed the advantages of cheap labor and of a high protective tariff, allied itself with the autocracy in demanding the preservation of order, and in turn received aid from the government for suppression of labor conflicts. By contrast the "small" bourgeoisie, which derived less tangible economic benefits from the Tsarist régime, opposed the forces of reaction and cherished a romantic longing for political liberty. While the more radical members of the intelligentsia pledged their allegiance to various revolutionary groups, the majority of the "small" bourgeoisie supported the Constitutional Democratic party (*Cadets*), led by professors and liberal landowners, which advocated universal suffrage, constitutional monarchy, and solution of the agrarian problem by expropriation of the landowners, who were to receive money compensation.

The rise of the middle class was paralleled by the transformation of many landless peasants, who had been absorbed by the new industries, into a class-conscious proletariat which numbered 3,000,000 on the eve of the Bolshevik *coup d'état* in 1917. The proletariat suffered the usual hardships of an industrial revolution—long hours of work, low wages, intolerable living conditions and brutal treatment on the part of employers and police. Deprived of all opportunity to voice their grievances through trade unions, prohibited by the government until 1906, the workers resorted to illegal "underground" organizations which eventually became affiliated with the Social Democratic party formed in 1898 by a group of radical intellectuals, notably Georgyi Plekhanov, who had popularized the writings of

Marx in Russia, and V. I. Lenin. Unlike the Social Revolutionaries, who devoted their attention mainly to the peasants, the Social Democrats concentrated their efforts on the industrial workers, whom they regarded as shock troops of the coming revolution. At the London Congress of 1903 the Social Democratic party split into two factions—the Bolsheviks, led by Lenin, and the Mensheviks, among whom was Lenin's former collaborator, Leon Trotzky. The Bolsheviks, who were in a minority in Russia but had a majority at the congress, favored a thorough-going revolution to be effected by violent means, while the Mensheviks advocated evolutionary methods and cooperation with the bourgeoisie for the overthrow of autocracy.

The ultimate success of the Bolsheviks appears to have been determined less by their numbers, which remained relatively small until 1917, or even by their close-knit organization, than by the driving force of Lenin, who combined an iron will and a profound knowledge of economic theory with a keen sense of political expediency, and whom neither defeat nor defection among his adherents could divert from preparations for the revolution. Born in 1870 of a family of well-to-do intellectuals, Lenin early in his youth discovered a lifelong source of inspiration in the writings of Karl Marx. Arrested in 1896 for revolutionary activities, and later deported to Siberia, he utilized his enforced leisure to analyze Russia's economic conditions in the light of Marxist doctrine. In 1900 he left Russia and settled in Zürich, where he founded a newspaper, *Iskra* (The Spark), which became the organ of the Bolsheviks. Except for a brief visit to Russia during the 1905 revolution, he remained abroad until 1917, immersed in studies which often appeared academic to his followers and practically isolated from direct contact with Russian workers.[4]

THE 1905 REVOLUTION

The various currents of social unrest which Tsarist repression had failed to subdue converged in the revolution of 1905, precipitated by Russia's defeat in the Japanese war. This revolution reached its climax in the general strike of October 1905, which completely paralyzed the country's economic life. The government, faced by determined opposition on the part of the liberal bourgeoisie, the proletariat and the peasants, issued a manifesto which promised a number of fundamental reforms, including the establishment of a *Duma* elected by democratic suffrage and the recognition of civil liberties. The October manifesto revealed a fatal lack of unity among the revolutionaries: the liberals, while pressing for a constitution, feared further acts of terrorism and were for the most part content to accept the government's program, while the Social Democrats, who under Trotzky's leadership had organized the first Soviet[5] of Workers' and Soldiers' Deputies in St. Petersburg, demanded the overthrow of the monarchy. This divergence of aims, which created an irreparable breach between bour-

[4] No definitive biography of Lenin has yet been published in English. The best available works are Valeriu Marcu, *Lenin* (New York, Macmillan, 1928); D. S. Mirsky, *Lenin* (Boston, Little, Brown, 1931); Leon Trotzky, *Lenin* (New York, Minton, Balch, 1925); and George Vernadsky, *Lenin, Red Dictator* (New Haven, Yale University Press, 1931). For other works on this period, *cf.* also V. I. Lenin, *The Iskra Period* (New York, International Publishers, 1929); Leon Trotzky, *My Life* (New York, Scribners, 1930); *idem., The History of the Russian Revolution* (New York, Simon & Schuster, 1932), 3 vols.

[5] The word *soviet* means council.

geoisie and proletariat, proved the death blow of the revolution. The army, which had meanwhile returned from the Far East, remained loyal to the government, and the country gradually returned to a state of political apathy from which it was not aroused until the industrial strikes of 1913–1914.

The 1905 revolution, however, was not entirely barren of results. While representation in the *Duma* was practically restricted to the propertied classes, and while its powers were constantly whittled down by the autocracy, this assembly nevertheless constituted Russia's first experiment in self-government since the *zemstvos*.[6] The agrarian disorders of 1905, moreover, had demonstrated the danger of a property-less peasantry. By the Stolypin reforms, 1906–1910, the peasants were consequently permitted to separate themselves from the *mir* and to take personal possession of land without compensation to the community. On the eve of the World War, nearly 25 per cent of the peasants in European Russia had left the *mir* and had received individual properties.

RUSSIA DURING THE WORLD WAR

The World War, which in Western states rallied all parties to the support of their respective governments, produced the opposite effect in Russia where, after the first outburst of patriotism, the bourgeoisie as well as the proletariat were soon alienated by the autocracy's incompetent military organization. The weak and obstinate character of Nicholas II de-

[6] The *zemstvos* were provincial councils established in 1864, on which the nobility, the town intelligentsia and the peasants were represented, and which exercised a certain degree of autonomy with respect to education, health and road construction.

feated the efforts of his more able collaborators to formulate a unified policy. A series of reactionary and ignorant ministers, who were at the mercy of Court circles dominated by Rasputin, Empress Alexandra's favorite, flitted rapidly across the political scene. Neither industry nor transportation proved equal to the demand for war material. All attempts of the liberal *zemstvos* and of civil organizations to supplement the government's inadequate preparations were viewed with suspicion and promptly suppressed. Hoarding of foodstuffs by the peasants, which became widespread after 1916, caused an acute food shortage in the cities, and increased the dissatisfaction of the army, whose morale had been shaken by military reverses. The bourgeoisie, which had hitherto opposed extreme measures, began to advocate the overthrow of the monarchy. Bread riots in the principal cities culminated in the revolution of March 1917. The Emperor was forced to abdicate, and power passed into the hands of the Provisional Government, composed of Constitutional Democrats and *zemstvo* leaders, with one Social Revolutionary, Alexander Kerensky, in its ranks.[7]

THE BOLSHEVIK COUP D'ETAT, 1917

The rule of this government of liberals who, content with political revolution, contemplated no fundamental social changes, was promptly challenged by the Soviets of Workers' and Soldiers' Deputies, which had been simultaneously organized by Social Revolutionaries and Social Democrats,

[7] For a study of Russia's political and social conditions on the eve of the March 1917 revolution, *cf.* Michael T. Florinsky, *The End of the Russian Empire* (New Haven, Yale University Press, 1931).

chiefly Mensheviks. The Provisional Government, undismayed by the fact that Russia lacked political experience and was then in the throes of a disastrous war, referred the solution of all pressing problems, including the land question, to a Constituent Assembly, to be elected by universal suffrage and convened in the autumn of 1917. Constitutionalism and democracy, however, had no meaning for the peasants, workers and soldiers, who demanded land, bread and peace at any price. The soviets, which after Lenin's return from exile in April had been gradually converted to the Bolshevik point of view, adopted the slogan "All power to the soviets!" and advocated withdrawal from a war in which, they claimed, the proletariat was being needlessly sacrificed to selfish capitalist schemes. The disorganization of the army, which had been subjected to able Bolshevik propaganda, practically suspended military operations after June 1917. Kerensky, who had meanwhile become Prime Minister, was unable either to control the soviets or to elaborate a concrete program which would have met the demands of the masses. The bourgeoisie failed to assume the leadership in this crisis, and offered no effectual resistance to the Bolshevik *coup d'état* of November 1917, which established the "dictatorship of the proletariat." The new government immediately announced its intention to terminate the war, nationalized land, took possession of banks and factories, separated the church from the state and the school from the church. The Constituent Assembly, which finally convened in January 1918 after perfunctory elections, was unceremoniously dissolved, despite the protests of Mensheviks and Social Revolutionaries.

The authority of the Soviet government, controlled by the Bolsheviks—who assumed the name of Communist party in 1918 [8]—was at first paramount only in Great Russia, notably the two capitals, Petrograd (rechristened Leningrad) and Moscow. No sooner had the government obtained a "respite" in the West by concluding a separate peace with Germany at Brest-Litovsk in March 1918 than it found itself confronted by several hostile "White" armies. These armies, recruited chiefly from officers, the bourgeoisie and the old bureaucracy, and aided by Allied expeditionary forces, disputed Soviet rule in North and South Russia and in Siberia until their final defeat in 1920.[9] The dangers of civil war and intervention were further increased by the threatened disruption of the Russian Empire, whose two hundred races and nationalities, differing widely in education, religion and economic development, had been held together before 1914 largely by a brutal policy of "Russification." [10] Finland had become an independent republic in 1917; the new states of Poland,

[8] The original name, "All-Russian Communist party (Bolsheviks)," was changed to "All-Union Communist party (Bolsheviks)" after the establishment of the Soviet Union in 1923.

[9] For a detailed account of this period, cf. A. L. P. Dennis, The Foreign Policies of Soviet Russia (New York, Dutton, 1924); Louis Fischer, The Soviets in World Affairs (two volumes, New York, Cape and Smith, 1930), Vol. I, Chapters I–VIII; General William S. Graves, America's Siberian Adventure (New York, Cape and Smith, 1931); United States, Papers Relating to the Foreign Relations of the United States, 1918, Russia (2 volumes, Washington, Government Printing Office, 1931), Vol. I.

[10] The population of the Soviet Union is at present composed as follows: Russians, 52.9 per cent; Ukrainians, 21.2 per cent; White Russians, 3.2 per cent; Kazaks, 2.7 per cent; Uzbeks, 2.6 per cent; Tartars, 2 per cent; Jews, 1.8 per cent; Georgians, 1.2 per cent; Azerbaidjan Turks, 1.2 per cent; Armenians, 1.1 per cent. Other racial and national groups constitute less than one per cent of the total population. American-Russian Chamber of Commerce, Economic Handbook of the Soviet Union (New York, 1931), p. 3.

Estonia, Latvia and Lithuania had been established on Russia's Western border; [11] Rumania, Russia's World War ally, had seized Bessarabia; White Russia, the Ukraine, the various peoples of the Caucasus, had sought to erect national states with foreign assistance. The spirit of local autonomy swept in the wake of civil war.

FORMATION OF THE SOVIET UNION

The disintegration of the former empire was not only contrary to Soviet doctrine, which envisaged a union of the world proletariat irrespective of national boundaries, but seriously threatened Communist plans for the economic reconstruction and industrialization of the country. This tendency had been partially stemmed in 1918 by the "free and voluntary union" of "the laboring classes of all nationalities" of Great Russia in the Russian Soviet Federated Socialist Republic, which became the nucleus of the future Soviet Union. The danger of territorial break-up was further lessened in 1920, when White Russia and the Ukraine, which had failed to secure independence, concluded treaties providing for military and economic union with the R.S.F.S.R. Similar agreements with the R.S.F.S.R. were signed in 1921 by Georgia, Armenia and Azerbaidjan, which a year later jointly organized the Transcaucasian Soviet Federated Socialist Republic. The Communist party, however, believed that the political bonds uniting the four soviet socialist republics were not yet sufficiently close. At the Tenth All-Russian Congress of Soviets in 1922, Joseph

[11] *Cf.* M. W. Graham, "Security in the Baltic States," *Foreign Policy Reports,* Vol. VII, No. 25, February 17, 1932.

Stalin, then People's Commissar for Nationalities, consequently urged the formation of a Union of Soviet Socialist Republics on the ground that economic reconstruction and the danger of capitalist attack necessitated a strong centralized government. The congress promptly adopted a declaration and a treaty of union, both of which were ratified by the first All-Union Congress of Soviets on December 22, 1922, and were promulgated on July 6, 1923.[12] This federation, originally composed of the R.S.F.S.R., White Russia, the Ukraine and the Transcaucasian S.S.R., was subsequently enlarged by the admission of the Turkmen and Uzbek Soviet Socialist Republics in 1925, and of Tadjikistan in 1929. The territories of the Russian Empire were thus united in "the first workers' republic of the world," from whose name all reference to its predominantly Russian character had been intentionally omitted.

The treaty of 1923, which until 1937 was also the constitution of the U.S.S.R., established a federation of six Union republics (to which the Tadjik S.S.R. was added in 1929). The territory and population of the Union republics are shown in the following table:[13]

[12] For the Russian text of the declaration and the treaty of union, cf. Union of Soviet Socialist Republics, *Sbornik Postanovlenii i Rasporiazhenii Raboche-Krestianskovo Pravitelstva S.S.S.R.* (Collection of Decrees and Regulations of the Workers' and Peasants' Government of the U.S.S.R.), Moscow, 1923, No. 1, p. 16. For an English text of these documents, cf. Walter R. Batsell, *Soviet Rule in Russia* (New York, Macmillan, 1928), p. 300. Since 1923 the laws of the Soviet Union have been published annually in *Sobranye Zakonov i Rasporiazhenii Raboche-Krestianskovo Pravitelstva S.S.S.R.* (Collection of Laws and Regulations of the Workers' and Peasants' Government of the U.S.S.R.), which appears in two parts, the first part containing laws and decrees, while the second contains administrative regulations and treaties with foreign states.

[13] *Handbook of the Soviet Union,* compiled by the American-Russian Chamber of Commerce (New York, Day, 1936), p. 3.

THE UNION OF SOVIET SOCIALIST REPUBLICS[14]
(as of January 1, 1933)

Union Republics	Area (square kilometers)	Population
Russian S.F.S.R.	19,707,000	113,991,100
Ukrainian S.S.R.	451,800	32,069,700
White Russian S.S.R.	126,800	5,439,400
Transcaucasian S.F.S.R.	185,600	6,888,300
Uzbek S.S.R.	172,000	4,928,400
Turkmen S.S.R.	443,600	1,182,200
Tadjik S.S.R.	143,900	1,192,100
U.S.S.R.	21,230,700	165,681,200

Under the new constitution drafted in 1936 by a special commission headed by Stalin, the Transcaucasian S.F.S.R. was broken up into three Union Republics—the Armenian, Azerbaidjan and Georgian Soviet Socialist Republics, and two new republics were created—the Kazakh and Kirghiz Soviet Socialist Republics—making a total of eleven Union republics, as contrasted with six under the 1923 constitution.

The Union government is entrusted not only with powers usually reserved to the central organs of a federation—conduct of foreign affairs, national de-

[14] The R.S.F.S.R. is composed of 11 autonomous republics and 15 autonomous regions; the Ukrainian S.S.R. contains one autonomous republic—Moldavia; the Transcaucasian S.F.S.R., until 1936, contained three republics—Georgia, Armenia and Azerbaidjan—three autonomous republics and two autonomous regions: the Tadjik S.S.R. contains one autonomous region. The autonomous republics which are found in the R.S.F.S.R., the Ukrainian S.S.R. and the Transcaucasian S.F.S.R. are little more than administrative divisions established on an ethnographic basis. While these republics enjoy a considerable degree of cultural autonomy, they are politically and economically subordinated to the government of the Union republic in which they are situated, and ultimately to the government of the U.S.S.R. The autonomous regions which are found in the R.S.F.S.R., the Transcaucasian S.S.R. and the Tadjik S.S.R. occupy an even less important position in the structure of the Union, and for the most part serve merely as organs of local administration.

fense, administration of the federal budget—but controls foreign and internal trade, and is authorized to establish a general plan of national economy, to formulate the general principles of education, to issue fundamental labor laws and to define the principles governing the development and use of land. These powers—until 1936—were vested in the All-Union Congress of Soviets, which under the new constitution will be called the Supreme Council of the U.S.S.R. In practice the Congress delegated its legislative powers to a Central Executive Committee which it elected, and its executive powers to a Council of People's Commissars, appointed by the Central Executive Committee. The Union republics, whose respective governments are similar to that of the Union, with a congress (now council), central executive committee (now replaced by a presidium) and council of people's commissars, retain the right of "free withdrawal" from the Union and sovereign authority over all matters not specifically reserved to the federal organs, including the administration of justice, health, education and social welfare. Despite this provision, all activities of the republics must conform with the policies of the Union government and the Communist party, and decrees of republican organs which infringe on the Union constitution may be repealed by the All-Union Congress.

The political centralization of the Union, which has been denounced by some critics as another form of "Russification" is justified by Soviet spokesmen on the ground that, while all national groups have a right to self-determination, this right must always be subordinated to the interests of the class struggle, which demands a centralized government during the period of socialism.[15] The Communist party, however, has always maintained that centralization should be "democratic" in character and should be accompanied by a wide degree of cultural autonomy. Unlike the Tsarist régime, the Soviet government encourages every national group, no matter how small, to develop its own language and literature, in the hope that education will strengthen the consciousness of proletarian solidarity. Obscure languages have been revived and transcribed, alphabets have been devised for dialects which formerly possessed no written literature, native languages have been introduced in the schools, courts and government institutions of various regions, and an effort has been made to select local officials from the native population. This policy which, according to Stalin, will facilitate the eventual assimilation of proletarian groups irrespective of nationality, has been hampered, on the one hand, by the chauvinism of the Great Russians, who demand the "liquidation" of all national cultures and the adoption of a single language for the whole Union and, on the other, by a drift toward local "nationalism" on the part of national groups in which "petty bourgeois" elements retain considerable influence. At the Sixteenth Congress of the Communist party in 1930 Stalin denounced both tendencies as deviations from the "party line," and demanded their eradication by the party.[16]

[15] *Cf.* V. I. Lenin, *Izbrannye Statyi po Nazionalnomu Voprossu* (Selected Articles on the National Question), Moscow, State Publishing House, 1925; Joseph V. Stalin, *Nazionalnye Momenty v Partyinom i Gosudarstvennom Stroitelstve* (National Questions in Party and State Construction), Moscow, State Publishing House, 1925.

[16] All-Union Communist Party, *Shestnadzatyi Syezd Vsesoyuznoi Communisticheskoi Partyi* (Sixteenth Congress of the All-

Despite the government's efforts to equalize the economic and cultural opportunities of the national groups composing the Union, the R.S.F.S.R., with ninety per cent of the country's territory and sixty-eight per cent of its population, continues to occupy a dominant position in the federation, while the Great Russians, who form sixty-five per cent of the Communist party, enjoy a marked preponderance in the federal administration.

CHAPTER I

MARXIST POLITICAL THEORY

THE political system established by the 1923 treaty has been, at one and the same time, denounced as a ruthless dictatorship and acclaimed as the only real democracy in the world. No general conclusions regarding the character of the Soviet government can be reached without a preliminary analysis of the theory, organization and functions of the Communist party, which occupies a pivotal position in the Soviet state.[1]

Russian communism, while daily adapted to the needs of the Soviet Union by timely interpretation, continues to derive its theoretical content from the works of Lenin,[2] which in turn are based on those

Union Communist Party, Stenographic Report, Moscow, State Publishing House, 1930, pp. 54–57.

[1] For the official history of the All-Union Communist party, cf. Emelyan Yaroslavsky, editor, *Istoriya VKP* (History of the All-Union Communist Party), four volumes, Moscow, State Publishing House, 1926–1930. *Cf.* also Gregorii Zinovyev, *Istoriya Rossiiskoi Communisticheskoi Partyi* (History of the Russian Communist Party), Moscow, State Publishing House, 1923.

[2] The first edition of Lenin's works, begun in 1920 and completed in 1926, consists of twenty volumes, published by the State Publishing House as *Sobranye Sochinenyi* (Collected Works).

of Karl Marx and his collaborator, Friedrich Engels. Lenin's principal contribution to political theory was not the introduction of new concepts, but his re-interpretation of Marxism, which he rescued from the sterile discussions of Marxist Socialists, and his practical application of a doctrine originally devised for highly industrialized states to a country pre-dominantly agricultural. The essential features of a workers' state may be found in Marx and Engels. It remained for Lenin to translate theory into action.

Unlike Hegel, who viewed the state as a mystical entity, the product of "the general progress of the human mind," Marx believed that the character of the state is determined primarily by the existing "material forces of production." The development of these forces, which shape not only the economic but the social and political structure of society, of-fers, according to Marx, the principal clue to the understanding of history. The forces of produc-tion, however, are not static: they undergo constant change and eventually conflict with existing property relations, within whose framework they have hith-erto developed, but which now act as intolerable

A second edition, which includes posthumous and hitherto un-published material, known as *Sochineniya* (Works), was begun by the Lenin Institute in Moscow in 1926, and will consist of twenty-five volumes when completed. A translation of the second edition, authorized by the Lenin Institute, is now in progress under the auspices of International Publishers, New York. Current bibliographies of all publications relating to Lenin and Leninism are contained in *Leniniana*, published annually by the Lenin Insti-tute. Moreover, a number of Soviet periodicals, of which the fortnightly *Bolshevik* is the most important, publish articles de-voted to interpretation of Lenin's writings. The outstanding ex-position of Lenin's doctrines is found in Joseph V. Stalin, *Lenin-ism* (London, Allen and Unwin, 1928). *Cf.* also Mirsky, *Lenin,* cited, p. 191 *et seq.*, and Max Eastman, *Marx, Lenin and the Revolution,* (London, Allen and Unwin, 1926).

fetters. This conflict precipitates a revolution, in the course of which the entire structure of society is eventually transformed.[3]

Applying Hegel's dialectical method to the analysis of social problems, Marx argued that history consists of class struggles, each social system, based on existing forces of production, creating an antithesis by which it is ultimately destroyed. Throughout the ages, he contended, freeman and slave, baron and serf, burgess and journeyman—"oppressor and oppressed"—have been arrayed each against the other.[4] The capitalist system, itself founded on the ruins of feudalism, merely intensifies the class struggle by dividing society into two irreconcilable camps—the bourgeoisie, which owns the means of production, and the proletarians, who must sell their labor to gain a precarious livelihood. Capitalism, the thesis, calls into being its antithesis, organized labor, by introducing collective methods of production, strict industrial discipline and universal literacy.[5] The establishment of large-scale industry, the expansion of commerce and navi-

[3] For Marx's only direct statement of the materialist conception of history, cf. Karl Marx, A Contribution to the Critique of Political Economy (Author's Preface), translated from the second German edition by N. I. Stone (New York, International Library Publishing Company, 1904). Cf. also, N. I. Bukharin, Historical Materialism (New York, International Publishers, 1925). For a recent commentary on Marxist theory, cf. Sidney Hook, Towards the Understanding of Karl Marx (New York, John Day, 1933).

[4] Karl Marx and Friedrich Engels, The Communist Manifesto (New York, International Publishers, 1930).

[5] Karl Marx, Capital, a Critique of Political Economy, translated from the fourth German edition by Eden and Cedar Paul (two volumes, New York, Dutton, 1930), Vol. II, p. 846; V. I. Lenin, Gosudarstvo i Revolutzia (The State and Revolution), Petrograd, "Life and Science," pp. 94–95. For an English translation of the latter work, cf. V. I. Lenin, The State and Revolution (London, Communist Party of Great Britain, 1925).

gation, the struggle of industrialized states for markets and raw materials, all tend to concentrate economic and political power in the hands of a few great capitalists, while the ranks of the proletariat are constantly swelled by the impoverishment of the lower middle class. Despite its power, however, the bourgeoisie fails "to cope with the abundance of the wealth which it has created," [6] and proves unable, during recurring periods of overproduction and unemployment, to provide security "for its slaves even within the confines of their slavish existence." [7] The proletarians, who "have nothing to lose but their chains," cannot hope to alter existing conditions by other than violent means. To seize the political machinery is not sufficient: the workers, under the leadership of their vanguard, the Communist party, must abolish the economic conditions which give rise to capitalism—private property and the exploitation of labor.[8] "The knell of capitalist private property sounds. The expropriators are expropriated." [9] The capitalist system is supplanted by its antithesis, the "dictatorship of the proletariat." Out of this conflict, according to Marx, a final synthesis—classless society—is evolved, with whose establishment "pre-history ends and history begins."

THE DICTATORSHIP OF THE PROLETARIAT

The appearance of a classless society, which is synonymous with communism, is preceded, according to Marx and Lenin, by a transition period known

[6] Marx and Engels, *The Communist Manifesto,* cited.
[7] *Ibid.*
[8] *Ibid.*
[9] Marx, *Capital,* cited, pp. 846–847.

as socialism, when the dictatorship of the proletariat
gradually socializes natural resources and means of
production, and may use all means at its disposal,
including violence, to extirpate the last remnants of
capitalism. During this period which, it is expected,
will be marked by bitter struggles between "a dying
capitalism and a communism which is being born," [10]
the state, conceived primarily as an instrument of
the ruling class, will continue to exist. Only when
classes have been completely destroyed will the
state become obsolete and slowly "wither away,"
until it is relegated, in Engels' phrase, to the mu-
seum of antiquities, along with the bronze axe
and the spinning-wheel.[11] Economic inequalities between intellectual work and manual labor will likewise persist under socialism; consequently goods
will be distributed among the citizens not according to need, but on the basis of work actually performed.[12]

Both Marx and Lenin argued that the dictatorship of the proletariat, while resorting to compulsion, will differ from its predecessor, the bourgeois
state, in one important particular: in contrast to
the latter, where a majority, the proletariat, had
been oppressed by a minority, the former will organize the masses of the people for the oppression
of a small group of exploiters. The workers' state,
they claimed, will thus be more truly democratic
than so-called Western democracies, where legal
provisions guaranteeing liberty and equality of

[10] V. I. Lenin, "Economics and Politics during the Period
of the Dictatorship of the Proletariat," *Sochineniya,* cited,
Vol. XV, p. 347.
[11] *Idem., Gosudarstvo i Revolutzia,* cited, p. 16.
[12] *Ibid.,* p. 87.

workers and employers alike are nullified in practice by the control which the propertied classes exercise over the schools, the courts, the press and the
ballot-box.[13] Nor is the "democratic" character of
the dictatorship of the proletariat modified, in their
opinion, by the restrictions which it places on the
freedom, not only of former exploiters, but even of
the ruling class. These restrictions are regarded as
a temporary expedient, which will be abandoned at
the termination of the class struggle.[14]

Neither Marx, nor Lenin before 1917, attempted
to describe the political structure of the socialist
state in any detail, beyond referring in laudatory
terms to the type of government established by the
Paris Commune of 1871, which both regarded as
the first step toward proletarian revolution.[15] Marx
expressed particular enthusiasm regarding the fact
that the Commune had been "not a parliamentary,
but a business corporation," combining executive
and legislative functions, and that deputies had been
selected not for their political views but for their
technical qualifications. Lenin indicated a prefer-
ence for a state organized on the model of a business enterprise, in which the class of professional
"rulers"—civil servants and politicians—would be
rapidly replaced by technical experts selected by the
laboring masses, in which all public functions would
be simplified and brought to the level of the average

[13] *Ibid.,* p. 82.
[14] Program of the All-Russian Communist Party, *Vossmoi
Syezd Rossiiskoi Communisticheskoi Partyi* (Eighth Congress
of the Russian Communist Party), March 18–23, 1919 (Stenographic Report, Moscow, "Communist," 1919), p. 341.
[15] Karl Marx, *Der Bürgerkrieg in Frankreich* (Berlin-Wilmers-
dorf, *Die Aktion,* 1919); Lenin, *Sochineniya,* cited, Vol. XII,
p. 163.

citizen's capacity, and whose defense would be entrusted to an army drawn exclusively from the
proletariat.[16]

The Marxist conception of political organization
in the "classless" society which will succeed socialism
has as yet been even less definitely formulated.
Inequality between intellectual and physical labor
will presumably disappear, production will be greatly
expanded, and social wealth will be distributed on
the principle of "from each according to his ability,
to each according to his needs." [17]   The population,
trained in the methods of collective production, will
learn to observe the elementary rules of collective
life, and the machinery of the state, designed primarily for compulsion, will be discarded in favor of
unqualified freedom and equality.[18] National barriers
will disappear as proletarian revolution spreads from
state to state, and the proletariat of the world, liberated from the capitalist yoke, will unite in one vast
community of producers.[19]

MARXISM AND THE SOVIET "CLASS" STATE

The development of the Soviet state since 1918
has, on the whole, followed the course indicated by
Marxist doctrine. The dictatorship of the proletariat,
controlled by the Communist party, has socialized
industry and over eighty per cent of agriculture, and
has transformed the state into a vast business enterprise operated by a hierarchy of soviets which com-
bine executive and legislative powers. During this
period, regarded as transitional, the class struggle,

[16] Lenin, *Gosudarstvo i Revolutzia,* cited, p. 46.
[17] *Ibid.,* p. 90.
[18] *Ibid.,* p. 84.
[19] No attempt is made in this book to give an analysis of the
economic theories of Marxism.

far from abating, was intensified by the sharp distinction drawn between four main social classes: the proletariat—workers and "poor" peasants; the "middle" peasants, potential allies of the proletariat, who had not yet been entirely won over to the socialist cause; employees and professional men, drawn chiefly from the old intelligentsia; and the former "exploiters"—aristocrats, bourgeoisie, private traders, priests and, after 1930, *kulaks*—who were known as the "disfranchised" (*lishentzi*).

The proletariat, composed of factory workers and farm laborers, was recognized as the ruling class, and was accorded various privileges with respect to food rations, housing, medical aid, recreation and education. This class, however, had not yet produced its own intelligentsia, and the government was consequently forced to rely on the services of "bourgeois" technical experts, the majority of whom were non-Communists, and until recently were suspected of nurturing counter-revolutionary sentiments. Distrust of the technical intelligentsia weighed like a millstone on Soviet industry: experts whose tasks called for the greatest initiative hesitated to make important decisions which, if unsuccessful for technical or other reasons, might lead to prosecution for counter-revolutionary crimes and eventual imprisonment, exile or death. Stalin attempted to remedy this situation in June 1931, when he declared that the government should henceforth seek not to suppress but to attract the technical experts who, in his opinion, were no longer as hostile to the Soviet régime as in the past. "It would be stupid and senseless," he said, "if we were now to look upon practically every engineer of the old school as if he were a potential criminal or 'wrecker.' "[20] Following Stalin's speech, a large number of engineers accused or convicted of counter-revolutionary activities were released from prison and encouraged to resume their work, with assurance that they would not be willfully prosecuted for technical errors. While many specialists now enjoy a standard of living equal or even superior to that of the workers and are urged to display greater initiative, some of them still remain agents, rather than collaborators, of the proletariat. Finally, the "disfranchised" were penalized for their connection with the Tsarist régime by deprivation of civic rights and social ostracism: they and their older children were practically barred from active participation in Soviet life and were doomed, as a class, to slow extinction.

This class demarcation which, according to Western critics, was the direct antithesis of democracy, was regarded by leading Communists as an inevitable corollary of the transition period, which must witness the final destruction of capitalist elements both in the economic system and in "the consciousness of men." Communist spokesmen declared that the progress of economic planning and the consequent growth of socialism had already mitigated the class struggle, and predicted the abolition of all classes under the second Five-Year Plan, scheduled to end in 1937. The fundamental political problem of the second Five-Year Plan, in their opinion, would be "the transformation of all the working population of the country into conscious and active builders of a classless socialist society."[21]

[20] Cf. Stalin's speech on "New Economic Problems," The Soviet Union Review, July-August 1931, p. 152.

[21] Cf. report on the second Five-Year Plan by Vyacheslav Molotov, president of the Council of People's Commissars of

With the triumph of collectivization, which by 1936 had eliminated the danger of further peasant opposition; the progress of production, not only in heavy industries, but in those devoted to the manufacture of consumers' goods; the resulting improvement in the food supply and the general standard of living; and the realization that the Soviet Union could defend itself against foreign attack if necessary—the Soviet government found it possible to relax the stringent curbs it had imposed on the population during the revolutionary period of storm and stress. The new constitution drafted in 1936 reflects this change in the government's attitude. While it does not materially alter the administrative system or relations between the government and the Communist party, it seeks to establish the equality of all citizens before the law, irrespective of social origin and economic status, and specifies the rights to be enjoyed by all within the framework of the socialist state.

LIBERTY UNDER THE SOVIETS

The dictatorship of the proletariat, as prophesied by Marx and Lenin, has not abandoned the use of force during the period of socialism, and the rights of all individuals, irrespective of class, have been subordinated to collective interests as interpreted by the Communist party. A vigilant secret police is charged with the task of checking all attempts to overthrow or openly criticize the government. Workers and technical experts are subject to "mobilization" and may be transferred at short notice from one weak "sector" of the industrial or agricultural

the U.S.S.R., at the Seventeenth Conference of the All-Union Communist party, February 4, 1932, *Izvestia,* February 5, 1932.

"front" to another.[22] While Soviet legislation permits the existence of religious associations of all sects and denominations, in practice religious groups constantly encounter serious obstacles to the prosecution of their activities. The right of association is granted only to professional or social groups which have the government's approval, and attempts to form non-Communist political organizations or even independent Communist factions are promptly suppressed. The expression of unorthodox political or economic views is barred in schools and universities. The press, the radio, the publication of books, are controlled solely by the government. Even literature and art are judged less by their intrinsic quality than by their willingness to depict the class struggle.

Stifling as these restrictions on individual liberty may appear to Western observers, they are justified in Soviet opinion by the exigencies of the class struggle and the wartime tension resulting from the application of the Five-Year Plan. It should be noted, moreover, that liberty as conceived in Western states played little or no part in the pre-revolutionary life of the Russian proletariat. The sense of individual dignity which the West inherited from the Renaissance and the Reformation was practically unknown to the Russian masses, brought up in a tradition of Byzantine subservience to autocracy and orthodoxy. Far from resenting the absence of rights they had never enjoyed, the workers now derive a real sense of power from the economic benefits which they receive and from their participation in

[22] For a translation of some Soviet labor laws, *cf.* Great Britain, *A Selection of Documents Relative to Labour Legislation in Force in the Union of Soviet Socialist Republics* (London, H. M. Stationery Office, 1931), Cmd. 3775, *Russia No. 1, 1931.*

innumerable conferences and elections. Furthermore, while even the workers must abstain from
criticism of the government and the Communist
party, they are encouraged to flay economic short-
comings under the guise of "self-criticism."

COMMUNISM AND THE AGRARIAN PROBLEM

While the structure of the Soviet state thus em-
bodies the principal features of Marxism, the special problems of the Soviet Union have necessitated
considerable modification of Marxist doctrine. Of
the various modifications introduced by Lenin and
his successor, Joseph Stalin, none has provoked such
bitter controversy within the Communist party as
that concerned with the solution of Russia's agrarian
problem. Convinced that the proletarian revolution
would first occur not in a highly industrialized state,
as predicted by Marx, but in a state where capitalism
was weakest, Lenin did not hesitate to proclaim the
dictatorship of the proletariat in a country eighty
per cent of whose population was composed of peasants eager to obtain private ownership of land. He
clearly perceived, however, that the rule of the
proletariat—workers and farm laborers—could be
successfully maintained in Russia only with the cooperation of the "middle" peasant (*seredniak*), distinguished from the so-called rich peasant (*kulak*)
by the fact that he is not an exploiter of labor.[23]

To achieve this end, Lenin advocated the industrialization and voluntary collectivization of agriculture which, in his opinion, would not only raise
agrarian productivity, but create an identity of interests between workers and peasants, and exter-

[23] Lenin, *Sobranye Sochinenii*, cited, Vol. XVI, p. 146;
Vol. XX, p. 361.

minate the seeds of capitalism in the village.[24] The Communist party, however, was divided regarding the policy best calculated to secure peasant participation in this program. Trotzky, who after Lenin's death in 1924 feared that the concessions granted to the peasants by the New Economic Policy would consolidate agrarian capitalism, urged drastic measures of repression against the *kulaks,* as well as intensive collectivization.[25] Stalin, Secretary-General of the party, contended in 1927 that Trotzky's policy, which he denounced as "Left Opposition," was premature, and would merely foment class war in the villages. Nevertheless, with the introduction of the Five-Year Plan in 1928, Stalin sought to hasten collectivization and to restrict *kulak* activities by methods strikingly similar to those advocated by the exiled Trotzky. These measures, in turn, were criticized by the more moderate elements of the Communist party, known as the Right Opposition, under the leadership of Rykov, president of the Council of People's Commissars, who wished for the time being to protect the interests of the more prosperous peasants. Stalin, however, denounced the protests of the Right Opposition as inspired by "petty bourgeois sentiments," obtained the recantation of Rykov and his associates in 1929, and proceeded to carry through his policy of collectivization and "liquidation" of the *kulaks,* with the result that over seventy-five per cent of the country's farms had been collectivized by the end of 1935.[26]

[24] *Ibid.,* Vol. XVI, p. 106; Vol. XVIII, Part I, pp. 143, 200.
[25] Leon Trotzky, *The Real Situation in Russia* (New York, Harcourt, Brace, 1928), p. 60 *et seq.*
[26] For Stalin's attack on Trotzky and "Trotzkyism," *cf.* Joseph V. Stalin, *Ob Opposizii: Statyi i Rechi, 1921–1927* (Regarding the Opposition: Articles and Speeches, 1921–1927), Moscow, State

CHAPTER II

THE COMMUNIST PARTY

INTERNAL conflicts and resulting modification of Marxist doctrine, however, have not impaired the outward unity of the Communist party, preserved by a close-knit organization, an iron discipline and a strict enforcement of the "party line." The Communist party has at present a total membership of 1,500,000. The relatively slow growth of the party is due, in part, to the rigid conditions required of candidates for admission, and in part to the searching control which the party exercises over its members through periodic investigations of their activities, known as "purges," which frequently result in the censure or expulsion of politically "alien" or passive elements.

THE COMMUNIST PARTY

The constitution of the party, adopted at its Fourteenth Congress in 1925,[1] draws a sharp dis-

Publishing House, 1928, and his political report to the Fifteenth Congress of the Communist Party in 1927, *Piatnadzatyi Syezd VKP* (Fifteenth Congress of the All-Union Communist Party). Stenographic Report, Moscow, State Publishing House, 1928, p. 68 *et seq. Cf.* also N. I. Bukharin, *Partiya i Opposizionnyi Blok* (The Party and the Opposition Bloc), Leningrad, "Priboi," 1927. For a detailed study of Soviet agrarian policy, *cf.* Vera M. Dean, "Russia's Agrarian Problem," Foreign Policy Association, *Information Service*, Vol. VI, No. 10, July 23, 1930.

[1] *Ustav VKP s Resolutziami Partsyezdov, Conferenzii i TSK VPK po Voprossam Partyinovo Stroitelstva* (The Constitution of the All-Union Communist Party with the Resolutions of Party Congresses, Conferences and of the Central Committee of the

tinction between the workers who, according to Communist doctrine, must serve as the vanguard of the proletariat and must form at least fifty-one per cent of the party,[2] and other groups of the population. Applicants for membership are consequently divided into three categories: 1. workers and Red Army soldiers (subdivided in turn into two groups —industrial workers engaged in physical labor, and non-industrial workers, including farm hands); 2. peasants and private handicraftsmen; 3. employees, professional men and others. Qualifications for admission range from a six months' period of probation, accompanied by two recommendations from party members of two years' standing for the first group of the first category, to a two-year period of probation and five recommendations from party members of five years' standing for the third category.

In recent years, however, the percentage of factory workers has declined, while that of peasants and other social groups has slightly increased. Of the total membership of the party in 1935, 50 per cent were workers, 20 per cent were peasants and

Party on Questions of Party Construction), Moscow, State Publishing House, 1926. For discussion of various questions concerning the organization of the party, cf. the stenographic reports of the sixteen party congresses, as well as the following: *Rossüskaya Communisticheskaya Partiya v Postanovleniach ye Syezdov, 1903–1921* (The Russian Communist Party in the Resolutions of its Congresses, 1903–1921), Moscow, State Publishing House, 1921, and *Rossiiskaya Communisticheskaya Partiya v Resolutaziach ye Syesdov i Conferenzii, 1898–1927* (The Russian Communist Party in the Resolutions of its Congresses and Conferences, 1898–1927), Moscow, State Publishing House, 1927. For discussion of current questions of party organization, cf. *Partiynoe Stroitelstvo* (Party Construction), a semimonthly organ of the Central Committee of the party; *Pravda* (The Truth), the party's daily organ; and such periodicals as *Bolshevik*.

[2] *Cf.* resolution of the Thirteenth Party Congress, 1924, *Ustav VKP,* cited, p. 106.

the rest were drawn from employees and intellectuals.[3]

Members of the Communist party are required not
only to obtain a thorough knowledge of Marxist
doctrine and to participate in all civic and party activities, but to observe a certain standard of personal conduct. They must abstain from excessive
drinking and other indulgences, and must in general
serve as an example to the rest of the population.
The Communists, regarded as the governing *élite*,
are industriously trained for their manifold tasks in
a series of special educational institutions ranging
from local schools of "political grammar" to the
Communist Academy and the Marx-Engels and
Lenin Institutes in Moscow. While both careerists
and incompetents may be found in the ranks of the
party, the Communists have on the whole shown
sustained zeal and enthusiasm, and have willingly
served as shock troops in the new enterprises
launched under the Five-Year Plan.

The Comsomol

The members of the Communist party will gradually be relieved at their posts by the new "shift"
now trained in the Communist League of Youth
(*Comsomol*), composed of 5,000,000 boys and girls
between the ages of fourteen and twenty-three. The
constitution [4] of the *Comsomol*, like that of the

[3] In 1930, 68.2 per cent of the party were industrial workers,
18.7 per cent peasants, and the rest employees and intellectuals.
Calendar-Ezhegodnik Communista na 1931 God (Calendar of the
Communist for 1931), Moscow, "The Moscow Worker," 1931,
p. 351.

[4] *Ustav i Programma Rossiiskovo Leninskovo Communi-
stecheskovo Soyuza Molodiozhi* (Constitution and Program of
the Russian Leninist Communist League of Youth), Moscow,
State Publishing House, 1926. *Cf.* also Balashov and Nelepin,
VLKSM za Desyat Let v Tzifrach (Ten Years of the Russian
Leninist Communist League of Youth in Figures), Moscow, "The

party, draws a distinction between proletarian and non-proletarian elements. Young workers and peasants are admitted without recommendations or previous probation, while youths of non-proletarian origin must undergo a year's probation, and present two recommendations from party or *Comsomol* members of two years' standing. The *Comsomols* are regarded as a leavening element in the young generation, whose vanguard they are destined to become. They are consequently encouraged to perfect their knowledge of Communist doctrine, to improve their health by sports and physical culture, to participate collectively in the political and economic activities of the community in which they live, and to prepare themselves for the defense of the country. While promotion from the *Comsomol* to the party is not automatic, young Communists trained under the Soviet régime, who know little or nothing of the country's pre-revolutionary history and are fired with enthusiasm for the Five-Year Plan, now predominate in the ranks of the party, bringing youthful energy and a boundless faith in ultimate success.

The Young Communists direct the work of their juniors, the Pioneers, an organization of children aged ten to sixteen, numbering 6,000,000 in 1935, which in turn leads a still younger group, the "Octiabrists," [5] which includes children from eight to

Young Guard," 1928; Andrei Shokhin, *Kratkii Ocherk Istoryi Comsomola* (Short Sketch of the History of the *Comsomol*), Moscow, "The Young Guard," 1926; Thomas Woody, *New Minds: New Men?* (New York, Macmillan, 1932), Chapter VI. The *Comsomol* has its own official organ, *Comsomolskaya Pravda*, modeled on the party *Pravda*, as well as a number of other newspapers and periodicals.

[5] The "Octiabrists," often referred to as "children of the revolution," are named in honor of the October (old style) revolution of 1917. The Pioneers were organized in 1922, and the "Octiabrists" in 1923.

ten years of age.[6] The work of the Pioneers and "Octiabrists," like that of the Young Communists, emphasizes the study of Communist principles, the performance of "socially useful labor," and elementary military training.

PARTY ORGANIZATION

The nucleus of the party is the cell (*yacheika*), which must include not less than three party members, and which may be formed in factory, village or office, or by Communists who are attached to no organized production unit. The function of the cell is to carry out party policies and decisions, to recruit and educate new members, to assist local party committees in propaganda work, and to participate actively in the country's political and economic life. Of a total of 39,321 party cells in 1928, 25.4 per cent were found in factories, 52.7 in villages, 18.5 in offices and enterprises, and 1.8 in educational institutions.[7]

Party cells elect delegates to the higher organs of the party, which correspond to the administrative divisions of the country. From the provincial and regional party congresses delegates are elected to the All-Union party congress, which is usually convoked once every two years [8] and which, according to the

[6] *Cf.* N. K. Krupskaya, *Deti Revolutzii* (The Children of the Revolution), Moscow, "The Young Guard," 1929; Woody, *New Minds: New Men?* cited, Chapter V. A certain overlapping of ages is allowed in all Communist groups, in order that a number of Young Communists may remain as leaders of the Pioneers, and that a number of Pioneers may serve as leaders of the "Octiabrists."

[7] All-Union Communist Party, Statistical Department of the Central Committee, *VKP v Tzifrach* (The All-Union Communist Party in Figures), Moscow, State Publishing House, 1929, p. 13.

[8] In the intermediate year the party usually holds an All-Union party conference, which is distinguished from the party congress principally by the fact that, while the latter is com-

party constitution, acts as the supreme organ of authority. The Congress, however, delegates its powers to a Central Committee which it elects, and which represents it during intervals between sessions. The Central Committee is at present composed of seventy-one members, and is divided into three sections: a secretariat; an organization bureau (*Orgbureau*), which is entrusted with administrative functions; and a Political Bureau (*Politbureau*) of ten members, which is concerned with the formulation of party policies.[9] The members of the *Politbureau* are nominally appointed by the Central Committee. In practice, however, their selection is determined by Stalin, Secretary-General of the party since 1922, himself a member of the *Politbureau*. While Stalin occupies no important post in the government of the Union, he exercises a decisive influence on both party and government policy. The *Politbureau* has no published statutes; its meetings, like those of the party congress, are not open to the public; and only its decisions, usually embodied in decrees countersigned by Soviet officials, appear in the Soviet press. It is generally known, however, that all fundamental problems of party and gov-

posed of delegates elected by the various party organizations. the former is attended only by party officials.

[9] The *Politbureau* is at present composed as follows: Joseph Stalin, Secretary-General of the Central Committee of the Communist Party; Michael Kalinin, senior chairman of the Central Executive Committee of the U.S.S.R.; Valerian Kuibyshev, president of the State Planning Commission; A. A. Andreyev, People's Commissar for Transportation; Vyacheslav Molotov, president of the Council of People's Commissars; Klimentyi Voroshilov, People's Commissar for Military and Naval Affairs; Sergey Kirov, Secretary of the Leningrad Regional Committee of the party; Lazar M. Kaganovich, Secretary of Central Committee of Communist party and of the Moscow Communist party committee, and Stanislav Kossior, General Secretary of the Executive Committee of the party in the Ukraine.

ernment policy are first threshed out in the *Polit-bureau,* and the latter's decisions regarding the "line" which the party will follow on all current questions are reported by the press. Such far-reaching developments as the introduction of the Five-Year Plan, the "liquidation" of the *kulaks* and the inauguration of a milder policy toward technical experts originated not with the organs of the Soviet government, but with the *Politbureau,* and were actually formulated by Stalin and his closest associates. This predominance of the party over the government, however, creates no real political conflict, since all leading Soviet officials are members of the party, while the majority of the members of the *Politbureau* occupy responsible government positions.[10]

At the Seventeenth Congress of the Communist party held in January and February 1934, it was proposed to obliterate all outward distinction between party and government by officially welding the two together and centralizing authority in the hands of party organs. The program of proposed reforms was submitted by Lazar M. Kaganovich, secretary of the Moscow Communist party committee and a close collaborator of Stalin, who is generally regarded as Stalin's most probable successor. Under this program, the Central Control Committee of the party and the Commissariat of Workers' and Peasants' Inspection—the control organ of the Soviet government[11]—were abolished. They

[10] The organization of the *Comsomol* is modeled on that of the party, with cells, rural, county, economic district, provincial and regional committees and an All-Union *Comsomol* Congress. The Pioneers are organized in brigades and detachments, while the "Octiabrists" are organized in divisions.

[11] *Cf.* p. 386.

were replaced by a Party Control Committee attached to the Central Committee of the party and a Soviet Control Committee attached to the Council of People's Commissars. The significant point of this reform is that both committees are elected by the congress of the Communist party, and that the Soviet government is thus directly subordinated to party control. Kaganovich also proposed to abolish party cells—with a view to centralizing authority in higher party organs—and to create a category of "sympathizers" drawn from the ranks of those who, although not yet ready to shoulder the responsibilities of party membership, are willing to cooperate loyally with the party.[12]

The constitution of the party describes party organization as "democratic centralism," and provides for "complete freedom" of discussion regarding controversial questions.[13] Once a decision has been reached, however, party discipline demands the cessation of discussion, and all party organs, as well as Communist "fractions" in non-party organizations (soviets, trade or professional unions, and cooperative associations), must immediately give effect to party mandates. Failure to follow party directions, and "other offenses recognized as criminal by the public opinion of the party," are investigated by a Central Control Committee, and are subject to penalties ranging from censure to expulsion from the party. Thus when Trotzky condemned Stalin's policies in 1927, he and some of his associates in the Left Opposition were expelled from

[12] *Cf.* theses of Kaganovich, *Izvestia,* December 31, 1933.
[13] *Cf.* also resolution of the *Politbureau* and of the Central Committee, December 5, 1923, *Ustav VKP,* cited, p. 86.

the party,[14] and subsequently exiled. Similarly, when Nicholas Bukharin, editor of the Communist organ *Pravda,* supported the Right Opposition, he was ousted from the *Politbureau* in 1929, and his fate was shared in 1930 by Rykov and Tomsky, chairman of the All-Union Council of Trade Unions, despite their recantation of the "Right heresy."

THE "PARTY LINE"

The severe treatment meted out to dissenters by what Trotzky described as the "party bureaucracy" is justified by Communist leaders on the ground that the "monolithic unity" of the party, which serves as a bulwark against capitalist reaction, can be maintained only by strict enforcement of the "Leninist party line." This line is not a rigid program which takes no cognizance of change of circumstances, but a flexible set of formulas determined by a concrete "historical situation" and designed to meet the special problems which each situation creates. Competent observers believe that the party line, while invariably supported by numerous quotations from Lenin's works, represents the policy which Stalin and his associates consider best adapted to existing conditions.

The centralization of party authority in the hands of the *Politbureau,* which Trotzky denounced as contrary to "inter-party democracy," [15] is regarded by

---

[14] *Cf.* resolution of the Fifteenth Party Congress, approving the decision of the Central Committee to expel Trotzky and his associates from the party. *Piatnadzatyi Syezd Vse-Soyuznoi Communisticheskoi Partyi* (Fifteenth Congress of the All-Union Communist Party), Stenographic Report, Moscow, State Publishing House, 1928, p. 1317.

[15] Trotzky, *The Real Situation in Russia,* cited, p. 111 *et seq.*

Communist leaders as the only method calculated to establish the leadership of the party, and consequently of the proletariat, among less class-conscious elements of the population. Only a disciplined, united party, they claim, can give effect to the aspirations of the laboring masses and lead them to decisive victory over capitalism.

THE THIRD INTERNATIONAL

The All-Union Communist party forms a "section" of the Third (Communist) International (*Comintern*), established in 1919 with headquarters in Moscow, in which fifty-eight Communist parties from as many states or colonies are represented.[16] The object of the Third International, according to its constitution, is to struggle with all means at its disposal, including violence, "for the overthrow of the international bourgeoisie and the establishment of an international Soviet republic, as a transitional stage toward complete annihilation of the state."[17] The Third International regards the dictatorship of the proletariat as the only institution capable of liberating mankind "from the horrors of capitalism," recognizes the Soviet government as "the historic form" of the dictatorship, and undertakes to support every Soviet republic, "wherever established."[18] The program adopted at the close of the Sixth Congress of the Third International in 1928 declared that Communist aims "can be accomplished only through

[16] The *Comsomol* similarly forms a "section" of the Communist Youth International, which is affiliated with the Third International.

[17] Constitution of the Third International adopted at its Fifth Congress in 1924, *Ustav VKP,* cited, p. 165.

[18] *Ibid.*

an overthrow by force of the whole existing social order."[19]

The supreme organ of authority in the Third International, according to its constitution, is the World Congress—which last met in 1935—in which the All-Union Communist party, despite its minority position, exercises a predominant influence. This congress delegates its powers to an Executive Committee of fifty-nine members, which it elects. Of the ten members of the *Politbureau* only Stalin, Secretary-General of the Communist party, is a member of the Executive Committee of the Third International, but others, including Molotov, president of the Union Council of People's Commissars, served as delegates to the Sixth World Congress of the *Comintern* in 1928. The decisions of the Executive Committee are binding on all "sections" of the Third International, including the All-Union Communist party, as well as on individual Communists throughout the world. While the All-Union Communist party, like other "sections," contributes dues to the Third International, there is no evidence that the latter receives financial aid from the Soviet government.

[19] *Izvestia*, September 5, 1928. Reports of the first two congresses of the Third International are available in Russian: *Pervyi Congress Communisticheskovo Internatzionala* (First Congress of the Communist International), March 2–19, 1919 (Petrograd, 1921); *Vtoroi Congress Communisticheskovo Internatzionala* (Second Congress of the Communist International), 1920 (Petrograd, 1921). Abridged reports of the Fourth and Fifth Congresses have been issued in English by the Communist Party of Great Britain. *Cf.* also *The Communist International between the Fifth and Sixth World Congresses, 1924–1928* (London, The Communist Party of Great Britain, 1928). *The Communist International*, the organ of the Third International, is published simultaneously in Russian, German, French and English. *Cf.* also A. Tivel and M. Kheimo, *Dessyat Let Cominterna v Resheniach i Tzifrach* (Ten Years of the *Comintern* in Decisions and Figures), Moscow, State Publishing House, 1929.

The internal conflicts of the All-Union Communist party, the *Comintern's* most active and powerful "section," have been reflected in the Third International, many of whose constituent parties, less disciplined than that of the Soviet Union, have split into Trotzky, Stalin and other factions. The policy of the Third International, however, has in recent years been determined by the Stalin "party line," notably with respect to the imminence of world revolution. The Communist conviction that the World War marked the beginning of a period of world revolution, which would witness the intensification of "capitalist contradictions" and the triumph of the proletariat, was gradually weakened by the failure of Communist uprisings in China and in the colonies. The program of the Sixth Congress of the *Comintern* echoed Stalin's conclusion that capitalism had been temporarily "stabilized," and declared that "the victory of socialism is possible in only a few countries, or even only in one individual country." The Third International thus accepted Stalin's decision that, for the time being at least, the Soviet government should concentrate its efforts not on fomenting revolution abroad, but on the task of "building socialism" at home. The Soviet government has meanwhile made every effort to dissociate its foreign policy, directed at establishing peaceful relations with capitalist states whose economic coöperation is needed for the prosecution of the Five-Year Plan, from the openly anti-capitalist program of the *Comintern*.

CHAPTER III

THE GOVERNMENT OF THE
SOVIET UNION

THE predominant position occupied by the Communist party in the Soviet state has occasioned no conflict of authority, since the party is in practice closely identified with the government.[1] The fact, however, that all significant decisions on Soviet policy emanate not from the constitutional organs of the Union, but from the councils of the Communist party, has gradually restricted the functions of the former to ratification and execution of party mandates. The 1936 constitution,[2] while democratizing the electoral procedure and introducing a "socialist" bill of rights, does not alter this fundamental relationship between government and Communist party, which it describes as "the vanguard of the toilers in their struggle for strengthening and de-

[1] Soviet literature on the structure of the federal government consists for the most part of works which merely expound the principal provisions of the Union constitution and make little or no attempt to give a critical analysis. Cf. I. N. Ananov, *Ocherki Federalnovo Upravleniva S.S.S.R.* (Sketches of the Federal Government of the U.S.S.R.), Leningrad, State Publishing House, 1925; G. S. Gurvich, *Sovetskoe Gosudarstvennoe Ustroistvo* (The Organization of the Soviet State), Moscow, "Soviet Power," 1930; V. I. Ignatiev, *Sovetskii Stroi* (The Soviet Order), Moscow, State Publishing House, 1928; D. A. Magerovski, *Soyuz S.S.R.* (The U.S.S.R.) Moscow, 1923. For an English work on the subject, *cf.* Walter R. Batsell, *Soviet Rule in Russia* (New York, Macmillan, 1929), which is valuable chiefly for its translations of Soviet laws and constitutions. For articles on current problems of government organization, *cf. Sovetskoe Stroitelstvo* (Soviet Construction), a monthly magazine published by the Central Executive Committee of the U.S.S.R. since 1926, and *Izvestia*, the daily organ of the Central Executive Committee.

[2] For text of the draft constitution, cf. *Izvestia,* June 12, 1936; *New York Times,* June 26, 1936.

veloping the socialist system," and as "the leading nucleus of all organizations of the toilers, both public and state."[3] To understand the changes envisaged by the new constitution, it is important to compare its provisions with those of the 1923 instrument.

The Soviet Union, according to the 1936 constitution, is a federation of eleven Union republics. In this federation Michael Kalinin, president of the R.S.F.S.R. and a member of the *Politbureau*, performs some of the ceremonial functions usually entrusted to the president of a Western republic, such as the reception of ambassadors. The constitution, however, makes no provision for a president, and entrusts all power to the Supreme Council of the U.S.S.R. (All-Union Congress of Soviets under the 1923 constitution), elected for four years, which is to be convened twice a year (instead of every two years as provided in 1923).

SOVIET BILL OF RIGHTS

The 1936 constitution declares that the Soviet Union is "a socialist state of workers and peasants," whose economic foundations rest on socialist ownership of the implements and means of production, "firmly established as a result of the liquidation of the capitalist system of economy, the abolition of private ownership of the instruments and means of production, and the abolition of exploitation of man by man." The constitution distinguishes between public property, controlled by the state—land, waters, forests, mills, factories, mines, railways, banks, means of communication, state farms, etc.; and private property, owned by individuals, such as income from work and savings, objects of domestic and household use, of personal use and comfort, in-

[3] Draft of 1936 constitution, Article 126.

dividual plots of land owned by collective farmers, together with their houses, productive livestock, poultry and minor agricultural implements. The constitution frankly acknowledges that the Soviet Union has reached the stage not of communism, but of socialism, and states that work is the obligation of every citizen capable of working, in accordance with the principle: "He who does not work shall not eat." In the Soviet Union, says the constitution, the socialist principle—"from each according to his ability, to each according to his work"—is now being realized.

In contrast to the 1923 constitution, which discriminated against non-proletarians and rigidly curtailed personal rights, the 1936 constitution contains a list of "citizens' basic rights and obligations." This list, at the same time, represents an analysis of the achievements claimed by the socialist state. Soviet citizens have the right to work—a right ensured "by the socialist organization of national economy, the steady growth of the productive forces of Soviet society, the absence of economic crises, and the abolition of unemployment." They have the right to rest —a right ensured "by the reduction of the working day to seven hours for the overwhelming majority of the workers, establishment of annual vacations with pay for workers and employees and provision of a wide network of sanatoriums, rest homes and clubs for the accommodation of the toilers." They have the right to material security in old age as well as in the event of sickness and loss of capacity to work —a right ensured "by the wide development of social insurance of workers and employees at the expense of the state, free medical aid, and the provision of a wide network of health resorts for the use of the toilers." They have the right to education—a right ensured "by universal compulsory elementary education, free of charge, including higher education by the system of state stipends for the overwhelming majority of students in higher schools, instruction in schools in the native language, and organization of free industrial, technical and agronomic education for the toilers at the factories, state farms, machine and tractor stations and collective farms." Women are accorded equal rights with men in all fields of economic, state, cultural, social and political life. The possibility of realizing women's rights is ensured "by affording women equally with men the right to work, payment for work, rest, social insurance and education, state protection of the interests of mother and child, granting pregnancy leave with pay, and the provision of a wide network of maternity homes, nurseries and kindergartens."

All citizens are assured equal rights, irrespective of their nationality or race, in all fields of economic, cultural, social and political life. Direct or indirect restriction of these rights or establishment of privileges for citizens on account of race or nationality, as well as propagation of racial or national exceptionalism or hatred and contempt, is punishable by law.

The church is separated from the state and the school from the church. Freedom to perform religious rites and freedom of anti-religious propaganda is recognized for all citizens. It should be noted that while, as in 1923, freedom of anti-religious propaganda is permitted, no similar freedom is granted for religious propaganda, thus severely handicapping the spread of religious doctrines.

"For the purpose of strengthening the socialist

system," the new constitution guarantees to all citizens freedom of speech, of the press, of assembly and meetings, of street processions and demonstrations. These rights are ensured by placing at the disposal of "the toilers and their organizations printing presses, supplies of paper, public buildings, streets, means of communication and other material conditions necessary to their realization." Citizens are granted the right of combining in various public organizations, but the formation of political parties other than the Communist party is not permitted. The inviolability of the person, of homes, and the secrecy of correspondence is assured. "No one may be subjected to arrest except upon the decision of a court or with the sanction of the prosecutor." The effect of this provision will depend entirely on the extent to which courts and prosecutors are prepared to respect the personal rights of individuals.

Every citizen of the U.S.S.R., for his part, is obliged to safeguard and consolidate public socialist property "as the sacred inviolable foundation of the Soviet system, as the source of wealth and might of the fatherland, as the source of the prosperous cultural life of all the toilers. Persons attempting to violate public socialist property are enemies of the people."

The spectacular trial of August 1936, in which sixteen alleged Trotzkyists—including the old revolutionary leaders Zinoviev and Kamenev—were found guilty of plotting to assassinate Stalin and his associates, and were subsequently executed, seriously undermined the favorable impression created abroad by the terms of the 1936 draft constitution. With the publication of this constitution, designed to align the Soviet Union on the side of European democracies in the anticipated struggle with Fascism, it had been expected abroad that non-Stalin elements might enjoy greater political freedom than in the past. Soviet commentaries on the constitution, however, soon made it clear that freedom of speech, assembly, etc., was to be reserved solely for loyal supporters of the Stalin government, and that surviving opposition elements—whether monarchists, social revolutionaries or Trotzkyists—would be no more permitted to share in the country's political life than lunatics, to use the expression of one Soviet writer. Some observers believe that, before inaugurating the new constitution, with its promise of a more abundant political life, the government found it advisable to put the people on their guard against opposition influence by a sensational public trial, intended to destroy Trotzkyism root and branch. In the opinion of Western liberals, however, this trial revealed how difficult it is for a dictatorship to father democracy.

SOVIET ELECTORAL PROCEDURE

The administrative system of the Union consists of soviets of "toilers'" deputies, grouped in a pyramidal formation, with village, town and factory soviets at the base and the Supreme Council (formerly All-Union Congress of Soviets) at the apex. The soviet, the only form of organization known to Soviet constitutional law, is a council elected by the "toilers" which exercises executive and legislative powers within its jurisdiction, and meets periodically to examine and ratify the acts and policies of government officials. During intervals between sessions, each soviet is represented by a central executive committee which it elects and, in the more important

administrative units, by a smaller body, known as
the "presidium."

Until the drafting of the 1936 constitution, the
Soviet electoral system bore a strikingly class character: the vote, under the 1923 instrument, was
granted only to the "laboring" population; and the
workers enjoyed an advantage over the peasants
with respect both to the number of delegates whom
they could elect and the manner in which they
elected them.

According to Soviet political theory, the vote is
not a right, but a social function, and constitutes the
most effective weapon for the protection of the economic interests of the laboring masses.[4] The vote,
formerly granted only to those who either earned
their livelihood by "productive work useful to society" or were enlisted in the Soviet armed forces,[5-6]
is to be exercised, under the new constitution, on
the basis of universal, equal and direct suffrage. All
citizens who have reached the age of eighteen may
now vote, irrespective of race or nationality, religion,
educational or residential qualifications, social origin,
property status and past activity. The category of
disfranchised, which under the 1923 constitution
affected some 8,000,000 persons for political or economic reasons, is thus abolished. The political category included all those directly or indirectly associated with the Tsarist order, notably members of

[4] S. M. Brodovich, *Sovetskoe Izbiratelnoe Pravo* (Soviet Electoral Law), Leningrad, State Publishing House, 1925; G. S. Gurvich, *Istoriya Sovetskoi Constitutzii* (History of the Soviet
Constitution), Moscow, Socialist Academy, 1923, p. 46.

[5-6] *Cf.* Article 64 of the constitution of the R.S.F.S.R.; Batsell,
Soviet Rule in Russia, cited, p. 80; and corresponding articles in
the constitutions of the other Union republics. Persons engaged in
domestic pursuits were included in the category of those perform-
ing productive work.

the Romanov dynasty, employees of the former police and gendarmerie, organizers of punitive expeditions, agents of counter-revolutionary governments, such as those of Kolchak and Denikin, officers and employees of the White armies, monks, nuns and clergymen of all religious denominations.[7] The category of persons disfranchised for economic reasons had proved very elastic, and reflected the government's economic policy at any given time. Broadly speaking, it included all those who employed hired labor for profit, who lived on an unearned income such as interest on capital, profits from industrial enterprises or real estate, etc., or engaged in private trade.[8] These general provisions were altered and amplified from time to time by the Union Presidium and by corresponding organs of the Union republics.[9] After 1925 disfranchisement based on economic considerations had been extended to *kulaks* (so-called "rich peasants") and to handicraftsmen employing hired labor. Petty traders and members of free professions engaged in "socially useful" work were exempt from disfranchisement.

The government had been careful to point out that lists of disfranchised persons should be drawn up exclusively by local electoral commissions on the

---

[7] Article 65 of the constitution of the R.S.F.S.R.; Instruction of the Presidium of the Central Executive Committee of the U.S.S.R. Regarding Elections to the Soviets, January 16, 1925, *Sobranye Zakonov i Rasporiazhenii Raboche-Krestianskovo Pravitelstva* (Collection of Laws and Regulations of the Workers' and Peasants' Government), 195, Part I, p. 103; Instruction of the Presidium of the Central Executive Committee of the U.S.S.R., September 28, 1926, *ibid.*, 1926, Part I, No. 66, p. 1209.

[8] Article 65 of the constitution of the R.S.F.S.R.

[9] Instructions of the Presidium of the Central Executive Committee of the U.S.S.R., January 16, 1925, and September 28, 1926, cited. It is estimated that 3.2 per cent of the total population in the villages of the R.S.F.S.R. were disfranchised in the 1931 elections.

basis of information furnished by local soviets, administrative organs or other unofficial groups.[10] Despite government regulations, however, local soviets frequently used their own discretion in according or withholding the franchise, and local officials on occasion resorted to disfranchisement for the purpose of avenging personal grievances.[11] Disfranchisement was regarded as a form of social ostracism, and was usually accompanied by deprivation of ration cards, medical aid and housing facilities, exclusion of children of the disfranchised from schools, and even eviction from village or city. To correct this tendency, the government had decreed in 1930 that the disfranchised and their families should not be subjected to material hardships, and that children of the disfranchised who had come of age since 1925 should be granted the vote provided they were independently engaged in socially useful labor.[12]

The details of elections, such as time, place and manner of procedure are fixed by electoral commissions appointed in each administrative unit by the latter's executive committee.[13-14] The electoral commissions are composed of from seven to twenty-one members—depending on the nature of the administrative unit—chosen from the local executive

[10] Instruction of the Presidium of the Central Executive Committee of the U.S.S.R., January 16, 1925, cited; Regulation of the Central Executive Committee of the U.S.S.R. for the Removal of Violations of the Electoral Legislation of the U.S.S.R., March 22, 1930, *Sobranye Zakonov,* cited, 1930, Part I, p. 360.

[11] "Zakon o Lishenii Izbiratelnych Prav i Narushenia Evo na Praktike" (The Law Regarding Disfranchisement and Its Violations in Practice), *Sovetskoe Stroitelstvo,* May 1930, p. 1.

[12] Regulations of the Central Executive Committee of the U.S.S.R. for the Removal of Violations of Electoral Legislation of the U.S.S.R., March 22, 1930, cited.

[13-14] Instructions of the Presidium of the Central Executive Committee of the U.S.S.R., Regarding Elections to the Soviets, September 28, 1926, cited.

committee, trade and professional unions, the Communist League of Youth, town soviets, peasant organizations, national minorities and the Red Army.

Voting takes place on an occupational rather than a territorial basis, electoral assemblies being held in factories, offices, trade union headquarters, collective farms and other production units. An exception to this general rule is made only for "unorganized" citizens, such as housewives and handicraftsmen, who vote territorially by districts. The advantage of this system, from the point of view of the Soviet government, lies in the fact that the voters do not disperse after the elections, but remain in close contact with each other, and are thus in a better position to exercise continuous control over their delegates, and recall them if necessary. A delegate may be recalled at any time on decision of the voters.[15]

Candidates may be nominated by social organizations and societies of the "toilers," Communist party organizations, trade unions, cooperatives, youth organizations and cultural societies. While under the 1936 constitution citizens are given the right to organize "for the purpose of developing the organizational self-expression and political activity of the masses of the people," no political party other than that of the Communists is permitted in the Soviet Union. Opposition groups and even factions of the party regarded as inimical to the "party line" are given no opportunity to present their views to the voters. Elections, which until 1936 were usually open, the vote being taken by a show of hands, will now be held by secret ballot.

Under the 1923 constitution, the workers enjoyed two distinct advantages over the peasants in every

[15] Draft of 1936 Constitution, Article 142.

election: towns and factory soviets were entitled to
one representative for every 25,000 voters, while village soviets could elect only one representative for
every 125,000 population; and the town and factory
soviets, composed predominantly of workers, elected
delegates directly to the All-Union Congress, while
delegates elected by the village soviets had to pass
through two intermediate stages—district and regional congresses—before reaching the All-Union
Congress. This difference in the voting rights of
workers and peasants was justified on the ground
that, during the transition period from capitalism
to communism, the class-conscious and politically
educated workers must assume leadership over the
backward peasant masses. It was argued that, when
the peasants had reached the economic and cultural
level of the workers, the existing differences between
the voting powers of the two groups would gradually
disappear.[16] This stage has now apparently been
reached, for the 1936 constitution provides for direct
elections from town and village soviets to the Supreme Council of the U.S.S.R.[17]

Despite the fact that non-Communists are elected
to the soviets, the latter are regarded primarily as
organs for the fulfilment of the "ideals, program and
orders" of the Communist party.[18] In the opinion of
Soviet writers, the soviet is an institution in which
workers and peasants are united with the vanguard

[16] S. M. Brodovich, *Sovetskoe Izbiratelnoe Pravo,* cited; F. A.
Shuiski, *Partiya i Sovety* (The Party and the Soviets), Moscow,
State Publishing House, 1927, pp. 47-48.

[17] Draft of 1936 Constitution, Article 139.

[18] Cf. *Izvestia,* December 7, 1930. The plenum of the Central
Committee of the Communist party declared in December 1930
that the soviets should become channels for the "party line,"
and should be irreconcilably hostile to both Right and Left "opportunism." *Ibid.,* January 16, 1931.

of the proletariat—the Communist party—under
the leadership of the latter.[19] Soviet spokesmen,
however, deny the contention of Western critics that
the soviets constitute a dictatorship not of the proletariat, but of the Communist party. They argue that
the soviets, through which the laboring masses are
for the first time in history admitted to active participation in the government, represent the highest
form of "proletarian democracy."[20] Elections to the
soviets are consequently viewed not as a sham procedure whose results are practically predetermined,
but as "the most important school for the political
education of the laboring masses."[21] Government
and party organs make every effort to acquaint the
masses with the rudiments of "political grammar"—
the Soviet constitution, the Communist party program and the Five-Year Plan. All available agencies
—schools, clubs, trade unions, the press, the radio,
the theatre, the movies—are enlisted in the gigantic
task of training a population, large numbers of
which are still illiterate, to exercise the function of
voting.[22] The elections themselves are utilized to
focus the attention of the masses on problems of
immediate importance, whether defects in transportation or the progress of collectivization: while
Soviet achievements are extolled, no attempt is
made to disguise existing difficulties. In short, the

[19] *Ibid.,* December 7, 1930; Shuiski, *Partiya i Sovety,* cited,
p. 53.

[20] Shuiski, *Partiya i Sovety,* cited, p. 54.

[21] Resolution of the Third Congress of Soviets of the U.S.S.R.
Regarding Improvement of the Work of the Soviets, May 20, 1925,
Sobranye Zakonov, cited, 1925, Part I, p. 544.

[22] For a detailed study of Soviet methods of political educa-
tion, cf. Samuel N. Harper, *Civic Training in Soviet Russia*
(Chicago, University of Chicago Press, 1929); *idem., Making
Bolsheviks* (Chicago, University of Chicago Press, 1931).

voters are constantly urged to take an active part in the work of a state whose policies, however, are ultimately controlled not by the elected soviets, but by the self-perpetuating inner group which rules the Communist party.

The Supreme Council of the U.S.S.R.

The Supreme Council (which as the All-Union Congress usually numbered about two thousand delegates, approximately seventy-five per cent of whom were Communists), is too unwieldy to exercise real power, and consequently meets only to receive reports by government officials on such subjects as foreign and domestic policy, the progress of the Five-Year Plan in various branches of national economy, and the status of the Red Army, to ratify the acts of the government, and to elect a presidium of thirty-seven members, which acts on its behalf in intervals between sessions.[23]

The Supreme Council, which has exclusive exercise of the legislative power, is composed of two chambers: the Council of the Union and the Council of Nationalities. The former is elected on the basis of one delegate for every 300,000 of the population, while the latter consists of delegates appointed by the supreme councils of the Union and autonomous republics and soviets in the autonomous provinces, on the basis of ten deputies from each Union republic,

[23] The All-Union Congress had met six times since the establishment of the Union—in 1922, when the only item on its agenda was the ratification of the treaty of union, in 1924, 1925, 1927, 1929 and 1931. The congresses of the Union republics generally meet once a year. For the work of the All-Union Congress of Soviets, cf. the stenographic reports of the six congresses held to date, published by the Central Executive Committee under the title *Syezd Sovetov S.S.S.R.* (The Congress of Soviets of the U.S.S.R.)

five from each autonomous republic, and two from each autonomous province.[24-25]

While the Council of Nationalities is charged with the special task of protecting the interests of the various national groups in the Union, the two chambers enjoy equal powers with respect to legislation. Projects of law are generally first presented by the Council of People's Commissars, individual commissariats and other government institutions to the Presidium, which after preliminary study submits them to the two chambers at a joint session. Debates on proposed legislation usually take place at separate sessions of the two chambers. A bill is considered passed when it receives a majority of the votes in each chamber.

Council of People's Commissars

While the legislative functions of the Supreme Council are in large part performed by the Presidium, its executive powers are exercised by the Council of People's Commissars of the U.S.S.R. (*Sovnarkom*), which it appoints at a joint session of the two chambers, and which corresponds to the cabinet of Western states.[26] According to Soviet law the people's commissars, whose position is similar to that of Western cabinet ministers, are appointed by and responsible to the Supreme Council. In practice the Communist party exercises a decisive influence over appointments to the Council of People's Com-

[24-25] Draft of 1936 Constitution, Articles 34 and 35.

[26] For the provisions governing the organization and functions of the Council of People's Commissars, cf. Chapter VI of the Union constitution and the decree of November 12, 1923, establishing the Council. *Sbornik Postanovlenii i Rasporiazhenii Raboche-Krestianskovo Pravitelstva S.S.S.R.* (Collection of Decrees and Regulations of the Workers' and Peasants' Government of the U.S.S.R.), 1923, No. 21, p. 340.

missars. In 1930 when Rykov, who had succeeded Lenin as president of the Council—a position analogous to that of premier in parliamentary governments—was censured by the party for his support of the Right Opposition, he was forced to resign in favor of Vyacheslav Molotov, a close adherent of Stalin, who continues to occupy that post.[27] The Council of People's Commissars is charged with the execution of all measures necessary for the general administration of the Union, preliminary examination of all projects of law submitted to the Presidium, and particularly those concerning the introduction of new or the increase of already existing taxes, and the preparation of the Union budget.

The Council of People's Commissars consists of two types of commissariats: All-Union Commissariats, which are common to the whole Union, and unified commissariats, which are duplicated in every Union republic.[28] The All-Union commissariats at present include defense (formerly war and navy), foreign affairs, foreign trade,[29] railways, communications (formerly posts and telegraphs), water trans-

[27] A few months later, when the party's attack on the "Right heresy" had somewhat abated, Rykov was permitted to return to the Council of People's Commissars as Commissar of Posts and Telegraphs.

[28] Decree on the General Act Organizing the People's Commissariats of the U.S.S.R., *Sbornik Postanovlenii i Rasporiazhenii,* cited, 1923, No. 21, p. 341; Batsell, *Soviet Rule in Russia,* cited, p. 599.

[29] The commissariats of foreign and domestic trade have undergone several transformations since the establishment of the Union. The decree of November 12, 1923 provided for an All-Union commissariat of foreign trade and a unified commissariat of internal trade, which was to take the place of the former commissariat of food. These two commissariats were combined in 1925 into a unified commissariat of foreign and domestic trade. In 1930, however, when the distribution of goods on the domestic market became particularly pressing, this commissariat was divided into the present commissariats of supply and foreign trade.

portation,[30] heavy industry; while the unified commissariats include food industry, light industry, timber industry, agriculture,[31] state grain and livestock farms, finance, internal trade, internal affairs, justice and health.[32-33]

Each of the All-Union commissariats maintains close contacts with the several Union republics through a representative named either by the Union commissariat or by the central executive committee of each republic. This representative, who usually acts in an advisory capacity, is responsible not only to the All-Union Council of People's Commissars, but also to the government of the republic to which

[30] In 1930, when transportation proved inadequate for the needs of an expanding industry and agriculture, the former All-Union commissariat of communications was divided into two commissariats—transportation (railways and roads) and waterways.

[31] The Commissariat of Agriculture was established in 1929, when the Soviet government launched its drive for collectivization. Until that time agriculture had been within the competence of the several republics.

[32-33] In August 1933 the Commissariat of Labor, which had hitherto functioned as a unified Commissariat, was merged with the Soviet trade unions. The Council of People's Commissars is at present composed as follows: President, V. M. Molotov; Foreign Affairs, M. M. Litvinov; Defense, K. E. Voroshilov; Foreign Trade, A. P. Rosengoltz; Transportation, A. A. Andreyev; Water Transportation, N. I. Pakhomov; Communications, A. I. Rykov; Heavy Industry, G. K. Ordjonikidze; Timber Industry, S. S. Lobov; Light Industry, I. E. Lubimov; Agriculture, M. A. Chernov; State Farms, M. I. Kalmanovich; Food Industry, A. I. Mikoyan; Internal Trade, L. Y. Veitzer; Finance, G. T. Grinko; State Planning Commission (*Gosplan*), V. I. Mezhlauk; Internal Affairs, G. G. Yagoda.

In 1930 the Union government abolished the Union republican commissariats of internal affairs on the ground that the functions of Western ministries of the interior are performed in the Soviet state by the Supreme Economic Council (since then divided into three commissariats—heavy and light industry, and lumber) and by the Commissariat of Agriculture, "laboratories of Soviet internal policy," and by organs of the Communist party. Cf. V. Vassiliev, "Likvidatzia Narodnych Commissariatov Vnutrennych Diel" (The "Liquidation" of People's Commissariats of Internal Affairs), *Sovetskoe Stroitelstvo,* January 1931, p. 35.

he is accredited. Each of the Union republics, in addition, maintains a permanent representative in Moscow, who may participate in the work of the All-Union Council of People's Commissars whenever the interests of his government are at stake.[34]

Unlike the All-Union commissariats, the unified commissariats perform their functions in the Union republics through corresponding commissariats appointed and dismissed solely by the central executive committee of each republic. The republican commissariats, however, must execute the directions of the unified commissariats, which supervise their work and may suspend or repeal their decrees.[35] The central executive committee of each Union republic, for its part, may suspend the application of decrees issued by unified commissariats when these conflict with the Union constitution or laws, or with republican legislation.

COUNCIL OF LABOR AND DEFENSE

It would be impossible, within the scope of this book, to examine the organization and functions of each Soviet commissariat in detail. Particular interest, however, attaches to those departments and commissions of the Council of People's Commissars which are concerned with the application of planned economy and with protection of the Soviet order— notably the Council of Labor and Defense, the State Planning Commission, the Commissariat of Workers' and Peasants' Inspection and the State Political

[34] Ananov, *Ocherki Federalnovo Ustroistva S.S.S.R.*, cited, p. 45 *et seq.*

[35] An exception is made for decrees of republican commissariats based on orders issued by the republican council of people's commissars; the only action which the unified commissariat may take with respect to such decrees is to register a protest against them with the All-Union Council of People's Commissars.

Administration. The Council of Labor and Defense
(STO) which, while not a commissariat, is attached
to the Council of People's Commissars, occupies a
pivotal position in the Soviet system, and may be
regarded as the general staff of the economic as well
as the armed forces of the Union.[36] Its principal
function is to formulate the economic and financial
plans of the Union, to alter these plans in accordance
with existing economic and political conditions, and
to exercise immediate supervision over the performance by the various commissariats of economic policies and measures concerning defense.[37] The importance of the STO may be measured by the fact
that Stalin, who had hitherto occupied no post in
the government, became a member of the STO in
1930.

The State Planning Commission

The planning functions of the STO are performed
by a special organ, the State Planning Commission
(*Gosplan*), which coördinates the plans of the several republics as well as all enterprises and undertakings in the Union, drafts "a common Union
perspective plan" in collaboration with a whole network of regional and local planning bodies, and supervises the execution of the plan.[38] The possibility

[36] The organization and functions of the Council of Labor and
Defense are defined in a decree of August 21, 1923: *Sbornik
Postanovlenii i Rasporiazhenii,* cited, 1923, No. 13, p. 216. An
English text of this decree is found in Batsell, *Soviet Rule in
Russia,* cited, p. 620.

[37] Arkhippov, *Zakon v Sovetskom Gosudarstve* (Law in the
Soviet State), cited, p. 106.

[38] The organization and functions of the State Planning Com-
mission are defined in a decree of August 21, 1923: U.S.S.R.,
Sbornik Postanovlenii i Rasporiazhenii, cited, 1923, No. 13. An
English text of this decree is found in Batsell, *Soviet Rule in
Russia,* cited, p. 618.

of establishing a system of "planned economy" which alone, in Lenin's opinion, would permit the transformation of Russia from a backward agricultural country into a modern industrial and socialist state, received serious consideration after 1920, when a plan for the electrification of the country was first elaborated. The *Gosplan*, charged with the examination and correlation of data on this subject, prepared a preliminary draft for a Five-Year Plan intended to cover the period 1927-1932. This draft, amended and corrected, served as the basis for the first Five-Year Plan, inaugurated on October 1, 1928.[39] The plan contained detailed programs for the development of every branch of national economy—industry, agriculture, finance, transportation, etc.—and for simultaneous development in all fields of social activity, notably education. The figures originally set by the plan, which include maximum and minimum "variants," are checked annually by

[39] The date on which the Five-Year Plan was scheduled to terminate was originally set as September 30, 1933; this date, however, was shifted in 1930 to December 31, 1933, when the fiscal year was changed to coincide with the calendar year, and then to December 31, 1932, when the slogan "The Five-Year Plan in Four Years" was introduced For the text of the Five-Year Plan, *cf.* U.S.S.R., *Piatiletnii Plan Narodno-Khozyastvennovo Stroitelstva S.S.S.R.* (The Five-Year Plan of National Economic Construction of the U.S.S.R.), 3 volumes, Moscow, "Planned Economy," 1929. For a summary of the Five-Year Plan in English. *cf. The Soviet Union Looks Ahead* (New York, Liveright, 1929). The economic aspects of the Five-Year Plan, which lie outside the scope of this book, have been analyzed in a number of works, the most valuable of which are W. H. Chamberlin, *The Soviet Planned Economic Order* (Boston, World Peace Foundation, 1931); Michael Farbman, *Piatiletka: Russia's Five-Year Plan* (New York, The New Republic, 1931); G. F. Grinko, *The Five Year Plan of the Soviet Union* (New York, International Publishers, 1930); and Calvin B. Hoover, *The Economic Life of Soviet Russia* (New York, Macmillan, 1931). For an official account of the results accomplished under the Five-Year Plan, *cf. Summary of the Fulfilment of the First Five-Year Plan* (Moscow, State Planning Commission of the U.S.S.R., 1933).

"control figures," prepared on the basis of actual results achieved during the past year, and these "control figures" in turn serve as a basis for altering the
estimates of the plan for the following year. The
first Five-Year Plan was regarded as but a prologue
to a vast program of economic development to be
elaborated in successive Five-Year Plans, the second
of which was approved in its main points by the
Seventeenth Conference of the Communist party in
January 1932 and is now in operation.

In addition to the organs specifically charged with
the administration of "planned economy," the commissariats of the Union and of the constituent republics, as well as subordinate government institutions, perform important planning functions in their
respective fields, subject to the control of the *Gosplan* and the STO. The administration and regulation of state industries, with the notable exception
of industries engaged in the production of foodstuffs, controlled by the Commissariat for Internal
Supply, were entrusted at first to the Supreme Economic Council, which was duplicated by economic
councils in the Union republics, and was responsible
to the Council for Labor and Defense. On January 5,
1932, however, the Supreme Economic Council was
broken up into three unified commissariats—heavy
industry, light industry and lumber.[40] Each of these
commissariats will now plan and supervise the work
of the plants, trusts and industrial combinations
within its field, will regulate the distribution of government credits among them, and will assist the
State Planning Commission with the preparation of
annual "control" figures. Similarly the Commissariat
of Foreign Trade, which applies the Soviet govern-

[40] *Izvestia,* January 5, 1932.

ment's foreign trade monopoly, annually draws up a plan of exports and imports in conformity with the country's economic condition.[41]

Financial Planning

Financial planning is entrusted to the Commissariat of Finance which, after consultation with other Union commissariats and with representatives of the Council of Labor and Defense, the State Planning Commission and the Union republics, annually prepares a "unified state budget"[42] which, like Western budgets, contains estimates of revenue and expenditures. The Union budget for 1936, submitted to the All-Union Central Executive Committee by the Commissar of Finance on January 14, 1936, estimated expenditures at 78,500,000,000 rubles.[43]

Soviet revenue is derived from two principal sources—taxation, and the income of various state enterprises and undertakings. The most profitable Soviet taxes are the business turnover tax, the agricultural tax, and customs duties. In addition, the Soviet government levies trade and industry, general income and excess profits taxes, as well as a special tax for cultural needs. The principal items in the non-taxation category are the income from transportation and the administration of posts and telegraphs, revenue derived from state industries,

[41] For a detailed analysis of the work of the Commissariat of Foreign Trade, *cf.* Vera M. Dean, "Foreign Trade Policy of the Soviet Government," F. P. A. *Information Service,* Volume VI, No. 20, December 10, 1930.

[42] S. A. Kotlyarcvski, *Budget S.S.S.R.* (The Budget of the U.S.S.R.), Leningrad, State Publishing House, 1925; *Idem, Budgetnoe Pravo R.S.F.S.R. i S.S.S.R.* (The Budget Law of the R.S.F.S.R. and the U.S.S.R.), Moscow, State Publishing House, 1924; Chamberlin, *The Soviet Planned Economic Order,* cited, p. 96.

[43] *New York Times,* January 14, 1936.

state credit institutions, internal trade—which is almost entirely controlled by the state—and state loans.

In 1936 about 48 per cent of the total Soviet budget was to be expended on the financing of national economy—industry (entirely controlled by the state), state and collective farms, transportation, posts and telegraphs; 8.3 per cent on education and social welfare; 19 per cent on national defense; 1.2 per cent on administration; and 15.7 per cent was to be contributed by the Union government to local budgets.[44]

The Soviet budget thus serves as an agency for collecting revenue from taxes and from profitable state enterprises, such as light industry, and for redistributing capital among state undertakings which are most in need of financial assistance, notably heavy industry and transportation. The financing of Soviet industry, trade and agriculture is effected through six main banks, all operated by the state, of which the State Bank established in 1921 is the most important. The State Bank issues banknotes (*chervontzi*), regulates currency circulation, and handles all short-term credits extended in the Soviet Union.[45] Long-term credits are granted to industry by the Long-Term Credit Bank for Industry and Electrification (*Prombank*), organized in 1928; to socialized agriculture by the *Selkhozbank* (Agricultural Bank); to cooperative organizations by the *Vsekobank* (All-Union Cooperative Bank);

[44] For analysis of Soviet budget for 1936, *cf.* report of G. F. Grinko, People's Commissar of Finance, to the all-Union Central Executive Committee, *Izvestia*, January 17, 1936.

[45] *Economic Handbook of the Soviet Union*, compiled by the American-Russian Chamber of Commerce (New York, Day, 1936), pp. 402-407.

to municipal public utilities and housing enterprises by the *Tsekombank* (Central Bank for Public Utilities). While the State Bank finances the bulk of foreign trade operations, the export of such raw materials as timber, oil, grain and dairy products, as well as industrial products, is financed in part by the *Vneshtorgbank* (Bank for Foreign Trade).

COMMISSARIAT OF WORKERS' AND PEASANTS' INSPECTION

The vastness and multiplicity of the tasks which the state would be called on to perform under socialism, and the consequent development of a stifling bureaucracy, have frequently been regarded as an insuperable obstacle to the establishment of an efficient socialist state. The extent to which the Soviet government is aware of this danger may be judged by the virulence of the "self-criticism" which is constantly directed against red tape and routine performance of administrative duties. The extirpation of bureaucracy which, if unchecked, might seriously jeopardize the country's economic life, is regarded as so important that a special organ, the Commissariat of Workers' and Peasants' Inspection (RKI), was charged until 1934 with the task of investigating the administration of all government institutions, of offering constructive criticism for improvement of the state apparatus, and of adjusting the latter to the needs of socialist construction.[46] The RKI was empowered to rationalize the technique of administration, to draft plans for changes in the

[46] The organization and functions of the Commissariat of Workers' and Peasants' Inspection are defined in a decree of November 12, 1923: *Sbornik Postanovlenii i Rasporiazhenii, 1923*, cited, No. 24, p. 386. For an English text of this decree, *cf.* Batsell, *Soviet Rule in Russia,* cited, p. 611.

structure of state organs and to coördinate their work, to examine and analyze Union and republican budgets, as well as all plans of production, to request information from government institutions and officials on matters under investigation, and to assist them in the selection and training of personnel. Finally, the RKI conducted periodic "cleansings" of the state apparatus, in the course of which the work of all government institutions was minutely checked, and employees who were found inefficient could be summarily dismissed, exiled or even shot.[47] Under the program of reforms proposed by Kaganovich, the RKI was replaced by a Soviet Control Committee elected by the Communist Party Congress.

THE OGPU

In its unremitting struggle against all administrative abuses, whether bureaucracy, negligence or counter-revolutionary "wrecking" and sabotage, the Soviet government is further assisted by the State Political Administrations (GPU) which were established in each of the Union republics following the abolition of the famous revolutionary tribunal, the Extraordinary Commission (*Cheka*) in 1922, and by the Unified Political Administration of the Union (OGPU), organized in 1923 and abolished in 1934.[48] The OGPU, which was attached to the Union Council of People's Commissars, was an extensive system of secret police, somewhat similar to the "Third

[47] For details of the "cleansing" procedure, *cf.* Kudryashev, "Predvaritelnye Itogi Chistki Sovetskovo Apparata v S.S.S.R." (Preliminary Results of the "Cleansing" of the Soviet Apparatus in the U.S.S.R.), *Sovetskoe Stroitelstvo*, May-June 1931, p. 1.

[48] The organization and functions of the OGPU are defined in a decree of November 15, 1923: *Sbornik Postanovlenii i Rasporiazhenii* (1923), cited, No. 22. For the English text of this decree, *cf.* Batsell, *Soviet Rule in Russia*, cited, p. 609.

Division" of the Tsarist chancellery, devoted to the suppression of political unrest, and was charged with the task of consolidating "the revolutionary efforts of the republics in their struggle against political and economic counter-revolution, espionage and banditism," and of protecting the frontiers of the Union.[49] Special military units, whose number is determined by the STO and which now total 45,000, were placed at the disposal of the OGPU, which could, without consulting the regular police or the courts, arrest, imprison, exile or sentence to death any person suspected of counter-revolutionary tendencies. The activities of the OGPU, whose president was appointed by the Union Presidium, were nevertheless subject to supervision by the Prosecutor of the Supreme Court of the Union, who could participate in the prosecution of persons accused by the OGPU.[50]

"Counter-revolutionary," as distinguished from ordinary, crimes are defined as acts which seek to weaken, undermine or overthrow the Soviet government, to endanger the external security of the Union or to injure the economic and political order established by the proletarian revolution.[51] Such crimes

[49] The special frontier units of the OGPU must combat all attempts to introduce arms or literature illegally into the country, or to cross the frontiers for the purpose of committing counter-revolutionary crimes. *Cf.* the decree of the Presidium of the Union Central Executive Committee, June 15, 1927, *Sobranye Zakonov* (1927), cited, Part I, p. 1219.

[50] *Cf.* Law Regarding the Supreme Court of the U.S.S.R. and the Prosecutor of the Supreme Court of the U.S.S.R., July 24, 1929, *Sobranye Zakonov* (1929), cited, Part I, p. 1000. For the functions of the Union prosecutor, *cf.* p. 386.

No official statistics have been published on the number of OGPU executions during the last few years. The first president of the OGPU was Felix Dzerzhinsky, former head of the *Cheka*, who was succeeded in 1925 by Vyacheslav Menzhinsky. The latter died in May 1934.

[51] *Cf.* Law Regarding State Crimes, Crimes against the Ad-

are held to include armed revolt; seizure of power at the center or in the provinces for the purpose of detaching territory from the Union or of violating Soviet treaties with foreign states; the maintenance of relations with foreign governments or their agents with a view to obtaining assistance for the overthrow of the Soviet government; the "wrecking" of industrial trade and credit enterprises in the interests of former bourgeois owners or of capitalist states; propaganda or agitation advocating the overthrow of the Soviet government or directly inciting to counter-revolutionary crimes, especially when it seeks to arouse religious or national prejudices; and failure to report any of the above crimes. The punishment prescribed in such cases ranges from various terms of imprisonment, the maximum being ten years, to permanent exile from the Union with confiscation of property, or shooting—the "highest measure of social defense."

The work of the OGPU was shrouded in the greatest secrecy; arrests were usually made by night, and practically no information regarding the subsequent fate of the arrested persons appeared in the Soviet press. Occasionally, however, when so-called "counter-revolutionaries" were brought before the ordinary courts, reference was briefly made in the act of accusation to preliminary investigations conducted by the OGPU. Such was the case in three spectacular public trials—the Shakta trial in 1928, when a number of engineers and mechanics, including three Germans, were accused of sabotage in the Donetz coal mines; the Ramzin trial in 1930, when

ministration and Counter-Revolutionary Crimes Especially Dangerous for the U.S.S.R., February 25, 1927, *Sobranye Zakonov* (1927), cited, Part I, p. 283.

eight engineers were accused of plotting to "wreck" various industries and to overthrow the Soviet government with the aid of their former bourgeois employers, then living abroad in exile, and of capitalist states, notably France;[52] and the Metropolitan-Vickers case in 1933, when a number of technicians, including six British engineers, were tried on charges of espionage, bribery and "wrecking" of the Soviet electrical industry.[53] These trials would indicate that, following the inauguration of the Five-Year Plan, when the economic activities of the Soviet state not only merged with its political activities but came to overshadow them in the public mind, and when the government had more to fear from economic failure than from political opposition, the OGPU gradually shifted its surveillance from "counter-revolutionary" movements such as "Trotzkyism," which it had worked to eradicate in 1927, to engineers and technical experts, particularly those formerly associated with the old régime. This surveillance, as indicated above, proved a serious obstacle to the development of Soviet industry. The position of the technical intelligentsia, however, was considerably improved in the summer of 1931, when

---

[52] Cf. Le Procès des Industriels de Moscou, 25 Novembre-8 Décembre 1930, Sténographie Intégrale des Débats du Procès des Industriels de Moscou (Paris, Librairie Valois, 1931). The act of accusation in the Ramzin trial stated: "In the course of the past two years the OGPU has discovered sabotage organizations in various branches of industry, one after the other. After the Shakta sabotage group, a sabotage organization was discovered in the People's Commissariat of Transportation. After sabotage in transportation came the discovery of sabotage organizations in the war and textile industries, in naval construction, economic construction, chemical products, the gold and petroleum industries, etc." Ibid., p. 1.

[53] For the official verbatim report of the trial, cf. The Case of N. P. Vivitsky et al. Charged with Wrecking Activities at Power Stations in the Soviet Union (Moscow, State Publishing House, 1933, 3 vols.).

Stalin declared that it would be "stupid and sense-less" to regard "practically every engineer of the old school" as a "potential criminal or 'wrecker.' "[54] In July 1934 the Soviet government abolished the OGPU and entrusted its functions to a Commissariat of Internal Affairs organized along civil rather than semi-military lines. This change appeared to indicate that the government had achieved a measure of internal stability permitting relaxation of political terrorism. Some observers, however, believe that the change was more nominal than real, and that the government will apply drastic measures whenever the Soviet system appears to be menaced by political opposition. When Kirov, a leading Communist, was assassinated in December 1935 the government promptly returned to the procedure of the OGPU in political cases. The accused were tried not by ordinary courts, but by the military tribunal of the Supreme Court of the U.S.S.R., and it was ruled that they were to be indicted one day before trial, that they were to be tried in the absence of both prosecutor and defense counsel, and that their sentences were to be carried out immediately after the verdict, from which there was no appeal. Foreign criticisms of this procedure were described as "slander" by Premier Molotov, who declared that "nothing but the harshest punishment" awaits enemies of the Soviet government.

THE SOVIET JUDICIARY

The regular courts, which deal with ordinary crimes, such as murder, and with civil actions, take jurisdiction over "counter-revolutionary" crimes

[54] *Cf.* Stalin's speech on "New Economic Problems," *The Soviet Union Review*, July-August 1931, p. 152.

only when these are referred to them by the Prosecutor. There being no system of federal courts,[55] justice is administered through the courts of the several Union republics. The soviet judiciary is not an independent organ of the government, but an administrative department charged with the defense of the social order established by the proletarian revolution against attacks by individuals or classes hostile to it.[56] In the early days of Soviet rule the judiciary was regarded as primarily an instrument of class justice. This conception, however, was somewhat modified after the introduction of the New Economic Policy in 1921, which tolerated the existence of the "petty bourgeoisie"—*kulaks* and private traders. While the courts continue to be guided by class policy in the administration of justice, they seek to protect all citizens, irrespective of social origin, against offenses of an anti-Soviet character, even when committed by workers or peasants.

The organization of the judiciary is uniform throughout the Union, and consists of a people's court, a regional court, and a Supreme Court in each Union republic.[57] Variations from this system to meet the cultural, administrative or economic needs of certain regions, may be made only with the consent of the Union Central Executive Committee— a provision which has been criticized as tending toward undue centralization.[58] The Soviet judicial system is based on two main principles—that the

[55] *Cf.* p. 394.

[56] Basic Principles of the Judicial Organization of the U.S.S.R., 1924, *Sobranye Zakonov* (1924), cited, Part I, p. 366.

[57] In the autonomous republics the Supreme Court is usually replaced by a court described as "principal" or "highest."

[58] N. V. Krylenko, *Sud i Pravo v S.S.S.R.* (Law and the Courts in the U.S.S.R.), Moscow, State Publishing House, 1927, p. 30.

courts must be simple and easily accessible to the
population, and that they must be so organized as
to permit the performance of judicial functions exclusively by persons elected by the soviets from the
laboring masses.[59] An early revolutionary decree
provided for the "democratic election" of judges—
presumably direct election by the population.[60] Subsequently, judges of the people's and regional courts
were appointed by the executive committees of the
regional congresses,[61] to which they were responsible
and by which they could be recalled, while the judges
of the Supreme Court of each Union republic were
appointed by the republican executive committee.
The 1936 constitution provides that people's courts
shall henceforth be elected by secret ballot for a
period of three years by citizens of the district, on
the basis of universal, direct and equal suffrage.
Candidates for the bench must have the right to
vote, must have served either in the judiciary[62] or
in workers' and peasants' professional or party organizations and, in the case of supreme court judges,
must have served as judges in the people's courts.

[59] *Ibid.*, p. 39.
[60] Decree No. 1 Regarding the Courts, November 24, 1917.
N. V. Krylenko, *Sudoustroistvo R.S.F.S.R.* (The Judicial Organization of the R.S.F.S.R.), Moscow, Juridical Publications of the
People's Commissariat of Justice, 1924, p. 209. Krylenko described
this decree as "a vestige of the liberal terminology of pre-revolutionary days." *Idem, Sud i Pravo v S.S.S.R.*, cited.
[61] Judges in people's courts may in some instances be appointed
by town soviets, cf. Judah Zelitch, *Soviet Administration of
Criminal Law* (Philadelphia, University of Pennsylvania Press,
1931), p. 54.
[62] This provision has been criticized by Krylenko, who argues
that a judge requires no qualification other than experience in
political or social work in workers' and peasants', professional or
party organizations. He demanded that the work of the courts be
simplified, so that every citizen possessing an average political
and cultural education could grasp the questions in litigation without difficulty. (Krylenko, *Sud i Pravo v S.S.S.R.*, cited, p. 47.)

The people's court, which is the basic unit of the judicial system, consists of a judge and two co-judges (or "judge jurors") who have equal powers with the judge in the administration of justice. The co-judges, each of whom serves not more than six consecutive days in one year, are chosen from a panel prepared by a special committee from lists of persons elected for that purpose by village, factory and other soviets. No special training or experience is required for the office of co-judge. Trial by jury, which had never been widely used in Tsarist Russia, is unknown in the Soviet Union. The jurisdiction of the people's courts, which serve as trial courts, is being constantly broadened, with the result that they now handle over seventy per cent of the total cases.

Territorial and provincial courts and courts of autonomous provinces, which under the new constitution are to be elected by the soviets of their respective regions for a period of five years, serve as courts of cassation and supervision for cases first tried in people's courts, and have original jurisdiction over counter-revolutionary crimes, offenses against the administration, crimes committed by officials in the exercise of their duties, economic offenses (such as malfeasance or misfeasance in office), and ordinary crimes against life, health, liberty and property.[63]

The supreme courts of the Union republics, which under the new constitution are to be elected by the supreme councils of the republics for a period of five years, serve as courts of cassation for cases referred to them from territorial and provincial courts, and have original jurisdiction over cases of exceptional

[63] Cf. Zelitch, *Soviet Administration of Criminal Law,* cited, pp. 68-71.

importance referred to them by the republican supreme council or the prosecutor of the republic, as well as over cases involving offenses in office committed by members of the republican government.

SUPREME COURT OF THE UNION

The Soviet Union has no federal judiciary as distinguished from the three types of courts found in the Union republics. The Union constitution, however, provides for a Supreme Court of the Union which, like other Soviet courts, is not an independent institution, but is "attached" to the Union Central Executive Committee.[64] The Supreme Court examines cases involving offenses committed in office by members of the Union government; deals with conflicts between the constituent republics, and may appeal against them to the Supreme Council of the U.S.S.R. on the ground that they contradict the general legislation of the Union or affect the interests of other republics; finally, at the request of the Supreme Council of the U.S.S.R., it renders opinions regarding the constitutional validity of acts and decrees of organs of Union and republican government. These opinions, however, have the force, not of a decision, but of expert legal advice, and may or may not be approved by the Supreme Council of the U.S.S.R.[65]

The Supreme Court consists of a president, a

[64] The organization and functions of the Supreme Court are defined in Chapter VII of the 1923 constitution, and in the Law Regarding the Supreme Court of the U.S.S.R. and the Prosecutor of the Supreme Court of the U.S.S.R., July 24, 1929, cited, which superseded the earlier law of July 14, 1924; also Chapter IX, *Courts and Prosecution,* of the Draft of the 1936 Constitution.

[65] Cf. Zelitch, *Soviet Administration of Criminal Law,* cited, p. 100.

deputy president and thirty judges, all elected by the Supreme Council of the U.S.S.R. for a period of five years, and is divided into three chambers—civil, criminal and military. That the Supreme Court is charged with the protection not only of the interests of the Union, but of those of the Union republics as well, is indicated by the fact that the presidents of the supreme courts of the seven republics participate in the plenary sessions of the court.

In addition to the regular courts, the Soviet Union has several courts and commissions which deal with special questions. Thus property disputes between organs of the government are examined by arbitral commissions attached to the Council for Labor and Defense, the economic councils of the republics and the regional soviets. Disputes concerning land organization are referred to land commissions, while infractions of the labor code are dealt with by special chambers of the people's courts. Cases of juvenile delinquency are examined by commissions on the affairs of minors, which are composed of representatives of the commissariats of justice, health and education in each of the Union republics. Finally, military crimes and serious breaches of military discipline come within the jurisdiction of military tribunals, whose decisions are subject to review by the military chamber of the Supreme Court of the Union.

The administration of law is supervised by the Prosecutor (*Procurator*) of the Supreme Court of the Union and by republican, regional and local prosecutors who, in addition to their courtroom duties, are authorized to inquire into the "legality of the acts of all government organs, economic institutions, public and private organizations and of private persons."[66] The Prosecutor of the Supreme Court of the Union, who is appointed by the Supreme Council of the U.S.S.R. and is responsible to it alone, also occupies the office of People's Commissar, or deputy commissar, of Justice. Republican prosecutors are appointed by the central executive committees of the republics and, in turn, name regional and local prosecutors. The Soviet prosecutor enjoys powers equal to those of the courts, and occupies a subordinate position only during trials, when he appears as one of the parties in both civil and criminal cases.

As there are no private lawyers, the defense of accused persons is entrusted to a "college of advocates" which functions under the direct supervision of the courts,[67] and must render legal aid to the population, either for a stipulated remuneration, or without charge when the court rules that the defendants are unable to pay. The "college of advocates," which is a semi-autonomous organization, has been criticized on the ground that it is inconsistent with the spirit of Soviet law, and that legal advice should be furnished to workers not by specialists, but by trade and professional organizations.[68]

Soviet law, as has already been noted, draws a sharp distinction between "counter-revolutionary" crimes, which are regarded as socially dangerous, and ordinary crimes against life and property.[69] The

[66] Basic Principles of the Judicial Organization of the U.S.S.R., 1924, cited, Section 63.

[67] *Ibid.*, Section 11.

[68] Krylenko, *Sud i Pravo v S.S.S.R.*, cited, p. 122.

[69] Fundamental Principles of the Criminal Legislation of the U.S.S.R. and of the Union Republics, October 31, 1924, *Sobranye Zakonov* (1924), cited, Part I, p. 372.

avowed purpose of Soviet criminal legislation is not revenge or punishment, but the prevention of crime and the re-training of criminals for normal life. As a result, the penalty for ordinary crimes is much lighter than for "counter-revolutionary" ones. Thus death sentences, which are frequent in cases of administrative or economic mismanagement, embezzlement of government funds and other acts considered as crimes against the state, are seldom pronounced in ordinary murder cases. Punishment usually takes the form of forced labor for not more than one year or imprisonment for a maximum of ten years, and deprivation of civic rights for a period not exceeding five years. The latter penalty carried with it disfranchisement and expulsion from trade and professional unions, whose members enjoy important privileges, including ration cards and the right of admission to coöperative stores.

The courts are instructed to differentiate between various crimes on the basis of motivation and of the social origin of the criminal. Thus severe punishment must be meted out when the crime has been committed for the purpose of restoring the "bourgeois" government or, if not aimed directly against the Soviet state or the working class, is potentially harmful to them; when the crime is motivated by greed or accompanied by unusual cruelty; and when the criminal was or is connected with the "exploiting" classes. Conversely, milder punishment is prescribed when the crime has been committed either in self-defense or for the protection of the Soviet government; when it has been dictated by hunger, want, or strong emotion, or has occurred as a result of ignorance; and when the criminal is either a worker or a peasant.[70] The Soviet government believes that, in the case of all crimes except those classified as counter-revolutionary, the offender should be reformed and re-trained for normal life rather than punished, and Soviet penal institutions are regarded by experts as models of human treatment.[71]

THE RED ARMY

While the Commissariat of Internal Affairs and the ordinary courts are charged with the protection of internal order, the external defense of the Soviet Union is entrusted to the Red Army of Workers and Peasants (RKKA) organized in February 1918.[72] During the period of civil war and intervention, when the Soviet government had to repulse attacks on several fronts, the Red Army numbered nearly five million men. The danger over, the government faced the task of demobilizing this army, organized almost overnight by Leon Trotzky, then People's Commissar of War, and releasing men for productive work, at the same time assuring the country's adequate defense. At the Ninth Congress of the Communist Party in 1920 Trotzky declared that the regular army should be limited in numbers. So limited an army, however, was not sufficient, in his opinion, for the defense of the Soviet Union's far-flung frontiers. He

[70] *Ibid.*

[71] For a discussion of Soviet prisons, *cf.* Elias Tobenkin, *Stalin's Ladder* (New York, Minton, Balch, 1933).

[72] For the history and organization of the Red Army, *cf.* A. Geronimus, *Partiya i Krasnaya Armiya* (The Party and the Red Army), Moscow, State Publishing House, 1928; I. Petukhov, *Partiinaya Organizatsiya i Partiinaya Rabota v RKKA* (Party Organization and Party Work in the Red Army of Workers and Peasants), Moscow, State Publishing House, Division of Military Literature, 1928; B. Tal, *Istoriya Krasnoi Armii* (The History of the Red Army), Moscow, State Military Publications, 1924.

therefore proposed to establish, in addition to the regular army, a territorial militia which would have the advantage that its members would remain in contact with production in fields and factories. The units of this militia should correspond to the country's administrative divisions, and should be actively supported by trade and professional unions. Under this system, every member of the population capable of bearing arms would eventually be included in a military unit and would receive some form of military training.[73] Trotzky's thesis was supported by his successor, Michael Frunze, who stated in 1925 that "the surest guarantee of peace is not only a pacific policy, but a strong Red Army," and that the Soviet Union needed a system of defense which, in time of war, would bring to the battlefield not only professional soldiers, but trained masses of workers and peasants as well.[74]

The complete realization of Trotzky's military scheme has so far been prevented by the country's cultural backwardness and by financial considerations. At the present time the Red Army is recruited on the basis of compulsory service for all men between the ages of nineteen and forty.[75] Every year some 1,200,000 men become eligible for service, of whom some 300,000 are rejected as physically unfit. Of the remaining number about 450,000 are accepted for a two-year term of active service, about half

[73] Russian Communist Party, *Deviaty Syezd Rossiiskoi Communisticheskoi Partyi* (Ninth Congress of the Russian Communist Party), March 29–April 4, 1920, Stenographic Report, Moscow, State Publishing House, 1920, p. 353 *et seq.*

[74] Union of Soviet Socialist Republics, *Tretii Syezd Sovetov S.S.S.R.* (Third Congress of Soviets of the U.S.S.R.), Twelfth Session, May 19, 1925, Stenographic Report, Moscow, Publications of the Central Executive Committee of the U.S.S.R., 1925, p. 488.

[75] Law Regarding Compulsory Military Service, September 16, 1925. *Sobranye Zakonov* (1925), cited, Part I, p. 850 *et seq.*

going into the regular army of 562,000, which includes land, sea and air forces, while half are taken into the territorial militia.[76] Persons enlisted in the militia continue their work in office, field or factory, but receive military training in their respective administrative districts and participate in annual manœuvres. In addition, voluntary courses in rifle practice, the use 'of gas masks and the operation of tanks and military lorries are organized for men who have failed to gain admittance to the army or to the militia, as well as for women and even children. These courses are sponsored primarily by two civilian organizations—*Avtodor*,[77] which is concerned with the development of transportation and the training of automobile drivers, and *Osoviachim*,[78] an organization of over 10,000,000 workers, Young Communists, students and women,[79] which seeks to increase the country's preparedness for air and chemical warfare.

While military service is compulsory for all citizens, the armed defense of the country is regarded as a privilege of the proletariat: as a result, the Red Army consists predominantly of workers and peas-

[76] W. H. Chamberlin, *Soviet Russia* (Boston, Little, Brown, Revised Edition, 1931), p. 127; *Calendar-Ezhegodnik Communista*, cited, p. 358; N. P. Vishnyakov and F. I. Arkhipov, *Ustroistvo Vooruzhennych Sil S.S.S.R.* (The Organization of the Armed Forces of the U.S.S.R.), Moscow, The Military Messenger, 1926.

[77] The full name of this organization is *Obschestvo Sodeistviya Razvitiyu Avtomobilisma i Uluchsheniyu Dorog* (Society for the Development of Automobilism and the Improvement of Roads).

[78] The full name of this organization if *Obschestvo Druzei Oborony i Aviazionno-Khimicheskovo Stroitelstva S.S.S.R.* (Society of Friends of the Defense and Aërial-Chemical Construction of the U.S.S.R.).

[79] S. Kamenev, "Na Strazhe Sozialisticheskovo Stroitelstva" (Protection of Socialist Construction), *Sovetskoe Stroitelstvo*, cited, No. 3, 1931, p. 19.

ants. Persons disfranchised for political or other reasons are assigned to rear guard units and, in addition, must pay a special military tax.[80] In 1934 peasants constituted 42.5 per cent of the army, while factory workers formed 45.8 and office employees 11.7 per cent. Nearly half of the army are Communists, 129,-000 being members of the party and 130,000 members of the *Comsomol*. The commanding personnel, which is recruited partly from soldiers who have received special training and partly from graduates of military schools, is also predominantly of working-class origin, and some seventy per cent are Communists.[81] While discipline is strictly enforced, officers enjoy no special privileges and their relations with the soldiers are unusually democratic in character.

The armed forces of the Soviet Union are controlled by the People's Commissar for Defense through the Revolutionary War Council, of which he is president and the Commander-in-Chief a member. This council has immediate supervision not only over the military staffs, but also over the Political Section (PUR), which directs education and propaganda in the army. By means of various courses, clubs, permanent and itinerant libraries and wall-newspapers the PUR, with the coöperation of Red Army party cells, supplies the rudiments of

[80] This tax goes into a fund for the assistance of invalids of the civil war and of the families of men called to active service. Citizens excused from military service on religious grounds may be used in time of peace for fighting epidemics or forest fires, while in time of war they may be organized into special units. Amendment to the Law Regarding Compulsory Military Service, February 8, 1927, *Sobranye Zakonov* (1927), cited, Part I, p. 223.

[81] *Calendar-Ezhegodnik Communista, 1931*, cited. p. 490. Tsarist officers constituted only 10.6 per cent of the Red Army in 1930, and 6.7 per cent of the higher commanding personnel.

literacy and "political grammar" to soldiers many of whom, especially peasants, come into the army illiterate. The Red Army thus serves as an important training-ground for communism.[82]

Critics of the Soviet government contend that a powerful Soviet army, which increased from 560,-000 in 1933 to 1,300,000 in 1936, and a defense appropriation of 14,800,000,000 rubles in 1936 (or 19 per cent of the total budget),[83] stand in marked contrast to the Soviet government's assertions that it desires peace and abhors war. The Soviet government, in reply, declares that it urgently desires peace and that the Red Army is designed, not for wars of national aggression, but for the defense of the first workers' republic against capitalist attack and, eventually, for the defense of the world proletariat. There can be little doubt that today, and for the immediate future, war would be directly contrary to Soviet interests, since it might seriously jeopardize the progress of the Five-Year Plan, and that Stalin was sincere when he said at the Sixteenth Congress of the Communist party in 1930: "Our policy is a policy of peace . . . We do not want a foot of alien soil, but we shall not surrender an inch of ours." To say that the Soviet Union has developed a sudden affection for capitalist states or lost interest in world revolution would be misleading. The Soviet government, however, is at present more absorbed in creating within the boundaries of the U.S.S.R. a socialist state which may serve as inspiration to workers throughout the world than in spreading the gospel of communism abroad.

[82] For a detailed study of the methods employed by the PUR, cf. Harper, *Civic Training in Soviet Russia*, cited.
[83] *New York Times*, January 14, 1936.

SPAIN UNDER THE REPUBLIC

PRIMO DE RIVERA DICTATORSHIP

PRIOR to the 1936 revolt, Spain had undergone two important governmental changes: the first on September 13, 1923, when General Primo de Rivera overthrew the Constitution of 1876 and established a dictatorship; the second on April 14, 1931, when the Republic was declared.

The dictatorship of Primo de Rivera was the product of social, economic and political conditions common to many European nations after the World War. These conditions had upset the balance of power between the old political parties, breaking them into factions which fought for the spoils of office without regard to the welfare of the people. The result was an almost complete breakdown of responsibility in government, and a notorious slackening of public morality. This period coincided with a military campaign in Morocco, the inept conduct of which led to the disastrous battle of Annual in 1921, in which the Spanish lost between twelve and fourteen thousand men. Responsibility for this disaster was placed at the door of the government, which was already unpopular, and to some extent at the door of the King. The attempt to investigate the Morocco venture was frustrated by the coup

d'état of 1923, and it has been generally believed—
although proof is lacking—that one of the motives
for Primo de Rivera's coup was to save the King
from being implicated in the course of an investigation.

Other reasons for the establishment of a dictatorship at that particular time were not lacking. The
post-war depression had struck Spain, depriving the
country of markets built up during the war, and
throwing thousands of workers out of employment.
The situation was particularly acute in Catalonia,
where the Anarcho-Syndicalists were strong, and
where a Separatist movement had kept the region
in a state of chaos for several years. Primo de Rivera
declared that the objects of his dictatorship were
purification of politics, termination of the Morocco
war, and restoration of social stability.[1]

Primo de Rivera's rule was in many respects a period of progress and prosperity for Spain, although
this prosperity, like that of other countries, could
not withstand the world depression of recent years.
The war in Morocco was brought to a successful
close. Considerable industrial development occurred
between 1923 and 1930 and the government sought
to encourage industry by building up the railroads
and roads, providing a better system of communication, and organizing a National Economic Council
to coördinate economic development. The financial
condition of the country was such as to permit
inauguration of a public works program sufficient

[1] *Cf.* Agnes Waddell, "Spain under the Dictatorship," Foreign
Policy Association, *Information Service,* September 4, 1929;
Gabriel Mauro Gamazo, *Bosquejo Histórico de la Dictadura*
(5th edition, Madrid, Javier Morata, 1930), gives a critical view
of Primo de Rivera; Enrique Díaz Retg, *España Bajo el Nuevo
Régimen* (Madrid, Ediciones Mercurio, 1928), is an estimate of
the régime from the "official" viewpoint.

to employ surplus workers, thus temporarily stemming the rise of revolutionary labor.

During the first five years of the dictatorship, 1923–1928, Primo de Rivera undoubtedly had the support of the majority of the people. A number of events, however, served to diminish his popularity after that date. Among these not the least important was the prolongation of his dictatorship, which had originally been planned to last only three months. Another reason was a campaign for restoration of the Constitution, fostered chiefly by the old politicians who wished to get back into office, which served to create popular feeling against the dictator. The repressive measures employed against government opponents, especially the newspapers and students, added to Primo de Rivera's unpopularity. The army, too, had been severely disciplined, with the result that the government lost its united support. Early in 1930 the growing unpopularity of the dictator, together with his failing health, precipitated his resignation.

Alfonso XIII then entrusted the government to General Dámaso Berenguer, a second dictator, whose rule proved to be unfortunate for the Monarchy. Primo de Rivera had been *simpático*, attracting great numbers of followers because of his personal qualities; Berenguer proved to be neither a good ruler nor a good politician. His one year in power merely succeeded in arousing public sentiment not only against dictators, but against the throne. He had been intimately connected with the King for a number of years, was partly responsible for the Annual disaster, and his appointment was ascribed to Alfonso's desire to continue a personal form of government. Anti-dictatorship sentiment became anti-Monarchist in character, and led to a revolt in December 1930 which, although unsuccessful, stimulated further revolutionary activity. Berenguer's belated attempts to return to constitutional methods were balked by the refusal of the Left forces to participate in elections, and he was forced to give way to Admiral Aznar early in 1931. Aznar proved even less capable than Berenguer; as a result anti-Monarchical sentiment reached fever heat, and the downfall of monarchy became inevitable.

Alfonso XIII fled Spain on April 14, 1931, leaving a new republic behind him.[2] Spain's First Republic had been ended by a military coup in 1874 after ten and a half months of ineffectual existence.[3] Would the Second Republic meet a similar fate? During the First Republic, Spain had been ruled in succession by four Presidents, none of whom had sufficient strength either in the Cortes or in the country to bring order out of the chaos left by the Monarchy. Would the Second Republic produce men of greater ability? The first Republic lacked organized parties strong enough to maintain it. Would the Second Republic develop such parties?

The First Republic had been a product of Liberalism, the Second Republic of Socialism combined with Liberalism. The prominence of the Socialists in Spain's second essay at republicanism served to raise a number of other questions. Would the Socialists succeed in dominating the new régime and use it to transform Spain into a socialist state?

[2] William E. Linglebach, "The Spanish Revolution," *Current History*, June 1931.

[3] Pio Zabala y Lera, *Historia de España, 1808–1923* (2 vols., Barcelona, Sucesores de Juan Gili, 1930) II, pp. 23–24; Joseph A. Brandt, *Toward the New Spain* (Chicago, the University of Chicago Press, 1933), pp. 173–353.

Would the Republic succumb in the end to reactionary forces, or would Spain, like Russia, carry through its revolution even at the cost of dictatorship? The program of the First Republic was entirely political in character. It sought to construct a new Spain without fundamentally modifying existing economic conditions. The presence of the Socialists in the Second Republic committed it to economic reforms. Were the Socialists strong enough to impose their program, or would they be placed in a position of responsibility while lacking adequate authority? These and many other questions confronted the new Republic.

The fall of Alfonso XIII and the establishment of the Republic were precipitated by the decisive victory of Republicans and Socialists in the municipal elections held throughout Spain on April 12, 1931.[4] This victory was brought about by a coalition of anti-Monarchical groups, some of which had been in

[4] For the electoral results, cf. Anuario Estadístico de España (Madrid, Instituto de Geografía, 1931), p. 482. In the whole of Spain 80,472 municipal councillors were elected by 5,440,103 voters, of whom 1,104,159, or about 20 per cent, lived in provincial capitals. This 20 per cent elected only 1,729 councillors, or about 2 per cent of the total. Of these 1,729 councillors the anti-Monarchists gained 1,065. If the cities had been allotted a number proportionate to their population, they would have named some 16,000 councillors. For example: Barcelona had one councillor for every 5,350 voters, Madrid one for every 4,620, while Soria, a small town in the conservative section of Spain, could boast of a councillor for every 150 voters, and Avila and Teruel, also small towns, had a councillor for every 165 voters. The number of councillors elected, therefore, did not represent the relative voting strength of Monarchists and anti-Monarchists. In all Spain 34,368 Republicans, 4,813 Socialists, 19,035 Monarchists, 67 Communists, 15,198 representatives of local parties, and 6,991 unclassified candidates were elected. All those not Republicans, Socialists or Communists were considered Monarchists. The Monarchists had, on this basis, 51.5 per cent of the total number of the councillors to 48.5 for the anti-Monarchists. The anti-Monarchists carried 46 of the 50 provincial capitals, however, and showed great strength in the large cities.

existence since the fall of the First Republic, while others were of recent origin.

When the returns of April 12, 1931, showed a decided republican victory in the principal cities and towns, the King was faced with the choice of yielding or maintaining himself by force.[5] General Berenguer, who was Minister of War in the Aznar cabinet, and General Sanjurjo, Commander of the Civil Guard, refused to repress the people. Failing to obtain the necessary support, the King left Madrid on the night of April 14, 1931. A Provisional Government, with Niceto Alcalá-Zamora as President, had already been formed.[6]

THE CONSTITUTIONAL CORTES

For three months after the establishment of the Republic, the Provisional Government ruled alone without the aid of a Cortes. In some cases the work of the Provisional Government was practically definitive, but all actions taken in the first three months had later to be ratified by the Cortes, and the election of this legislative body was one of the first concerns of the new government. Before the elections to the Cortes, scheduled for June 28, 1931, the government took a new electoral census, lowered the voting age from 25 to 23, and fixed the representation at one deputy for every 50,000 of population, making the total number of deputies 470 and giving the urban centers more equitable representation.[7]

[5] Comte de Romanones, "La Republique en Espagne," *Revue des Deux Mondes* (Paris), July 15, 1931.

[6] The final scenes are given in what is probably a fairly accurate account by Julián Cortés Cavanillas, *La Caída de Alfonso XIII* (Madrid, Librería de San Martín, 1933), p. 207 *et seq.*

[7] In the last Cortes of the Monarchy, which had 404 deputies, the rural districts were favored. Under the new apportionment, Barcelona gained 12 and Madrid 13 representatives, and other

Practically the only issue presented to the people
was approval or disapproval of the Revolution. The
sharp differences which were to develop later had
not yet come into the open, and the Republicans
and Socialists presented a coalition ticket. The
opposition consisted of a few remnants of the
old political parties. The Monarchists presented no
ticket, but the Agrarian and Basque-Navarre parties represented the forces of the old régime. The
Socialist-Republican coalition won a decisive victory.[8] The opposition elected about 60 deputies
drawn from the Agrarians, the Basque-Navarre
party, and independents of known Right leanings.
There was also a small group on the Left which later
turned Communist. The new Cortes assembled on
July 14, 1931.[9]

CHAPTER II

BUILDING A NEW SPAIN

THE early accomplishments of the Spanish Republic were considerable, when the difficulties and
opposition which it faced are taken into consideration. The Cortes framed one of the most progressive

urban centers made gains while some of the country districts
either remained stationary or lost. For the pre-Republic figures,
cf. España (Madrid, Espasa-Calpe, 1925), pp. 524–27; for Republican figures, cf. Ley Electoral, published in the Biblioteca Oficial
Legislativa, Vol. XXVI, by Editorial Reus (Madrid, 1920 and
1933).

[8] The Socialists elected 116 deputies; the Radicals 90; the
Radical Socialists 60; the Progressives (Right Republican of
Alcalá-Zamora and Miguel Maura) 22; the Republican Action
30; the Federals 17; the Galician Left 16; and the Catalan
Left 43. Luz (Madrid), March 3, 1932; Anuario, cited, 1931,
p. 487. These figures include the deputies chosen in subsequent
supplementary elections.

[9] El Sol (Madrid), and other Spanish papers printed the
proceedings of the Cortes.

of modern constitutions. The army was reorganized, two-thirds of its officers retired, its technical equipment improved and much of its political significance removed. Church and State were separated, the Jesuits dissolved and their property expropriated, the property of the Church nationalized, the religious orders submitted to a law of associations, and forbidden to engage in commerce or industry, or to teach. Civil marriage and divorce were made legal.

In the field of social legislation the Republic made notable achievements. A complete new system of laws was designed to give the worker full protection of labor and wages. Workers were guaranteed rights of collective bargaining, protected by the *Jurados mixtos* and the Labor Delegates, and given the benefits of social insurance. The Labor Department was reorganized in such a way that it afforded a real protection to the worker. The Agrarian Reform Law, which legalized redistribution of land, had begun to operate by the autumn of 1933. The Catalan question, for centuries a source of trouble, was handled in a way that made a definite solution seem possible by distributing administrative powers between the state and the region. A tremendous stride toward revolutionizing the schools was made by the establishment of more than nine thousand new schools, the reorganization of the normal schools and the general increase in the pay of teachers. For the first time in the history of Spain thousands of poor children were placed in the classroom. Finally, the Republic began the building of important public works such as irrigation projects, hydroelectric plants, highways, electrified railways, port facilities, and houses for the poor.

THE CONSTITUTION

Spain's new political structure as outlined by the Constitution [1] consisted of a single-chamber Cortes elected for four years, a President elected for six years, a Supreme Court and a Tribunal of Constitutional Guarantees. The President was empowered to appoint a Premier who, with his Cabinet, was responsible for the program of the government, as in England and France. The Constitution broke abruptly with Spain's past, declaring that "Spain is a democratic republic of workers of all classes." Reversing the policy followed for centuries, it declared that "the Spanish State has no official religion," and established freedom of worship, [2] right of divorce, civil marriage and lay education. Property was subject to expropriation for social uses, and the state might intervene in the direction and control of industry, or nationalize public utilities. It was declared that "Spain renounces war as an instrument of national policy," and provided that the President might wage war and make peace "subject to the conditions prescribed in the Covenant of the League of Nations."

Spain became a federative, although not necessarily a federal, republic by Article 8, providing that "regions constituting autonomous governments" may be established and frame a charter which "the Spanish State shall recognize . . . and uphold . . .

[1] For English text, cf. *Current History,* June 1932.
[2] Article 27 of the Constitution provides: "Freedom of conscience and the right to profess and practice freely any religion are guaranteed in Spanish territory, provided public morals are safeguarded. . . . All denominations may observe their rites privately. Public celebration of the rites of a sect in each case must be authorized by the Government." *Current History,* June 1932, p. 377.

as an integral part of the national law." This allowed such regions as Catalonia, Galicia and the Basque provinces to organize governments competent to handle local affairs, and set up standards for determining which powers should be held by the central government and which by the regions. Such regions were not considered to be sovereign states voluntarily surrendering their prerogatives to the central government. Article 18 provided that "all powers not explicitly granted in the charter of an autonomous region shall be considered as reserved to the Spanish State."

Among the most revolutionary provisions of the Constitution were those relating to the Church. In addition to the provisions mentioned above, the Constitution stated that "all religious denominations shall be considered as associations subject to special laws," withdrew the state subsidy hitherto granted the Church and empowered the Cortes to dissolve religious orders dangerous to the state. The Constitution also limited their rights of commerce, industry and teaching, and the Cortes might confiscate their property.

Conflict over the status of the Church caused the first break in the revolutionary coalition. The Socialists had called for the "ultimate destruction of the Church," and had demanded a provision in the Constitution stating that "all religious orders shall be expelled and their property seized." [3] Alcalá-Zamora and Maura were opposed to such drastic action and favored a moderate policy. As finally adopted, the Constitution chose a middle course, calling for dissolution of the Jesuits, but leaving the status of the other orders to decision by the

[3] *El Sol* and *New York Times*, October 14, 15, 1931.

Cortes. Alcalá-Zamora and Maura, however, resigned in protest against the anti-clerical articles and a new government was formed by Manuel Azaña on October 14, 1931.

Other important Articles of the Constitution extended the vote to all citizens 23 years of age or over, guaranteed freedom of speech and the press, and provided against arbitrary arrest. The right to expropriate property with compensation and "the socialization of property . . . under the same conditions" left the way open to nationalization of wealth, but was in reality a conservative measure which did not satisfy the Socialists. The statement that "work in its diverse forms is a social obligation and shall enjoy the protection of the law" and the provisions for social insurance indicated Socialist influence.

ARMY REORGANIZATION

For more than a century Spain had been at the mercy of an army which was more a political than a military instrument. The King's debt to the army was great, and every attempt to correct abuses which had crept into its organization was halted by the danger of offending it. Primo de Rivera's mistake in antagonizing a portion of the army, as has already been pointed out, was one of the principal causes for the success of the Revolution.

Not only did Republican Spain owe little to the army, but the army as organized and officered in 1931 was a distinct threat to the Republic. If the Monarchist officers, of whom there were many, should seize control of the army, a quick restoration of the Bourbons might be possible. Manuel Azaña, Minister of War, decided that the army must be immediately taken out of politics and made into a weapon for national defense. "In the reform of the army," he said, "the object has been a very simple one, though non-existent up to this time: it has been nothing other than to endow the Republic with a military policy." [4] One of his first moves was to repeal the Law of Jurisdictions which gave the army the right to try all who criticized it.[5] All officers were required to pledge allegiance to the Republic or resign, and to rid the army of surplus officers Azaña decreed that those who wished might retire on full pay.[6] Azaña suppressed the eight or ten captains-general, and supplanted the Supreme War and Naval Council with a court for trying military and naval cases only. He subsequently decreed that any retired officer convicted of taking part in politics should lose his pension. Largely as a result of these measures during the first two and a half years of the Republic's life, the army exerted little if any pressure on the government.

Azaña was also determined to equip the Spanish army for future conflicts. The declaration in the Constitution that "Spain renounces war as an instrument of national policy" and makes a declaration of war "subject to the conditions prescribed in the Covenant of the League of Nations" was generally hailed as a great step in internationalism, and justly so. But war, and not peace, was implied in this article of the Constitution. It was a declaration that Spain would not remain neutral in any future conflict in which the League might take part.

[4] Manuel Azaña, *Una Política* (Madrid, Espasa-Calpe, 1932), pp. 141-172.
[5] *New York Times,* April 18, 1931.
[6] *The Statesman's Yearbook, 1933; Anuario Estadístico, 1931,* p. 490; *Extracto de organización militar de España,* July 1, 1933.

AGRARIAN REFORM

Spain's most important problem remained the establishment of a prosperous agriculture. Although a notable increase had taken place in industry and the towns had assumed greater importance, some 75 per cent of the people still depended directly on agriculture for a living. In the past Spain had not cultivated all of its soil nor the best of it. About 60 per cent was left uncultivated, and only 27 per cent was cropped each year.[7] This situation had arisen "because access could not be had to much of the good land" and the result had been that "the agricultural classes have had to cultivate other, bad land that should be used for forest."[8] It may be said, in general, that in the southern and western part of Spain land was held in enormous estates, only partly cultivated, while northern, northwestern, and to some extent parts of eastern Spain suffered from excessive division of the land into small farms. The great estates were cultivated largely by landless farm workers who had been completely at the mercy of the landlords, while the regions where small farms abounded were cultivated by renters, share croppers and leaseholders who were frequently dispossessed on any convenient pretense. Even where they owned their land and might not be dispossessed, their farms were usually too small to produce a crop sufficient for the needs of a family.

This situation created a problem which the Monarchy was unable to solve, and on the solution of which the future of the Republic depended. The

[7] Pascual Carrión, *La Reforma Agraria* (Madrid, Editorial Pueyo, 1931), p. 13ff.
[8] *Ibid.*

economic status of farm workers was extremely low and their social condition even worse. Few if any schools were available, and in some provinces illiteracy in rural sections reached 85 per cent. The peasants lived in small villages and hamlets reached in many cases neither by railroad, highway nor telephone. Their cultural life was practically nonexistent, and their political hopes were stifled by systematic falsification of electoral results.

The explanation of why this system prevailed and why Spain had done so little to alleviate it must be sought in its origin. Before the nineteenth century Spain was still almost completely feudal in its agriculture. The land belonged to the great military orders, the Church, the nobility and the municipalities. But in practically every case the peasants held rights in the municipal common, in the church lands or in the land belonging to the nobility; and the privilege of grazing sheep, cows or burros on certain public lands was established by custom and law.

This system was radically altered in the past century. Beginning in 1811 and extending on through to 1888 a series of disentailment and mortmain laws were passed.[9] According to Costa these laws took from the "needy" of Spain and gave to the "legislators" five important interests in the land: the right of pasturage, the ecclesiatical tithe, a part of usufruct on the inheritances of the Church, the village lands, and the municipal commons. The passage of these laws meant for the capitalists, he says, "the acquisition of more than half of the Peninsula for the tenth of its value." These laws threw thousands

[9] Joaquín Costa, *La Tierra y la Cuestión Social* (Vol. IV. of the *Biblioteca Económica, Obras Completas* of Costa. Madrid, Biblioteca Costa, 1915).

of peasants off the land, or reduced them to the status of rural proletariat.

The old feudal estate and feudal practices continued to exist side by side with the new domains. Many towns, villages, and individuals paid dues just as they did in the Middle Ages. Most of the good land of Spain was still owned by a few people, either under old title, or through title acquired during the nineteenth century.[10] In some cases this ownership consisted of hundreds or even thousands of small farms. For example, Cáceres Province had twelve owners with 19,000 acres each. "Forty proprietors, the majority resident in Madrid, [had] greater wealth in the province of Salamanca than 100,000 inhabitants of 150 towns."

Moreover, the landlords of Spain, through their economic power, were able to control political life, despite the existence of universal suffrage. Francisco Cambó, political leader and Catalan industrialist, has described the system adopted. He says:

"Everybody was given the right to vote; but, as there were very few citizens prepared to exercise this right—and as the great majority of these few figured in the parties opposed to the régime—there was organized, systematically, the falsification of the suffrage by the creation of *caciquismo*. A contractor of the rudimentary and non-existent public opinion was situated in each province, with branches and agencies in every town and village. He supplied the votes which the citizens did not cast, and made way with those cast by rebellious citizens; it was his

[10] For a discussion of Spain's land problem, *cf.* Salvador de Madariaga, *Spain* (New York, Scribner, 1930); Pascual Carrión, *Los Latifundios de España* (Madrid, Francisco Beltrán, 1932), entire; Pazos y Garcia, *op. cit.*

job to assure the triumph of the candidates named by the government. In exchange, the contractor of public opinion was the representative of the government in his district, of just any government; the magistrates and judges were at his command and it was he in reality who administered justice; the treasury official and the district attorneys were subject to his authority and it was he, in reality, who decided the amount of the taxes, and who should pay them; the governor of the province and the mayors were subject to his will . . . and even if the bishop and the parish priests were not, a large number of the canons were, since he had it in his power to name them." [11]

While some technical and social progress took place before 1931, agrarian conditions were still deplorable. The need of reform was urgent, and the Cortes framed the Agrarian Reform Law with a double aim in view: to distribute the soil more equitably and to endow it with the necessary technical assistance, such as irrigation projects, for scientific cultivation; and to build in Spain a new social and political order through improvement of the condition of the rural population.

Owing to opposition from vested interests, the agrarian law was not passed until September 1932. A year was allowed for preliminary study, including a census of the workers, thus delaying actual application of the law until September 1933. The law created an Institute of Agrarian Reform and endowed it with fifty million pesetas a year. [12] Fourteen provinces where the large estates were numerous were

[11] Quoted from Cortes Cavanillas, *op. cit.*, pp. 14–15.
[12] For the Agrarian Reform Law and the Decree, *cf. Gaceta de Madrid,* September 21, 23, 25, and November 5, 1932.

the first to come under the law, but large estates wherever located could be expropriated. No compensation was allowed for feudal estates, but other lands were to be paid for by capitalizing the value shown on the tax records at the rate of 5 per cent for farm incomes up to 15,000 pesetas. The rate then rose to 20 per cent for incomes of 200,000 pesetas and over. The expropriated lands were to be distributed to individual farmers or to associations of farm workers for collective farming, and vacant lands formerly embraced in the large estates were to be colonized and towns built on them. The law provided that "once in possession of the land, the communities will decide by majority vote whether the land is to be worked individually or collectively, and if individually, will proceed to divide and distribute it, taking into account the nature of the land, the capability of the rural families and other factors that will contribute to the maintenance of the economic equality of the members." The land so distributed belonged to the state and the occupant might be dispossessed for abuse of the property, but the Institute was obligated to give compensation for improvements made by the occupant. The Institute also encouraged the formation of coöperative societies for purchasing food, farm machinery and other necessities, and for securing credit.

"All feudal contributions whether in money or in kind [were] abolished without right of indemnification," and a great many charges known as *foros* and *subforos* levied against the land heretofore were subject to revision, as well as the special obligation known as the *rabassa morta* collected in Catalonia. The basic reform was supplemented by a great many auxiliary laws intended to correct any weaknesses it might show in practice. The establishment of irrigation systems, the construction of new roads, agricultural schools and experimental farms were a part of the general scheme of building a new agrarian system.

REGIONAL PROBLEMS

One of the serious problems which the Provisional Government had to face from the first was that of separatism. Four hundred years' effort toward unification had not deprived Catalonia, Galicia and the Basque provinces of their desire to regain the autonomous rights they had once enjoyed. The Monarchy had failed to settle this question, and the First Republic had been torn apart by inability to reconcile the claims of the various regions. Catalonia had been converted from mild, conservative regionalism to violent separatism by the policy of the dictatorship, and would not coöperate with the revolutionaries until promised a satisfactory settlement of its demands. When the revolution came in April 1931, Catalonia established the Catalan Republic. Colonel Maciá announced that Catalonia would be one of the states of the "Federated Spanish Republic." He was persuaded to retreat from this position by President Alcalá-Zamora, on the promise that the Cortes would consider a Catalonian Statute, prepared in Catalonia and approved by a plebiscite. This statute was drafted by a Catalan Assembly known as the Generality,[13] ratified overwhelmingly by the people and presented by Colonel Maciá to the Spanish Cortes on August 14, 1931.[14] Discussion

[13] For full text, cf. El Sol, July 14, 1931.
[14] Ibid., August 14, 1931.

of the Constitution was in progress at the time, and President Alcalá-Zamora suggested that it should take precedence over the Statute, a suggestion which was adopted. The Catalans manifested much impatience over this delay, but the Statute did not come up for discussion until May 1932, and was not finally approved until September 1932.[15]

Catalonia was defined in the Statute as an "autonomous region within the Spanish State."[16] The principal contention of the Catalans, however—that Catalonia was to be considered an independent region delegating certain of its prerogatives to the Spanish state—was denied. The powers granted Catalonia over finances, police, justice, education and social services were extensive, but both in the Constitution and in the Statute the rights of Catalonia were enumerated, and it was declared that the state reserved those not specifically granted. The Statute did not meet the demands of all Catalans. A rather numerous Left Wing demanded much greater freedom.[17]

The Basque provinces were not so successful as Catalonia in pressing their demands. Their first efforts to frame a Statute met with failure because of internal dissensions, and only in November 1933 was their Statute approved by a plebiscite, while it did not reach the Cortes until January 1934.[18]

[15] *La Prensa* (New York), December 30, 1931, January 11, March 4, September 26, 1932.
[16] *Gaceta,* September 21, 1932.
[17] *El Sol,* August 21, 1933.
[18] *La Prensa* (New York), November 7, 1933. Autonomy was finally granted the Basque Provinces only on October 1, 1936.

CHURCH AND STATE

That the relations of the State and the Church would be altered under the Republic was evident from the beginning. The only question was how the change would be brought about, and to what extent the Church would be deprived of the privileges it had enjoyed for centuries under the Monarchy. Until 1857 education had been practically the exclusive right of the Church, and a law promoting popular state education passed in that year became a dead letter because of Church opposition. In 1931 half of the children who were in school were being educated by the Church, while both state and municipal schools were under its supervision. Hospital work, nursing, charity and many other functions were still the prerogatives of the Church, and their general deficiency could largely be attributed to the inability of the Church to meet the needs of the nation, and its consistent opposition to further state intervention in these fields. The reputed wealth of the Church had also fanned popular animosity. The Church was tax exempt and received compensation from the state for lands it had lost in the nineteenth century. Its wealth had identified the Church with the capitalist system precisely at a time when both Socialism and Anarcho-Syndicalism were gaining ground. Thus the Church had incurred the enmity of Liberals and Republicans, who considered it an obstacle to education, and of the laboring classes, which objected to its great wealth. Long-standing animosity toward the Church dating from the nineteenth century [19] flared up again in a series

[19] Zabala (*Historia de España,* cited, I, p. 314) says that the people attacked the monasteries in 1834 killing "one hundred religious."

of riots which began on May 11, 1931. Dozens of churches and monasteries were burned or destroyed, and the total property damage amounted to some five million dollars.

The anti-clerical attitude of the Republic soon became apparent. Even the most conservative members of the Provisional Government favored separation of Church and State. Provincial governors were ordered to absent themselves from church services, and negotiations were opened with the Vatican. President Alcalá-Zamora announced late in May, however, that "the Government will not adopt any definite policy toward the Church before a duly elected Cortes can work out the delicate problem of separation of Church and State." [20] It has already been noted that the Constitution provided for such a separation and empowered the government to supplement the Constitution by laws governing religious orders, church property, marriage and divorce. The Cortes had been given a clear mandate to dissolve the Jesuits, a step considered essential because of the growth of the religious orders during the twentieth century.[21] In January 1932 the Cortes dissolved the

[20] *New York Times,* May 30, 1931.
[21] Increase in number of clergy in Spain 1900–1930:

Year	Monks	Nuns	Total	Total per 10,000 Population
1900	12,142	42,596	54,738	29.42
1910	13,539	46,357	59,896	30.02
1923	17,210	54,605	71,815	33.16
1930	20,642	60,758	81,400	34.54

Anuario, 1931, p. 664.

Number of communities of religious orders in 1930 and to what dedicated:

	Teaching	Charity	Contemplation	Other	Total
Monks ..	514	35	147	326	1,022
Nuns ...	1,432	1,128	863	463	3,886

Anuario, 1931, p. 667.

Jesuit order and seized its property. At the same
time the cemeteries were secularized and religious
burial prohibited unless provided for in the will of
the deceased. The appropriation formerly given to
the Church by the state was cut by one-third in the
1932 budget, and was to have ended entirely after
November 1933.[22] A law permitting divorce was
passed in February 1932, giving the civil courts jurisdiction over such cases. Divorce was allowed by
mutual consent after two years of marriage, but
where divorce was granted for cause the guilty party
might not marry until one year after the final decree.[23] In June 1932 a law provided that "from the
date of the publication of the present law only one
form of marriage is recognized—civil marriage."[24]
Another decree provided that "the ecclesiastical
corps of the army is dissolved."[25]

These measures provoked bitter opposition to the
Cabinet and the Republic. By midsummer 1932
the Catholics were strongly united in the *Acción
Católica,* a non-political body for the defense of the
Church, and the *Acción Popular,* a political party
intended to unite all supporters of the Church. The
measures adopted against the Church aroused the
sympathy of some of the republican parties for the
views of *Acción Católica.* Miguel Maura with his
Conservative party carried on a campaign against the
Azaña government, and Alejandro Lerroux, although
still professing anti-clericalism, objected to the manner in which the anti-clerical legislation had been applied. These forces were not strong enough to stop
the attack on the Church, however, and in December

[22] *Cf.* p. 449.
[23] *Gaceta,* May 12, 1932.
[24] *Ibid.,* July 4, 1932.
[25] *Lu* (Paris), July 22, 1932.

1932 a law restricting the religious orders was presented to the Cortes. Owing to the bitter opposition and the obstructionist tactics of its opponents,
it was not finally approved until June 1933, and
when approved provoked a crisis in the government.
The law [26] confiscated the property of the orders,
estimated with other church property at $500,000,-
000.[27] It also enforced the "prohibition of the practice of industry, commerce or teaching" as provided
in Article 26 of the Constitution. According to its
terms, all primary teaching was to be taken out of
the hands of the orders by December 31, 1933,
and all other instruction by October 1933.[28] This
last provision led to the publication of a pastoral [29]
by the bishops of Spain in which attendance of state
schools was strictly forbidden, and the families of
the faithful were ordered to send their children to
Catholic schools.[30] The religious orders also sought
to evade the law by the organization of corporations
for teaching, and one of Spain's most prominent intellectuals complained of the "increasing prosperity
of the extinguished Company of Jesus which, under

[26] For full text of the law, cf. La Información (New York),
June 7, 1933.

[27] Ibid., May 19, 1933, and New York Times, June 6, 1933,
give this estimate.

[28] The Republic has created 9,620 schools, and 665 kindergartens. It has raised the pay of about 85.5 per cent of its
teachers, and in two years approximately 481,000 students were
placed in school. The total amount of money dedicated to education by the state increased from 209,861,049 pesetas in 1931 to
310,798,204 pesetas in 1933. For the important work done in
education by the Republic, cf. Rodolfo Llopis, La Revolución en
la Escuela (Madrid, M. Aguilar, 1933); and Boletín de Educación (Ministerio de Instrucción Pública, Enero-Marzo, 1933),
pp. 174ff.

[29] For a copy of the Pope's encyclical condemning this law
and of the bishop's pastoral, cf. En Estas Horas de Tribulación,
a pamphlet published by the Asociación de propagandistas Cató-
licos de Campostela (Santiago), 1933.

[30] New York Times, June 4, 1933.

a different title, multiplies the number of its schools and prepares itself to enjoy a splendid, though subterranean, existence." [31]

THE REVOLUTION IN THE SCHOOLS

Spain made considerable progress in education between 1874 and 1931; but educational conditions were highly unsatisfactory. Most of the progress came after 1902, when the educational reform of that year placed a far greater portion of the burden of education on the state. Previously the Church played a far more important part in education than the state. Despite the progress made, however, some 45 per cent of the people were still unable to read and write in 1931. The Church schools catered principally to the classes able to pay school fees, and only the very poor went to the primary schools maintained by the state and the municipalities. These were frequently inferior, inadequately housed, and poorly equipped. The teaching staff was deficient in training, and the pay too small to attract the best talent. The Church schools were not required to maintain a high standard for teachers, and too many of their teachers were more zealous than capable. Though Spain had some very excellent schools, both Church and state, there were not enough of them to educate the entire nation. It was estimated in 1931 that some 27,000 schools would be needed to supply the needs of the children not enrolled in any school.

The Republic has attacked this problem with considerable vigor. From 1931 to 1933 some 9,620

[31] Américo Castro, "La cuestión religiosa en España," *El Sol*, August 12, 1933.

schools were created, more than the Monarchy had
established in the previous seventeen years. Formerly most schools were one-teacher units; the Republic established 2,619 classes in grade schools.
Some 665 kindergartens were established throughout Spain and in the province of Madrid alone
some 514 new schools were founded, while Barcelona
established 592. At the same time the Republic
has raised the pay of some 86.5 per cent of its
teachers and licensed many new instructors.[32] Sup-
plying new teachers was not so difficult as it was
supposed to be. The failure of the state to provide
a sufficient number of primary schools in the past
had left a great number of high school and college
graduates without a career. The increase in the
number of monks and nuns in teaching during this
century also tended to prevent many graduates from
finding positions. Spain had some 15,000 teachers
with the necessary titles for teaching and ready to
begin when schools were available.[33]

Not only in the creation of schools did the Republic carry on its educational program, it was necessary also to give the teachers better training. To
accomplish this, *cursillos,* or short courses, were organized for the new and old teachers. Approximately
20,000 prospective teachers were enrolled in the
courses designed to prepare them for examinations
as teachers, and 20,000 teachers already in service
took advantage of these courses to prepare them-

[32] *Boletín de Educación,* Ministerio de Instrucción Pública,
Enero-Marzo, 1933, pp. 174ff. Pay for teachers was increased from
2,000 up to 3,000 pesetas in the lower grades. Total teacher pay
rose from 116 million to 169 million pesetas between 1931 and
1933. Some 31,775 teachers out of 36,680 received a higher salary
than they had under the Monarchy.

[33] Rodolfo Llopis, *La Revolución en la Escuela.* Madrid,
M. Aguilar, 1933, p. 244.

selves for advancement. Some 18,500 in 1931 and 22,000 in 1933 made application for courses preparatory to the examinations for teachers. The Normal Schools, 54 in number, were placed on a higher standard and a School of Pedagogy created in the University of Madrid. To bring the whole nation in line with the program, the corps of supervisors was reorganized and some 165 new members added, dropping the ratio of teachers to each inspector from 173 in 1931 to 131 in 1933.

Outside the schools another form of education was carried on. Many of the rural districts of Spain lacked any contact with the cultural world, and, to reach these, traveling schools, museums, dramas, and cinemas were instituted. These "schools" traveled from town to town, organizing and giving classic Spanish dramas, showing cinemas to children and grown-ups who had never seen them before, carrying copies of the finest sculpture and painting of Spain, and seeking to implant in the people a desire for learning. Music was carried to them by means of gramophones and radios. Libraries to the number of 1,487 were established. Around the Normal Schools and other institutions of learning numbers of "residencias" or homes for the students were built. The total amount of money dedicated to education by the state increased from 209,861,049 pesetas in 1931 to 310,798,204 pesetas in 1933.[34]

The credit for the Educational Reform must go principally to Marcelino Domingo, first Minister of Education, and to Fernando de los Ríos, the one-time Columbia University professor, who succeeded him in that place. Both men had traveled and

[34] *Presupuestos Generales del Estado,* Ministerio de Hacienda, 1931 and 1933.

studied educational systems abroad, and were prepared for the work they assumed.

THE REPUBLIC AND LABOR

Organized labor played a leading part in establishing the Republic, and expected to be rewarded for its services. The Socialists especially were under obligation to the workers for their support, and the inability of the Socialists to carry out all their promises greatly contributed to the unpopularity they incurred in 1933. The labor legislation of the Republic,[35] however, constituted a great improvement and may be attributed mainly to Largo Caballero, Socialist Minister of Labor, and Indalecio Prieto, Socialist Minister of Public Works.

A law of Labor Contracts [36] gave the laborer an effective collective bargaining instrument. National employment offices were provided and all private offices closed.[37] The law of *Términos Municipales*,[38] called by Largo Caballero [39] "the most revolutionary of the Republic because it safeguards the political rights of the working class, subjugated before to the economic tyranny of the *cacique*," [40] was particularly effective. It created a classified register of workers in

[35] Spain has ratified some thirty conventions recommended by the International Labor Office, twenty-two of them since the establishment of the Republic. In most cases the appropriate legislation has been enacted, but this work was slowed up by the crisis in the government beginning in the spring of 1933. For these conventions, *cf. Los convenios Internacionales de trabajo y su ratificación por España* (Madrid, Ministerio de Trabajo, 1932).

[36] *Labor realizada desde la proclamación de la República hasta el 8 de septiembre de 1932* (Ministerio de Trabajo, 1932), pp. 59 ff.

[37] *Ibid.*, pp. 71ff.

[38] *Ibid.*, pp. 27.

[39] *El Sol*, October 3, 1933.

[40] A political boss.

each municipality [41] and forbade the importation of workers from other municipalities until all local residents of any given occupation were employed. Its object was to prevent the importation of workers in order to lower wages or, as was customary under the Monarchy, to turn an election to the advantage of the *cacique*. None of the legislation of the Republic was more bitterly attacked, and the propertied classes cited it in every petition and at every congress as an assault on their rights.

Republican contributions to labor also include a National Unemployment Fund [42] and a Law of Labor Associations.[43] Coöperatives of consumers, laborers, merchants and farmers were established, but such coöperatives could not transact business except with their own members, and the Ministry of Labor was empowered to audit their accounts.[44] A new eight-hour-day law raised the pay for overtime from 20 to 25 per cent of the regular wage and empowered the Minister of Labor to cut the day to six hours or even less in mines and other exhausting occupations.[45] The accident compensation law was modified to supplant the single payment for injuries by a series of payments ranging from 9 to 75 per cent of the usual wage, according to character of the accident, and guarantee the payments to the laborer by a national fund.[46] Agricultural laborers were also protected by accident in-

[41] The Spanish municipality embraces all of the country to the next municipal boundary, thereby including farming as well as urban territory.

[42] *Gaceta*, May 27, October 2, 1931.

[43] *Labor Realizada*, pp. 85ff.

[44] *Ibid.*, pp. 95ff.

[45] *Gaceta*, July 2, 4, 1931.

[46] *Ibid.*, October 12, 1932, and February 2, 7, 1933.

surance.[47] An Act of May 26, 1931, which modified an older law, made maternity insurance obligatory for employers and allowed a rest period before and after childbirth.[48]

Obviously, whatever benefits labor was to obtain from the Republic would depend on the machinery established to supervise labor legislation.[49] With this in mind, Largo Caballero centralized the Ministry and charged the Minister with final responsibility for law enforcement. The first responsibility for enforcement of labor legislation, however, was placed on the Labor Delegates [50] (*Delegado de Trabajo*) of each province, who were invested with full authority, including the authority over labor formerly exercised by the provincial governors. No labor association could function until its charter was approved by the Delegate, and he might impose fines or suspend such associations. The most important function of the Delegate was to act as the administrative officer for the Minister in each province and to impose penalties for infraction of the labor laws.[51]

Labor disputes and strikes were directly in the hands of the *Jurados mixtos*,[52] juries composed of six representatives of both workers and employers. This idea was not new, but an innovation introduced in Spain made such juries a powerful weapon for the protection of labor. This innovation came in the selection of the president. If the twelve men agreed unanimously, they could choose the presi-

[47] *Ibid.*, June 13, August 30, 1931.
[48] *Los Convenios*, p. 23; *Gaceta*, September 9, 1931.
[49] *Labor Realizada*, *passim*.
[50] *Gaceta*, May 15, 1932.
[51] *Gaceta*, June 24, 1932.
[52] *Ibid.*, November 28, 1931.

dent; in case they disagreed, this power was exercised by the Minister of Labor. Since the Minister was a Socialist and himself a worker, for more than two and a half years the juries had presidents who sympathized with the worker's point of view. This situation brought a united protest from merchants, industrialists and landlords. In a number of cases heavy fines were imposed on employers for failure to obey the decisions of the juries, and in Madrid the entire directorate of the Merchants' Committee was arrested late in June 1933, and the *Círculo de la Unión Mercantil,* an organization corresponding somewhat to a Chamber of Commerce, was closed. This action naturally caused a protest of the propertied classes, and throughout the summer there was intense activity looking to the union of all merchants, manufacturers and landlords against the labor policy of the Republic. A *Junta Central,* or Central Committee, was formed in July, and among its strongest resolutions were those against the Minister of Labor himself and against the Labor Delegates and the *Jurados mixtos.*[53] No small share of the responsibility for the almost complete paralysis of the legislation of the Republic during the summer of 1933 and the subsequent fall of the Azaña Ministry rests on this Central Committee and its representatives in the Cortes.

One aspect of the labor situation was handled in a way which brought strong criticism of the Republic from friend and foe alike. A considerable unemployment problem faced the new government from its first day. Many of the unemployed were

[53] *El Sol,* July 1, 15, 19, 20, 21, 31, and *Luz,* September 6, 1933, and also other dates give a picture of this controversy from the owners' point of view; *El Socialista* (Madrid) may be consulted for the workers' side of the question.

concentrated in a few of the large cities, and their discontent had played an important part in the establishment of the Republic. To check this discontent, the government launched a public works program which many considered ill-advised and badly planned. Madrid began an extensive project designed to connect the three railways stations by an underground tunnel and endow the city with a complete underground system of transportation. Road-building, electrification of the railroads, irrigation projects, and many other much needed improvements were also started. These cannot be criticized on the ground that they were not beneficial, but the cost was enormous and the projects frequently seemed designed more to give jobs than to construct needed public works. Whether the Socialists were entirely responsible for this public works program, costing more than 860,000,000 pesetas in 1933, the fact that Indalecio Prieto, a Socialist, was Minister of Public Works caused the blame to fall on them.

ECONOMIC AND FINANCIAL CONDITIONS

Enormous sums of money were necessary for the work of the Republic at a time when Spain was feeling the effects of the world depression. When the Republic was established, hundreds of landlords immediately declared that they would not cultivate their lands. This crisis was largely overcome by a decree forcing cultivation, but the Republic did not entirely escape the effects of systematic sabotage by the landlords.

Another economic difficulty concerned the flight of capital. For several months after April 1931, the nobles and rich bourgeoisie of Spain systematically exported their capital. The peseta, which at its lowest was worth 10.34 cents in 1930, sank to below 8 cents under the Republic. The Monarchy, moreover, had bequeathed to the Republic an enormous public debt, amounting to more than 21,000,000,000 pesetas,[54] and a chronic budgetary deficit, together with an unfavorable trade balance. Moreover, the world price of Spain's chief products—olive oil, wine, cork, oranges, flax, and iron and copper ores—declined almost continuously from 1931 to 1933.

Spanish exports fell from 2,299,700,000 pesetas in 1930 to 990,300,000 in 1931 and to 742,300,000 pesetas in 1932.[55] Through the first eight months of 1933 this decline continued, exports falling from 664,014,000 pesetas for the January-August period in 1931 to 434,568,000 pesetas for 1933.[56] There was a slight increase in the volume of goods shipped in this period, but the lower prices kept the net return to Spain far below that of former years. Internal conditions reflected this loss of foreign trade. Industrialists and farmers alike alleged that they could not keep up employment and wages in the face of falling prices. Attempts to cut wages were made at a time when the worker expected to receive better pay, and when the reorganized Labor Department was backing the workers in their demands. Hundreds of strikes and labor disputes further threw the economic system out of joint.

In spite of the depression, the budgetary appropriations of the Republic steadily rose. Total ex-

[54] *El Sol*, April 1, 1932.
[55] These figures are taken from *Resumen Mensual . . . del Comercio exterior de España*, published by the *Ministerio de Hacienda*, and from the *World Almanac, 1931–1933*. The two sources do not agree in all cases but are approximately the same.
[56] *El Sol*, October 11, 1933.

penditures for 1930 were 4,012,500,000 pesetas, leaving a deficit of 158,240,000 pesetas that year. The deficits for 1931 and 1932 were 508,830,000 pesetas and 711,730,000 pesetas,[57] respectively, while the expenses for 1933 were 4,427,281,490—leaving a deficit of 484,663,244 pesetas.[58] To meet this deficit the Republic had to increase the public debt inherited from the Monarchy. This was done by the flotation of bonds totalling 1,385,000,000 pesetas to October 1933.[59]

CHAPTER III

THE SWING TO THE RIGHT

THE Republic accomplished its reforms only by overcoming great difficulties. From the beginning it was forced to meet bitter opposition from both the Left and the Right. Three forces slowed up the republican program: the Anarcho-Syndicalist *Confederación Nacional del Trabajo,* which directed the labor opposition; the reactionary group; and the Cabinet which, being a coalition, was constantly forced into compromises in order to maintain a semblance of unity.

ANARCHO-SYNDICALIST AND COMMUNIST REVOLTS

Spain became a republic at a time when depressed economic conditions were causing a renewal of strike activity. Before the establishment of the Republic, strikes were fostered by the Socialists, Anarcho-

[57] *El Financiero* (Madrid), June 6, 1933.
[58] *El Sol,* January 16, 1934.
[59] *Ibid.,* August 23, 1933; *La Prensa* (New York), October 23, 1933.

Syndicalists and Communists, but when the Socialists became a part of the governing coalition most
of their efforts were expended in securing a peaceful
settlement of labor troubles through the Socialist
Minister of Labor. Both Anarcho-Syndicalists and
Communists, however, increased their agitation, and
on four occasions attempted the overthrow of the
Republic by revolution.

Serious strike activities began in June 1931, and
the first determined effort at revolution was made
by the Anarcho-Syndicalists, probably aided by the
Communists, in July 1931.[1] A seven-day battle was
fought in Seville from July 18 to 25, with over a
dozen persons killed and a hundred or more
wounded. This movement failed, but strike activities were not ended. Martial law was frequently declared, and by October 1931 Prime Minister Azaña
found it necessary to resort to a law known as the
Defense of the Republic granting the government
exceptional powers.[2] Arbitrary arrests and holding
of prisoners without charge became common. Some
nine thousand political prisoners were in jail by the
summer of 1933, when this law was supplanted by
another, called the "Law of Public Order," [3] giving
the government the right to suspend constitutional
guarantees and arrest people considered dangerous
to the state.

Such drastic action was considered necessary to
meet continued opposition, but did not succeed in
ending strikes and Left opposition. A second revolt
began in January 1932, and was crushed after hard
fighting, while a third serious effort of the Left

[1] *El Sol,* July 15 to 26, 1931.
[2] *Ibid.,* October 15 to 21, 1931.
[3] *Gaceta,* July 30, 1933.

occurred in January 1933, and cost the lives of some fifty workers and soldiers. A fourth revolt occurred December 8, 1933. The government's policy of strike-breaking provoked a decided reaction among the workers. The fact that the Socialists were represented in the government gave strike-breaking the appearance of war between the Socialists and Anarcho-Syndicalists.[4]

OPPOSITION FROM THE RIGHT

The Monarchists and other conservative groups were demoralized in the early days of the Republic, but began to reorganize without delay. Their weakness in the Cortes, where they had only 60 out of 470 deputies, prevented any really effectual opposition to the republican program during the first year and, frightened by the socialist legislation of the Cortes, they attempted a revolution in August 1932. The movement failed completely, and the Right groups after that time depended on political action to regain their lost privileges.

Political opposition proved more effective than armed revolt. The formation of the *Acción Católica* for the defense of the Church, and of the *Acción Popular* for political action, has already been noted. The organization of the *Confederación Española de Derechas Autónomas* brought the Right forces into still closer alignment. Originally the Right was represented only by the Agrarian and Basque-Navarre parties. In 1931 and 1932, however, many regional parties were organized for the defense of the conservative interests, and the C.E.D.A. came

[4] *Cf. El Sol* or other Spanish papers of corresponding date for these revolts. The four major ones have been reported in New York papers, and all of them in *La Prensa* (New York).

into existence in February 1933 to give them
strength.[5] The C.E.D.A. proposed to revise the Constitution, repeal the anti-clerical laws, abolish the
Agrarian Reform and put an end to the preponderant
influence labor had exercised since April 1931. In
many of these aims the C.E.D.A. was ably seconded
by the Central Committee of the merchants, industrialists and landlords.[6] In addition to the Right
forces included in the C.E.D.A., Spain had a Fascist movement directed by José Primo de Rivera,
son of the former dictator. The Fascists, openly opposed to the Republic, declared that they would rule
in Spain even if they had to gain power by armed
revolution. They were not as yet numerically
strong, but the experience of Italy and Germany
indicated that only a short length of time was necessary for the development of a powerful Fascist
movement.

POLITICAL REALIGNMENTS IN 1933

One of the most important forces working for reaction was the split in the coalition cabinet. The
divergent elements composing the cabinet had been
able to unite only because all agreed on one minimum demand—overthrow of the King. Once these
elements were in power their differences on political,
economic and religious matters came into the open.
Only fear of reaction or further revolution kept the
inevitable split from occurring sooner than it did.
President Alcalá-Zamora and Miguel Maura represented the conservative point of view, their revo-

[5] The Carlists, who have been active since 1833, are followers of Don Carlos, brother of Ferdinand VII, who pretended
to the throne against Isabel II.
[6] Cf. p. 425.

lutionary aims going little further than overthrow of the King and establishment of a democratic republic. Both were Catholic, both represented the land-owning classes, and both had recently been converted to Republicanism. The return to constitutional government satisfied their principal revolutionary demands. Their conflict with the Provisional Government over the Church issue has been noted.

Slightly to the Left at the beginning stood Alejandro Lerroux and Martínez Barrio of the Radical Republican party. Lerroux had for years been the outstanding opponent of the Monarchy and the Church. With the King gone and the Church divested of many of its privileges, he became a fighter without opponents. For a time he coöperated with the government, but in December 1931 his conservative economic ideas caused him to refuse to coöperate with the Socialists, and his stand in favor of centralism as opposed to federalism in government ranged him against the Catalans. He withdrew from the coalition at that time and joined the opposition. The remaining members of the coalition— the Republican Action, Socialists, Catalans, Galicians and Radical Socialists—managed to hold together until 1933, but their ideas were widely divergent and the program of the Republic was seriously held up by constant disagreement and compromise. Azaña was able to keep the Republican-Socialist alliance together only because he could drive the Republicans to accept measures of a more socialistic character than they wanted, and could presuade the Socialists to accept less than they had originally demanded. But neither side was satisfied. The Republicans resented the laws presented by the Socialists, while the latter, closely pressed by Anarcho-Syndicalists and Communists and unable to fulfill their promises to the workers, became alarmed at the prospect of losing their followers and began to talk of revolt and dictatorship. In other words, the character of the political struggle had changed radically by midsummer 1933. The main question was no longer Monarchy or Republic, but whether the Republic was to be bourgeois or socialist in character.

That a political crisis was approaching was evident after April 1933, when elections were held in about one-third of the municipalities. According to Spanish law, unopposed candidates were allowed to take office at the time of the elections of 1931 without the formality of a vote. The April 1933 elections were held to fill these places with new and duly elected officials, and the government parties won less than one-third of the municipal councillors, causing the opposition parties, both Republican and those of the extreme Right, to call on the Azaña cabinet to resign.[7] This reverse at the polls was

[7] It is probably correct to interpret the elections as an anti-government vote, but not necessarily as anti-Republican. The elections were held where 29,804 municipal councillors were seated in accordance with Article 29 of the law in 1931. In 1931 there were 13,940 Republicans, 887 Socialists, 6,065 Monarchists, 10 Communists, 6,043 representing local parties and 2,859 unclassified candidates so seated. This shows that about 50 per cent were either Republicans, Socialists or Communists, all anti-Monarchical, while the other 50 per cent was considered at the time to be Monarchical. Complete returns are not yet available for April 23, 1933. The newspaper *C.E.D.A.* of May 20, 1933, shows that the government parties won 4,356 places, the anti-government Republicans 4,108, and the Right 6,481. This gives the Right 43.36 per cent of the total. *El Sol* (Madrid) gave the vote as 5,048 for the government, 4,206 for the anti-government republicans, and 4,954 for the Right, according to *Current History*, July 1933. Complete returns on this basis would give the Right only 43 per cent of the vote in the districts in which it had 50 per cent in 1931.

followed by a cabinet crisis early in June 1933. President Alcalá-Zamora forced the Azaña Ministry to resign, but Azaña was returned to office when all efforts to form a cabinet without him and the Socialists failed. His new cabinet was never strong. During the summer its weakness became more and more evident, and by August the program of legislation was almost completely paralyzed by the break-up of the Republican-Socialist coalition.

Azaña, who had been accustomed to apply the cloture rule to force his measures through, now found this procedure impossible, and was obliged to compromise not only with the opposition Republicans but with the Agrarians, avowed enemies of the régime. The explanation of this situation lies in the division of his supporters. The Federal party was split, and discontented with the Azaña program; the Catalan Left was absorbed in regional affairs; the Galician Left was disgruntled over the slowness with which the regional aspirations of Galicia were granted, and was opposed to the Azaña Ministry because of a projected treaty with Uruguay which injured its cattle interests; the Radical-Socialist party was engaged in an internal struggle for leadership which soon split it into a pro-Socialist wing headed by Marcelino Domingo, and an anti-Socialist wing under the leadership of Gordón Ordás.

The eventual fall of the Ministry was inevitable, but it was hastened by a second set of elections. The Constitution provides that the Tribunal of Constitutional Guarantees shall have, in addition to other members, one judge from each of fifteen regions elected by the municipal councillors. The elections held on September 3, 1933, resulted in a second defeat of the government.[8] This development caused the resignation of Azaña and the formation of a ministry under Lerroux on September 13. The Republican parties which had refused to coöperate with Lerroux against the Socialists in June now accepted places in his ministry. Lerroux did not survive the first vote of confidence on October 3, however, and President Alcalá-Zamora entrusted the formation of a coalition of Republicans, excluding the Socialists, to Martínez Barrio of the Radical party. The President granted this ministry a dissolution of the Cortes and set general elections for November 19, 1933, with a supplementary election to be held on December 3 in districts where no candidate received the 40 per cent of the total vote required by law.

The significance of this general election was evident. Spanish voters, including 6,000,000 women who were to vote for the first time, were to have the first real opportunity to express their opinion of the Republic. At the time of the election of the Constituent Cortes in 1931 the economic principles of the various parties were so vague that the voters did not know for what program they were voting. This uncertainty had cleared up by 1933, and four chief alternatives were before the people: [9] the extreme Right represented by the C.E.D.A., organized by Gil Robles; the Right Center represented by Lerroux and Maura; the Republican Left with Azaña

[8] The government elected only five of the fifteen judges elected by the regions. *Cf. El. Sol,* September 5, and *La Nacion* (Madrid), September 5, 1933. *La Nacion* gives incomplete returns showing 12,910 pro-government votes against 34,193 anti-government votes. The Radical party (Lerroux) elected four judges, and the extreme Right, six.

[9] *La Prensa,* November 13, 1933; and *El Sol,* November 17, 1933.

as the outstanding figure; and the Socialists. In general, all of the Right parties were grouped around the C.E.D.A., while the Left were badly divided. The C.E.D.A., for example, allied itself with the Fascist organization, and with the *Lliga Regionalista,* the conservative Catalan party headed by Francisco Cambó; the Radical party of Lerroux, the Radical-Socialists of Gordón Ordás and the Conservative party of Miguel Maura went on the ballot together. The conservative, almost reactionary, character of this alliance is demonstrated by the adhesion of Melquiades Alvarez of the Liberal Democratic party, a former Minister of Alfonso XIII, and of Santiago Alba, another former Minister, both of whom joined Lerroux on the ground that he gave the best hope 'for a "united anti-Marxist party." The conservative character of the Radical party was also demonstrated by its alliance in certain electoral districts with the C.E.D.A., an alliance aimed at the Socialists. Azaña allied his Republican Action with the Independent Radical-Socialists of Marcelino Domingo, and with the Galician and Catalan Left. The Socialists went on the ballot alone, except for very limited coöperation with some of the Left parties in a few provincial districts.

The Right and Right Center parties won a sweeping victory.[10] The alignment in the newly elected Cortes was almost the exact reverse of that in the former Cortes. Where the Right had been able to elect barely 60 deputies in 1931, the Left elected less than a hundred in 1933. Some reaction had been expected and predicted before the election, but that the Right would win so completely was a surprise even to the leaders of the Right parties. Approximately two-thirds of the deputies were members of

[10] *Cf.* p. 468.

the C.E.D.A., whose principles were those of the Monarchy, or of the group centered around Lerroux, whose program was distinctly conservative.

The Republican parties of the Left, including the Republican Action with Azaña at its head, the Independent Radical Socialists under the lead of Gordón Ordás, and the Federals, were practically exterminated, dropping from a membership of well over a hundred to a mere handful. Considerable disorder occurred during the elections and charges of unfair tactics were numerous. Botella Asensi, Minister of Justice in the Martínez Barrio cabinet, resigned as a protest against the policy of the Prime Minister and alleged that Lerroux had an understanding with the extreme Right. This charge was given plausibility by Lerroux's action in withdrawing his candidate from the supplementary election held in Madrid on December 3, leaving the field to the extreme Right and the Socialists. The latter, who lost half of their representatives, also protested against irregularities in the elections, and Largo Caballero threatened that any attempt by the Right to take possession of the government and destroy the work done by the Republic would be met with armed revolution and a dictatorship along Communist lines.

The new Cortes met on December 7, 1933, and immediately became the battle ground for Right and Left, the former demanding the repeal of many of the essential reforms of the Republic. The formation of a government was entrusted to Alejandro Lerroux of the Right Center, but he depended for his majority on the votes of the Right parties, especially the Agrarians led by Martínez de Velasco and the Popular Action led by José María Gil Robles. This dependence forced him to present measures for abolition of the law of *Términos Municipales*, and modification of the character and functions of *Jurados mixtos*. The cabinet also proposed to appropriate some 30 millions of pesetas annually for the rural clergy and to send Pita Romero, Minister of Foreign Affairs, to Rome to study the terms for a new concordat.

These measures aroused the apprehensions of both the moderate and the extreme Left, who saw the entire revolutionary program threatened. The Anarcho-Syndicalists seized the opportunity to revolt, and while they were defeated the seriousness of the fighting—in which more than a hundred were killed and several hundred wounded—indicated that they had lost none of their aggressiveness. The republican Left, under the lead of Azaña, continued to advocate democratic methods, while the Socialists remained badly divided on the question of tactics.[11] Julián Besteiro and Fernando de los Ríos advocated evolutionary socialism. Indalecio Prieto attempted to revive the Republican-Socialist Conjunction, while Largo Caballero called for a dictatorship of the proletariat. The Right matched the Left in threats of dictatorship. José Primo de Rivera began a vigorous campaign of Fascist propaganda calling for destruction of the democratic régime, and Gil Robles prophesied that "sooner or later power will be given to the Right so that they may save Spain from a semi-Sovietic dictatorship of the extreme Left." On January 1, Largo Caballero directed a shaft at Primo de Rivera, declaring: "We Socialists will join with the Communists and Anarchists if the Fascists attempt to establish a dictatorship in Spain."[12]

[11] *El Sol,* December 8-17, 1933.
[12] *La Prensa,* January 2, 1934.

The belligerency of both sides was increased by the realization that the November 1933 elections had not been so complete a victory for the Right as at first supposed. The Socialists and the Left could point out that, while they had scarcely one-fifth of the deputies in the Cortes, their popular vote amounted to about half the total.[13] Another indication of the strength of the Left was offered by the municipal elections held in Catalonia on January 14, 1934, in which the Catalan Left decisively defeated the conservative parties. The violence attending this election indicated the increasingly bitter feeling between the parties, and as the Right realized their increasing weakness they showed more tendency to let force settle the issue.[14]

Meanwhile the struggle within the Socialist party came to a head with the resignation of the Executive Committee of the General Workers' Union, which had been dominated by Besteiro, and the election of a pro-Largo Caballero committee which believed in revolution.[15] Prieto seemed converted to this point of view also, and on February 4 declared that the time had come for the Socialists to study the program to be followed "when they had seized power."[16] The Right parties seemed determined to force the Left into revolt before the projected "united front" of radical labor parties could be formed. This was done by repeal of the measures passed while the Left was in office and by the constant attempt of Gil Robles to force the labor leaders into statements that would make them subject to prosecution.

[13] *Journal des Nations,* January 31, 1934.
[14] *El Sol,* January 16, 17, 1934. Colonel Francisco Macia, the leader of the Catalan Left party, died on December 25, 1933.
[15] *La Prensa,* January 29-31, 1934.
[16] *Ibid.,* February 5, 1934.

CHAPTER IV

CONSERVATIVES IN POWER

THE elections of November and December 1933 ushered in a two-year period during which Spain's Right and Center forces were to hold the reins of power. In contrast to the previous biennium (1931-1933) of Socialist-Left Republican dominance, with its definite program of reforms, its continuing agitation for change and progress, its fever of strikes and other expressions of unrest, this term was characterized by a trend toward reaction and, for a time, by relative tranquillity. Many of the hard-won gains of the preceding régime were nullified. Political action, however, was hindered by almost kaleidoscopic changes in governments and reigning confusion in the Cortes. The revolt of October 1934 punctuated the period with the somber threat of civil war.

The veteran politician, Alejandro Lerroux, headed the cabinet, which entered office on December 19. The new government, composed principally of members of the Radical party, was granted the backing, although not the active collaboration of a majority of the Right groups. Gil Robles and his Catholic followers, without formally committing themselves to a renunciation of monarchist leanings, agreed to support Lerroux on the basis of the repeal of the law of *Términos Municipales,* amendment of the agrarian reform and of the legislation governing the *Jurados Mixtos* (industrial juries of workers and employers), modification of laws affecting the church and education, and eventual reform of the Constitution.

Fulfillment of these pledges was promptly initiated. A law granted clergy in office at the establishment of the Republic in April 1931 two-thirds of their salaries for the current year. Religious schools were permitted to continue their activities; the State, it was alleged, was not yet in position to carry forward education without their aid. Negotiations looking toward resumption of full relations were opened with the Holy See, and Foreign Minister Pita Romero journeyed to the Vatican as Ambassador Extraordinary. Agrarian reform was paralyzed and the law of *Jurados Mixtos* was modified by a decree which decreased the influence of labor in these bodies. But any prospects of limiting the autonomy achieved by Catalonia were balked by a decisive victory of the *Esquerra*, or Catalan Left party, in the *Generalidad* elections of January 14, 1934.

A minor cabinet crisis at Madrid led to the resignation of three Radical ministers on March 1, but Premier Lerroux formed at once a new government substantially of the same political color as the preceding. This régime enjoyed only a seven weeks tenure, and fell on April 25. Its resignation was occasioned by an amnesty bill, which proposed to pardon all those charged with political offenses committed prior to December 3, 1933. This act would have principally benefited former Monarchist supporters, including General Sanjurjo and José Calvo Sotelo, Finance Minister of the Primo de Rivera dictatorship.[1] Although the measure met vigorous

---

[1] It did not release all the imprisoned Anarchists, many of whom had been jailed following the revolt of December 9, 1933. More than 8,000 were reported to have remained in prison. M. Dashar, *The Revolutionary Movement in Spain* (New York, Libertarian Publishing Society), p. 20.

left-wing opposition in the Cortes, it was finally passed on April 20. For some days, however, President Alcalá-Zamora withheld his approval. He finally signed the law, but at the same time submitted to the Cortes a memorandum outlining at length his objections to the legislation. By this maneuver he opened himself to attack from both Right and Left. His memorandum to the Cortes with its implied rebuke to the cabinet forced the resignation of Lerroux.

The latter was succeeded three days later by another Right-Center coalition, headed by Ricardo Samper of Valencia. The new cabinet contained all but four of the members of the previous Lerroux ministry. Despite the fact that this régime was chiefly noted for its "masterly inactivity," it remained in office for almost five months. Its do-nothing policy and its conciliatory attitude on certain regional questions progressively estranged its supporters on the Right. An extended controversy between Madrid and Catalonia marked the summer of 1934, concerning an agrarian law approved by the Catalan *Generalidad*.[2] This *Ley de Cultivos* was designed to open the way for gradual purchase by the *rabassaires* or tenant farmers of the small plots they cultivated. It gave them the right after 18 years of labor to buy the land held under lease, facilitating division of great estates, whose origin in many cases dated from the Middle Ages. The law created arbitration tribunals with authority to settle the differences between landed proprietors and the *rabassaires*, including reinstatement of evicted tenants,

[2] For the Catalan text, cf. *Lleis de Catalunya*, Volume XI, "Llei de Contractes de Conreu" (Barcelona, Llibreria Castells, 1934).

permitting the latter to pay landowners only half of pre-1931 rentals. This legislation drew vigorous protests from the landed proprietors.

The law was submitted to the Tribunal of Constitutional Guarantees, Spain's final court of appeal; and this body by a small majority found against it, not on the ground that it violated the Constitution, but rather that the Catalonian parliament lacked competence to legislate in this field. Premier Samper declared himself in accord with the decision of the Tribunal. But the *Esquerra*, in control of the government at Barcelona, refused to yield. Its deputies withdrew from the Cortes on June 12 and were followed by the Basque Nationalists.[3] The Catalonian parliament repassed the rejected measure with an additional article making it retroactive to the date of its original promulgation in April. Despite the provocative tactics of Barcelona, Samper followed a conciliatory course and prepared a compromise formula which was discussed in the Cortes on June 25. No action was approved, however; and when parliament adjourned for the summer on July 3, it left the dispute in the hands of the cabinet, granting it a vote of confidence "to resolve the conflict existing in Catalonia, in strict accord with the precepts of the Constitution and the Statute."[4] Conversations between Madrid and Barcelona were in-

[3] The local authorities in the Basque provinces were involved in a dispute with the central government concerning their traditional rights to lay their own taxes and pay a lump sum annually to Madrid. For a succinct review of this controversy as well as that with Catalonia, cf. E. Allison Peers, *The Spanish Tragedy* (New York, Oxford University Press, 1936), pp. 153-59.

[4] *Cf.* Francisco Casares, *La C.E.D.A. Va a Gobernar* (Madrid, Gráfica Administrativa, 1934), p. 250. This book, by a journalistic supporter of Gil Robles, provides a running comment on political developments from the November 1933 elections to October 1934.

itiated, but agitation continued in Catalonia. The Catalan proprietors organized a great pilgrimage to Madrid on September 8, chartering ten special trains, and voiced a long protest against the land legislation. In reply the Socialist, Syndicalists and Communists called a two-day general strike in the capital. Traffic was stopped and factories closed. This controversy over the agrarian law, which called into question the extent of Catalonia's autonomous rights, played an important part in determining the rôle which the region was to play in the events of October 1934.

Meanwhile the Samper government was under attack for other causes by both Right and Left. On August 1 the Socialist General Union of Workers (U.G.T.) issued a manifesto charging that the Socialist press had been consistently persecuted, Socialist meetings broken up, and municipal councils controlled by Socialists had been dissolved. Prices had risen steadily and wages fallen, thus lowering the working man's standard of living. Gil Robles had also been proclaiming that the time was near when he, at the head of Popular Action, would assume power. Despite the fact that his followers constituted the largest single group in the Cortes, they had not yet been accorded any cabinet portfolios. This was due in part to the distrust and personal dislike which, according to report, President Alcalá-Zamora felt toward the youthful leader of the Catholic forces. But a more important factor was the suspicion widespread among the Left parties concerning the loyalty of Gil Robles and his adherents to the Republic.

In 1933 the Vatican had published the Encyclical *Dilectissima Nobis*, which lamented "the provocations and vexations of the enemies of the church," but continued: "All know that the Catholic Church, being in no manner bound to one form of government more than another, provided always that the rights of God and of the Christian conscience are safeguarded, finds no difficulty in accommodating itself to the various civil institutions, be they monarchic or be they republican."[5] Following this declaration, the Catholic daily, *El Debate,* carried an editorial on December 15, 1933, which viewed the Pope's message as indicating to Spanish Catholics the possibility of adjusting themselves to republican institutions. It argued for political action by the Right forces, defining it as "political action of Catholics and as Catholics," a phrase which subsequently became the leading note for the Popular Action party. Working on this basis, Gil Robles won over the vast majority of Catholics to support the Lerroux government, much to the chagrin of the Monarchists and the Rivera Fascists.

But the Left forces could not forget that Gil Robles, a former Monarchist, had shown himself frankly anti-republican as a member of the Constituent Cortes. He had refused to vote for the Constitution when it was approved. He was looked upon in many quarters as the representative of the Jesuits, and thus excited the distrust traditionally associated with that order. Moreover, in the 1933 elections Popular Action had supported in various districts a joint ticket with the Monarchists.[6] On February 4, 1934, however, Gil Robles—in a speech at Seville—called on all his followers to pledge allegiance to

[5] Quoted in Lawrence A. Fernsworth, "Back of the Spanish Rebellion," *Foreign Affairs* (New York), October, 1936.
[6] Cf. Luis Araquistain, "October Revolution in Spain," *Foreign Affairs* (New York), January, 1935.

the Republic, that the way might be opened for Popular Action to participate in the cabinet.[7] He had repeatedly affirmed, both before and after this date, that when the time was ripe, he and his adherents would accept cabinet posts and serve the Republic faithfully.[8] But the loyalty he proffered was clearly pragmatic and opportunist; his party, moreover, never met the demands of their opponents to renounce completely desire for a monarchical restoration. Consequently the sincerity of their devotion to the Republic continued to be suspected by Left-Republican and labor forces.[9] These groups feared, furthermore, that attainment of power by Catholic Popular Action would presage restoration of the old order, destruction of the labor movement, repeal of anti-clerical and agrarian legislation, and ultimately establishment of a clerical-Fascist régime. Gil Robles professed faith in ideas of "Christian democracy" similar to those preached by Dollfuss in Austria. The crushing of Socialism in the latter country had stirred apprehension in Spain, and labor leaders feared that Gil Robles, if given an opportunity, would suppress their organizations and set

[7] *New York Times,* February 5, 1934.

[8] Cf. Casares, *La C.E.D.A. va a Governar,* cited, pp. 109, 122, 123, 185, 221.

[9] Gil Robles was first and foremost a Catholic; in that capacity he was willing to support any régime which accorded the Church what he considered its due place. The equivocal character of his attitude toward the Republic is indicated by an interview given in 1936 to *Diario Español* of Buenos Aires, which was published also in *La Vanguardia* of Barcelona for June 2, in which he declared: "For us Democracy is a transitory means of influencing the politics of the country. . . . What I do is to find a supporting base on whatever offers itself to me in order to transform it and, if necessary, to destroy it. I do not refer to such an insignificant and transitory thing as the form of the government. but to the problem of the fundamental change of the country." (Quoted by Fernsworth, "Back of the Spanish Rebellion," cited.)

up a Workers' Front resembling the *Arbeitsfront* which Dollfuss had created in Austria.[10]

Left-wing leaders warned on September 23 that the entry of representatives of Catholic Popular Action into a new cabinet would be the signal for revolution.[11] This threat was received all the more seriously in view of the discovery earlier in the month of deposits of arms and munitions in Socialist hands, both at Madrid and in Asturias. Minister of Interior Salazar Alonzo charged that Left-wing groups had expended 5,000,000 pesetas on war stocks.[12]

The Revolt of October 1934

When the Cortes reconvened on October 1, Gil Robles attacked Premier Samper's statement on the Catalan question and declared that the government had made "weak and disgraceful concessions to a rebellious region."[13] Loss of Popular Action support made the fall of the Samper government inevitable. Three days later, on October 4, Lerroux succeeded in forming another cabinet. But the inclusion within it of three members of the Catholic Popular Action party set off the spark of revolt.[14]

[10] Gil Robles had visited Austria in the summer of 1933 to study the tactics of Dollfuss. In September he attended the Nazi Congress at Nuremberg. Apparently impressed by this trip with the value of the large popular demonstrations, he called a concentration of Popular Action Youth for April 22, 1934 at the Escorial near Madrid, one of the most important centers of Spain's conservative traditions. But a general strike in the capital seriously hampered the success of this demonstration. For the 19-point creed approved at the Escorial, cf. Casares, *La C.E.D.A. va a Gobernar*, cited, pp. 207, 208.

[11] *New York Times*, September 24, 1934.

[12] *New York Times*, September 15 and 24, 1934, and *La Prensa* (New York), September 20, 1934.

[13] *New York Times*, October 2, 1934.

[14] It included, in addition, seven Radicals, two Agrarians, one

At the news of the Lerroux-Gil Robles cabinet, the chiefs of all the Republican parties—save only Lerroux' own Radicals—protested to President Alcalá-Zamora, and on October 5 formally withdrew their support from the government. General strikes were called in various parts of Spain by the Socialist General Union of Workers and by the Workers' Alliances, in which Socialists, Communists and independent groups of workers and peasants had joined. The revolt, whose leadership was attributed principally to Socialists, began without a centralized plan and in reality proved to be "a series of provincial insurrections." It was a triangular affair, with its principal points at Madrid in the center, Catalonia to the east and Asturias to the north. In the capital and other centers the strike was supported by the Socialists and Communists, but found the Anarcho-Syndicalists divided in sympathies.[15] The strike order did not apparently make clear whether a pacific movement or an armed insurrection was intended, and this ambiguity weakened the thrust. But in Madrid activities were tied up for eight days; serious strikes also broke out in Valencia and in Viscaya.

To Catalonia the Lerroux-Gil Robles government represented a double challenge. It threatened the hard-won autonomy of the region, and endangered

Liberal Democrat and one representative of Orga (Galician Left). *La Prensa* (New York), October 5, 1934.

[15] The Anarcho-Syndicalist National Labor Confederation (C.N.T.) took part in the strike movement at various points. "The leaders of the C.N.T. did not issue an official strike proclamation and that is why the trade unions of the Anarcho-Syndicalists did not take an active part in the strike movement in most districts. The C.N.T. stood at attention, ready as always to support the fight against fascism; but they did not want to be merely pawns in a strike movement which was essentially directed by the socialist alliances." M. Dashar, *The Revolutionary Movement in Spain* (New York, Libertarian Publishing Society), p. 21.

the position of the Catalan government, whose principal support was drawn from the Esquerra, a Left-wing party of the lower middle-class and the workers. It also menaced the rights of labor. The situation thus favored common action by the Catalan government and the Workers' Alliances. The latter were the first to move and declared a general strike in Barcelona on October 5.[16] This strike won the sympathetic cooperation of the peasants, who had strongly resented the efforts of the large land-owners and of the Madrid government during the previous summer to nullify the Catalan agrarian law. The *Generalidad*, however, hesitated to take a decisive step.[17] The general strike demonstrated the popular support available for a movement of revolt, but carried with it the threat of potential social revolution, which if loosed might sweep the *Generalidad* from power. The workers had organized a Red Army 10,000 strong, and were demanding arms. By the evening of October 6, however, delay was no longer possible and at 8 o'clock Companys proclaimed from the balcony of the government palace the establishment of the Catalan State as part of a yet-to-be-created Spanish Federal Republic.[18] Such a step would insure greater freedom for Catalonia,

[16] At first it was supported only by the adherents of the Workers' Alliance in the transport services, by employees in shops and offices and by the lower middle-class. The C.N.T. did not give the strike its backing; its adherents continued at work and "were chased out of their shops by force of arms" to make the strike general. Dashar, *The Revolutionary Movement in Spain*, cited, pp. 21, 22.

[17] Within the *Esquerra* a struggle was in process between Companys, representing the creed of democracy and traditional republicanism, and Dencás, Minister of Interior, with tendencies toward separatism, and a Catalan fascism. Cf. Joaquín Maurín, *Hacia la Segunda Revolución* (Barcelona, Gráficos Alfa, 1935), p. 130.

[18] For the full Catalan text of the speech of Sr. Companys, cf. *Bulletin of Spanish Studies* (Liverpool), 1935, Vol. XII, pp. 11-12. Companys did not seek separation from Spain, as charged

without definitive separation from the rest of Spain. It was a move designed to channel the revolt along political rather than social lines. Apparently it was launched in the expectation that Madrid would show some disposition to compromise, and that the dispute would be settled by negotiation. Had Companys appealed to arms, he could have counted on the support of the 3,000 armed Catalan police and the 7,000 *escamots* or militia of the *Esquerra* in Barcelona. To oppose these, General Domingo Batet, commander of the regular army forces in Catalonia, had 5,000 soldiers. But Companys chose to win the support of Batet by negotiation. This was refused. Batet brought out his troops, shelled several government buildings, promptly forced the surrender of the *Generalidad* palace, captured Companys and other leaders, and by October 7 had crushed the insurrection. Two days later the workers returned to their tasks.

The rebellion proved most serious in the mountains of Asturias to the north where it lasted for two weeks. In this region had developed one of the best-organized and most aggressive labor movements in all Spain. Moreover, here alone did the workers present a solidly united front; the Workers' Al-

by the Lerroux government. On the afternoon of October 6, former Premier Azaña, then in Barcelona, was consulted on the wisdom of Catalonia's projected move and advised against it. He was subsequently arrested for alleged complicity in the revolt and imprisoned for 80 days. But the charges were finally thrown out by the courts. Cf. Manuel Azaña, *Mi Rebelión en Barcelona* (Madrid, Espasa-Calpe, 1935). On February 20, 1935 the Popular Action party presented a second set of charges against Azaña, accusing him of complicity in gun-running prior to the Asturias revolt, and of conspiring against the Republic in other ways. But after long investigation, the Cortes failed to support the accusations by the necessary majority, and they fell to the ground. Cf. Peers, *The Spanish Tragedy*, cited, p. 179.

liance included Anarcho-Syndicalists as well as Socialists and Communists. The general strike was declared on the night of October 4, and from the first the movement was one of open armed resistance. The miners constituted the nucleus of the revolt; and their organization centered at Mieres, south of Oviedo.[19] A Workers' Militia was formed. On the morning of the 6th Oviedo was attacked. The City Hall and the local branch of the Bank of Spain were seized. The dynamite factory at Mongaya and the plant for small artillery at Trubia fell to the rebels; later also the Vega rifle factory.[20] But the government troops, who numbered originally some 2,000 in the region, held out in Pelayo barracks in Oviedo, where much ammunition had been stored.

Meanwhile, the workers with their revolutionary committees had taken over local government in the area. Proclamations were issued calling the proletariat to arms, prohibiting pillage, confiscating supplies of food and clothing for equitable distribution among the populace. Money was abolished, and the Supply Committees of the revolutionaries controlled and directed all distribution. Hospitals and collective kitchens were organized. A Socialist Republic in embryo was established.[21]

[19] The Miners' Union was reported to have had 27,251 members in the region; of these approximately 20,000 were Socialists, with the remainder divided between Communists and Anarcho-Syndicalists. *La Revolución en Asturias* (México, Ediciones Defensa Roja, 1935), p. 9.

[20] This contained 21,115 rifles, 198 machine guns and 281 submachine guns. Much of the ammunition, however, had been transferred to Pelayo barracks, and lack of this later handicapped the Workers' Militia. Cf. Maurín, *Hacia la Segunda Revolución,* cited, p. 153.

[21] For a detailed story of the revolt by a resident of Oviedo, cf. *La Prensa* (New York), October 22, 1934.

But while the workers of Asturias had wagered their all on the issue of battle, the revolt in Catalonia had capitulated, and the movement in Madrid had fallen far short of a revolutionary offensive. With all hope lost for a nation-wide rising, the Workers' Alliance of Oviedo decided on a "strategic retreat." The army troops in the region, together with the Civil and Assault Guards, had proved unable to suffocate the insurrection. The government consequently had introduced the Foreign Legion and Moors from Africa. These reached Oviedo on October 12, but street fighting continued behind barricades until the 19th. On that day a pact between General López Ochoa, government commander, and Belarmino Tomás, workers' leader, ended the struggle, although guerrilla bands carried on for some time longer in the mountains. During the struggle the city was shelled by artillery and bombed from the air; many of its finest buildings, including the university, were destroyed or gutted by fire.[22]

Atrocities on both sides were reported in the course of the fighting.[23] The revolutionists were accused of murdering and maltreating priests and Civil Guards. The Foreign Legion and the Moors, brought into a region which centuries before had been Spain's last Christian stronghold during the period of Mohammedan rule in the peninsula, were charged with wantonly killing and torturing many defenseless civilians, including women and children.[24] Estimates placed the number of killed in the revolt at 1355,

---

[22] For an account of the government's campaign against the rebels, cf. General López Ochoa, *Campaña Militar de Asturias en Octubre de 1934* (Madrid, Editorial Yunque, 1936).

[23] Cf. *New York Times*, October 29, 1934.

[24] *La Revolución de Asturias*, cited, pp. 12 ff.

with 2951 wounded.[25] Following the defeat of the movement, Spain's prisons were crowded with 30,000 offenders. Reports that prisoners were brutally beaten and tortured were frequent.[26] Among those imprisoned were 14 deputies in the Cortes, including ex-Premier Manuel Azaña, President Companys of Catalonia, and Francisco Largo Caballero, Socialist leader.

Although Largo Caballero and other Left leaders had long threatened rebellion and quantities of arms had been imported and distributed among labor and other groups, the leadership of the October revolt was patently ineffective. The revolutionary elements lacked cohesion and a centralized direction; the movement failed to enlist the cooperation of many important groups. The Anarcho-Syndicalist were largely passive, as was also the lower middle-class. The peasants offered small participation. No support was won in the army, or among the ranks of the Civil and Assault Guards.

CHAPTER V

THE STORM CLOUDS GATHER

THE failure of the October revolt served to strengthen the Right as against the Left, the large landowners and industrialists as against the workers and peasants, the church as against the anti-cleri-

[25] A. Ramos Oliveira, *The Drama of Spain, 1931-1936* (London, The National Council of Labour), p. 11.
[26] Cf. statements by Félix Gordón Ordás, Deputy in the Cortes from León, Vicente Marcos Miranda, Deputy from Valencia and Fernando de los Ríos, Socialist and former cabinet minister. The English text of the greater part of these documents is given in Leah Manning, *What I Saw in Spain* (London, Gollancz, 1935).

cals, and centralism as against regionalism. The Socialists, who were reputed to have organized the
rebellion, lost perhaps more heavily than any other
group. Their most important leaders were in prison
or exile, their municipal councilors had been ousted,
their newspapers suspended or heavily censored;
many labor organizations were broken up. On the
other hand, the Right parties had consolidated their
ranks and strengthened their position; and the cabinet whose formation had provoked the revolt, continued to hold the reins of power. In December a
few resignations brought a reshuffling of portfolios,
but no fundamental change in party representation.

Catalonia suffered severely for its part in the revolt. Hundreds of arrests were made. Autonomous
rights were reduced; Madrid took back control of
policing, taxation, and the administration of justice.
In the Cortes, the Monarchist deputies demanded
that the Catalan Statute be completely annulled.
But this proposal failed to win the support of either
the Radicals or the C.E.D.A. It was finally decided
to suspend the Statute until the Cortes should approve its restoration. A Governor-General was temporarily to exercise the functions of the *Generalidad*
president.[1]

The Lerroux government sought in general to follow a moderate policy in the liquidation of the October revolt. But a rift in the reigning coalition

[1] In April 1935 Catalonia recovered a limited autonomy, including the restoration of control over various public services.
Madrid, however, continued to exercise responsibility for public
order. Later, a new regional council—made up of representatives
of the conservative Lliga, C.E.D.A. and Radicals—took office
in the *Generalidad*. Companys and six of his associates were
condemned by the Tribunal of Constitutional Guarantees—by a
vote of 14 to 7—to thirty years' imprisonment. Cf. Peers, *The
Spanish Tragedy*, cited, p. 178.

developed over the application of death penalties, decreed by military tribunals for the chiefs of the insurrection in Asturias. By the end of March two leaders had already been executed and twenty more were under sentence. Among the latter was Teodomiro Menéndez, a Socialist deputy. While in prison, he had unsuccessfully attempted suicide, an effort which served sharply to dramatize before public opinion the fate of these political defenders. The Radicals favored a reprieve for the condemned; but the cabinet representatives of the Catholics, the Agrarians and the Liberal Democrats voted to apply the death penalty. The Radical majority carried the day, and in consequence on March 29, 1935 the ministers of the other parties resigned. A week's negotiations brought as a curious result the organization of another Lerroux cabinet, in this case composed principally of members of the Radical party, with no representation of Popular Action. Such a government could command only minority support in the Cortes and it remained in office barely a month.

The members of Popular Action confidently expected their leader, Gil Robles, to head the succeeding cabinet. But late in April Lerroux again emerged as Premier. The Catholics, however, could boast of five ministers, including Gil Robles himself in the War portfolio. It was announced that in addition to the budget, the new régime would give principal attention to reform of the 1931 constitution. This document had carried a provision permitting revision after it had been in force for four years (i.e., after December 8, 1935) by the vote merely of an absolute majority in the Cortes. In July 1935 the cabinet issued its version of the reforms needed. These included modification of the articles on religion, education, and regional autonomy, elimination of the provision authorizing expropriation of private property, limitation of the powers of the President, reform of the Tribunal of Constitutional Guarantees and restoration of the Senate.[2] The proposals affected many of the reforms previously achieved by the Socialists and Left-Republicans and stirred new apprehension in the ranks of those groups.

In the field of public finance, attention turned toward the budget. Since 1932 no budget had been presented to the Cortes. Joaquín Chapaprieta, Minister of Finance, determined on a program of immediate economies, presentation of a budget in October 1935 and balancing of the budget for the year 1936-1937.[3] At his suggestion, the Cortes approved a Law of Restrictions, which aimed at drastic economies in government bureaucracy, abolishing many offices, and cutting salaries and allowances. This was to go into effect in October. But on September 18 two Agrarian ministers resigned from the government in protest against the return of public services to Catalonia, and this move provoked a general cabinet crisis. Chapaprieta, who was a political independent, became Premier, heading a cabinet composed of only nine ministers—three Radicals, three Cedistas (of whom Gil Robles was one), the chief of the Agrarian party and a representative of the Catalan Lliga (Right). The new régime reaffirmed support of public economy and early Constitutional reform. It announced intentions of attacking the Republic's economic maladies, resulting from an

[2] Cf. Peers, *The Spanish Tragedy*, cited, pp. 180, 181.
[3] For 1934 the approximate deficit had amounted to 750,000,000 pesetas. Cf. Emilio Ruiz, "La política presupuestaria radical-cedista," *Leviatán* (Madrid), July 1935, p. 40.

unfavorable balance of trade, chronic budget deficits and continuing unemployment. But within five weeks, Lerroux, who had filled the post of Foreign Minister, was forced to resign as the result of a gambling scandal.[4] The attempt to balance the budget failed when Popular Action refused to support a program of heavy taxes on the rich. Loss of this group's backing led to the fall of Chapaprieta on December 9, the sixth cabinet crisis within a year. Although Gil Robles still headed the largest party in the Cortes, President Alcalá-Zamora again passed him over—this time in favor of Manuel Portela Valladares, a Center politician. The latter formed an interim ministry, whose principal responsibility was to be the holding of general elections, which could no longer be postponed. After two weeks in office, this government resigned,[5] but was reconstituted under the same Premier on the last day of 1935. Constitutional guarantees were reported restored for the first time in two years.

The Popular Front and the February Elections

The six weeks of the campaign period witnessed a unification of forces on both Right and Left. The former drew together into what they termed an anti-Marxist alliance, and proclaimed themselves the de-

[4] Daniel Straus, a Mexican, charged that bribery had been involved in the grant of gambling concessions at San Sebastián and Majorca. Inquiry by a parliamentary commission found evidence against a nephew of Lerroux and three other Radical deputies. Lerroux himself was not directly accused. Cf. *New York Times,* October 20, 26, 27, 29, 1935. In December, Antonio Nombela published charges relating to government approval of a steamship company's indemnity claim for 7,450,000 pesetas. These involved Guillermo Moreno Calvo, formerly an under-secretary in the Lerroux cabinet. *Ibid.,* December 1, 9, 1935.

[5] Six ministers desired to be free of cabinet responsibility during the coming campaign. *New York Times,* December 31, 1935.

fenders of Law and Order. The latter, emulating the example which France had set in July 1935, organized a Popular Front. Its leader was Manuel Azaña, whose popular prestige had been steadily rising, following the twice repeated failure of his opponents to prove their charges against him. The Popular Front linked together, for cooperation in a common program and against the common threat of semi-Fascist and Monarchist reaction, the moderate liberals of the Left-Republican parties and all the labor groups, save only the majority of the Anarcho-Syndicalists. Specifically the Popular Front pact, which was signed on January 16, 1936, included the following organizations: among bourgeois parties, the Republican Left of Azaña and the Republican Union of Martínez Barrio; the Socialist party, with its trade union counterpart, the General Workers' Union; the National Federation of Socialist Youth; the Communist party; the Syndicalist party—led by Angel Pestaña—a faction of Right-wing Syndicalists willing to support political action; and the Workers' Party of Marxist Unification (P.O.U.M.), a semi-Trotzkyite group with its principal strength in Catalonia. The pact was to provide the basis for joint action in the election campaign, and also for the "norm of government which the Left-Republican parties are to carry out, with the support of labor forces, in the event of victory."[6]

Since this program constituted the official platform of the Popular Front and later was to be attacked by the Rebel leaders as "communistic," a somewhat detailed examination may be in order. The agreement was divided into ten sections. The first

---

[6] *El Sol* (Madrid), January 16, 1936. This issue published the full text of the Popular Front program.

called for a sweeping amnesty, directed toward free-
ing the 30,000 political prisoners who had been held
in confinement since October 1934. It also pledged
reinstatement to the hundreds of thousands who had
lost their jobs for political reasons in both public
and private employment. Section two promised
maintenance and enforcement of the Constitution,
reform of the courts and investigation of abuses
charged to the police and armed forces. In section
three, devoted to agrarian questions, the Left-Republicans refused to support the Socialist demand
for nationalization of land, but instead offered to the
peasants a new tenancy law, reduction in taxes and
rents, and other advantages. The law compensating
grandees whose estates had been seized was to be
repealed. The fourth section advocated a certain degree of government regulation of industry and commerce. Section five called for an extensive program
of public works; the Left-Republicans, however,
declined to accept the principle of an unemployment
dole advocated by the workers' representatives. In
section six, which related to finance and banking,
the Left-Republican parties stopped short of the
nationalization of banking demanded by the labor
parties, but agreed to stricter regulation both of
the Bank of Spain and private banking, and in addition pledged tax reforms. The seventh section dealt
with social legislation, promising reorganization of
industrial arbitration, minimum wages, employment
offices, and general stimulus of welfare agencies. Section eight advocated development of public education, supervision of private schools and wider access
to middle and higher education by working-class
students. The two final sections promised re-estab-

lishment of the principles of regional autonomy and
declared that in international policy, Spain would
be guided by the Covenant of the League of Nations. In this platform the moderate views of the
middle-class parties clearly predominated over the
more radical demands of labor. It was a program
of liberal reform, but by no means one of social
revolution.

In the elections of February 16 and the run-off
poll on March 1, the Popular Front scored a decisive victory. It elected approximately 258 deputies
in the Cortes, to 62 representatives of the Center
parties, and 152 of the Right. The returns, as compared with those of the 1933 elections, were as shown
on page 469.[7]

The popular majority of the Left parties, which
has been the subject of considerable controversy,
was much less impressive than their gains in the
Cortes. Including the figures for the Basque Nation-

[7] The 1933 figures are taken from República Española. Con-
greso de los Diputados, Biblioteca, *Boletín de Información Bibli-
ográfica y Parlamentaria de España y del Extranjero* (Madrid),
November-December 1933, p. 1069; the 1936 figures from *ibid.*,
January-February 1936, pp. 121-48. For the most important individual parties, the changes were as follows:

LIBERAL AND LABOR PARTIES	1936	1933	Gain or Loss
Republican Left (Manuel Azaña)	82	11	+71
Esquerra (Catalan Left)	21	17	+ 4
Socialist party	89	59	+30
Communist party	14	1	+13

CENTER AND RIGHT PARTIES			
Radical party (Alejandro Lerroux)	8	101	—93
Agrarian party	13	31	—18
C.E.D.A. (Gil Robles)	98	115	—17
Lliga (Catalan Right)	11	26	—15
Monarchist parties	23	36	—13

Liberal and Labor Parties*	1936	1933	Gains
Liberal or Left-Republican parties	148	32	116
Labor parties	110	60	50
	258	92	166

Center and Right Parties			Losses
Center parties	62	173	111
Right parties	152	196	44
	214†	369‡	155

* Most of these supported the 1936 Popular Front.

† The Cortes has a total of 473 deputies; this count indicates one seat still in dispute.

‡ There were 12 vacancies when this count was taken in December 1933.

alists (132,247), who are now supporting the Popular Front government, the liberal and labor groups had a total of 4,206,156 votes, as compared with 3,783,601 for the Right parties, and 681,047 for the Center. The Popular Front owed much of its triumph to the solid vote of labor; even the Anarcho-Syndicalists overcame their traditional aversion to political action and went to the polls, hoping to secure amnesty for their imprisoned comrades through a Popular Front victory; many middle-class voters, dissatisfied with the record of the Center-Right governments and fearful of Fascist aggression against the republic, also supported the victorious coalition.[8]

As soon as the Left victory became known, demand was promptly voiced for immediate fulfillment

[8] Spain's electoral law was so framed that a united minority, by a coalition agreement among its constituent parties, could defeat a disunited majority. This fact explains the wide discrepancy between the Cortes figures and the popular returns, both in the 1933 and the 1936 elections.

of the Popular Front's most urgent platform pledge
—that of an amnesty for political prisoners. Riots
within the prisons and mass demonstrations in the
cities augmented the popular clamor. Rumors that
an army coup might cheat the Popular Front of
the fruits of victory further stirred unrest. The Portela government decreed a "state of alarm"—modified martial law—and reimposed a press censorship.
When these steps proved insufficient to calm the
growing agitation, the cabinet resigned on February
19 and President Alcalá-Zamora appointed Manuel
Azaña to head a new ministry. His cabinet was composed entirely of middle-class representatives, members of Republican Left and Republican Union. The
Socialists were unwilling to accept seats in a cabinet
in which bourgeois parties sat. They would remain
outside the government, exerting continual pressure
on the administration to carry out its platform
pledges, while at the same time retaining freedom
of action to stage a coup, should the situation be
favorable, for establishment of a Socialist republic.
The party also needed time to deal with dissensions
within its ranks. It was divided into three factions.
Francisco Largo Caballero on the Left, who had
abandoned former "reformist" principles to take a
position close to the Communists, argued for violent
seizure of power by the proletariat; in the Center,
Indalecio Prieto opposed violence and favored an
evolutionary and parliamentary program toward the
Socialist commonwealth; even farther to the Right,
Besteiro led a third faction, relatively weak in comparison with the other two.

Azaña promptly published the amnesty decree desired, and the jails were rapidly emptied of their

thousands of political offenders.[9] This was followed
on February 28 by a second decree authorizing reinstatement of all workers whose revolutionary sympathies had lost them their jobs; employers were
required to pay compensation for the time lost.

The Road to Rebellion

The forces of social unrest were prompt to take
advantage of the excited state of the popular temper. In the cities Leftist demonstrations of victory
were attended by the burning of churches and convents—for many decades a recurrent phenomenon
in Spanish history. The political clubs and newspaper offices of Fascist and Monarchist groups were
sacked and pillaged. The government followed a passive policy toward these outbreaks, largely, it would
appear, due to the fear that repression might further
excite mob feeling. It was hoped that the movement,
if left to itself, would soon run out; but this, un-
fortunately, did not prove to be the case.

Unrest in the agricultural districts—especially in
western and southern Spain—took the form of forcible seizure of the large estates by the impatient
peasants. For five years they had waited for the
land which had been promised them. It had taken
the Republic almost a year and a half to pass its
agrarian reform law, which went on the books in
September 1932. From that date until the end of
1934 only 12,000 peasants had been allotted plots.

[9] The Premier had originally announced that amnesty must
wait until the Cortes could meet and pass a bill. But popular
pressure was so strong that within twenty-four hours of this
statement the decree had been issued by the Executive. The
permanent delegation of the old Cortes (which represented Parliament when the latter was not sitting), with a majority from the
former Center-Right coalition, recognized the dangers of the
situation and sanctioned the Premier's step.

The Center and Right forces, following their triumph in November 1933, promptly threw out of gear the machinery for agrarian distribution which was just getting under way. This was followed by a law of August 1, 1935, which required full compensation for all land expropriated from the grandees.[10] Then only 50,000 pesetas were appropriated annually for such compensation. The practical effect of this law was to stop entirely distribution of land. The victory of the Popular Front markedly speeded up agrarian reform. By the end of March 70,000 *yunteros* (so-called because they owned their own *yuntas* or yokes of mules or oxen, with which they tilled their rented plots) had been assigned land for cultivation.[11] But many peasants remained unsatisfied. It would soon be too late for the spring sowing. Under the leadership of the Socialist Agricultural Federations, various groups proceeded to direct action. One incident in the southwestern province of Badajoz is thus described:

"At 5.00 a.m. on March 25, organized groups of labourers armed with ropes, spades and other implements mustered secretly and trooped out from 150 of the 163 villages of the province; they proceeded—many of them on their donkeys, of course —to the neighbouring big estates and calmly marked out the strips which they proposed to occupy for cultivation under the new land settlement system. Then, after a lusty cry of '*¡Viva la República!*' they

[10] This legislation, together with the sections of the 1932 laws still left in force, was published as the law of November 9, 1935. *Gaceta,* November 19, 1935. Lands previously expropriated without compensation were declared only under temporary occupation, and rent was to be paid to the owners from the date of seizure.

[11] For the decrees in question, dated March 3 and 14, cf. *Boletín del Instituto de Reforma Agraria* (Madrid), March 1936, pp. 195-204.

marched back to their villages, held a demonstration
meeting in front of the local Government Building,
and then sent a commission to get formal approval
for their land-taking, their case being that they had
been promised the land in the Government election
programme, but that all kinds of bureaucratic obstacles were being put in their way."[12] In some cases
the act was accepted and legalized with considerable
dispatch; in others, the peasants were dislodged from
the land taken. But the widespread agitation stimulated governmental action. On March 20 a decree
had declared of "social utility" and thus subject to
expropriation all farms situated in districts (*términos
municipales*) possessing the following characteristics: great concentration of property; a high proportion of peasants in relation to the total population;
a low ratio of available land in comparison with the
number of peasants; prevalence of extensive cultivation.[13] On June 18 the law of August 1, 1935, was
repealed and the 1932 reform legislation declared
again in force.[14] Up to June 1936 land had been
provided for 90,000 peasants, representing with their
families a population of half a million persons.

On March 16 peasants occupied two estates belonging to Niceto Alcalá-Zamora. But a greater mis-
fortune than this was in store for the President of
the Republic. His efforts to strengthen Center forces
and to steer a middle course between the violently

[12] W. Horsfall Carter, "Spain To-day," *The Listener, 1936,*
Vol. XV, pp. 797-99, 826; quoted in Peers, *The Spanish Tragedy,*
cited, p. 197.

[13] For the text, cf. *Boletín del Instituto de Reforma Agraria,*
cited, March 1936, pp. 206-07. This decree was based on a provision curiously included in the reactionary law of August 1, 1935,
permitting expropriation of farms declared to be of "social
utility."

[14] *Ibid.,* June 1936, p. 643. This number contains (pp. 664-87)
a review of the Republic's agrarian policy for 1931-1936.

antagonistic Right and Left had earned for him the active ill will of both groups. The latter were particularly hostile, blaming him for the repressions they had suffered following the October 1934 revolt. It was now decided that the President must be ousted. The Socialists took the initiative, Indalecio Prieto making the principal speech in the Cortes against Alcalá-Zamora. The Right forces felt no strong devotion to the Executive, and on the decisive ballot abstained from voting. Alcalá-Zamora's withdrawal was forced by a motion which the Cortes approved on April 7, declaring that the President had unnecessarily dissolved the previous parliament on January 7. Under Article 81 of the Spanish Constitution the President may dissolve the Cortes twice during his six-year term, but parliament has the right to review the necessity of the second dissolution, an unfavorable decision involving automatic dismissal of the Executive. Diego Martínez Barrio, presiding officer of the Cortes, temporarily succeeded to the Presidency. Elections were held on May 10[15] and Azaña was named the new President. Santiago Casares Quiroga became Prime Minister, heading a cabinet similar in composition to the previous one.

But political and social ferment continued. The masses, disillusioned by the meager gains they had received at the hands of the bourgeois Republic, were becoming increasingly radical. The temper of the Madrid workers was revealed on April 17, when the Syndicalists—numerically weak in the capital—

[15] The President was named by an Electoral College, a body made up of the 473 deputies in the Cortes and an equal number of electors chosen by popular vote. These latter were elected on April 26 in a poll which the Right parties boycotted to a large degree.

succeeded in instigating a general strike, which was carried through against the opposition of the Socialist and Communist leaders, normally the recognized chiefs of the labor movement. This was only one of an epidemic of strikes. On June 16 Gil Robles charged in the Cortes that since the February elections there had been 113 general and 218 partial strikes.

A wave of murders by gunmen and political assassinations further alarmed public opinion. The victims included José María Maura, an insurance official of Bilbao and brother of three outstanding political leaders; Alfredo Martínez, a physician of Oviedo; En Miquel Badià, one of the chiefs of the October revolt in Catalonia.[16] Luis Jiménez de Asúa, Socialist professor and vice-president of the Cortes, was shot at as he was leaving his Madrid home. He escaped, but his bodyguard was killed. Some of the slayings were attributed to Leftist gunmen; others to Fascist assassins. Of all the Right groups, the Spanish Phalanx, Spain's self-proclaimed Fascists, who were led by young José Antonio Primo de Rivera, had shown themselves most aggressive since the February elections. They hoped possibly to enlarge the relatively small number of their adherents by strong-armed action. There seems little doubt of their responsibility for much of the violence.[17] The government ordered the Phalanx dissolved; Primo de Rivera and hundreds of other Fascists were imprisoned. But still the disorders continued.

[16] Cf. Peers, *The Spanish Tragedy*, cited, p. 195.

[17] In July the Madrid police reported discovery of Fascist documents, which carried instructions for directing the activities of hired agitators. District leaders were instructed "to promote and foment the greatest possible number of strikes, especially in the public services." *New York Times*, July 7, 1936.

In the June 16 speech of Gil Robles already al-
luded to, the leader of Catholic Action summed up
the history of the previous four months by declaring
that in that period 269 persons had been killed, 1500
others seriously injured, and that 251 churches had
been burned or partially destroyed.[18]

CHAPTER VI

CIVIL WAR

IN MID-SUMMER the long series of political killings came to a climax. At 10 o'clock on Sunday evening, July 12, José del Castillo, lieutenant in the
shock police, was shot down in front of his Madrid
home—supposedly by Fascists. Members of this
group believed him responsible for the slaying a few
months earlier of a cousin of the Fascist chief, José
Antonio Primo de Rivera. At 3 o'clock the following
morning, members of the shock police appeared at
the home of José Calvo Sotelo, Monarchist leader
and Finance Minister under the former Primo de
Rivera dictatorship.[1] He was taken away in a police
van, and an hour later his dead body was left with
the porter of a Madrid cemetery. The killing of this
brilliant orator and politician provoked violent protests from the Monarchists, Fascists and allied
groups. That evening President Azaña suspended the
sessions of the Cortes for one week and decreed extension of the state of alarm for thirty days.

Four days later, on July 17, the civil war began

[18] *New York Times,* June 17, 1936.
[1] In December 1934 Calvo Sotelo had been reported as attempting to initiate a movement for the simultaneous restoration of
the Monarch and the establishment of a Fascist corporative state
on Italian lines. Cf. *New York Times,* December 6, 9, 23, 1934.

with the rise of a number of regiments in Spanish Morocco against the government. The leader of the movement, General Francisco Franco, flew to Morocco from the Canary Islands where he had been stationed as Governor. With the backing of the Foreign Legion, Moorish contingents and regular army troops, the Insurgents made themselves masters of Spanish Morocco with little resistance. The following day the rebellion spread to Spain itself. By the 19th garrisons under the leadership of prominent generals had mutinied in all parts of the country. General Queipo de Llano had revolted at Seville. In the north General Emilio Mola, and at Saragossa General Miguel Cabanellas, had risen against Madrid. In Majorca General Goded had declared for the rebellion and then flown to Barcelona. On July 20, however, General José Sanjurjo, friend of former King Alfonso and leader of the unsuccessful Monarchist coup in 1932, was killed when the airplane which was carrying him to Spain crashed near Lisbon. He was reported to have been the choice of revolutionary leaders for supreme chief of the new movement.[2]

The Rebel generals were supported, it was estimated, by 90 per cent of the officers and perhaps two-thirds of the army rank and file. The army forces stationed in Spain numbered approximately 100,000; those in Africa 35,000, of whom almost 9,000 were Moors and 13,000 in the Foreign Legion.[3] In

[2] Before the revolt General Sanjurjo had passed several weeks in Berlin, in contact with German leaders. *Manchester Guardian,* August 5, 1936.

[3] Cf. *Anuario Militar Español, 1935* (Madrid), pp. 130-33. For a description of the rôle played by the Moors in the civil war, cf. Frank L. Kluckhohn, "With the Moors on the March in Spain," *New York Times Magazine,* November 22, 1936.

addition, a good part of the Civil Guard or constabulary, whose total strength was 32,000, went over to the revolt. The government was thus left with a small remnant of the army, a portion of the Civil Guard—whose loyalty was none too certain—and of the shock police or Assault Guards, numbering 17,-000. The army air force and the navy in part, also remained loyal. In the latter the officers' plan to turn the vessels over to the Rebels was balked by the determined opposition of the crews.[4]

But at best these forces were utterly inadequate to stem the tide of revolt. The only alternative to immediate capitulation was mobilization of the masses in the Left-wing labor groups. With the help of these organizations, Socialist and Communist workers and later Anarcho-Syndicalists were given arms. A Popular Militia approximately 50,000 strong —undisciplined and hastily organized, but with the enthusiastic strength of a mass movement—now stood behind the government.

But this step led to a cabinet crisis; in fact Madrid had three Premiers within the span of 24 hours. Early on Sunday morning, July 19, Casares Quiroga resigned, discredited by his failure to foresee and prepare against the revolt. President Azaña, instead of organizing a ministry fully representative of the Popular Front, called on the moderate Diego Martínez Barrio, Speaker of the Cortes, to form a government. But this régime lasted only a few hours. The Premier refused to sanction arming the masses, and for this and other reasons the cabinet was denied the support of the labor unions. Martínez Barrio consequently gave way to José Giral, an obscure

[4] The rôle of the navy in the civil war is briefly reviewed by Hanson W. Baldwin, *New York Times*, November 22, 1936, p. 38.

politician and friend of Azaña. The new Prime Minister was manifestly only a figurehead through whom the President would actually govern. The Giral cabinet was limited to Left-Republicans and included no Socialists or other labor representatives.

Following seizure of Spanish Morocco and victory in the provincial capitals, the generals had apparently planned that, in the third stage of the revolt, the troops at Madrid would rise and overturn the republican régime. But the arming of the masses upset their calculations. On July 19, when sporadic fighting began in the capital, armed workers were on the streets in force. They met the attacks of Fascist desperadoes who drove madly about, firing from automobiles at the police and militia. On the following day the troops in Montaña and Carabanchel garrisons mutinied. The air force at Cuatro Vientos and the soldiers in the Getafe and Vicalvaro cantonments were also involved. All the artillery was in the hands of the Insurgents and in addition the bolts of 70,000 spare rifles had been taken secretly to Montaña barracks. The government was limited to one heavy gun and two field pieces found at repair shops, and 5,000 rifles. Many of the troops in Montaña garrison were out of sympathy with the rebellion; and after a few hours' struggle the barracks was captured by workers' militia, Civil Guards and police. Madrid had been saved for the government.[5] The strife led to the burning of churches and convents. Following their victory, members of the Popular

[5] A vivid and detailed account of events in the capital during the first days of the revolt is given in the *New York Times,* August 5, 1936. For pictures of Barcelona and Valencia as well as Madrid in the same period, cf. *International Press Correspondence* (London), August 15, 1936, pp. 987 ff. Robert Neville reports life in Granada from July 18 to August 14 in the *New York Herald Tribune,* August 30, 1936.

Militia drove through the streets shooting wildly in delirious enthusiasm. In Barcelona also, armed workers crushed the rebellion in a three-day conflict. General Goded was forced to surrender, and by July 22 the Loyalist forces were in control.

The revolt at its inception appeared to be purely a military movement. Whatever other elements were involved in the conspiracy,[6] the initiative for the rebellion clearly lay with the generals. Many of these belonged to a secret officers' association, the *Unión Militar Española*, which had originally been organized in 1929 to conspire for the overthrow of the Primo de Rivera dictatorship.[7] On March 15, 1936 army chiefs were reported to have issued a virtual ultimatum to Premier Azaña threatening that the armed forces would take matters into their own hands unless the civil authorities took effective steps to quell riots and end destruction of property. Meanwhile the government, on its side, was concerned about the loyalty of many of the officers. On April 17 a law was introduced providing that all officers known to have been active in political affairs be retired from the army immediately on pension, while

[6] Reports that a military-Fascist revolt was under preparation had been current for some time. Calvo Sotelo was declared to be the civil politician most closely in touch with the army officers. It is also charged that Gil Robles, when Minister of War in 1935, had entered into close relations with army leaders and ordered maneuvers in the Guadarrama Mountains, to facilitate construction of fortifications later used by the Rebel forces moving on Madrid. Cf. Gannes and Repard, *Spain in Revolt*, cited, p. 74.

[7] Lawrence Fernsworth ("Back of the Spanish Rebellion," *Foreign Affairs*, October 1936) quotes from one of its recent pronunciamentos. This document is described as "a violent exhortation to military men to 'save Spain' from an 'international plot' to 'pulverize' it and 'promote the ruin of religious sentiment, and of the Spanish family, of capital, of labor . . .'"

those already on the retired list who had engaged in such activity were to be deprived of their pensions.[8] On the ensuing day, the War and Interior Ministries initiated a general shake-up in the high commands; officers suspected of Monarchist or Conservative sympathies were dismissed or transferred to distant posts. General Francisco Franco, who had been Chief of Staff under the Gil Robles ministry and previously had commanded the Foreign Legion in Morocco, was "exiled" to the Canary Islands; General Goded was dispatched to the Balearics. General López Ochoa, allegedly one of the *Unión* members, was arrested by the Popular Front government on May 12, 1936, charged with unnecessary cruelty in suppressing the 1934 revolt in Asturias. At the beginning of July, Casares Quiroga, then Minister of War as well as Premier, ordered General Gómez Morato, Commander-in-Chief in Morocco, to remove the majority of Foreign Legion officers from their posts. Resentment at these steps was supposedly the prime motive for the conspiracy; control of the armed forces by the ruling clique of generals was clearly menaced. The murder of Calvo Sotelo appears to have been only the immediate cause of the revolt; it precipitated an outbreak which was premature by two months, according to report.[9]

The movement began without a program. In a manifesto issued at the outbreak of the revolt, General Franco attempted to justify the Rebels' action by proclaiming that anarchy had been rife; he emphasized the prevalence of strikes, assassinations and disorder, and declared that "the forces of public

[8] Cf. *New York Times*, April 18, 1936.
[9] Cf. W. Horsfall Carter, "Spain and the Social Revolution," *International Affairs* (London), September-October 1936, pp 647-70.

order remain held to their garrisons by authorities who intend to dishonor them." But beyond announcing a crusade against foreign "isms" and a general campaign in favor of "fraternity, liberty and equality," the generals did not seem ready to proclaim their goals.[10]

Although supported by the Monarchists, the Insurgent leaders early declared their loyalty to republican principles.[11] Later Franco denied that the Rebels wished to establish a Fascist government in Spain, but declared that, if victorious, they would set up a temporary military régime and then propose the prompt drafting of a new liberal constitution, which would assure justice to middle-class property holders as well as to the working class. He added: "We propose to see that long-needed social reforms are pushed forward in Spain. As far as the church is concerned, we intend to allow complete freedom of worship, but under no conditions will we permit the church to play a part in politics. We started the revolt only after it had become self-evident that the government was playing into the hands of the Communists and extreme Socialists and that there was no justice for others."[12]

The Moors, Foreign Legion, regular army troops and Civil Guards under the control of the Rebels were augmented by civilian volunteers—the Fascist followers of Primo de Rivera and Carlists, especially in the north. Churchmen and large landowners gave

[10] *New York American*, July 22, 1936.
[11] Cf. statements of General Miguel Cabanellas, head of the Burgos Junta (*New York Herald Tribune*, July 26, 1936), and of General Emilio Mola (*New York Times*, August 5, 1936). The latter refused to permit the enlistment of Prince Juan in his forces, and was reported to have ordered the arrest of any member of the royal family who appeared in his jurisdiction.
[12] *New York Times*, August 9, 1936.

sympathy and active support. Many Right politicians also backed the movement. On its outbreak
Gil Robles fled to France, but soon passed to Portugal where he was reported serving as purchasing
agent for the generals. On August 29 he appeared at
Rebel headquarters in Burgos to declare: "I am with
Spain and Spain is here."[13]

In the field the Rebel armies at first made slow
progress and their plan of campaign for convergent
action on Madrid suffered a serious breakdown.
Government control of the navy hampered Franco's
transport of troops from Morocco, forcing him to the
slow process of shuttling them across in airplanes,
with the help of occasional transports which succeeded in evading the loyal vessels. At the end of
the first two weeks the Rebels held in the south the
valley of the Guadalquivir, with the cities of Cór-
doba, Seville and Cadiz. But their control outside
the garrisoned centers was tenuous; they had as yet
been unable to organize an effective field force, and
the great mass of peasants and farm laborers in
the area was openly hostile. In the north the Insurgents controlled important cities; under General Mola they had in the field an active army and
the movement had the support of the mountaineers
of Navarre and the small farmers of old Castile. But
the advance of Mola's force was stopped by government militia in the Guadarrama Mountains. While
the Rebels had cut Madrid's communications with
the north, their own rear was threatened by the
government's control of the Asturias, including the
important seaports of Santander, San Sebastián,
Irún and the industrial center of Bilbao. Every road
out of Madrid was reported blocked at the end of

[13] *New York Herald Tribune,* August 30, 1936.

the first week, but subsequently the government captured Albacete, thus opening rail service south-eastward to Cartagena and Valencia, and through the latter to Barcelona. Westward also service had been restored almost to the Portuguese border near Badajoz. In the east, forces from Barcelona were attacking the Rebels in Saragossa.

By this time the Rebels were reported to be receiving effective aid from Italy and Germany in the form of bombing planes, artillery and other supplies.[14] Government superiority in the air—its own antiquated equipment had apparently been augmented by receipt of approximately a hundred planes from France—was soon to be ended. On August 8 General Franco arrived at Seville to direct a Rebel drive northward.[15] His troops had to battle against peasant sniping from the hills, and determined resistance from workers' militia in the towns and villages. But on August 14 the city of Badajoz fell to the advancing Moors and Legionnaires. This opened an important gateway to Portugal and cleared the way for General Franco's forces to contact the northern army of General Mola. The latter meanwhile, checked in the Guadarrama Mountains, had diverted some troops for a campaign against Irún and San Sebastián. Irún was vigorously defended, despite reports of friction between Anarcho-Syndicalists and Basque Nationalists—the latter conservative and Catholic. The city, almost reduced to ashes, fell on September 4 after a bitter struggle. A week later San Sebastián was captured. The fall

[14] Cf. Vera M. Dean, "European Diplomacy in the Spanish Crisis," *Foreign Policy Reports*, December 1, 1936, pp. 224, 226.

[15] He had opened recruiting among the Moors in Africa, but the results were declared disappointing, due to native unwillingness and lack of money. The situation in the province forced the retention there of 12,000 troops. *New York Times*, August 14, 1936.

of these centers relieved pressure on the rear of Mola's forces, and—more important still—closed for the government not only its main gateway to France, but also its principal line of communication through that friendly country between the northern front and Catalonia. While the Rebels were registering these important gains, government forces had made little progress against Saragossa, and a Catalan expeditionary force had been routed in Majorca with heavy losses. In Madrid Rebel air raids had become almost a nightly occurrence.

On the day marked by the fall of Irún, the "grave situation of the civil war" led to a cabinet change at Madrid. The Giral ministry was replaced by a much stronger and more representative government under Francisco Largo Caballero, dynamic Left-wing Socialist. His cabinet was made up of six Socialists— including the more moderate Indalecio Prieto—two Communists, three left-Republicans and one representative each from the Catalan *Esquerra* and the Basque Nationalists. Thus for the first time since the victory of the Popular Front in the February elections, the government had the active collaboration of all its supporting groups—with the sole exception of the Anarcho-Syndicalists.

The first step of the Largo Caballero cabinet was to unify military command. General José Asensio was made chief of all government troops in central Spain. The authorities had already begun to transform the Popular Militia into a regular republican army. The pay of each soldier-worker had been fixed at 10 pesetas daily. But many of the militia were still poorly equipped, fighting at times with shotguns and revolvers. Discipline was faulty; authority was divided between officers and political delegates, named by the various labor organizations. From the first the militia chose their own officers, but only after considerable delay were these new leaders given any technical military instruction.[16]

The Popular militia, despite individual courage and heroism, was unable to present an effective resistance to General Franco's disciplined Moors, Foreign Legionnaires and regulars. The government forces were clearly at a disadvantage in aircraft, tanks, artillery, modern machine guns and war machinery of all sorts. The Rebels, moreover, were superior in tactics and unity of command. Thus, despite small numbers—Franco was reported to have no more than 15,000 effective troops, and General Mola only about 10,000 in the north—the Rebels advanced steadily northward, from Badajoz to Cáceres, and thence northwestward up the Tagus Valley toward Madrid. After hard fighting, Talavera de la Reina was captured. On September 22 Franco crushed 30,000 Loyalists at Maqueda, "largely by means of airplanes that flew at a height of ninety feet and used machine guns on the Leftist columns and positions."[17] By this time government forces were reported seriously handicapped by lack of pursuit planes and experienced pilots.

From Maqueda, 40 miles from Madrid, Franco diverted part of his force southward for the relief of the beleaguered Alcázar in historic Toledo. On September 24 the government loosed a reported 240,-000,000 cubic yards of water from the Alberche River dam to sweep down over the Insurgent's army. But this desperate measure had only a temporary effect. Franco's advance continued and on Septem-

[16] For a description of the militia in the field around Saragossa, cf. articles by Walter Duranty in *New York Times*, September 1, 2, 1936.

[17] *New York Times*, September 23, 1936.

ber 27 the Moors entered Toledo, from which their ancestors had been expelled many centuries before. The 70-day siege of the Alcázar was lifted. Since July 20, 1,100 men—cadets, officers and troops—and some 400 women and children had held out in this ancient fortress. Repeatedly the government offered safety to the women and children. The diplomatic corps, led by the Chilean envoy, journeyed from Madrid to Toledo to transmit the government's offer of mercy through a loud speaker. But all advances were rebuffed by the Rebels. Finally the government pledged that the lives of all would be spared if they abandoned the Alcázar. Only after this offer was refused, did the investing forces supplement their artillery bombardment by the explosions of mines of TNT. Still the defenders refused to surrender. During the siege 139 were killed, 430 were seriously and 150 slightly wounded. Less than 300 of the Rebels passed through this ordeal unscathed; their food supply of horse and mule meat was almost exhausted. But their spirit was indomitable, and on September 27 they sallied out of the fortress and fought to join hands with deliverers.

At the end of September, it was estimated that the Madrid and Barcelona governments controlled about one-third of the territory and half the population of the country. Spain's 49 provinces were divided as follows:

	Population	Area in Sq. Kilos.
Government-controlled, 18 provinces, mostly in east and northeast........	11,520,000	175,293
Rebel-controlled, 17 provinces, in north, west and south.............	7,850,000	155,857
Fighting in 14 provinces, in north, northeast, west and south............	6,770,000	172,752[18]

[18] New York Times, September 30, 1936.

General Francisco Franco's *de facto* leadership of
the Insurgent cause was formalized by the Rebel
Junta on September 30, when at Burgos he was
made practical dictator, being named "Chief of the
Government of the Spanish State," "Generalisimo
of the national forces of land, sea and air" and
"Commander-in-chief of the armies in the field."[19]
The Junta declared payment of interest on the public debt suspended until "the political conditions of
the Government of the Spanish Nation permit it,"
called up the reservists of the 1933, 1934 and 1935
classes (estimated to number 50,000 men), requisi-
tioned the properties of various companies whose
directors were considered opposed to the "noble
ends" sought by the Junta, outlawed all political
organizations which had formed part of the Popular
Front since the call for the February elections, prohibited for the time being all political activities, particularly on the part of workers' or employers' organizations, replaced the republican flag by Spain's
traditional red and yellow emblem, and declared
that since public schools were no longer secular, religious instruction would be compulsory.[20] Agrarian
reform was suspended, and all properties on which
the program of distribution had not been carried
through to the final legal point—especially those
which had been subdivided or occupied after the

[19] *Boletín Oficial de la Junta de Defensa Nacional de España*
(Burgos), September 30, 1936, Decree 138. The Rebel officers had
organized their government at Burgos on July 24, under the title
of the National Defense Junta of Spain. General Miguel Cabanellas served as president. General Franco was then named general-
in-chief of the Army of Morocco and Southern Spain, and General
Emilio Mola general-in-chief of the Army of the North. *Ibid.,*
July 25, 1936. This source is hereafter cited as *Boletín.*
[20] *Ibid.,* August 11, 17, 25, 29, 30, September 4, 16, 24, 28. In
the school curriculum, sports were to include "pre-military instruction." The study of Portuguese, Italian and German was to
be expanded. *Ibid.,* September 28, 1936, Order 207.

victory of the Popular Front—were to be returned to their former owners.[21]

During October the Insurgents pressed closer to the capital. On the 17th, Madrid's only remaining railroad line to the coast was cut at Castillejos, 34 miles from the capital. On the 21st, Navalcarnero fell, the government's last stronghold on the west. By the end of the month the Insurgent lines formed an immense "C" around the capital, running from Sigüenza on the northeast to Escorial on the north and thence south to Aranjuez. In the capital itself, government militia were reported to number 100,-000. Food supplies had run short. Fortifications were under construction; large gangs of men were digging trenches and laying barbed wire. On the 16th, Premier Largo Caballero was declared "supreme chief of the military forces of Spain" and Foreign Minister Alvarez del Vayo named "General Commissioner for War," with four assistants representing the Socialist, Syndicalist and Communist unions. The purpose of this move was to tighten government control of the militia and other armed forces.[22]

The Spanish civil war became more clearly an international struggle, with Italy, Germany and Portugal backing the Rebels, and the Soviet Union and—to a much lesser degree—France supporting the government. Foreign correspondents with the "Nationalist" army reported that its backbone was now Italian, German and Moorish. The Insurgents, who had only 20 to 30 planes when the revolt began, could boast of more than 100 Italian and German aircraft, and 40 Italian tanks; the Moorish troops were equipped with foreign ammunition. Italian of-

[21] *Ibid.*, August 30, Decree 74; September 26, Decree 128; September 28, Decree 133.

[22] Cf. *Gaceta de Madrid*, October 16, 1936.

ficers in their own national uniforms were to be seen at many points along the Insurgent lines. Observers reported that advances against the poorly armed militia were generally heralded by artillery and airplane bombardment. "Large Caproni airplanes, sometimes three or four at a time, appear with fighting Fiat escorts. . . . The Rebels' tanks then advance, half a dozen at a time, moving rapidly, circling easily, pouring fire on the open lines of the militia and crossing right up to and over trenches, wherever these exist."[23] Where the militia occupied villages, these were outflanked and captured by pincer movements. Madrid had undoubtedly received assistance from the Soviet Union and France, but observers declared that "this aid has been neither so complete nor so effective as that vouchsafed to the Insurgents by others."[24] By the end of October, however, it became evident that the government had obtained—presumably from the Soviet—substantial supplies, particularly planes and tanks. On the 29th Premier Largo Caballero called on the militia to initiate a counter-offensive and declared: "We are already in possession of formidable mechanized equipment. We have tanks and a powerful air force."[25] Following this appeal, the government troops succeeded in driving back the Rebels from three to four miles at certain points.

Despite the military successes of the Insurgents,

[23] *New York Times,* October 23, 30, 1936. The Spanish Embassy in Paris asserted that Italian forces dominated the Balearic Islands. It was reported that Italian inf⸗ntry had been landed; 112 Italian bombers and pursuit planes were ready to attack Barcelona; and 8 Italian submarines were prepared to leave their base at Genoa, to aid the Rebels. *The Times* (London), October 28, 1936.

[24] *New York Times,* October 30, 1936.

[25] *Le Temps* (Paris), October 31, 1936.

two factors cast doubt on the political strength of their movement. First, serious differences on policy existed between three principal groups—the military, the Monarchists, and the Fascists. Franco and some of his fellow officers now inclined toward establishment of a corporative state based on the army. He apparently favored breaking up the great estates and curbing the Church's influence in politics.[26] But the Monarchists and their allies, the large landowners, desired to balk reform of the land system and to restore the Spanish throne. With the general aims of the Spanish Fascists or Phalanxists who formed an important part of the Rebel militia,[27] Franco seemingly sympathized. But he regarded them as extremists and potential rivals of the military for dominance of political life.[28] In September they had published a program, calling for the repudiation of the capitalist system, nationalization of banks and public utilities, division of the large holdings and state regimentation of agriculture, and government domination of the Church. They also declared against "permitting the military to dictate Spanish politics."[29]

The second political weakness affecting the Rebel movement was its lack—outside of Navarre and Old Castile in the north—of popular support. De-

[26] Cf. Frank L. Kluckhohn, "Franco Wages War with a Light Heart," *New York Times Magazine,* November 8, 1936.

[27] The eventual withdrawal of the Moors and Foreign Legion from Spain—they could not be used for a permanent army of occupation without provoking extreme opposition—would leave the Fascists far outnumbering the regular army.

[28] To hamper the growth of political fascism, General Franco had ordered on August 14 that no one in the Rebel militia should continue membership in a political organization. *New York Times,* August 15, 1936.

[29] *New York Times,* September 7, 1936.

spite the fact that much of the territory around
Mérida and Cáceres had been in Insurgent hands
for seven weeks, one correspondent reported at the
end of October:

"So violent has been the sniping and guerrilla
warfare back of General Franco's lines that in the
past ten days he has opened a reign of terror along
the whole Rebel line from Maqueda, near Madrid,
through Talavera de la Reina to Badajoz. . . . An
impartial observer is forced to the conclusion that
General Franco's movement is extremely unpopular
with the bulk of the people, who regard it as an
attempt of the privileged class to turn the clock back.
Only foreign aid has made the Rebel success to date
possible."[30]

By this time "terror" and atrocities had become
almost a commonplace in the Spanish struggle. Its
ruthless and fanatical cruelty rivalled that of a religious war. The medieval practice of holding hostages was revived. Both Rebels and Loyalists have
been guilty of large-scale executions. Not all by any
means can be explained as mob actions—committed
in moments of frenzy—such as the events of September 25 in Bilbao, when a Rebel air raid which
killed 100 persons was avenged by a furious rabble
which attacked and slaughtered 60 Fascist hostages.[31] Loyalists and labor supporters massacred
thousands of Fascists, landowners, clericals and
Church adherents, and members of Right-wing
parties. On October 3 a Vatican City dispatch alleged that approximately 400 priests or male Church
officials and about 100 nuns had been killed; some

[30] *Ibid.*, October 30, 1936.
[31] *Ibid.*, September 26, 1936.

500 were missing; about 1,000 others had fled the country.[32] In Madrid, Barcelona and other cities members of the upper classes were taken from their homes by armed workers, never to be seen alive again. Anarchists in Valencia admitted to one correspondent that there had been 1500 clandestine executions of alleged Fascists.[33] Another reported that up to December 25,000 had been slain in Madrid. Under cover of general disorder private grudges were often liquidated in blood. In the villages of southern Spain, many murders were listed of Civil Guards, employers and property-owners, professional men, relatives of the clergy and army men, and other Right sympathizers. On the approach of Insurgent forces, prisoners were shot in jails or in some instances reported burned alive.[34]

It is reasonably clear, however, that in numerous cases Loyalist authorities endeavored to curb popular violence. In Barcelona the Anti-Fascist Committee of Fifteen early sought to end assassinations and to punish those guilty therefor. In Madrid on August 30 the Anarcho-Syndicalists' National Confederation of Labor denounced those who, garbed as its members or militiamen, indulged in individual reprisals or in arrests motivated by personal hatred.[35] In an effort to end these irregular actions and at the same time satisfy a widespread demand for prompt action against government enemies, Popular Tri-

[32] *Ibid.*, October 4, 1936. Cf. also Michael Williams, "How Many Slain?" *Current History*, December 1936.
[33] Lawrence A. Fernsworth, in *New York Times*, November 8, 1936, and Wm. P. Carney, *ibid.*, December 7, 1936.
[34] *A Preliminary Official Report on the Atrocities, committed in southern Spain in July and August, 1936.* . . . The Committee of Investigation appointed by the National Government at Burgos (London, Eyre and Spottiswoode), 1936.
[35] *New York Times*, August 1, 31, 1936. Cf. also *The Times* (London), October 3, 1936.

bunals were set up, composed of members of the judiciary together with representatives of workers' organizations. Defective as the administration of justice might be under such auspices, these agencies represented an advance over indiscriminate killings.[36]

With the Rebels, however, wholesale execution of opponents has been a definite policy, and has cost the lives of far more victims than Moorish "atrocities."[37] As early as July 30 Colonel José Palacios, Rebel commander with the army of the north, declared: "I take no prisoners. Anybody other than uniformed soldiers of the Spanish Army caught by me carrying arms finds the death he deserves."[38] General Franco, holding that all those voting for the Popular Front were *ipso facto* Communists, has carried out in the territories conquered by his troops a policy of so-called "necessary elimination." It is thus described by an American correspondent:

"Insurgent troops kill the ringleaders of the Left forces as soon as they capture any town. Then they leave the place in peace for about a week, during which agents investigate. Finally they start rounding up those who supported the Loyalist cause or who are suspected of having done so. These persons are led to cemeteries, where they are shot in

[36] For a description, possibly somewhat idealized, of one of these tribunals, cf. *International Press Correspondence* (London), October 17, 1936.

[37] Following the capture of Talavera de la Reina by the Insurgents, Walter Duranty reported: "The Moors, with curved knives, massacred, raped and looted in Talavera—I talked with refugees and what they said was dreadful—to their heart's content." *New York Times*, September 13, 1936. The Moors have consistently been given the privilege of looting the centers they capture.

[38] *New York Herald Tribune*, July 31, 1936.

groups of about twenty throughout several days and nights."[39]

A particularly large-scale massacre took place when Badajoz fell to the Insurgents on August 14. As fast as Loyalists were captured they were lined up for mass executions. Men were stopped in the street, and their shirts ripped back; if their right shoulders showed rifle bruises, they were hurried off to the firing squad. Two militiamen discovered among the crowd in the cathedral were reported shot on the steps of the altar. Estimates placed the number killed at 1200 to 4000.[40]

By November 7 the Insurgents' advance had carried them to the city limits of Madrid, and the battle for the capital began. Hopes that it would fall easily were soon disappointed by the determined resistance of the defenders. On the western side of the city the attackers were stopped along the line of the Manzanares River. Franco then attempted a flanking movement to the northwest, seeking to occupy the *Casa de Campo*, formerly a royal hunting preserve, and University City, on which several million dollars had been expended in recent years to build a modern educational center. But the Rebels were

[39] Frank L. Kluckhohn, who accompanied Franco's forces for several weeks, *New York Times,* October 11, 1936. Robert Neville reports a similar policy, as carried out in Granada. The executions took place in the cemetery, and the caretaker finally went mad. *New York Herald Tribune,* August 30, 1936. The Governing Board of the Madrid Bar Association accused the Insurgents of killing 9000 workers and peasants in Seville and shooting 2000 in Saragossa. Many Leftist deputies were executed. *La Libertad* (Madrid), September 30, 1936.

[40] *The Times* (London), August 17, 1936. Some of the more youthful victims asked to be comforted by priests before being shot. "Whereupon, priests on the Rebel side dropped their guns, changed their uniforms for Catholic raiment and officiated." *New York Times,* August 17, 1936. Jay Allen gives an especially graphic account of the fall of Badajoz in the *Chicago Tribune,* August 30, 1936.

balked here also, in large part due to the work of
the anti-Fascist International volunteers, a group
of Russians, Poles, anti-Fascist Germans and Italians, and French Leftists. The defenders were further reinforced by the arrival of 5000 Catalan
militia. Additional efforts to extend the wings of the
attacking forces both north and south resulted in
failure, and a counter-attack by the Loyalists against
the Rebel positions in the *Casa de Campo* led to the
centering of the struggle along the 10-mile front on
the west. The downtown section of the capital was
shelled by artillery and repeatedly bombed by air
raids. At the end of the month the Mayor of Madrid
announced that between November 8 and 28 the toll
from Insurgent planes had been 365 killed and 1936
injured.[41]

The Rebel threat to Madrid had led on November 4 to reorganization of the cabinet. Since early
September the government had been dominated by
the Socialists, whose strength among labor groups
had long centered in the capital. But the Anarcho-
Syndicalists were demanding a voice in public affairs
commensurate with their strength. Recognizing apparently that the fall of Madrid would menace next
their strongholds in Catalonia, the Anarcho-Syndicalists finally waived their anti-political scruples
and named three representatives in the government,
among them the outstanding leader, Juan Oliver.
Three days later the Loyalist government transferred its seat to Valencia.[42] The capital was left in
charge of General José Miaja and a council of Defense, representing the various labor and Left-Re-

[41] *New York Times,* December 1, 1936.
[42] On October 19 President Azaña had arrived in Barcelona for
an indefinite stay. Azaña has subsequently remained in Catalonia,
taking little part in political activity.

publican groups in the Popular Front. This move brought the central authorities into closer geographical relations with Barcelona, where their authority had become a mere shadow in the course of the civil war, and emphasized anew the importance of Catalonia to the Loyalist cause.[43]

In Catalonia the struggle for power among rival proletarian groups had been more intense, but a degree of working unity had been achieved earlier than at Madrid. Three principal groups sought the support of the masses. The Anarcho-Syndicalists had traditionally predominated in the region. But their position of leadership was threatened by the Socialists, who had made important gains since the outbreak of the July rebellion. The United Socialist Party of Catalonia (PSUC) held the same close relation to the Catalan General Workers' Union (UGT) as the Iberian Anarchist Federation (FAI) to the National Confederation of Labor (CNT). In addition there was the semi-Trotzkyite Workers' Party of Marxist Unification (POUM).[44] This party, which claimed to have increased its supporters to 45,000, criticized the willingness of the Socialists to cooperate with bourgeois organizations toward a moderate "democratic" revolution, and demanded unity among proletarian groups to carry through an

[43] Catalonia had established practical independence of activity in at least five important departments of government: military defense, public order, finance, economy and education. It had also created a Secretary of Exterior Relations. In conversations at Valencia in January 1937 the Barcelona delegates reasserted their doctrine of "a Catalan state within a federal republic." Previously Premier Tarradellas had declared that Catalonians "aspire to fuller liberty" than that conceded in the Statute of Autonomy. *New York Times,* January 4, 1937.

[44] For a brief discussion of these groups, cf. Charles A. Thomson, "Spain: Issues Behind the Conflict," *Foreign Policy Reports,* January 1, 1937, pp. 249, 250.

immediate and radical social revolution. The Socialists, however, asserted that in the crisis of civil
war the fundamental problem was to forge common
action toward victory. Working unity was essential
not alone in political and military activities, but
even more so in the everyday problems of factory
adjustment for development of a war industry. The
situation required, it was alleged, subordination of
doctrinal differences to practical cooperation, between both Socialists and Anarcho-Syndicalists, and
also with the lower middle-class. Given the prevalence of small factories in Catalonia, collaboration
of the technicians and directive personnel in this
group was indispensable. Hence the civil war, ran
the argument, represented a struggle between democracy and fascism, rather than one phase of the
world-wide conflict between socialism and fascism,
as the POUM asserted. Among the share-croppers
and tenant farmers, the Union of Rabassaires and
Workers constituted a fourth party estimated to
have 35,000 members.[45]

LABOR TAKES POWER IN CATALONIA

From the beginning of the civil war the proletarian bodies attained considerable political as well
as economic influence in Catalonia. Every city and
town, had its Committee of Anti-Fascist Militias.
In the Central Committee, formed at Barcelona on

[45] Other agrarian organizations were the Peasants' Union, affiliated with the CNT and composed solely of agricultural laborers,
and the Federation of Land Workers, affiliated with the UGT.
This agency possessed a reported membership of 500,000 farm
workers in all Spain, but was of small importance in Catalonia.
For a review of the agrarian question in the region, cf. *The
Spanish Revolution* (Barcelona), October 21, 28 and November
4, 1936. This publication, issued in English, is the weekly organ
of the POUM.

July 22, the labor organizations named ten representatives, the middle-class Republicans four, and
the peasants one.[46] This agency exercised more real
authority than the regional government, or Generalidad, which was largely reduced to the function
of a political rubber stamp.

But the committee represented a unity of action
more apparent than real. Each party jealously retained exclusive control of its own militiamen and
of the factories and other agencies which its members had occupied.[47] Bickering and recrimination
were rife. The rivalry brought several shifts in the
cabinet of the Generalidad. On July 31 Juan Casanovas formed a government, dominated by the *Esquerra* but containing three Socialists. This régime
sought to assume control of the various militia
groups and provoked the opposition, particularly,
of the Anarcho-Syndicalists. The Socialists then
withdrew from the ministry; and a cabinet reconstituted by Casanovas, almost entirely from the
Esquerra, held office until September 26.

On this date the proletarian organizations gained
control of the Generalidad government, with a majority of the seats in a new cabinet headed by José
Tarradellas of the *Esquerra*. The Anarcho-Syndicalists consented to enter the ministry with three
representatives, thus anticipating a similar step
taken in November at Madrid. The new régime
issued a proclamation pledging coordination of all

[46] The proletarian delegates were divided as follows: 3 of the
CNT; 2 of the FAI; 3 of the UGT; 1 of the PSUC; 1 of the
POUM. Of the four middle-class delegates, three represented the
Esquerra and one the more conservative Catalan Action.
[47] On this period, cf. M. E. Ravage, "Hopeful Catalonia," *The
New Republic,* December 9, 1936. The CNT, for example, was
accused of running the street cars, buses and taxicabs as "its own
property."

forces for victory, and establishment of obligatory service and discipline in the militia. Following organization of this cabinet, the Central Committee of Anti-Fascist Militias at Barcelona declared itself dissolved and turned over its powers to the civil régime.[48]

Although proletarian influence in the Generalidad was thus augmented, the dissolution of the Committee of Anti-Fascist Militias was criticized as signifying abandonment of the purpose to create a new Red Army. The armed forces were left in the hands of many officers who, it was argued, in the event of a Loyalist victory, would be more closely linked to bourgeois Republicans than to the working class.

On October 22 the Anarcho-Syndicalists and Socialists took an important step toward even closer collaboration. Leaders of the Iberian Anarchist Federation and the CNT pooled their differences with those of the United Socialist party and the UGT, and issued jointly a 15-point pact which covered most of the popular grounds of dispute and outlined the general structure of a future society.[49] Pledging support to the Generalidad, this declaration announced: "We are in favor of collectivization of production, i.e., expropriation without indemnification of the capitalists, and transfer of such property to the community. We are in favor of collectiv-

[48] For the full list of the cabinet and its announced program of government, cf. La Vanguardia (Barcelona), September 27, 1936. The stress of military necessity was apparently responsible for the end thus put to the period of "dual power," during which—according to Marxist theory—the nascent proletarian régime, while not openly attacking bourgeois government, should gradually absorb its powers.

[49] For text, cf. El Noticiario Universal (Barcelona), October 23, 1936.

ization of all that is necessary for the war." But socialization of small industries was opposed "except in case they belong to Fascists or answer urgent needs of the war." In the case of foreign enterprises, compensation was advocated to the amount of capital invested. Land, according to the statement, "belongs to the local governments, and we assure individual cultivation to those who are not disposed to do so collectively. The sale, exchange and purchase of products will be carried out through the Agricultural Unions." Dwellings, except small urban properties, were to become the property of the local governments. Nationalization of banks was favored. Domestic production and foreign commerce were to be subject to state regulation. A single military headquarters "coordinating the action of all the fighting forces" was favored to win the war. Catalonia's practical independence from control by the central government was evidenced by a clause declaring: "We are in favor of establishing a basis of political, economic and military collaboration with the Spanish government if and when all the organizations represented by us participate in it." Good feeling between the two rival labor federations— CNT and UGT—was to be safeguarded by a pledge of "freedom of labor organization and joint action to suppress all kinds of compulsion."

Despite these steps, friction continued among the governing groups, particularly between the United Socialist party (PSUC) and the POUM. The conflict came to a head in mid-December, and on the 17th a new ministry was formed under Tarradellas. In this the proletarian masses were represented, not by their political parties as such—both the PSUC and the POUM were excluded, in a purported effort to avoid further rivalry—but through their labor federations. The CNT had four and the UGT three seats. The bourgeois *Esquerra* was assigned three ministers, and the agrarian Union of Rabassaires one. Soviet influence, it was reported, had contributed to the ousting of the POUM from the government. The POUM asserted that it was the only real revolutionary party in Spain and announced plans to found, in cooperation with Swedish, German and Italian Socialists and the British Independent Labour party, a Fifth International, which should follow a policy independent of both Stalin's and Trotzky's influence.[50]

SOCIAL REVOLUTION

Internal struggles among the workers had not prevented them from carrying forward a program of practical socialization. As already noted, the large land-holders had succeeded through support of Franco in stopping agrarian reform in the regions controlled by the Rebels. The labor organizations, on their part, by backing the established governments at Madrid and Barcelona, made distinct advances toward their goal of fundamental economic and social reform. From the outset of the revolt groups of workers took the initiative in occupying factories and other properties, and later forced the authorities to legalize these steps. In the country the peasants seized lands, declared rents and dues abolished and sometimes burned land titles. In many cases war needs were the primary factor which induced extension of government control. As early as July 28 a decree of the Ministry of Industry and Commerce at Madrid provided for a committee with authority over all industries. Before a month had

[50] *New York Times,* January 3, 1937.

passed, government intervention in 600 plants was reported at the capital. These included heavy industries, transport, large commercial and distributive enterprises such as stores, restaurants and hotels, public utilities, and various factories and businesses whose owners were reported to have fled.[51]

In Catalonia the proletarian groups were even more aggressive than at Madrid. Decrees were obtained assuring the masses a 40-hour week, 15 per cent wage increases, debt moratorium, suspension of evictions, and 25 per cent decreases in rents. Many large factories, department stores and shops were taken over by labor groups and run by workers' committees. Public utilities suffered the same fate, as did the Ford and General Motors assembly plants. Both the Barcelona and the Madrid governments, however, pledged ultimate compensation for foreign property seized.[52]

The real situation with regard to socialization was decidedly spotty in character. Procedure had been substantially *de facto,* and had varied from district to district, from town to town and even from factory to factory. Where the workers were aggressive and well-organized, the business prosperous and the owners or managers unpopular, labor control might be promptly and completely established. Under different conditions, the owners' prerogatives might suffer little or no curtailment.[53]

Various economic decrees had attempted to estab-

[51] *New York Times,* August 24, 1936 and *International Press Correspondence,* October 17, 1936.

[52] The value of United States investments in Spain is estimated at $80,000,000, of which $64,000,000 is represented by the National Telephone Company, a subsidiary of the International Telephone and Telegraph Company.

[53] For descriptions of actions in individual communities and factories, cf. Generalitat de Catalunya, *Comunicat de Premsa* (Barcelona), December 11, 1936, and *The Spanish Revolution,* cited, December 2, 1936, pp. 2, 7.

lish legal uniformity for what was in fact an exceedingly chequered situation. Of these the most sweeping in Catalonia was a measure of October 24, which declared: "The principle of the economic-social organization of big business shall be collective production. The substitution of collective for private property, as understood by the Council of the Generalidad, means the collectivizing of the property, that is to say the capital, of large enterprise, while allowing private property in consumption goods and small industry to remain."

The decree provided for the obligatory socialization of all commercial and industrial enterprises employing more than 100 workers, and authorized socialization of smaller concerns on certain conditions. The executive management of the socialized companies was to be placed in the hands of a Council of Enterprise, elected by a general meeting of the workers. The Council in turn would appoint a director, responsible for the active management of the concern. Compensation was assured for foreign interests represented in industry, but it was prescribed that this should be "calculated in national currency"; compensation for domestic interests was left subject to later determination.

In industries and businesses not socialized, organization of a workers' committee of control was declared obligatory. This committee was to have jurisdiction over working conditions, receipts and expenditures, and control of production, and to examine the company's balance sheet and yearly statement.

Provision was also made for the formation in each industry of a General Council, which would regulate total production in the light of consumption requirements and other factors, organize sales centers and "negotiate banking facilities and credit." The decisions of the General Councils were to be compulsory.[54] These Councils in separate industries were to be coordinated by a Council of Economy for all Catalonia, which had been originally established by a decree of August 11.

Thus the workers, organized in factory and industrial groups, rather than the state, were to hold ownership of the large-scale means of production. The function of the state was principally to be one of regulation and coordination. In Catalonia it was evident that the Anarcho-Syndicalist emphases on liberty and local self-government would materially modify realization of the Marxist program for centralized administration of economic life.

SPAIN—VORTEX OF INTERNATIONAL CONFLICT

Meanwhile international tension over the Spanish struggle continued to increase. The Soviet Union, following its declaration to the London committee on October 23 that it would not consider itself bound by the non-intervention agreement "to any greater extent than the remaining participants," had changed its policy toward the Loyalists. Various observers reported an increasing flow of Russian supplies to the government. The extensive influence exercised at Madrid by Marcel Rosenburg, Soviet Ambassador, and at Barcelona by Soviet Consul-General Antonov-Ovseenkov became a subject of comment.[55] While Premier Largo Caballero contin-

[54] *Diari Oficial de la Generalitat de Catalunya,* No. 302, October 28, 1936, pp. 373-76. A partial English text is given in *The Spanish Revolution,* cited, November 4, 1936.

[55] Cf. *New York Times,* January 3, 1937; and especially article by William P. Carney, *ibid.,* December 7, 1936. This correspondent

ued to maintain that the government forces sought maintenance of a parliamentary republic rather than establishment of a soviet régime, he sent a New Year's message to the Soviet Union in which he declared: "The Spanish working class is forever united with the Russian workers. . . . The proletariat of Spain will always strive during the war and after the war is over to follow the example of your great country."[56]

Germany and Italy had staked their prestige on the success of the Rebels even more than the Soviet Union had done with respect to the Madrid government. On November 18 the two Fascist powers, without waiting for Franco to capture Madrid, recognized the Burgos Junta—not merely as a belligerent but as the legal government of Spain.[57] On November 27 the Largo Caballero government appealed to the League, invoking Article XI of the Covenant. It alleged that international peace was being endangered by the "armed intervention of Italy and Germany."

The most alarming factor in the situation was the rapid increase of German "volunteers" in Spain. On December 1, 5000 German re-enforcements for

declared that the Soviet Ambassador enjoyed a voice concerning cabinet appointments, frequently attended cabinet meetings and had vetoed proposals that Madrid be abandoned without resistance. He asserted: "Far in advance of Russia's decision to aid the Spanish government openly . . . Russian war materials, including trucks, planes, tanks and munitions, were reported in the Madrid press as being received by the Loyalist forces." The Soviet Union concluded two commercial treaties with the Valencia and Barcelona governments in November 1936. But M. Litvinov denied that the Soviet Union wished to establish a Soviet state in Spain. Cf. *New York Times*, November 29, 1936.

[56] *Journal des Nations*, November 25, 1936, and *New York Times*, January 2, 1937.

[57] Portugal had broken off diplomatic relations with the Madrid government on October 23.

the Rebels landed at Cadiz. By Christmas, according to many reports, the number had approximately
doubled. General Faupel, appointed German chargé
at Burgos, was said to have informed Hitler that
Franco needed at least 40,000 additional troops to
assure Rebel victory. The possible creation of a Nazi
standing army in Spain seriously menaced the Mediterranean interests, not only of Britain and France,
but Italy. Dominance of the Fascist powers in Spanish Morocco and on the Balearic Islands[58] might
easily interfere with British imperial communications in time of war. Possession of Majorca by a non-
Spanish power would block the sea-routes between
France and its African possessions. Moreover, the
establishment of German hegemony in Spain would
mean that France would be forced to provide for
defense of its Pyrenean frontier. This direct threat
to the vital interests of the two Western democracies
increased their former concern to prevent the Spanish conflict from precipitating a general European
war. Nor did Italy, despite its previous cooperation
with Germany in aiding the Rebels, welcome the
emergence of the Reich as a Mediterranean power.

On December 4 a Franco-British suggestion to extend the non-intervention agreement to cover foreign volunteers destined for either Spanish faction
was blocked by Germany, Italy and Portugal. A
proposal to end the civil war by mediation also met
with failure.

[58] A number of German officers are reported to have resided
for some time at Tetuán. Their relation to a pan-Arab conference, which opened on October 21 in that city, attracted considerable attention. (*Journal des Nations,* November 30, 1936.)
It has been frequently rumored that, under a secret treaty nego-
tiated in 1926 between Mussolini and the Spanish dictator, Primo
de Rivera, Italy had been ceded a base on the Balearic Islands.
(*L'Afrique Française,* Paris, August-September 1936, p. 475.)

The increasing flow of German troops to Spain led
Britain and France to act again on December 27,
when they addressed notes to Berlin, Rome, Lisbon
and Moscow, stressing the dangers involved in the
continued shipment of "volunteers." Meanwhile,
negotiations between Rome and London, consummated in the accord of January 2, 1937, had apparently opened for Italy an easier road toward assurance of its position in the Mediterranean than
support of General Franco could offer. In an exchange of notes annexed to the treaty Count Ciano,
Italian Foreign Minister, confirmed the British government's understanding that: "So far as Italy is
concerned the integrity of the present territories of
Spain shall in all circumstances remain intact and
unmodified." Anglo-Italian agreement on such a
pledge was interpreted as barring not only Italian
occupation of the Balearic Islands or German seizure of other Spanish territory, but also creation of
an independent Socialist or Communist state in
Catalonia under Russian or French protection. The
agreement led some observers to forecast withdrawal
of Rome's assistance to the Rebels, although on
January 3 it was reported that 5000 armed Italians
had disembarked from three Italian warships at
Cadiz within the past few days.[59]

Activity of German naval vessels in Spanish

[59] *New York Times,* January 4, 1937. Four days later it was
estimated that 50,000 foreigners of 12 nationalities were in Spain.
Of these the Rebels were reported to have, exclusive of Moors
and the Foreign Legion, nearly 30,000—including 14,000 Italians,
12,000 Germans and 4,000 Portuguese, Irish and other nationalities. On the government side, the International Brigade on the
Madrid front numbered 8,000 foreigners, with 10,000 others in
training behind the lines. Eighty per cent of Franco's air forces, it
was estimated, was German, 15 per cent Italians and 5 per cent
Spaniards. Half the Loyalist airmen, it was reported, were French
and half Russian, with a few of other nationalities. Cf. article by
Webb Miller, *New York Herald Tribune,* January 8, 1937.

waters further complicated the situation. On December 24 a Loyalist cruiser seized the German steamer *Palos*. The vessel was subsequently released, but the Loyalists retained alleged war materials found in the cargo and one Spanish passenger, accused of being a Rebel agent. Berlin claimed that the *Palos* had been seized on the high seas, and in "reprisal" German war craft captured one Spanish freighter and forced another ashore by shell fire. The Valencia government declared these steps represented an "act of war" and announced it would resist further aggression by German vessels.

Meanwhile the issuance by the American State Department on December 28 of an export license for approximately $3,000,000 worth of used airplanes and airplane motors to the Spanish Loyalists was viewed as threatening the neutrality policy which had been adopted by the United States. The existing Neutrality Act did not apply to civil wars. On convening in January, however, Congress promptly approved legislation, signed by President Roosevelt on January 8, authorizing the executive to extend the law to the Spanish struggle. Earlier, Washington had exerted moral influence to prevent arms shipments to either side, in accordance with a statement by Under Secretary Phillips on August 7 that the United States would "scrupulously refrain from any interference whatsoever in the unfortunate Spanish situation."[60]

CONCLUSION

Six months from its outbreak, the war in Spain had clearly taken on a threefold character. It was not only a military conflict between contending

[60] United States, Department of State, *Press Releases*, August 15, 1936.

Spanish factions, but also a deep-cutting social struggle, with the forces of revolutionary change aligned against those of reaction. Moreover, the Iberian Peninsula had become the vortex for Europe's swirling tides of international rivalry. Power politics and clashing ideologies had led to German and Italian aid for the Rebels, and Soviet aid for the Loyalists. Thus, foreign interference served to intensify the bitterness of domestic conflict.

In military operations, the Rebels to date have held the initiative, and the Loyalist forces have been consistently on the defensive. If for the moment the element of foreign interference is ignored, long-term factors apparently favor the government cause. Its gold reserve of approximately $700,000,000[61] gives it the advantage in financial resources. With Catalonia and Asturias in its hands, it controls the areas of major industrial production. Valencia and Catalonia also are important agricultural regions. Further, Franco's evident dependence on foreign troops indicates that the government commands far wider popular support than the Rebels. The army officers who initiated the revolt, had apparently planned a coup whose success would be assured automatically by the wholesale defection of Spain's entire military machine. But their calculations miscarried because of two unforeseen developments. A sufficient minority of the armed forces remained loyal to afford the government some organized support. Moreover, a rising of the popular masses in countless villages,

[61] The Rebels were believed to be financing their campaign principally from three sources: (1) "voluntary" contributions from Fascists, Monarchists, clericals, and large landholders and industrialists such as Juan March; (2) control of foreign exchange for products exported from their territories; (3) credits from Germany and Italy. Those from the former were reported to total $180,000,000. *New York Times,* January 10, 1937.

as well as in cities like Madrid, Barcelona and Valencia, balked the plans of the militarists. The Rebels early achieved advantage, due to superiority in professional leadership, in organization and discipline, and in modern equipment. Their advance reached the limits of Madrid early in November, but since that time they have been held at the city's gates. Meanwhile the discipline of the Loyalist troops has markedly improved, and their armament has been augmented.

The popular strength of the government cause is based in large part on its pledges of social reform— already partly redeemed—as opposed to the Fascist and reactionary tenets espoused by the Rebels. At the start of the rebellion Madrid's Popular Front government was composed entirely of liberal Republicans; not a Socialist or Communist held a seat. But now the Loyalist régimes, both at Valencia and Barcelona, are dominated by proletarian groups. Growing unity prevails. The Socialists and Anarcho-Syndicalists, long bitter rivals with radically different approaches to social reconstruction, have gone far toward pooling their differences. With them also are linked the middle-class parties. In Catalonia, where the middle-class is particularly important, this group under the leadership of President Companys has aligned itself, not with the Fascists as in Germany, Italy and Portugal, but with the industrial proletariat and the peasants. This fact may prove of far-reaching significance. The Loyalists have taken definite steps toward a socialized economy. At Madrid war needs have been an important factor in this trend. The process has been carried even further in Catalonia where it points toward establishment of a new social order. Developments to date forecast a hybrid Anarcho-Socialist régime in which large enterprises would be collectivized, but small enterprises would be permitted, for a time at least, to continue under private operation modified by a considerable degree of government and labor supervision.

The transformation of the civil war into a social struggle may spell doom for Spanish democracy in its bourgeois political phase. Depending on which side wins, it may be replaced either by a military-Fascist dictatorship, supported by foreign troops and financial aid; or possibly by some sort of federal system, linking together a number of semi-autonomous regional administrations characterized by various degrees of socialization.

The international character of the Spanish struggle, however, complicates all attempts to chart its future course. To term it a civil war has involved a misnomer practically from the start. To what degree the Rebels had entered into relations with Germany and Italy prior to the revolt is not yet clear. In any case, within two weeks of its inception, General Franco had received airplanes and other military supplies from the Fascist powers. Russian assistance to the government came only after these nations had taken the initiative with the Rebels, and Soviet aid was not appreciably large until November. Supplementing the shipment of supplies, "volunteers" later poured into Spain to strengthen both factions. Early in January it was estimated that the Rebels had been re-enforced by 30,000 foreigners, exclusive of the Moors and the Foreign Legion. On the government side there were approximately 20,000 foreign troops.[62]

[62] *New York Herald Tribune*, January 8, 1937.

This foreign aid apparently proved decisive at two points in the struggle. Following the Rebels' early failure to take Madrid and Barcelona, their cause seemed lost until the arrival of German and Italian aid strengthened their hand. Conversely the appearance of the International Brigade and the receipt of Soviet munitions and supplies probably saved Madrid, when it was on the point of falling to the Insurgents early in November.

But the international phase of the Spanish war may determine not alone the outcome of that struggle. It has been said: "In certain measure, the Iberian Peninsula has served to catalyze European conflicts. It has precipitated them, in the double sense of the word."[63] No nation, apparently, is willing to provoke a general war for the sake of its stake in Spain. Yet, in the absence of more effective curbs than those provided by the London Non-Intervention Committee, international rivalry may serve materially to prolong the Spanish conflict and, with it, a continual menace to European peace.

[63] Jean Rollin, "La Guerre civile en Espagne," *Politique Etrangère* (Paris), October 1936, p. 78.

INDEX